C000128597

Social Work Decision-Making:
A Guide for Childcare Lawyers

Second Edition

Social Work Decision-Making:
A Guide for Childcare Lawyers

Second Edition

Elizabeth Isaacs
Barrister
St Ives Chambers, Birmingham

Carmel Shepherd
Children's Guardian
Local authority panels chair
Trainer and consultant

Family Law

Published by Family Law
A publishing imprint of Jordan Publishing Limited
21 St Thomas Street
Bristol BS1 6JS

Whilst the publishers and the author have taken every care in preparing the material included in this work, any statements made as to the legal or other implications of particular transactions are made in good faith purely for general guidance and cannot be regarded as a substitute for professional advice. Consequently, no liability can be accepted for loss or expense incurred as a result of relying in particular circumstances on statements made in this work.

© Jordan Publishing Ltd 2012

All rights reserved. No part of this publication may be reproduced, stored in a retrieval system, or transmitted in any way or by any means, including photocopying or recording, without the written permission of the copyright holder, application for which should be addressed to the publisher.

British Library Cataloguing-in-Publication Data

A catalogue record for this book is available from the British Library.

ISBN 978 1 84661 254 1

Typeset by Letterpart Ltd, Reigate, Surrey

Printed in Great Britain by CPI Antony Rowe, Chippenham and Eastbourne

We dedicate this book to the one and only Dr Lili Nir, the dearest of friends, who has died far too prematurely for us.

ACKNOWLEDGMENTS

This book could not have been written without continued advice and support from our families, friends and colleagues. Between us we have over 50 years' experience in what can sometimes seem like a quagmire of social work and family law. Those people who have contributed to our knowledge and discussions are too numerous to mention. We are also afraid that we might offend the one person we forget to mention, albeit unintentionally.

This book is owed to them all.

FOREWORD

The authors of this valuable book have used the experience and insight that they collectively have into the overlapping realms of social work and childcare law to produce a clear and accessible guide for lawyers into the professional world of the local authority social worker. Collected within this volume, seasoned children's lawyers will find an explanation for, and a route map through, many of the 'best practice guidance', local authority circulars and public inquiry reports which, I suspect, exist in an unfocussed way on the edges of the lawyer's radar screen. This material is catalogued, explained and put into context in order to assist lawyers in understanding what they, and the courts, may expect from social work professionals. This work is, however, much more than that, containing, as it does, a comprehensive description of the structures and processes within a social services children's department. The aim, which is certainly achieved, is to inform the lawyer (both experienced and novice) so that he or she may better understand the work of the social worker and their role in an ongoing case. This Second Edition is timed so that it includes reference to the new court rules, central government guidance and regulations, together with the recommendations of both the Munro Review of Child Protection and the Family Justice Review. There is much within these pages that will be of use, but I suspect that the most thumbed section will be that on how to analyse social services decision-making. Positive and productive use of this work is likely to improve the professional practice of both the lawyers and the social workers who appear in childcare proceedings.

Andrew McFarlane
March 2012

PREFACE

We pondered long and hard about how to introduce the second edition of this book. We wondered whether in fact it would be easier to say what it's not. It's *not* a book to be read straight through from cover to cover. It's *not* the sort of book to take with you on holiday. It's *not* the kind of thing you would want to read in bed.

However, to start a book by drawing attention to the negatives is a big professional no no.

In the same way, it would be unprofessional for a social worker to start by identifying the negatives in the families with whom they work. In good social work practice there should be no negatives. Families have strengths, as we all do. Families also face challenges – poverty, inequality, addiction, violence and so on. Best practice for social workers assessing and working with families aims to work with them to overcome such challenges.

The first edition of this book grew out of increasing requests to both of us, during training courses and at court, to explain issues in social work practice to people who were unfamiliar with some of the principles, procedures and terminology regularly used by social workers. Those questions were about the intricacies and procedural conundrums relating to social work, as well as the broader issues. The first edition of the book aimed to be a manual to help lawyers understand the social work witness, to make sense of what they are supposed to do, and to understand how social workers should think, plan, assess, analyse and make decisions about children and their families.

The second edition is written following 4 years of considerable legal, social and political change. Social workers are subject to greater pressure than ever before which inevitably affects the preparation, planning and presentation of their work. Lawyers are faced with an ever-increasing raft of legislation, guidance and good practice documents relating to social work. This rapidly changing context shows no sign of slowing down. Understanding social work terminology, procedure and practice remains a key element of the childcare lawyer's toolkit.

So the book remains a reference book, a manual, for you to dip into whenever you need to prepare for a case. While we hope it continues to demystify the inner workings of social work practice, we would only recommend taking it to bed or to the pool at your peril.

The law is as stated at 1 January 2012.

Carmel Shepherd
Elizabeth Isaacs
March 2012

CONTENTS

TABLE OF CASES

References are to paragraph numbers.

TABLE OF STATUTES

References are to paragraph numbers.

TABLE OF STATUTORY INSTRUMENTS

References are to paragraph numbers.

Chapter 1

THE LEGAL FRAMEWORK

INTRODUCTION

1.1　The Children Act 1989 (CA 1989) created a single coherent framework to deal with the private and public law relating to children. It aims to strike a balance between the rights of children to express their wishes on decisions made about their lives, the rights of parents to exercise their responsibilities towards their children, and the duty of the state to intervene where the child's welfare requires it.[1]

1.2　The CA 1989 is based on the belief that children are generally best looked after within the family, with their parents playing a full part in their lives and with least recourse to legal proceedings. The principles underpinning social work practice are informed by the CA 1989 (reinforced in the Children Act 2004), and can be summarised as follows:

- safeguarding children and promoting their welfare;

- recognising parental responsibility (and the ability of unmarried fathers to share that responsibility by agreement with the mother, by joint registration at birth, or by court order);

- providing family support and services to children in need, including services for disabled children, to enable children to remain in their own homes as far as possible;

- taking account of race, culture, language, religion and disability;

- working in partnership with children and their families;

- the local authority's duty (unless not reasonably practicable or consistent with the child's welfare) to promote contact between a looked after child and his or her parents (or relevant others);

- the local authority's duty to return a child looked after by them to his or her family unless it is not in the child's interests;

- giving due weight to children's wishes and feelings.

---

[1]　Department for Education *The Children Act 1989 Guidance and Regulations*, vol 1: court orders (July 2011).

SECTION 1 – THE STATUTORY LEGISLATION

1.3   The statutory legislation most relevant to work to safeguard and promote the welfare of children is as follows:

- Children Act 1989 (Pts I, III and IV);

- Children Act 2004;

- Children (Leaving Care) Act 2000;

- Adoption and Children Act 2002; and

- Children and Young Persons Act 2008.

The duty to promote and safeguard children's welfare

1.4   The CA 1989 places a duty on local authorities to promote and safeguard the welfare of children in need in their area. The primary focus of legislation about children in need is on how well they are progressing and whether their development would be impaired without the provision of services.

1.5   Section 17 of the CA 1989 deals with the general duties of local authorities to safeguard and promote children's welfare. Local authorities carry the lead responsibility for establishing whether a child is in need and for ensuring that services are provided to that child as appropriate.

1.6   This does not necessarily require local authorities themselves to be the provider of such services. Section 17(5) of the CA 1989 enables the local authority to make arrangements with others to provide services on their behalf.

1.7   CA 1989, ss 17(1) and (10):

'(1)   It shall be the general duty of every local authority …

    (a)   to safeguard and promote the welfare of children within their area who are in need; and
    (b)   so far as is consistent with that duty, to promote the upbringing of such children by their families,

by providing a range and level of services appropriate to those children's needs.

(10)   … a child shall be taken to be in need if –

    (a)   he is unlikely to achieve or maintain, or to have the opportunity of achieving or maintaining, a reasonable standard of health or development without the provision for him of services by a local authority under this Part;

(b)   his heath or development is likely to be significantly impaired, or further impaired, without the provision for him of such services, or

(c)   he is disabled ...'

1.8   The thrust of the government guidance[2] remains that only in exceptional cases should there be compulsory intervention in family life, for example where necessary to safeguard a child from significant harm. Such intervention should, as long as it is consistent with the child's safety and welfare, support families in making their own plans for the welfare and protection of their children. As well as being responsive to children's direct requests for help and advice, professionals also need to engage with parents at the earliest opportunity when doing so may prevent problems or difficulties becoming worse.

1.9   Children have varying needs that change over time. Judgments about how best to intervene when there are concerns about harm to a child will often, and unavoidably, entail an element of risk – at the extreme, of leaving a child for too long in a dangerous situation or of removing a child unnecessarily from his or her family. The government's guidance in *Working Together* makes it clear that the way to proceed in the face of uncertainty is through competent professional judgments, based on a sound assessment of the child's needs and the parents' capacity to respond to these (including their capacity to keep the child safe from significant harm) and the wider family circumstances.[3]

1.10   Where it appears to a local authority that there is a child within its area who is in need, para 3 of Sch 2 to the CA 1989 enables the local authority to assess that child's needs. At the same time as carrying out an assessment under this part of the CA 1989, account should be taken of assessment requirements contained in any other legislative framework. This could include an assessment of the needs of a disabled person under the Chronically Sick and Disabled Persons Act 1970, the Disabled Persons (Services, Consultation and Representation) Act 1986, or an assessment of the child's special educational needs under the Education Act 1996 Pt IV.

1.11   Section 17(4A) of the CA 1989[4] requires local authorities, where practicable, to take account of children's wishes and feelings before determining what services to provide or what action to take.

1.12   CA 1989, s 17(4A) (as amended):

'(4A)   Before determining what (if any) services to provide for a particular child in need in the exercise of functions conferred on them by this section, a local authority shall, so far as is reasonably practicable and consistent with the child's welfare –

---

2   Department for Children, Schools and Families (DCSF) (now DfE) *Working Together to Safeguard Children – A Guide to Inter-agency Working to Safeguard and Promote the Welfare of Children* ('*Working Together*') (TSO, 4th edn, 2010) (or can be downloaded from www.education.gov.uk/publications).

3   *Working Together*, para 1.10.

4   As amended by s 53(1) of the Children Act 2004.

(a)   ascertain the child's wishes and feelings regarding the provision of those services; and

(b)   give due consideration (having regard to his age and understanding) to such wishes and feelings of the child as they have been able to ascertain.'

1.13   *Working Together* requires local authorities (in common with all organisations that provide services or work with children and young people), to:

- have senior managers who are committed to children's and young people's welfare and safety;

- be clear about people's responsibilities to safeguard and promote children's and young people's welfare;

- check that there are no known reasons or information available that would prevent staff and volunteers from working with children and young people;

- have procedures for dealing with allegations of abuse against members of staff and volunteers;

- make sure staff get training that helps them do their job well;

- have procedures about how to safeguard and promote the welfare of young people; and

- have agreements about working with other organisations.

1.14   The guidance in *Working Together* makes it quite clear that safeguarding and promoting the welfare of children is the responsibility of the local authority when working in partnership with other public organisations, the voluntary sector, children and young people, parents and carers, and the wider community. A key objective for local authorities is to ensure that children are protected from harm. Other functions of local authorities that make an important contribution to safeguarding are housing, culture and leisure services, and youth services.

The duty to work together with other agencies

1.15   Section 27 of the CA 1989 also places a specific duty on local authority services and health organisations to co-operate in the interests of children in need. An underlying principle of the CA 1989 is to encourage such collaboration between agencies in order to achieve a holistic view of a child's needs. It is not sufficient for the local authority simply to identify and consider specific problems; rather, the local authority must take account of other services provided by other agencies, including voluntary organisations, and should facilitate the provision of services by others which the local authority may provide.

1.16 CA 1989, s 27:

> '(1)   Where it appears to a local authority that any authority or other person mentioned in subsection (3) could, by taking any specified action, help in the exercise of any of their functions under this Part, they may request the help of that other authority or person, specifying the action in question.
>
> (2)   An authority whose help is so requested shall comply with the request if it is compatible with their own statutory or other duties and obligations and does not unduly prejudice the discharge of any of their functions.
>
> (3)   The persons are –
>
> (a)   any local authority;
>
> (b)   any local education authority;
>
> (c)   any local housing authority;
>
> (d)   any health authority; and
>
> (e)   any person authorised by the Secretary of State for the purposes of this section.'

1.17   The guidance in Working Together reinforces this duty by linking the safeguarding and promotion of children's welfare – and in particular the protection of children from significant harm – to the need for effective joint working between agencies and professionals that have different roles and expertise. Individual children, especially some of the most vulnerable children and those at greatest risk of suffering harm and social exclusion, will need coordinated help from health, education, early years, children's social care, the voluntary sector and other agencies, including youth justice services.

1.18   In order to achieve this joint working there need to be constructive relationships between individual workers, promoted and supported by a strong lead from local authority members and effective local coordination by the Local Safeguarding Children Board in each area.

1.19   For those children who are suffering, or likely to suffer, significant harm, joint working is essential to safeguard and promote their welfare.

The duty to carry out an investigation

1.20   Section 47 of the CA 1989 places the local authority under a duty to make enquiries in certain circumstances to decide whether it should take any action to safeguard or promote the welfare of a child.

1.21   CA 1989, s 47:

> '(1)   Where a local authority –
>
> (a)   are informed that a child who lives, or is found, in their area –
>
> > (i)   is the subject of an emergency protection order; or
> >
> > (ii)   is in police protection; or

(b)   have reasonable cause to suspect that a child who lives, or is found, in
their area is suffering, or is likely to suffer, significant harm,
the authority shall make, or cause to be made, such enquiries as they
consider necessary to enable them to decide whether they should take any
action to safeguard or promote the child's welfare.'

1.22   Very often social work assessments need to depend on building a picture
of the child's needs and the capacity of their parents or wider family to care for
them on the basis of seeking information from many sources. The local
authority social worker, in carrying out assessments, should do his or her
utmost to secure willing co-operation and participation from all professionals
and services by being prepared to explain and justify the local authority's
actions and to demonstrate that the process is being managed in a way that can
help to bring about better outcomes for children.

1.23   Sections 47(9), (10) and (11) of the CA 1989 place a statutory duty on
any local authority, any local education authority, any local housing authority,
and any health authority, to help it in carrying out its social services functions
in undertaking s 47 enquiries (unless it would be unreasonable in all the
circumstances of the case). The Local Safeguarding Children Board (LSCB)
has an important role to play in cultivating and promoting a climate of trust
and understanding between different professionals and services.[5]

The duty to work with children

1.24   Section 47(5A) of the CA 1989[6] requires local authorities, where
practicable, to take account of children's wishes and feelings before
determining what action to take during investigations.

1.25   The revised guidance in *Working Together* (2010) confirms the approach
to be taken by social workers in situations when it is not possible to ascertain
the child's wishes and feelings. In those circumstances professionals should
record in writing why it was not reasonably practicable or consistent with the
child's welfare to elicit his or her wishes or feelings.[7]

1.26   CA 1989, s 47(5A):
'(5A)   For the purposes of making a determination under this section as to
the action to be taken with respect to a child, a local authority shall, so far as
is reasonably practicable and consistent with the child's welfare –
(a)   ascertain the child's wishes and feelings regarding the action to be
taken with respect to him; and
(b)   give due consideration (having regard to his age and understanding) to
such wishes and feelings of the child as they have been able to
ascertain.'

---

[5]   *Working Together*, para 5.63.
[6]   As amended by s 53(3) of the Children Act 2004.
[7]   *Working Together*, para 1.17.

1.27 The guidance in the *Framework for the Assessment of Children in Need and their Families*[8] provides the structure for helping to collect and analyse information obtained in the course of s 47 enquiries.

1.28 The 2008 Laming review of the progress across England to implement effective arrangements for safeguarding children[9] reiterated the importance of frontline professionals getting to know children as individual people and, as a matter of routine, considering how their situation feels to them.

1.29 The Ofsted evaluation of Serious Case Reviews conducted between 1 April 2007 and 31 March 2008 highlighted the importance of seeing children as individuals:

> '... the failure of all professionals to see the situation from the child's perspective and experience; to see and speak to the children; to listen to what they said, to observe how they were and to take serious account of their views in supporting their needs [is] probably the single most consistent failure in safeguarding work with children.'

1.30 A further Ofsted evaluation of Serious Case Reviews conducted between 1 April and 30 September 2010 confirmed this and repeated the persistent criticism that professionals did not speak to the children enough. This recent evaluation highlighted five main messages with respect to the participation of children:

- the child was not seen frequently enough by the professionals involved, or was not asked about their views and feelings;

- agencies did not listen to adults who tried to speak on behalf of the child and who had important information to contribute;

- parents and carers prevented professionals from seeing and listening to the child;

- practitioners focused too much on the needs of the parents, especially on vulnerable parents, and overlooked the implications for the child; and

- agencies did not interpret their findings well enough to protect the child.

1.31 Many of these findings are borne out in the research looking specifically at children's contact with social workers. Recent research commissioned by the Office of the Children's Commissioner[10] reported that significant proportions of children are not seen alone by their social worker, have minimal relationships

---

[8]   The Department of Health *Framework for the Assessment of Children in Need and Their Families* (TSO, 2000).
[9]   *The Protection of Children in England: A Progress Report* HC 330 (TSO, 2009).
[10] The Office of the Children's Commissioner *Don't make assumptions – Children and young people's views of the child protection system and messages for change* (2011).

with them, rarely see or discuss their reports or assessments and do not know why critical decisions are taken about their future care. A clear message from children (and their parents) is that they value continuity in their relationships with professionals. For some children, there is also the problem of the bewilderingly large number of professionals who get involved in their case. In one case study cited in the research a 4-year-old child was noted to have met 46 new adults in her first 6 months in the care system.

The Children and Young Person's Act 2008

1.32   The Children and Young Persons Act 2008 came into force in November 2008 and fulfils the commitments made in the White Paper, *Care Matters: Time for Change*.[11] The new legislation extends the statutory framework for children in care in England and Wales and is intended to ensure that children in care are able to share the same aspirations as those in supportive family homes by receiving high quality care and services which are focused on and tailored to their needs. The new legislation is intended to improve the stability of children's placements and improve the educational experience and attainment of young people in local authority care or about to leave care. Most of the changes are incorporated into the statutory framework by additions or substitutions in the Children Act 1989 and the Care Standards Act 2000.

1.33   Key elements of the Children and Young Persons Act 2008 include:

•   enabling local authorities to operate a different model of organising social care by discharging (although not delegating) social work functions to other bodies (any such arrangements must be exercised in favour of qualified social workers);

•   strengthening the role of the independent reviewing officer (IRO);

•   obliging local authorities to visit young people in their care;

•   ensuring that there will be a designated member of staff at maintained schools whose specific responsibility it will be to promote the educational achievement of children in care who attend that school;

•   ensuring that looked-after children (up to 18) are not moved out of an existing placement before they are ready;

•   requiring the local authority to provide assistance to young people in care or who have recently left care to pursue education and training;

•   improving the stability of placements for children in care, limiting 'out of authority' placements, and securing higher placement standards; and

---

[11]   Cm 7137 (2007).

- improving the support for family and friend carers, including allowing local authorities to make longer-term financial payments to family carers in circumstances where otherwise the child would be accommodated by the local authority, where this would be appropriate.

SECTION 2 – THE ROLE OF THE LOCAL AUTHORITY

The local authority's duty in relation to children and families

1.34 Local authorities are obliged to comply with statutory guidance issued under s 7(1) of the Local Authority Social Services Act 1970 (LASSA 1970) when carrying out their duties relating to children and families, unless there are exceptional circumstances which justify a variation.

1.35 LASSA 1970, s 7(1):

> 'Local authorities shall, in the exercise of their social services functions, including the exercise of any discretion conferred by any relevant enactment, act under the general guidance of the Secretary of State.'

1.36 If the local authority fails to follow statutory guidance (issued under the LASSA 1970, s 7(1)), in relation to any function under the CA 1989, the Secretary of State has the power to declare them in default.

1.37 The statutory inquiry into the death of Victoria Climbié[12] and the first joint Chief Inspectors' report on safeguarding children[13] highlighted the lack of priority status given by local authorities (as well as other agencies) to safeguarding children. The government's preliminary response to these findings was set out in the Green Paper, *Every Child Matters*, and was enacted in the Children Act 2004[14] which includes the provision for a Children's Commissioner.[15]

1.38 The role of the Children's Commissioner is defined in s 2 of the Children Act 2004 as:

- having the function of promoting awareness of the views and interests of children in England;

- encouraging people exercising functions or engaged in activities affecting children to take account of their views and interests;

- advising the Secretary of State on the views and interests of children;

---

[12] *The Victoria Climbié Inquiry Report* (TSO, 2003).
[13] The Department of Health *Safeguarding children: a Joint Chief Inspectors report on arrangements to safeguard children* (TSO, 2002).
[14] In force since 15 November 2004.
[15] Children Act 2004, s 2.

- considering or researching the operation of complaints procedures so far as relating to children;

- considering or researching any other matter relating to the interests of children;

- publishing reports on any matters considered or researched by him or her;

- ensuring that children are made aware of his/her function and how they may communicate with him or her; and

- consulting children, and organisations working with children, on the matters he or she proposes to consider or research.

1.39   The mission statement of the Children's Commissioner states that:[16]

'We will use our powers and independence to ensure that the views of children and young people are routinely asked for, listened to and that outcomes for children improve over time. We will do this in partnership with others, by bringing children and young people into the heart of the decision-making process to increase understanding of their best interests.'

1.40   The most important provisions of the new legislation in this wider context are:

- the duty for local authorities to make arrangements to promote co-operation between the local authority, each of the local authority's relevant partners and such other bodies (or people) working with children in the area as the local authority considers appropriate (CA 2004, s 10);

- the setting up of Local Safeguarding Children Boards (CA 2004, ss 13–16).

Interagency working and *Working Together*

1.41   The revised legislation envisages a *shared responsibility* and the need for *effective joint working* between agencies and professionals with different roles and expertise in order to protect children and promote their welfare. Effective joint working is reliant on constructive relationships between individual practitioners, promoted and supported by the commitment of senior managers to safeguard and promote the welfare of children, and reliant on the establishment of clear lines of accountability.

1.42   Achieving good outcomes for children requires all those with responsibility for assessment and the provision of services to work together

---

[16]   Mission statement of the Children's Commissioner available at www.childrenscommissioner. gov.uk.

according to an agreed plan of action. Effective collaboration requires organisations and people to be clear about:

- their *roles and responsibilities* for safeguarding and promoting the welfare of children;

- the *purpose* of their activity, the decisions that are required at each stage of the process and the planned outcomes for the child and family members;

- the *legislative basis* for the work;

- the *protocols and procedures* to be followed, including the way in which information will be shared and recorded within agencies and across professional boundaries;

- which organisation, team or professional has *lead responsibility*, and the precise roles of everyone else who is involved, including the way in which children and family members will be involved; and

- the *timescales* (set down in regulations or guidance) that govern the completion of assessments, making of plans and timing of reviews.

1.43 *Working Together to Safeguard Children* is the key piece of statutory guidance issued under the LASSA 1970, s 7(1),[17] which provides a clear framework of guidance about how individuals and organisations should work together to safeguard and promote the welfare of children.

1.44 *Working Together* was first published to accompany the CA 1989 and was revised and published in April 2010 in its fourth edition. The revised guidance takes account of the changes in safeguarding policy and practice since the previous edition was issued in 2006. The government has indicated that it will be subject to consultation about further revisions in 2012.

1.45 *Working Together* is intended to provide a national framework within which agencies and professionals at local level – individually and jointly – draw up and agree on their own ways of working together to safeguard and promote the welfare of children. It applies only to England.

1.46 Part 1 is statutory guidance. Part 2 is non-statutory practice guidance. Non-statutory guidance is not underpinned by any legal duty and does not give rise to any binding obligations on the part of the local authority. However, any non-statutory guidance is recognised as a standard of good practice and any variation from non-statutory guidance needs to be explained and justified.

---

[17] See n 2.

1.47 We suggest that all parts of *Working Together* are required reading for lawyers working in the field of public law childcare.

1.48 The guidance in *Working Together* is addressed to:

- all practitioners and front-line managers who have particular responsibilities for safeguarding and promoting the welfare of children;

- senior and operational managers in organisations that are responsible for commissioning or providing services to children, young people, parents and carers; and

- senior and operational managers in organisations that have a particular responsibility for safeguarding and promoting the welfare of children.

1.49 The theme of interagency working is not new. Formal procedures for agencies and professionals working together have been in place since the 1950s,[18] but as institutions, organisations, boards and partnerships evolve, responsibilities and lines of accountabilities change with them.

1.50 The Cleveland Inquiry Report 1987 included recommendations about interagency co-operation that seem just as relevant 25 years later:[19]

> 'We strongly recommend the development of inter-agency co-operation which acknowledges no single agency – Health, Social Services, Police or voluntary organisation – has the pre-eminent responsibility in the assessment of child abuse ... Each agency has a prime responsibility for a particular aspect of the problem. Neither children's nor parents' needs and rights can be adequately met or protected unless agencies agree a framework for their interaction.'

1.51 The Munro Review final report 2011[20] recently confirmed that one of the strengths in the English child protection system is the extent to which the many agencies and professions work together to coordinate their work with children and families.

1.52 An essential tenet of the CA 1989 and the first edition of *Working Together* was that promoting and safeguarding the welfare of children is not just the responsibility of the local authority; an integrated approach by all relevant agencies working together is a fundamental element of good practice.

---

[18] Home Office, Ministry of Health & the Ministry of Education *Joint circular from the Home Office, Ministry of Health and Ministry of Education. Children neglected or ill-treated in their homes* (1950).

[19] The Department of Health and Social Security *Report of the Inquiry into Child Abuse in Cleveland 1987* (HMSO, 1988), rec 8(a).

[20] *The Munro Review of Child Protection: Final Report – A Child-Centred* System, Cm 8062 (2011), para 6.30.

1.53 This was reinforced by Lord Laming in the Victoria Climbié Inquiry Report, where improving the way key people and bodies safeguard and promote the welfare of children was deemed crucial to improving outcomes for children:[21]

'The support and protection of children cannot be achieved by a single agency ... Every Service has to play its part. All staff must have placed upon them the clear expectation that their primary responsibility is to the child and his or her family.'

1.54 In the report into the death of Victoria Climbié, Lord Laming concluded that 'the suffering and death of Victoria was a gross failure of the system'.

1.55 Section 11 of the Children Act 2004 places a duty on key persons and bodies to make arrangements to ensure that in discharging their functions, they have regard to the need to safeguard and promote the welfare of children.

1.56 The thrust of government guidance and thinking around interagency working has therefore been clear for over 20 years – all organisations working with children and families share a commitment to safeguard and promote children's welfare. For many agencies this is underpinned by a statutory duty or duties.

1.57 This theme continues to lie at the heart of the guidance in the latest edition of *Working Together*:[22]

'Everyone shares responsibility for safeguarding and promoting the welfare of children and young people, irrespective of individual roles. Nevertheless, in order that organisations and practitioners collaborate effectively, it is vital that all partners who work with children – including local authorities, the police, the health service, the courts, professionals, the voluntary sector and individual members of local communities – are aware of, and appreciate, the role that each of them play in this area.'

1.58 The updated and revised 4th edition of *Working Together* also incorporates 23 of the 58 recommendations made by Lord Laming in his 2009 report which considered the progress being made across the country to implement effective arrangements for safeguarding children following the Peter Connolly (Baby Peter) case.[23]

1.59 There are three key elements in the Laming recommendations which reinforce and enhance the existing approach to interagency working:

- *An integrated approach* – the inherent difficulties facing the local authority social worker are set out explicitly, and it is made clear that safeguarding

[21] Paragraphs 17.92 and 17.93.
[22] *Working Together*, para 2.1.
[23] *The Protection of Children in England: A Progress Report* published 12 March 2009 HC 330 (TSO, 2009).

measures should not be seen in isolation from the wider range of support and services available to meet the needs of children and families:[24]

> 'Judgements on how to intervene when there are concerns about harm to a child will often, and unavoidably, entail an element of risk – at the extreme, of leaving a child for too long in a dangerous situation or of removing a child unnecessarily from his or her family. The way to proceed in the face of uncertainty is through competent professional judgements, based on a sound assessment of the child's needs and the parents' capacity to respond to these – including their capacity to keep the child safe from significant harm – and the wider circumstances.'

- *A shared responsibility* – safeguarding and promoting children's welfare (in particular, protecting them from harm) depends fundamentally on effective joint working between agencies and professionals with different roles and expertise. All agencies and professionals (including, of course, the local authority) should:

    - be alert to potential indicators of abuse or neglect;
    - be alert to the risks of harm posed to children by individual abusers, or potential abusers;
    - prioritise direct communication and positive relationships with children, ensuring children's wishes and feelings underpin assessments;
    - share and help to analyse information so that an assessment can be made of whether the child is suffering or is likely to suffer harm, their needs and circumstances;
    - contribute to whatever actions are needed to safeguard and promote the child's welfare;
    - take part in regularly reviewing the outcomes for the child against specific plans; and
    - work co-operatively with parents (unless this is inconsistent with ensuring the child's safety).

- *The child in focus* – as already indicated, professionals persistently fail to see the situation from the child's perspective and experience, to see, speak or listen to children, observe how they were and to take serious account of their views in supporting their needs in their safeguarding work with children. The importance of empathy and insight into children's and families' lives is therefore given increased emphasis in the revised guidance. Ways of effective action to keep the child in focus include:

    - developing a direct relationship with the child;
    - obtaining information from the child about his or her situation and needs;
    - eliciting the child's wishes and feelings about their current and future situation;

---

[24] *Working Together*, para 1.10.

- providing children with honest and accurate information about the current and possible future situation;
- involving the child in key decision-making;
- providing appropriate information to the child about his or her right to protection and assistance; and
- ensuring children have access to independent advice and support.

1.60 Chapter 5 of *Working Together* provides guidance on what should happen if somebody has concerns about the welfare of a child (including those living away from home), and in particular, concerns that a child may be suffering, or may be at risk of suffering, significant harm. It also sets out the principles which underpin work to safeguard and promote the welfare of children.

1.61 The guidance in the *Framework for the Assessment of Children in Need and Their Families*[25] should be followed when undertaking assessments on children in need and their families. This is discussed in detail in Chapter 5 of this book.

Local Safeguarding Children's Boards (LSCBs)

1.62 The current accountability structure for child protection in local areas was prescribed in the Children Act 2004 with the statutory positions of Director of Children's Services (DCS) and Lead Member for Children's Services being designated as the respective key points of professional and political accountability within the local authority. Around these key positions other services, such as the police and health, play key roles through local partnership structures, ie the Children's Trust Board and the LSCB.

1.63 LSCBs replaced the old Area Child Protection Committees from 1 April 2006. Guidance about the LSCB role and functions is set out in chapter 3 of *Working Together*.

1.64 LSCBs are primarily scrutiny bodies which monitor whether local partners, through the Children's Trust Board, are effectively safeguarding and promoting the welfare of children and young people in their local area. Like the Children's Trust Board, the LSCB is a statutory body. As part of their scrutiny function each LSCB produces and publishes an annual report about safeguarding and promoting the welfare of children in its local area, and submits a copy of this report to the Children's Trust Board. The majority of LSCBs are independently chaired, meaning that they are in a better position to provide scrutiny and challenge to the local authority and its Children's Trust Board partners.

---

[25] The Department of Health *Framework for the Assessment of Children in Need and Their Families* (TSO, 2000). See Chapter 5.

1.65   Although the LSCB coordinates the effectiveness of arrangements to safeguard and promote the welfare of children in that locality, the LSCB is not accountable for the operational work of the Board's partners. Each Board partner retains its own existing lines of accountability. The government's plans for maintaining the roles of LSCBs and the Children's Trust Boards remains unknown at the time of writing (December 2011).

1.66   The LSCB is the key statutory mechanism for agreeing how the relevant organisations in each local area will co-operate to safeguard and promote the welfare of children, and for ensuring the effectiveness of what they do.

1.67   There are three main elements of the LSCB role:

- to engage in activities that safeguard all children and aim to identify and prevent maltreatment, or impairment of health or development, and ensuring that children are growing up in circumstances consistent with safe and effective care;

- to lead and coordinate arrangements for responsive work to protect children who are suffering, or at risk of suffering, maltreatment; and

- to lead and coordinate proactive work that aims to target particular groups.

1.68   County level and unitary local authorities are responsible for establishing an LSCB in their area and ensuring that it is run effectively. LSCBs should have a clear and distinct identity within local children's trust governance arrangements. It is the responsibility of the local authority to appoint the chair of the LSCB.

1.69   In an overall analysis of the social work relating to a child and/or family, we suggest that lawyers should consider whether the local authority's work has complied with the LSCB policies and procedures for that area.

SECTION 3 – GOOD PRACTICE IN SAFEGUARDING AND PROMOTING CHILDREN'S WELFARE

Definition of safeguarding and promoting welfare

1.70   Safeguarding and promoting the welfare of children is defined in *Working Together*[26] as:

- protecting children from maltreatment; and

- preventing impairment of children's health or development; and

---

[26]   *Working Together*, para 1.20.

- ensuring that children are growing up in circumstances consistent with the provision of safe and effective care and undertaking that role so as to enable those children to have optimum life chances and to enter adulthood successfully.

1.71 Protecting children from maltreatment is important in preventing the impairment of health or development. The prevention of impaired health or development is necessary to ensure that children are growing up in circumstances consistent with the provision of safe and effective care. These aspects of safeguarding and promoting welfare are cumulative, and all contribute to positive outcomes for children and young people.

1.72 All children deserve the opportunity to achieve their full potential. *Working Together* identifies five outcomes for children and young people that are key to their well-being:[27]

- Stay safe.

- Be healthy.

- Enjoy and achieve.

- Make a positive contribution.

- Achieve economic well-being.

1.73 To achieve these five outcomes, children need to feel loved and valued, and be supported by a network of reliable and affectionate relationships. If they are denied the opportunity and support they need to achieve these outcomes, children are at increased risk not only of an impoverished childhood, but of disadvantage and social exclusion in adulthood. Abuse and neglect pose particular problems.

1.74 The five outcomes are confirmed throughout the provisions of the Children Act 2004. In particular, the Children's Commissioner's functions include the duty to be concerned with the views, interests and well-being of children in relation to the five outcomes.[28]

The key processes underpinning social work with children and families

1.75 The aim of social work with children and families is to:

- optimise the chances of children achieving the five outcomes; and

---

[27] *Working Together*, para 1.1.
[28] Children Act 2004, s 2(3).

- achieve improvements in the lives of children in need.

1.76   Four key processes underpin social work with children and families,[29] each of which has to be carried out effectively. These processes are:

(1)   assessment;

(2)   planning;

(3)   intervention; and

(4)   reviewing.

Child protection social work

1.77   Child protection social work refers to the activity that is undertaken to protect specific children who are suffering, or are at risk of suffering, significant harm. Effective child protection is essential as part of the local authority's wider work to safeguard and promote the welfare of children.

1.78   The four social work processes (assessment, planning, intervention and reviewing) start from the point at which concerns about a child are referred to a statutory organisation with the ability to take action to safeguard and promote the welfare of children.

1.79   *Working Together* sets out the detail of each of these social work processes. Although the guidance in *Working Together* is not intended as a detailed practice guide, it does set out clear expectations about the ways in which agencies and professionals should work together to safeguard and promote the welfare of children.

Time for change – The Munro Review

1.80   One of the recurring themes in the professional, academic and political evaluation of social work practice in the last two decades or more is the concern that social work has become too prescriptive. Some commentators feel that policies, procedures and guidance have perhaps gone too far in dictating to social workers what they must do, when and how, thus impacting adversely on the ability of the social worker to exercise their own professional judgments and ability to analyse and make reliable conclusions from the assessments and information they have gathered in relation to any case they work with.

1.81   At the same time, but not unrelated to the professional debates about the 'professionalism' v 'bureaucratisation' of social work practice, the current coalition government has called for a general reduction of 'red tape' in the

---

[29]   *Working Together*, chapter 5.

functions of the state and is considering various different means of reducing and/or amending the way in which the state intervenes in family life.

1.82 It is in this context that the government commissioned Professor Eileen Munro in June 2010 to conduct an independent review of child protection in England.[30] Three reports were produced by the Munro Review.

1.83 The Munro Review began by examining how the current position in relation to child protection had evolved. The review's first report described the child protection system in recent times as one that has been shaped by four key driving forces:

- the importance of the safety and welfare of children and young people and the understandable strong reaction when a child is killed or seriously harmed;

- a commonly held belief that the complexity and associated uncertainty of child protection work can be eradicated;

- a readiness, in high profile public inquiries into the death of a child, to focus on professional error without looking deeply enough into its causes; and

- the undue importance given to performance indicators and targets which provide only part of the picture of practice, and which have skewed attention to process over the quality and effectiveness of help given.

1.84 The Munro Review report defines eight clear principles of a good child protection system:

- The system should be child-centred. Everyone involved in child protection should pursue child-centred working and recognise children and young people as individuals with rights, including their right to participation in decisions about them in line with their age and maturity.

- The family is usually the best place for bringing up children and young people, but difficult judgments are sometimes needed in balancing the right of a child to be with their birth family with their right to protection from abuse and neglect.

- Helping children and families involves working with them and therefore the quality of the relationship between the child and family and professionals directly impacts on the effectiveness of help given.

---

[30] Munro Report of Child Protection, *Part One: A Systems Analysis* (October 2010), *Interim Report: The Child's Journey* (February 2011) and *Final Report: A Child-Centred System* (May 2011), Department for Education.

- Early help is better for children because it minimises the period of adverse experiences and improves outcomes for children.

- Children's needs and circumstances are varied so the system needs to offer equal variety in its response.

- Good professional practice is informed by knowledge of the latest theory and research.

- Uncertainty and risk are features of child protection work: risk management can only reduce risks, not eliminate them.

- The measure of the success of child protection systems, both local and national, is whether children are receiving effective help.

1.85 The Munro Review's first report concluded that these forces have come together to create a defensive system that puts so much emphasis on procedures and recording that insufficient attention is given to developing and supporting the expertise to work effectively with children, young people and families.

1.86 The Review's second report considered the child's journey through the child protection system – from needing to receiving help – to show how the system could be improved. It concluded that instead of 'doing things right' (ie following procedures) the system needed to be focused on doing the right thing (ie checking whether children and young people are being helped).

1.87 The Review's final report set out proposals for reform which, taken together, are intended to create the conditions that enable professionals to make the best judgments about the help to give to children, young people and families. This involves moving from a system that has become over-bureaucratised and focused on compliance to one that values and develops professional expertise and is focused on the safety and welfare of children and young people.

1.88 Practitioners and their managers told the Munro Review that statutory guidance, targets and local rules have become so extensive that they limit professionals' ability to stay child-centred. The Munro review concluded that the demands of bureaucracy have reduced social workers' capacity to work directly with children, young people and families, and that services have become so standardised that they do not provide the required range of responses to the variety of need that is presented.

1.89 As a result, the Munro Review recommended a radical reduction in the amount of central prescription to help professionals move from a compliance culture to a learning culture, where they have more freedom to use their expertise in assessing need and providing the right help.

1.90 The Munro Review recommended that the government revise statutory, multi-agency guidance to remove unnecessary or unhelpful prescription and focus only on essential rules for effective multi-agency working and on the principles that underpin good practice. A relevant example is the recommendation that the prescribed timescales for social work assessments should be removed, since they distort practice: 'helping children is a human process. When the bureaucratic aspects of work become too dominant, the heart of the work is lost'.

1.91 The Munro Review also reinforced that the underlying principle of timeliness is important and should be applied to the whole process of helping a child or young person, not just the early stage of assessment. The review proposed that, with the reduction of prescription, leaders in local authorities should have more autonomy but also more responsibility for helping their staff to operate with a high level of knowledge and skills. The review asked local authorities to take more responsibility for deciding the range of services they will offer, defining the knowledge and skills needed and helping the workers develop them. For example, a local authority wishing to implement a particular evidence-based way of working with children and families needs to consider what changes might be needed in the training, supervision, IT support and monitoring to enable this to be carried out effectively. To keep the focus on the quality of help being given to children and young people, local authorities need to pay close attention to the views and experiences of those receiving services and the professionals who help them.

1.92 A key recommendation of the Munro Review is that the government should revise the statutory guidance, *Working Together to Safeguard Children* and *The Framework for the Assessment of Children in Need and their Families* and their associated policies, to:

- distinguish the rules that are essential for effective working together, from guidance that informs professional judgment;

- set out the key principles underpinning the guidance;

- remove the distinction between initial and core assessments and the associated timescales in respect of these assessments, replacing them with the decisions that are required to be made by qualified social workers when developing an understanding of children's needs and making and implementing a plan to safeguard and promote their welfare;

- require local attention is given to:

  - timeliness in the identification of children's needs and provision of help;
  - the quality of the assessment to inform next steps to safeguard and promote children's welfare; and
  - the effectiveness of the help provided;

- give local areas the responsibility to draw on research and theoretical models to inform local practice; and

- remove constraints to local innovation and professional judgment that are created by prescribing or endorsing particular approaches, for example, nationally designed assessment forms, national performance indicators associated with assessment or nationally prescribed approaches to IT systems.

1.93 The Munro Review's recommendations and analysis about the obstacles to working in partnership with families, and the analysis about reasons for reform of the assessment process are discussed further in Chapters 5 and 6. The extent to which the government will embrace and implement the recommendations of the Munro review remains unclear at the time of writing (December 2011).

SECTION 4 – WHAT LAWYERS NEED TO KNOW ABOUT SOCIAL WORK

1.94 Childcare lawyers who act in public law care proceedings will at some stage encounter social workers. Lawyers representing children and families may need to cross-examine social workers or local authority workers such as family centre staff, contact supervisors or fostering social workers. Lawyers working and/or acting for local authorities will represent social workers directly as their professional clients. Whichever party is represented, it is inevitable that lawyers will hear frequent reference to social work terminology during a case, such as panels, core assessments or kinship carers.

1.95

What do lawyers need to be able to identify?

- What are the issues in the case?

- Are any directions needed for the filing of further factual evidence by any party?

- What are the issues requiring the assistance of proposed expert evidence or further assessment?

- Who is to conduct any further work?

- What type of expert is needed?

1.96 Over time lawyers will inevitably grow to develop an understanding of the principles underlying social work terminology. However, many lawyers, particularly those who are newly qualified or inexperienced, often find it hard to make informed choices about case planning or to challenge proposals put forward by other more experienced or knowledgeable lawyers.

1.97 We suggest that an understanding of the principles and expectations of good social work practice, and knowing the sources of such material, cannot only boost a lawyer's confidence but can be critical in planning the most effective case strategy for clients. Without a clear knowledge of the principles involved in social work assessment, planning and intervention, a lawyer's case strategy will be limited, weakened and inevitably open to challenge.[31]

> 'Child protection professionals are constantly making judgments that impinge on the rights of parents to be with and relate to their children and the parallel right of children to their parents. The stakes are high and child protection decision-making needs to be as explicit as possible and be available for review and scrutiny.'

SECTION 5 – UNDERSTANDING THE WHOLE PICTURE

1.98 As already discussed, social work practice does not exist in a legal vacuum. It is subject to numerous volumes of guidance and an ever-changing regulatory framework. To the uninitiated this framework can appear confusing, muddled and impenetrable. However, closer examination of the guidance and regulatory framework reveals a logical and unified theory underpinning the government's approach – the ultimate in 'joined-up' thinking. For example, the timetabling in the *Framework for Assessment* is informed by the timetabling in *Working Together* – see Chapter 5.

1.99 The primary role of the lawyer during public law proceedings is of course to represent the best interests of the client. In doing so, it is essential that the lawyer is able to participate fully in all the negotiations and discussions between advocates that take place outside court (either informally or during specially convened meetings for advocates or professionals).

1.100 Without an understanding of the requirements of the 'joined-up' process, it can be difficult to challenge proposals by other parties that may be made in discussions during such meetings in court proceedings. Such proposals, particularly if suggested by confident and experienced professionals (lawyers, social workers or experts such as psychologists or psychiatrists) may appear 'friendly' and can often seem inevitable or necessary, but may not, upon closer examination, actually be in the client's best interests.

1.101 A clear and detailed understanding of the existing or proposed decision-making (either by the local authority or by other professionals already instructed, such as independent social workers, psychologists or psychiatrists) is essential in helping lawyers to understand how such proposals actually do affect the client. Such an understanding will help in planning the case strategy and ultimately in persuading the court on behalf of the client's case. The

---

[31] The Munro Review Final Report (May 2011) at para 6.30.

decisions that have *not* been made are just as critical as the decisions that *have* been made in helping formulate an effective case strategy (for example, identifying the critical gaps in a social worker's core assessment may form the basis of an argument for a further, independent assessment of the client's parenting ability, or identifying the broad scope of an initial kinship assessment may help protect the local authority from an application for an independent assessment which would cause unnecessary delay in planning for a child).

1.102

Summary

Understanding social work can:

- boost confidence for newly qualified or inexperienced lawyers

- help in planning the most effective case strategy

- provide a benchmark for understanding the elements of good practice in assessment, planning and intervention

- insulate the case against challenge

- enable effective participation in advocates' or professionals' meetings outside court

- enable a critical analysis of past and present social work assessment, planning and intervention

- help in identifying deficiencies and omissions in the local authority's past and present conduct of the case

- enable lawyers to identify the work needed to remedy such deficiencies or omissions

Chapter 2

SOCIAL WORK IN PRACTICE

SECTION 1 – THE COMMON ASSESSMENT FRAMEWORK (CAF)

2.1   The statutory guidance to the Children Act 2004 aims to:

- integrate services for children from 0 to 19 with agencies working across professional boundaries; and

- coordinate support around the needs of children and young people.

2.2   These services are to be provided by:

- using common processes and language to meet those needs in the best possible way;

- focusing on prevention and early intervention; and

- providing better support to parents and families.

2.3   The Common Assessment Framework (CAF) is the standardised approach developed by the Department of Education and Skills (now Department for Education) to conduct an assessment of a child's *additional* needs and decide how those needs should be met. The non-statutory guidance relating to the CAF is set out in *The Common Assessment Framework: Guide for Service Managers and Practitioners*.[1]

2.4   The CAF is a four-step process whereby practitioners can identify a child's or young person's needs early, assess those needs holistically, deliver coordinated services and review progress. The CAF is designed to be used when:

- a practitioner is worried about how well a child or young person is progressing (eg concerns about their health, development, welfare, behaviour, progress in learning or any other aspect of their well-being);

- a child or young person, or their parent/carer, raises a concern with a practitioner;

---

[1]   The Department for Education and Skills *The Common Assessment Framework: Guide for Service Managers and Practitioners* (TSO, 2007) (available from www.cwdcouncil.org.uk).

- a child's or young person's needs are unclear, or broader than the practitioner's service can address.

2.5   The process is entirely voluntary and informed consent is mandatory, so families do not have to engage and if they do they can choose what information they want to share. It is not intended that children and families should feel stigmatised by the CAF; indeed they can ask for a CAF to be initiated.

2.6   The CAF process is not a 'referral' process but a 'request for services'.

2.7   The CAF should be offered to children who have additional needs to those being met by universal services. Unless a child is presenting a need, it is unlikely the CAF will be offered. The CAF is used to enable the practitioner to assess needs.

2.8   The CAF is not intended to apply to situations where an immediate statutory or specialist assessment is needed. The CAF is not a risk assessment. Although the CAF may lead to core assessments, any serious concerns regarding child protection matters should normally be referred immediately to specialist services (ie qualified social workers).

2.9   *Additional needs* is a broad term used to describe all those children at risk of poor outcomes (see the five outcomes detailed in Chapter 1). An estimated 20% to 30% of children have additional needs at some point in their childhood, requiring extra support from education, health, social services or other services. This could be for a limited period, or on a long-term basis. It is the group of children for whom targeted support within universal settings will be most appropriate (ie settings that are intended to meet the needs of all children). This group includes children who:

- have needs that are not being met by their current universal provision; and

- would benefit from an assessment to help a practitioner:

    – understand the child's needs;
    – determine whether other services should be involved in providing support for the child; and
    – engage further services for the child.

2.10   The CAF will not be appropriate for the majority of children. Most children are progressing satisfactorily towards the five outcomes with the support of universal services.

The purpose of the CAF

2.11   The CAF is intended to:

• promote more effective identification of additional needs, particularly within universal services;

• identify children's additional needs at an earlier stage;

• provide a simple process for a holistic assessment of a child's needs and strengths, taking account of the role of parents, carers and environmental factors on their development;

• enable practitioners to agree, with the child and family, the level of appropriate support; and

• improve integrated working between agencies by promoting coordinated service provision for children.

2.12   The needs of children and families are seen to lie along a continuum as set out in the figure below, supported by flexible and responsive services which become increasingly targeted and specialist, according to need.

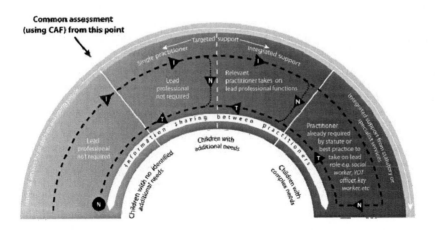

2.13 This book is about social workers' decision-making in relation to children with complex needs (rather than the additional needs provided for by the CAF). These are the children who meet the threshold for statutory involvement:

- children who are the subject of a child protection plan;

- looked-after children;

- care leavers;

- children for whom adoption is the plan;

- children with severe and complex special educational needs;

- children with complex disabilities or complex health needs;

- children diagnosed with significant mental health problems; and

- young offenders involved with youth justice services (community and custodial).

2.14 The practitioners completing the CAF will be known as *assessors* or *lead professionals*. Every local authority is required to recruit and train suitable staff to act as lead professionals and carry out CAF assessments. These workers are most likely to be:

- health visitors;

- special educational needs teachers;

- nursery nurses;

- youth workers;

- school nurses;

- speech therapists.

Such lead professionals are unlikely to be qualified social workers.[2]

2.15 As a tool for early intervention, the CAF is appropriate for use at an earlier stage than a specialist assessment, ideally enabling most issues to be

---

[2]   This change in the approach to assessments of children and their families may be compared to changes that have occurred within the NHS where hospital nurses have been given training and authority to carry out tasks previously undertaken by doctors, or within schools where unqualified teaching assistants were introduced to carry out some teaching tasks directly with children.

resolved before they require specialist assessment. Complex, targeted and/or specialist services will need to work with the universal services (eg housing, education and health) to provide support to children who have additional needs identified through common assessment.

2.16 Over time it is intended that the CAF should become the main generic method for early assessment. It is intended that any specialist assessments would supplement the information provided by the CAF. Professionals working with children with complex needs will receive the completed CAF assessment forms. The information in the CAF forms will:

- inform (and may reduce the scale of) the core assessment; and

- replace the initial assessment in many local authorities.

The CAF process

Step 1 – Preparation

2.17 This involves recognising the potential needs of the child and then discussing the situation with the child and family (and involving parents or carers unless this is not appropriate). The lead professional may talk to a manager, colleagues or others – possibly those already involved with the child. It is important that the lead professional find out whether a common assessment already exists. After reviewing the existing information, the lead professional will decide whether to undertake a common assessment with the agreement of the child or family, as appropriate.

Step 2 – Discussion

2.18 This involves completing the assessment with the child and family, making use of information already gathered from the child, family or other practitioners, and completing a consent statement. At the end of the discussion the lead professional should be able to understand the child's needs, and what can be done to help.

Step 3 – Delivery

2.19 This involves agreeing actions that the lead professional's service (or the family) can deliver, and considering what may be needed from other services. It is important to recognise that the CAF does not give the lead professional the ability to guarantee a service from another organisation without consulting that organisation.

Delivery of services following the CAF

2.20 The CAF should assess the additional needs of the child and family and identify the possible range of services from different agencies that could best meet those needs.

2.21 Local authorities have set up multi-agency panels to receive completed CAF assessments. These panels act as a gate-keeping mechanism to:

- monitor the quality of assessments;

- allocate resources (in accordance with agreed thresholds) to implement the plans arising from such assessments;

- identify key responsibilities for each agency involved with the child and family;

- allocate an agency to act as lead professional.

2.22 Good communication between agencies is essential to ensure that:

- the relevant services are delivered;

- ongoing support is provided; and

- these actions are reviewed as appropriate.

2.23 If a review concludes that the assessed additional needs of the child and family have been met, the current assessment process will come to an end. If it is identified that the child still has additional needs, the lead professional will coordinate further discussion between the relevant agencies and with the child and family. It may be that in these circumstances a further common assessment will be required.

The CAF Form

2.24 A pre-assessment checklist has been produced as an aid for professionals in deciding whether a CAF assessment is appropriate. The checklist guides the lead professional through consideration of the five outcomes in relation to the child. When undertaking a common assessment, practitioners should consider:

(1) how well a child is developing, including their health and progress in learning;

(2) how well parents or carers are able to support their child's development and respond appropriately to any needs;

(3) the impact of wider family and environmental elements on the child's development and on the capacity of their parents and carers.

2.25

Development of child

- Health

    – general health
    – physical development and speech
    – language and communications development

- Emotional and social development

- Behavioural development

- Identity, including self-esteem, self-image and social presentation

- Family and social relationships

- Self-care skills and independence

- Learning

    – understanding
    – reasoning and problem solving
    – participation in learning
    – education and employment
    – progress and achievement
    – aspirations

2.26

Parents and carers

- Basic care, ensuring safety and protection

- Emotional warmth and stability

- Guidance, boundaries and stimulation

2.27

> **Family and environmental**
>
> •   Family history, functioning and well-being
>
> •   Wider family
>
> •   Housing, employment and financial considerations
>
> •   Social and community elements and resources, including education

Information sharing during the CAF assessment

2.28   The CAF aims to enable and support better information sharing about the needs of children. As such it is intended to form part of a range of services to support children and families as early as possible and in a preventative way. All sharing and storing of information about children and families must comply with the Data Protection Act 1998. The lead professional should explain to the child and/or parent how the information in the assessment could, or will, be shared, and seek their consent. In most circumstances, a practitioner should only record and share CAF information with the informed consent of the child or parent. The child and parent should be given copies of relevant documents as appropriate. It is important that the assessor or lead professional:

•   obtains informed consent;

•   ensures that the information shared is accurate and up to date;

•   shares the information securely with those people who need to see it;

•   works with children and parents to agree how information is recorded, used and shared;

•   obtains explicit consent (where possible) if the information held or shared is sensitive[3] and, if the practitioner has ongoing contact, reviews the consent regularly; and

•   follows agreed local policies for recording and renewing consent.

2.29   A young person aged 16 or over (or a child under 16 who has the capacity to understand and make their own decisions about what they are being asked) may give consent. Children aged 12 or over may generally be expected to have sufficient understanding. Otherwise, a person with parental responsibility should be asked to consent on the child or young person's behalf.

---

[3]   Explicit consent can be obtained orally or in writing (but preferably in writing, for example, through a signature on the CAF recording form).

2.30 Confidential information is information that is sensitive, not in the public domain or readily available, and that has been provided in a relationship where the person giving it understood that it would not be shared with others. Confidential information should only be recorded on the CAF form if the child or parent explicitly agrees to this. If there is particular information that the child or parent does not want recorded on the form or shared with others, it should be recorded only in confidential case records.

2.31 During the course of a CAF discussion, the lead professional may gather information that they believe needs to be shared without consent (because consent has been refused or because it would be inappropriate to seek consent). In this case, the lead professional will need to consider whether the information is confidential (see above). If the information is not confidential, and the lead professional judges the disclosure to be *necessary* to fulfil a legitimate purpose, they may disclose the information.

2.32 Sharing of confidential information without consent may be justified:

- where there is *evidence* that the child is suffering or is at risk of suffering significant harm; or

- where there is *reasonable cause* to believe that a child may be suffering or is at risk of suffering significant harm; or

- to *prevent* significant harm arising to children and young people or serious harm to adults, including through the prevention, detection and prosecution of serious crime.

2.33 'Serious crime', for the purposes of the CAF guidance, means any crime that causes or is likely to cause significant harm to a child or young person or serious harm to an adult.

2.34 In cases where a lead professional decides to share information without consent, they should record the reasons for doing so.

SECTION 2 – THE TASK OF THE SOCIAL WORKER

2.35 Social workers work with, on behalf of, or in the interests of people to enable them to deal with personal and social difficulties, and to obtain essential resources and services:[4]

'The purpose of social work is to enable children, adults, families, groups and communities to function, participate and develop in society. Social workers

---

[4]   The Central Council for Education and Training in Social Work *Rules and Requirements for the Diploma in Social Work* (1995).

practise in a society of complexity, change and diversity, and the majority of people to whom they provide services are amongst the most vulnerable and disadvantaged in that society.'

2.36 The College of Social Work (operational from January 2012) defines social work as the 'safety net' of society, and the task of the trained and qualified social worker as being to:[5]

'... intervene in private and/or family life in order to protect individuals from harm to themselves or to others, and to promote human development and security, social inclusion and participation across the lifespan.'

2.37 Social workers have core values for carrying out their work. These values are defined as:

- to respect, promote and uphold the human, legal and civil rights of the child and adult;

- to respect and uphold the equality, worth and diversity of all people, respecting their individuality, privacy and dignity;

- to protect people from discrimination and prejudice; and

- to enable people to have personal autonomy, independence, choice and control.

2.38 Social work requires professionals to use effective communication, build trust, develop and maintain strong relationships with people who use services and carers, understand their relationships and their connections, and to know about the resources available in the wider community. The College of Social Work defines these as the crucial attributes of a social worker which will help to enable change in people's lives.

2.39 Social work is practised, whenever possible, in partnership with children, adults, families and communities and tries to improve the personal, practical, psychological and social aspects of people's lives.

2.40 Social workers have specific duties in respect of children under the Children Act 1989 and the Children Act 2004. They have a general duty to safeguard and promote the welfare of children in need in their area and – provided this is consistent with the child's safety and welfare – to promote the upbringing of such children by their families, by providing services appropriate to the child's needs. They should do this in partnership with parents, in a way that is sensitive to the child's race, religion, culture and language and that, where practicable, takes account of the child's wishes and feelings. Services might include day care for young children, after-school care for school children, counselling, respite care, family centres or practical help in the home.

---

[5]   College of Social Work website (2012) www.collegeofsocialwork.org.

2.41 Social workers act as the principal point of contact for children about whom there are welfare concerns, beyond the identification of additional needs. They may be contacted directly by children, parents or family members seeking help, by concerned friends and neighbours, or by professionals and others from statutory and voluntary organisations. The need for support should be considered at the first sign of difficulties, as early support can prevent more serious problems developing.

2.42 Children have varying needs that change over time. Judgments on how best to intervene when there are concerns about harm to a child will often, and unavoidably, entail an element of risk – at the extreme this may mean leaving a child for too long in a dangerous situation or may mean removing a child unnecessarily from his or her family.

2.43 The way for social workers to proceed in the face of such risk and uncertainty is through competent professional judgments, based on a sound assessment of the child's needs, the parents' capacity to respond to those needs – including their capacity to keep the child safe from significant harm – and the wider family circumstances. Social workers use such assessments to produce effective plans for safeguarding and promoting children's welfare. Effective measures to safeguard children are those that also promote their welfare. They should not be seen in isolation from the wider range of support and services already provided and available to meet the needs of children and families.

2.44 Individual children, especially some of the most vulnerable children and those at greatest risk of social exclusion, will need coordinated help from health, education, children's social care, and possibly the voluntary sector and other agencies, including youth justice services. Safeguarding and promoting the welfare of children, and in particular protecting them from significant harm, therefore depends on effective joint working between social workers and professionals from other agencies who have different roles and expertise.

2.45 The tasks and responsibilities for social workers include assessment, planning, intervention and the provision of services.

SECTION 3 – FAMILY GROUP CONFERENCES

2.46 Family group conferences (FGCs) originated in New Zealand as a response to:

- concerns about the disproportionate number of Maori children known to the social work department and in the populations of children in care; and

- concerns that many Maori children were placed trans-racially with White families.

2.47 A report, Puao-te-Ata-tu, written in 1986 by the Ministerial Advisory Committee on a Maori Perspective for the New Zealand Department of Social Welfare identified the existence of institutional racism within the Department of Social Welfare. This report informed the subsequent implementation of the Children, Young Persons and Their Families Act in New Zealand (1989). As originally conceived, FGCs involve the child or young person, their representative, the parents, extended family members, other people nominated by the family, the referring care and protection worker and possibly other participants but generally not legal representatives. The focus is on empowering the family to make their own decision about the care of the child or children. In New Zealand the use of FGCs is mandatory before child protection proceedings although this has given rise to concern.

2.48 The Children Act 1989 in the UK was introduced during the same period. The two Acts reflect broad similarities in philosophy and approach, although the New Zealand legislation recognised more powerfully the central role of families. Both Acts however aimed to reduce the role of the state in family life and to enable families (more widely defined) to be supported and empowered to care for their children.

2.49 The principles of consultation with families and of working in partnership were enshrined in the Children Act 1989. The New Zealand legislation, however, gave a more central role in decision-making to the family via the FGC model, and shifted the balance away from professionals to the family. In New Zealand an FGC must be convened as the first means for planning and making decisions about the protection and welfare of children.

2.50 The Family Rights Group was commissioned by the Department of Health in the 1990s to devise a training pack on working in partnership with families. The Family Rights Group considered the developments of FGCs in New Zealand as offering a genuine new model for working effectively in partnership with families.

2.51 In essence the FGC model offered a way of valuing the expertise and commitment of families whilst ensuring that the thinking and planning about children is informed by professionals' specialist knowledge and skills. The Family Rights Group has successfully campaigned to promote the use of FGCs in the UK, and in 1993 government funding was secured to develop the work over a 3-year period.

2.52 FGCs have been encouraged in England and Wales in recent years. Most (possibly all) local authorities now offer some form of FGC service. There is a variety of commissioning models and the use of the technique varies between local authorities. FGCs aim to develop a care plan for the child that involves wider family members. They follow a prescribed format and the use of private family time is mandatory. FGCs are usually recommended as a pre-court intervention, although they can be offered during proceedings and can help resolve a case through negotiation. In England and Wales they are usually seen as a means to avoid proceedings, in contrast to other jurisdictions where they may be used to arrive at binding plans later endorsed by the court.

The requirements for local authorities to consider using FGCs

2.53 The Public Law Outline (PLO)[6] requires the local authority to adopt a similar approach to the New Zealand model of convening an FGC as the first means of planning and making decisions about the protection and welfare of children. Local authorities should consider convening an FGC before making an application for a care order.

2.54 *Preparing for Care and Supervision Proceedings,*[7] the Best Practice Guide non-statutory guidance, makes it clear that FGCs could be considered at a pre-proceedings meeting as an appropriate step to assist identification of wider family support.[8]

2.55 The PLO guidance endorses the FGC model as an important opportunity to engage wider friends and members of the wider family at an early stage of concerns about a child, either to support the parents or to provide care for the child, whether in the shorter or longer-term. In either case, FGCs can reduce or eliminate the need for the child to become looked after. In presenting a care plan to court in any application for a care order the local authority will be required to demonstrate that it has considered family members and friends as potential carers at each stage of its decision-making.[9] The new Practice Direction[10] encourages the greater use of FGCs as not all local authorities currently make use of this practice. Local authorities are required to include minutes of family group meetings with their other documentation upon issuing care proceedings.[11] However, there is no detailed practice guidance about FGCs given the wide-ranging nature and scope of the model. It is important to recognise that there are no fixed timescales or circumstances for FGCs. They are a planning and decision-making process that can take place at any time when a plan has to be made.

2.56 The Family Justice Review considered FGCs and its extent in different forms in most local authorities in England and Wales in its interim report (April 2011). It found that most respondents to the Review were strongly supportive of FGCs.

---

[6]   Revised and replaced by the *Practice Direction Public Law Proceedings Guide to Case Management* in force from 6 April 2010, and are now incorporated into the Family Procedure Rules at *Practice Direction 12A: Public Law Proceedings Guide to Case Management* which came into force on 6 April 2011 – see Chapter 4.

[7]   Ministry of Justice, August 2009.

[8]   See Chapter 4.

[9]   Department for Children, Schools and Families *The Children Act 1989 Guidance and Regulations* vol 1: court orders (2nd edn, 2008), para 3.8.

[10]   *Practice Direction: Guide to Case Management in Public Law Proceedings* (January 2008).

[11]   See Public Law Outline (PLO) Pre-Proceedings Checklist in *Practice Direction: Guide to Case Management in Public Law Proceedings* (January 2008), para 10. See also Chapter 4.

2.57   The Family Justice Review final report (November 2011) concluded that FGCs have real potential to add value and can be useful in terms of their effect on delay in care proceedings, although more research is needed about their effectiveness, quality and cost to identify what works best in which circumstances. Pending stronger guidance as a result of such research, the Family Justice Review recommended that the government and judiciary encourage the use of FGCs as one of the alternatives to conventional court proceedings.[12]

The general principles

2.58   The key concept underpinning the FGC is that the family knows best. The family, widely defined, is believed to have the information, knowledge, skills and resources to identify welfare and protection issues within their family, and find the most appropriate solutions to overcome their problems. The task of the social worker is then to assist the family in implementing their chosen solution.

Definition of the 'family'

2.59   The term 'family' is widely defined for the purposes of an FGC and may include any significant others who are not necessarily blood related. It may include friends and/or advocate for the child. It is assumed that all family members, including the child, grandparents and other extended family members will be invited to attend the FGC. Only in rare circumstances will any member be excluded from attending. It is also usually assumed that an FGC is not viable if all participants are members of the one household (eg single parents with no other family members).

The process of FGCs

2.60   An FGC is a decision-making forum enabling the family to take responsibility for planning for the needs of their children.

FGCs consist of four stages:

Stage 1

2.61   Appointment of an *independent coordinator* who is not involved with the family or with the day-to-day service provision of local authorities. The coordinator identifies who is in the family and invites them to the conference at a venue of their choice (more details below).

---

[12]   Family Justice Review Final Report, Ministry of Justice, Nov 2011 paragraph 3.171.

Stage 2

2.62 Presentation by the *information giver* – professionals involved with the family, usually the social worker, are invited to the conference to share their information and knowledge of concerns with the family and answer any questions. They should prepare a written report to which the family could refer during their private time.

Stage 3

2.63 Professionals leave the conference, leaving the family to plan how best they can meet their child(ren)'s needs, including proposals for monitoring and evaluation. The coordinator is available to assist the family.

Stage 4

2.64 Professionals rejoin the conference to hear the solutions offered by the family and make any necessary arrangements for implementation. Professionals may reject the plan of the family only with clear evidence that the child(ren) may be suffering significant harm.

The role of the information giver

2.65 Social workers should be clear about the issues to be addressed when writing their reports, and giving their presentations to the conference. In particular, they should include:

- an outline of the concerns in respect of each child, which should be stated in a respectful, clear and concrete manner;

- the context (in brief) of these concerns;

- what, if any, are the current childcare plans in respect of each child;

- what areas the family's care plan *must* address – social workers should be clear about the 'bottom line';

- what resources, if any, are already being used by the family;

- what other resources might be available or helpful to the family (from within the local authority and/or the private and voluntary sector) and how the family can get access to them.

The role of the coordinator

2.66 On receiving a referral, the coordinator's first task will be to map out the extended family and friends, starting with the child(ren). The coordinator will need to ensure that they explain to family members their role and independence.

2.67 The way in which this task is approached will obviously depend to a large extent on the age of the child. Generally speaking, coordinators should expect to see the child with the parents first before meeting with him or her alone. It is important to establish who the child sees as their special friend within the family network, or even beyond.

2.68 As a general principle, families should be encouraged to spread the net as widely as possible to include everybody within the family, whether or not they are in regular contact with each other.

2.69 The second task is to invite those people identified as being part of the family's network to the conference. As far as possible, this should be done by means of a personal visit, since it is likely that many, if not all the family members, will need help in preparing themselves for the conference. It is not unknown for coordinators to invite family members from abroad, with the local authority giving financial assistance. Family members have a right to choose a venue and time that suits them.

2.70 It is the responsibility of the coordinator to clarify with the referring social worker which professionals are to be invited as information givers and then to ensure that they are invited.

What happens at the FGC?

2.71 The coordinator will chair the start of the meeting and will ensure that the family have all the necessary information from the professionals. The family is charged with four tasks:

- to decide whether they disagree with any of the concerns raised by the professionals;

- to devise and agree a plan to meet the child's needs;

- to agree how this plan will be reviewed;

- to agree contingency plans if the original plan is not working.

2.72 It is important for the coordinator and the professionals to leave the conference to enable the family to deliberate in private. The coordinator returns at the family's request to help them to formally record the plan. It is important that the coordinator does not comment on the family's plan. The job is just to help them record it point by point, identifying resources needed, responsibility for action, any arrangements for monitoring or review and timescales. The coordinator will then need to establish with the family who is to present the plan to the professionals and agree with those people how they would like the coordinator to help in this.

The presentation of the plan

2.73 The coordinator and family members will meet with the professionals to present the family's plan and negotiate resources. There are no particular guidelines for this stage, other than that the coordinator has the general responsibility to ensure that the family plan receives a fair hearing and that the professionals do not try to undermine or even sabotage it. It may occasionally be necessary to remind the professionals of the prior commitment only to reject the family's plan if it can be clearly shown that the plan places the child at risk of significant harm.

What happens after the FGC?

2.74 It is the coordinator's responsibility to ensure that everyone concerned has a copy of the plan that has been agreed and recorded. The plan should also identify by whom and how the plan is to be monitored and evaluated. At times there may be a need to convene another FGC.

2.75 The key elements of FGCs are that they:

- operate as a primary planning and decision-making forum;

- allow a wide definition of the family;

- represent an inclusive model which includes children;

- enable advocacy for the child;

- ensure that family members outnumber professionals; and

- facilitate the chosen language of the family.

SECTION 4 – SOCIAL WORK RECORDS

The importance of social work records

2.76 *Working Together*[13] provides clear guidance as to the role of record keeping within the local authority's decision-making and planning for children.

---

[13] Department for Children, Schools and Families (DCSF) (now DfE) *Working Together to Safeguard Children – A Guide to Inter-agency Working to Safeguard and Promote the Welfare of Children* ('*Working Together*') (TSO, 4th edn, 2010).

Well-maintained records are an essential element of good professional practice. Safeguarding and promoting the welfare of children requires information to be brought together from a number of different sources and careful professional judgments to be made on the basis of this information.

2.77 Clear and accurate records help social workers by:

- ensuring that there is a documented account of an agency's or professional's involvement with a child and/or family;

- providing a clear focus of work;

- enabling effective communication across agency and professional boundaries;

- providing continuity when individual workers are unavailable or changed;

- allowing managers to monitor and supervise work;

- providing evidence for investigations and assessments; and

- providing evidence for court proceedings.

2.78 Analysis of social work records should ensure that records are clear, accessible and comprehensive.

2.79 Good records should include:

- specific decisions (where decisions have been endorsed by a manager or taken jointly across agencies this should be made clear);

- clear evaluations and analysis of information;

- notes of work carried out clearly, concisely, accurately and in straightforward language;

- name of social worker or manager who made critical decisions; and

- details of the source of information received from other professionals.

2.80 Records should differentiate between:

- fact;

- opinion;

- judgment; and

- hypothesis.

2.81 Local authorities should ensure that records are stored safely and can be retrieved promptly and efficiently.

SECTION 5 – SUPERVISION OF SOCIAL WORKERS

The importance of social workers' supervision

2.82 Working to ensure children are protected from harm requires sound professional judgments to be made by social workers. It is demanding work that can be distressing and stressful. Supervision is particularly crucial within the assessment process:[14]

> 'Collecting information which will help explain what is happening to children and their families and making sense of that information are key tasks in the assessment process. These tasks require knowledge, confidence and skill, underpinned by regular training and professional supervision.'

2.83 Effective supervision is important because it:

- ensures that practitioners fully understand their roles, responsibilities and the scope of their professional discretion and authority;

- ensures that the key social work processes (assessment, planning, intervention and reviewing) are being carried out consistently and in accordance with regulations, statutory guidance, Local Safeguarding Children's Boards and organisational procedures;

- promotes good standards of practice and ensures that practice is soundly based;

- provides support and guidance to individual staff members;

- promotes the retention of good quality staff;

- ensures accountability of individual staff members; and

- helps identify the training and development needs of practitioners, so that each has the skills to provide an effective service.

2.84 Supervision should include:

- an opportunity for the supervisor and social worker to reflect on and evaluate the work planned or carried out;

---

[14] The Department of Health *Framework for the Assessment of Children in Need and Their Families* (TSO, 2000), para 4.2.

- an opportunity for the supervisor to scrutinise the content and quality of the work planned or carried out;

- an opportunity for the supervisor and the social worker to analyse the strengths and weaknesses of the practitioner;

- the provision of coaching, development and pastoral support;

- the provision of independent and objective advice and expertise;

- an opportunity for the endorsement of the social worker's judgments at certain key points in the process of a case;

- record of key decisions within the child's case records.

2.85 The Munro Review Final Report (May 2011) reiterates that critical appraisal of the assessment and planning for a child and family should be seen as central to good practice in reducing error. Ideally this should be part of the local authority culture and seen, not as a personal attack on the individual social worker, but as an outsider helping to pick up the unseen spots or offering a new angle on the problem. The Munro Review makes it clear that supervision is one context in which this can happen: it should not be limited to this but something that colleagues or fellow professionals are able to do. The more punitive and defensive the culture, the harder it is for anyone to accept flaws in their reasoning.[15]

2.86 Social workers should have access to advice and support from:

- peers;

- supervisors;

- managers; and

- specialist consultants (inside and outside the local authority).

---

[15]   *The Munro Review of Child Protection: Final Report – A Child-Centred* System, Cm 8062 (May 2011), para 6.30

Chapter 3

THE REFERRAL TO THE LOCAL AUTHORITY

SECTION 1 – SOURCES OF REFERRAL

3.1   A wide range of professionals or other individuals may make referrals about children to the local authority. The following paragraph lists the professionals likely to make referrals.

3.2   There are numerous possible sources of information for lawyers to consider regarding disclosure about referrals to the local authority, for example:

- social workers from other local authorities;

- social workers or staff from voluntary organisations;

- nursery staff;

- teachers;

- youth workers;

- health visitors;

- the police;

- domestic violence refuge staff;

- GPs;

- speech therapists;

- hospital staff (including Accident and Emergency staff and paediatricians);

- school nurses;

- probation officers;

- prison officers;

- child minders;

- CAMHS (Child and Adolescent Mental Heath Service) staff;

- community psychiatric nurses (CPNs) involved with parents or other family members;

- psychiatrists;

- psychologists; and

- substance misuse workers involved with parents or other family members.

3.3   Referrals can also be made by friends, family or neighbours of the child and family (explicitly or anonymously).

3.4   Referrals can be made electronically, in writing, telephone or by direct face-to-face visits to the local authority's offices. In some circumstances, practitioners in other agencies may have undertaken a Common Assessment (using the Common Assessment Framework – see Chapter 2) because they had concerns about a child and were trying to ascertain how best to help, or the findings from the Common Assessment may have caused them to be concerned about a child's welfare.

SECTION 2 – RESPONSIBILITIES OF STAFF IN OTHER AGENCIES

3.5   Staff members who have concerns about a child should discuss these with their manager, a named or designated health professional or a designated member of staff, depending on the organisational setting. Concerns can also be discussed – without necessarily identifying the child in question – with senior colleagues in another agency in order to develop an understanding of the child's needs and circumstances.

3.6   If, after discussion, these concerns remain, and it seems that the child and family would benefit from other services – including those from within another part of the same agency – decisions should be made about to whom to make a referral.

3.7   If the child is considered to be, or may be, a child in need under the Children Act 1989, the child should be referred to the children's services social work team. This includes a child who is believed to be, or may be at risk of, suffering significant harm. If these concerns arise about a child who is already known to the local authority, the allocated social worker should be informed of these concerns.

3.8 *Working Together*[1] provides that staff should:

- never delay emergency action to protect a child from harm;

- always record in writing concerns about a child's welfare, including whether or not further action is taken;

- always record in writing discussions about a child's welfare;

- at the close of a discussion, always reach a clear and explicit recorded agreement about who will be taking what action, or that no further action will be taken.

3.9 The Common Assessment Framework (CAF) offers a basis for early referral and information sharing between organisations and provides a structure for the written referral from other agencies. Professionals who phone the local authority should confirm their referrals in writing within 48 hours.

3.10 For lawyers there are clear implications of the guidance relating to referrals from other agencies, particularly in terms of the later analysis of the local authority's decision-making and issues of disclosure. Lawyers should consider seeking disclosure of documents relating to referrals, not just from the local authority, but also from other agencies. Cross-referencing this information against existing evidence may be particularly revealing. For example, it may become clear that there is a repeated pattern of referrals about a child from school that have not been dealt with efficiently or effectively by the local authority, or it may become clear that concerns by another agency are not properly substantiated when cross-referenced against other evidence.

SECTION 3 – THE RESPONSE TO REFERRALS

3.11 When a parent, professional, or another person contacts the local authority with concerns about a child's welfare, it is the responsibility of the local authority to clarify specific matters with the referrer (including self-referrals from children and families).

3.12 There is a clear expectation of what should be achieved by the local authority at the end of any discussion or dialogue about a child between the local authority and the referrer.

---

[1] Department for Children, Schools and Families (DCSF) (now DfE) *Working Together to Safeguard Children – A Guide to Inter-agency Working to Safeguard and Promote the Welfare of Children* ('*Working Together*') (TSO, 4th edn, 2010).

3.13

What should the local authority clarify when a referral is received?

- *Who* is the child and family: name, address, date of birth, gender, school or nursery, chosen language, any communication issues, siblings, carers, and significant others, religion, ethnic origin, disability, who has parental responsibility and their names and addresses, if different from the above

- *What* is the nature of the concern(s) or alleged injuries (including the location and size of injuries where appropriate, as well as the context leading the referrer to make contact with the department)

- *When* the incident(s) occurred, and what the child said and to whom about it, and whether anyone had witnessed what had happened

- *How* the referrer has explained to the child and / or any other person this referral to the department

- *Patterns* need to be considered when reading files and evaluating information to enable a decision to be made as to whether it is possible to form a hypothesis at this stage

- *Professional network* – it is essential to get details of professionals and other agencies involved. Non-professional referrers have a right to refer children anonymously

- *Context* – establish the context in which the incident or concerns occurred and take into account any significant pressures the child and / or family are experiencing

---

3.14

What should the local authority have achieved by the end of the referral process?

- Acknowledged a written referral within one working day of receipt of the referral

- Discussed the referral with the referring professional

- Discussed the referral with any other relevant agencies (including the police, where a criminal offence may have been committed against a child)

- Considered information held in existing local authority records

- Considered the referral on the basis of the available evidence:

  – Are there concerns about the child's health and development?
  – Is there actual or potential harm to justify an initial assessment to establish whether this child is possibly a child in need?

- Convened (if sufficient evidence) an immediate strategy discussion between the police, local authority children's social care and other agencies as appropriate if emergency action should be taken to safeguard and promote the welfare of a child

- Made a decision and plan for the next steps of action within one working day of receipt of the referral

- Made a written record of the decision and the reasons for the decision (even if no further action is to be taken) within one working day of receipt of the referral consistent with the information set out in the Referral and Initial Information Record (RIIR)

- Given clear information to referrer about:

  – proposed action (with reasons) which may include:

    - proceeding with s 47 investigation
    - referral to other agencies
    - the provision of advice or information
    - no further action
  – proposed timescales
  – action to be taken by whom

SECTION 4 – PARTNERSHIP DURING THE REFERRAL PROCESS

3.15 Issues of partnership with children and families can often be forgotten during the referral process. Lawyers should take care to analyse the actions of social work professionals during the early stages of referral and action as follows:

- Parents' permission, and the child's permission where appropriate, should be sought before discussing a referral about them with other agencies, unless seeking permission may itself place a child at increased risk of significant harm.

- When responding to referrals from a member of the public rather than another professional, the local authority should only disclose personal information about referrers, including identifying details to third parties, with the consent of the referrer.

- In all cases where the police are involved, the decision about when to inform the parents (about referrals from third parties) will have a bearing on the conduct of police investigations.

- Where the local authority decides to take no further action in response to a referral from a member of the public, feedback should be provided to the referrer in a manner consistent with respecting the confidentiality of the child.

- In deciding whether there is a need to share information, professionals should consider any duty of confidentiality to the child. The professional may lawfully share information if the child consents or if there is a public interest of sufficient force. This must be judged by the professional on the facts of each case:

  - where there is a clear risk of significant harm to a child, or serious harm to adults, the public interest test will almost certainly be satisfied; and
  - in cases where practitioners need to share some confidential information in order to make decisions or take action, the information shared should be proportionate.

3.16 New information may be received about a child or family where the child or family member is already known to the local authority. If the child's case is open, and there are concerns that the child is or may be suffering harm, then a decision should be made about whether a strategy discussion should be initiated. In these circumstances, it may not be necessary to undertake an initial assessment before deciding what to do next. It may, however, be appropriate to undertake a core assessment or to update a previous one, in order to understand the child's current needs and circumstances and inform future decision-making.

SECTION 5 – KEEPING RECORDS

3.17 Social workers should record all information about a referral in the Referral and Initial Information Record (RIIR). Guidance for social workers about the approach to using the RIIR is contained in the statutory guidance *The Framework for Assessment: guidance notes and glossary for Referral and Initial Information Record, Initial Assessment Record and Core Assessment Record.*[2]

3.18 The RIIR begins the process of systematic information gathering about children in need and their families. This process is continued in the Initial Assessment and Core Assessment Records. The records have been designed to provide an integrated framework for the process of recording and analysing information in line with the *Framework for Assessment: Practice Guidance.*[3]

3.19

What are the purposes of the Referral and Initial Information Record (RIIR)?

- Records the reason for the referral or request for services to the local authority

- Enables social workers to gather together all essential information about the child including:

  - culture, ethnicity, religion
  - household composition
  - parental responsibility
  - agencies currently involved with the child and family
  - any disabilities

- Records the nature of the local authority's response to the referral

- Records the nature of the responses by other agencies to the referral

---

3.20 Some referrals can be dealt with by the provision of information and advice or a referral to another agency. When referrals require a response from a local authority then an initial assessment should be carried out.

---

2   Department of Health (2000).
3   Department of Health (2000).

RIIR SECTION	SOCIAL WORKER'S RESPONSE
Reason for referral/request for services	Brief details about the reason for the referral or request for services.
Further action	Details about • what action has been taken, and • what action is planned, by whom and from which agency. This includes the decision to take no further action. The referral should be collated with previous referrals and/or case files, which should be consulted. The information in those documents should be considered as part of the analysis and decision-making processes.
Signature and date	The social worker who has completed the referral should always sign and date the record. The record should then be passed to the relevant manager to confirm the action recommended (in accordance with the local authority's own policies).

Chapter 4

LOCAL AUTHORITY INVESTIGATIONS

SECTION 1 – THE SECTION 47 INVESTIGATION

The legal framework

4.1 Section 47 of the Children Act 1989 (CA 1989) provides for the local authority's duty to investigate and make enquiries in relation to children within its area. Where a local authority:

- is informed that a child who lives, or is found, in its area:

    - is the subject of an emergency protection order (EPO); or
    - is in police protection; or
    - has contravened a ban imposed by a curfew notice within the meaning of chapter 1 of Part 1 of the Crime and Disorder Act 1998; or

- has reasonable cause to suspect that a child who lives, or is found, in its area is suffering, or is likely to suffer, significant harm,

the authority shall make, or cause to be made, such enquiries as they consider necessary to enable them to decide whether they should take any action to safeguard or promote the child's welfare.

4.2 In *Re S (Sexual Abuse Allegations: Local Authority Response)*,[1] it was held that the test to be applied under s 47 is 'quite low' and does not require conclusions or facts to be established on the balance of probabilities. The test in s 47 is 'reasonable cause to suspect'.

4.3 *Working Together*[2] provides guidance on what should happen if somebody has concerns about the welfare of a child (including those living away from home), and in particular concerns that a child may be suffering, or may be at risk of suffering, significant harm. It also sets out the principles that underpin work to safeguard and promote the welfare of children.

---

[1]   [2001] 2 FLR 776.
[2]   Department for Children, Schools and Families (DCSF) (now DfE) *Working Together to Safeguard Children – A Guide to Inter-agency Working to Safeguard and Promote the Welfare of Children* ('*Working Together*') (TSO, 4th edn, 2010) 5.

4.4 In *Birmingham City Council v AG and A*,[3] the court considered the impact of the local authority's failure to consider an enquiry under s 47 following the death by starvation of a young child and the severe neglect, physical abuse and malnutrition of her siblings. It was held that the lack of a coordinated response from all the relevant professionals involved with a family meant that each professional carried out his or her own duties in isolation, information had not been passed on and relevant connections had not been made.

The purpose of the s 47 inquiry

4.5 The purpose of the local authority's enquiries conducted under s 47 is to determine whether action is needed to promote and safeguard the welfare of the child or children who are the subject of the enquiries. The *Framework for Assessment*[4] provides the structure for helping to collect and analyse the information gathered (see Chapter 5).

4.6 There are several specific duties placed upon local authorities during the conduct of the s 47 investigation:

- the s 47 investigation must be directed in particular to establishing whether the local authority should make any application to the court, or exercise any powers under CA 1989 with respect to the child (s 47(3)(a));

- where a child has already been made subject of an EPO and is not in local authority accommodation, then the local authority should direct its enquiries to establishing whether it would be in the child's best interests to be in local authority accommodation (s 47(3)(b));

- if during the course of the investigation, the local authority concludes that it should take a certain course of action to safeguard or promote the child's welfare, then it must take that action so far as it is within its powers and reasonably practicable for it to do so (s 47(8)); for example, issue court proceedings, or offer services to the child and his family.

4.7 In *Birmingham City Council v AG and A*,[5] the local authority was roundly criticised for shortcomings in the initial assessment visit to the family. It was held that the social worker's visit had been insufficient for the purposes even of an initial assessment: the only mandatory enquiry was seeing the children, which included observation and talking with the child in an age-appropriate way. The welfare issues, which should have been at the forefront of any social work enquiries with the family, had not been considered at all.

---

3   [2010] 2 FLR 580.
4   Department of Health *Framework for the Assessment of Children in Need and Their Families* (TSO, 2000).
5   [2010] 2 FLR 580.

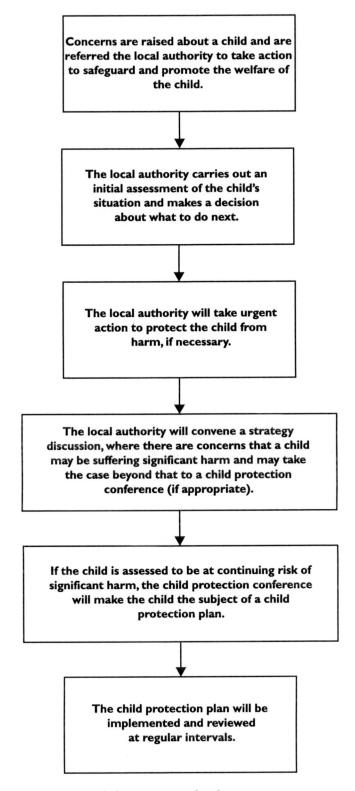

The local authority's response to referrals

Working with other agencies

4.8   The professionals conducting s 47 investigations should do their utmost to secure willing co-operation and participation from all professionals and services, by being prepared to explain and justify their actions, and to demonstrate that the process is being managed in a way that can help to bring about better outcomes for children. The Local Safeguarding Children Board (LSCB) has an important role to play in cultivating and promoting a climate of trust and understanding between different professionals and services.

4.9   The requirement for the local authority to consult other agencies during all its investigation and assessment processes is well established as a theme in both the CA 1989 and in all the accompanying guidance (but particularly within *Working Together*):

- s 47(5) provides that the local authority must consult the local education authority if it appears during the course of enquiries that there are matters relating to a child's education;

- ss 47(9) and (11) (and *Working Together*) impose a duty on a number of public bodies (including any local authority, local education authority, housing authority, health authority or NHS trust) to assist the local authority with its inquiries if called on to do so (unless to assist would be unreasonable in the circumstances: s 47(10)).

4.10   LSCBs should have in place a protocol agreed between the local authority and the police, to guide both organisations in deciding how child protection enquiries should be conducted, and the circumstances in which joint enquiries are appropriate.

4.11

Analysing the local authority's actions during s 47 investigations

- Has the local authority considered whether any application to the court should be made?

- Has the local authority considered whether it could exercise any powers under the CA 1989 with respect to the child? For example:

  - the use of s 8 orders
  - the use of an exclusion orders attached to an emergency protection order (EPO) (s 44A) or to an interim care order (ICO?) (s 38A)
  - the use of s 17 powers to assist children in need

- Has the local authority taken any action recommended to safeguard or promote a child's welfare?

- Has the local authority consulted other relevant agencies (such as the police, schools, health visiting service, GP, nurseries, other local authorities) during the investigation?

- Does the local authority's s 47 assessment include contributions from other relevant agencies?

- Have the basic principles for investigation and assessments been adhered to by the local authority?

- Have the wishes and feelings of the children been sought?

SECTION 2 – THE STRATEGY DISCUSSION

4.12 If the s 47 investigation gives the local authority reasonable cause to suspect that a child is suffering, or is likely to suffer significant harm, the local authority should arrange a strategy discussion involving the local authority and the police, and other agencies as appropriate (for example, school and health), in particular any referring agency.

4.13 The strategy discussion should be convened by the local authority and those participating should be sufficiently senior and able to make decisions on behalf of their agencies. If the child is a hospital patient (in-patient or out-patient) or receiving services from a child development team, the medical consultant responsible for the child's health care should be involved, as should the senior ward nurse if the child is an in-patient. Where a medical examination may be necessary or has taken place a senior doctor from those organisations providing services should also be involved.

The timing of a strategy discussion

4.14 Some LSCBs have defined specific timelines for strategy discussions within their local child protection procedures. However, a strategy discussion may take place at any point following a referral, or at any other time (for example, if concerns about significant harm emerge in respect of child receiving support under s 17).

The purpose of a strategy discussion

4.15   The strategy discussion should be used to:

- share available information;

- agree the conduct and timing of any criminal investigation;

- decide whether a core assessment under the CA 1989, s 47 should be initiated, or continued if it has already begun;

- plan how the s 47 enquiry should be undertaken (if one is to be initiated), including the need for medical treatment, and who will carry out what actions, by when and for what purpose;

- agree what action is required immediately to safeguard and promote the welfare of the child, and/or provide interim services and support. If the child is in hospital, decisions should also be made about how to secure the safe discharge of the child;

- determine what information from the strategy discussion will be shared with the family, unless such information sharing may place a child at increased risk of significant harm or jeopardise police investigations into any alleged offence(s); and

- determine if any legal action is required.

4.16 Any information shared at the strategy meeting, all decisions reached, and the basis for those decisions, should be clearly recorded by the chair of the strategy discussion and circulated within one working day to all parties to the discussion. The local authority should record such information in the Record of Strategy Discussion.

4.17 Any decisions about taking immediate action should be kept under constant review. Section 47 enquiries may run concurrently with police investigations concerning possible associated crimes. The findings from the assessment and/or police investigation should be used to inform plans about future support and help to the child and family. They may also contribute to legal proceedings, whether criminal, civil or both.

The format of the strategy discussion

4.18 A strategy discussion may take place at a meeting or by other means (for example, by telephone). In complex types of maltreatment a meeting is likely to be the most effective way of discussing the child's welfare and planning future action. More than one strategy discussion may be necessary. This is likely to be where the child's circumstances are very complex and a number of discussions are required to consider whether and, if so, when to initiate s 47 enquiries, as well as how best to undertake them. Such a meeting should be held at a convenient location for the key attendees, such as a hospital, school, police station or children's services office.

Joint investigations between the local authority and the police

4.19 Each LSCB should have in place a protocol for the local authority and the police, to guide both agencies in deciding how s 47 enquiries and associated police investigations should be conducted jointly, and in particular, in what circumstances s 47 enquiries and linked criminal investigations are necessary and/or appropriate. When joint enquiries take place, the police will take the lead for the criminal investigation and the local authority will take the lead for the s 47 enquiries and the child's welfare. While no rigid rules apply, it is desirable that interviews with young children should be conducted as soon as possible after any allegations are first made.[6] Where a child has been interviewed on a number of occasions, the court may later attach a diminishing weight to what is said by the child in the later interviews.[7] It is normally undesirable for a parent to be present with the child during an interview, and the interviewing social worker and/or police officer should avoid using questions which force or lead the child or young person's responses. Any joint child protection interview conducted by police and social services must follow the guidance *Achieving Best Evidence in Criminal Proceedings* (which replaced the previous Memorandum of Good Practice in March 2002).[8] Adherence to the good practice described in the guidance is voluntary. Although the guidance relates solely to criminal proceedings, *Achieving Best Evidence* (ABE) represents a detailed distillation of the good practice that has developed for the interviewing of children and the principles are applicable to care (and indeed private law) cases.

---

[6] *Re D (Child Abuse: Interviews)* [1998] 2 FLR 10; *Re M (Sexual Abuse Allegations: Interviewing Techniques)* [1999] 2 FLR 92.

[7] *Re E (A Minor) (Child Abuse: Evidence)* [1991] 1 FLR 420; *Re D (Child Abuse: Interviews)* [1998] 2 FLR 10.

[8] *Achieving Best Evidence in Criminal Proceedings: Guidance for Vulnerable or Intimidated Witnesses, including Children* (Department for Education, Department of Health, March 2011) (can be downloaded from www.cps.gov.uk and www.homeoffice.gov.uk).

4.20

Analysing the strategy discussion

- Were people from a range of relevant agencies invited to participate in the strategy discussion?

- Did the relevant people participate in the strategy discussion?

- If the child was medically examined, was a senior medical practitioner involved in the strategy discussion?

- Did the strategy discussion take place sufficiently promptly following the referral (or notification of concerns about the child to the local authority)?

- Was the information provided and the decisions reached (including any decision to take no further action) during the strategy discussion clearly recorded in the Record of Strategy Discussion?

- Was any provision made at the strategy discussion for review of the decisions reached?

- Was any joint investigation between the police and the local authority conducted in accordance with the LSCB protocols?

- Were any recommendations made about whether to interview any child under the ABE guidance?

- Has a decision been made in relation to parental participation in the investigation process?

SECTION 3 – ASSESSMENT DURING THE SECTION 47 INVESTIGATION

4.21 As already identified, the objective of the local authority's s 47 investigation is to determine whether action is required to safeguard and promote the welfare of the child or children who are the subjects of the enquiries.

4.22 The local authority should carry out the s 47 investigation by completing a core assessment in respect of the child. The core assessment should be led by a qualified and experienced social worker. The *Framework for the Assessment of Children in Need and their Families* provides the structure for helping to collect and analyse information obtained in the course of s 47 enquiries – see Chapter 5. The local authority may already have gathered preliminary information via an initial assessment or Common Assessment Framework (CAF) assessment. Alternatively, the local authority may have decided to proceed directly to a core assessment (for example, in a case where the child is well known to the local authority or where the issues to be investigated are clearly serious or complex).

Interviews with the child during the s 47 assessment

4.23 The social worker (and police if necessary) should aim to carry out separate interviews with the child who is the subject of concern (where appropriate in view of the child's age and understanding). When children are first interviewed, the nature and extent of any harm suffered by them may not be clear, nor whether a criminal offence has been committed. It is important that even initial discussions with children are conducted in a way that minimises any distress caused to them, and maximises the likelihood that they will provide accurate and complete information. It is important, wherever possible, to have separate communication with a child. Leading or suggestive communication should always be avoided. Children may need time, and more than one opportunity, in order to develop sufficient trust to communicate any concerns they may have, especially if they have communication difficulties, learning disabilities, are very young, or are experiencing mental health problems. If the child is unable to take part in an interview because of age or understanding, alternative means of understanding the child's wishes or feelings should be used, including observation where children are very young or where they have communication impairments.

4.24 Exceptionally, a joint enquiry or investigation team may need to speak to a suspected child victim without the knowledge of the parent or caregiver. Relevant circumstances could include:

• the possibility that a child would be threatened or otherwise coerced into silence;

• a strong likelihood that important evidence would be destroyed;

• the possibility that the child in question did not wish the parent to be involved at that stage, and is competent to take that decision.

4.25 In all cases where the police are involved, the decision about when to inform the parent or caregiver will have a bearing on the conduct of police investigations, and the strategy discussion should decide on the most appropriate timing of parental participation.

SECTION 4 – *ACHIEVING BEST EVIDENCE* INTERVIEWS

4.26 In accordance with the guidance in ABE,[9] all joint interviews with children should be conducted by those with specialist training and experience in interviewing children. Additional specialist help may be required where:

- the child does not speak English at a level that enables him or her to participate in the interview;

- the child appears to have a degree of psychiatric disturbance but is deemed competent;

- the child has an impairment of some sort;

- interviewers do not have adequate knowledge and understanding of the child's racial, religious or cultural background.

4.27 Consideration should also be given to the gender of interviewers, particularly in cases of alleged sexual abuse.

4.28 The ABE guidance describes generic good practice in interviewing victims and witnesses, and in preparing them to give their best evidence in court. The status of the guidance is advisory and does not constitute a legally enforceable code of conduct.

4.29 The guidance considers preparing and planning for interviews with witnesses, decisions about whether or not to conduct an interview, and decisions about whether the interview should be video-recorded or whether it would be more appropriate for a written statement to be taken following the interview. It covers the interviewing of witnesses both for the purposes of making a video-recorded statement and also for taking a written statement, their preparation for court and the subsequent court appearance. It applies to both prosecution and defence witnesses and is intended for all persons involved in relevant investigations, including the police, adults and children's social care workers, and members of the legal profession.

4.30 Key general points in the revised guidance include the following:

- The needs of vulnerable witnesses should be identified as early as possible during the criminal justice process, and the information recorded and passed on to the CPS. The early identification of a vulnerable witness will improve the quality of an investigation by assisting the witness to give information to the police and assist the legal process by helping the witness give their best evidence in court.

- Any visually recorded statement must be of good quality so that where a prosecution takes place this can be conducted as effectively as possible.

---

[9] Department for Education, Department of Health, March 2011.

- Training alone for practitioners is unlikely to be effective – there should be a means of quality assuring interviews on an ongoing basis while developing, maintaining and enhancing the skills of interviewers.

- Vulnerable witnesses need support from the moment they experience or witness a crime, and support needs to be sustained throughout the whole process of reporting the crime, making a statement, pre-trial preparation, entering court procedures, and post-trial.

- Specialist training should be developed to interview witnesses with particular needs. This should include interviewing child witnesses, traumatised witnesses and witnesses with a mental disorder, learning disability or physical disability impacting on communication. Such training should include working with intermediaries. However, training alone is unlikely to deliver effective performance in the workplace. Training needs to be set in the context of a developmental assessment regime. Such a regime should deliver a means of quality assuring interviews, while developing, maintaining and enhancing the skills of interviewers. The regime should be supported by an agreed assessment protocol. In the case of police interviewers, such a protocol should take account of the National Occupational Standards for interviews with witnesses developed in Skills for Justice. Agencies regularly involved in conducting interviews with witnesses should have the necessary policies, procedures and management structures in place to quality assure interviews on an ongoing basis.

The structure of the ABE guidance

4.31 The ABE guidance sets out in detail the various stages that should be included within the planning, conduct and evaluation of an effective interview with a child or vulnerable witness.

Planning and preparation for interviews

4.32 The importance of planning cannot be overstated. Even if the circumstances necessitate an early interview, an appropriate planning session that takes account of all the information available about the witness at the time and identifies the key issues and objectives is required. It is important that, as far as possible, the case is thoroughly reviewed before an interview is embarked upon to ensure that all issues are covered and key questions asked, since the opportunity to do this will in most cases be lost once the interview(s) have been concluded.

4.33 The planning information should be used to set the objectives for the interview and determine the techniques used within the phased interview. The planning information should also be used to decide:

- the means by which the interview is to be recorded;

- who should conduct the interview and if anybody else should be present (including social support for the witness);

- if anybody should monitor the interview (eg investigating officer, supervising officer, specialist/interview adviser, etc) and who will operate the equipment;

- the location of the interview;

- the timing of the interview;

- the duration of the interview (including pace, breaks and the possibility of more than one session); and

- what is likely to happen after the interview.

4.34 Setting clear objectives for the interview is important because they give direction to the interview and contribute to its structure. The interview objectives should focus on the alleged incident or event(s), and any case-specific information important to the investigation.

4.35 The aim of the interview should be to achieve all the objectives that are set for it while being as concise as reasonably possible.

Conducting the interview

4.36 The basic goal of an interview with a witness is to obtain an accurate and reliable account in a way which is fair, is in the witness's interests and is acceptable to the court. Over the years, many professionals have recommended the use of the phased approach of interviewing, starting with a free narrative phase and then gradually becoming more and more specific in the nature of the questioning in order to elicit further detail.

4.37 However, inclusion of a phased approach in the ABE guidance should not be taken to imply that all other techniques are necessarily unacceptable or to preclude their development, nor should the phased approach be regarded as a checklist to be rigidly worked through. The phased interview was primarily developed for interviewing witnesses who are reasonably articulate, and the ABE guidance emphasises that flexibility is the key to successful interviewing.

4.38 Nevertheless, phased interviewing should not be departed from by interviewers unless they have discussed and agreed the reasons for doing so with their senior manager(s) or an interview adviser.[10]

4.39 For all witnesses, interviews should normally consist of four main phases:

---

[10]   See Association of Chief Police Officers *National Investigative Interviewing Strategy* (2009).

- phase 1 – establishing rapport;

- phase 2 – free narrative account;

- phase 3 – questioning; and

- phase 4 – closing the interview.

4.40 The planning phase prior to interview should provide guidance to the interviewer about what might be achieved in each of the four main phases of the interview. No interview should be conducted without prior, proper planning. A typical interview structure diagram is set out at figure 3.1 in the ABE guidance.

4.41 The ABE guidance defines the various types of question which may be used in interviews and distinguishes them in terms of how directive they are. The guidance is clear that questioning should, whenever possible, commence with open-ended questions and then proceed, if necessary, to specific-closed questions. The guidance sets out the difficulties for witnesses in being asked multiple questions, and confirms that forced-choice questions and leading questions should only be used as a last resort.

4.42 It is important that the interviewer asks only one question at a time, and allows the witness enough time to complete their answer before asking a further question. Patience is always required when asking questions, particularly with developmentally younger children who will need time to respond. Interviewers should not be tempted to fill pauses by asking additional questions or making irrelevant comments. Sometimes, silence is the best cue for eliciting further information; but it can also be oppressive and care needs to be taken in the use of this technique. It is important also that the interviewer does not interrupt the witness when they are still speaking. Interrupting the witness may suggest to them that only short answers are required.

4.43 Some children will experience difficulty if, without warning, the interviewer switches the questioning to a new topic. To help witnesses, interviewers should indicate a topic change by saying, for example 'I'd now like to ask you about something else'.

4.44 Many children will have difficulty with questions unless they are simple, contain only one point per question, do not contain abstract words or double negatives, and lack suggestion and jargon.

4.45 It is important that interviewers check that witnesses understand what has just been said to them by asking the witness to convey back to the interviewer (where this is possible) what they understand the interviewer to have just said. If they do not understand a question some children will nevertheless attempt to answer it to the best of their ability by guessing at what is meant, possibly producing an inappropriate reply.

4.46   The information requested in questions should always take account of a child's stage of development. Many concepts that are taken for granted in adult conversation are only acquired gradually as children develop. Therefore, questions that rely upon the grasp of such concepts may produce misleading and unreliable responses from children, which can damage the overall credibility of their statements in the interview. Concepts with which children have difficulty include:

- dates and times;

- length and frequency of events; and

- weight, height and age estimates.

Such concepts are only gradually mastered. For the concept of time, for instance, telling the time is learned by the average child at around 7 years of age, but an awareness of the days of the week and the seasons does not occur until at least a year later. Age norms are only a guide and it should be anticipated in the planning phase whether a particular child is likely to perform above or below such norms.

4.47   After the interview is concluded, there should also be a process of evaluation. Evaluation should take account of both the information obtained *and* the interviewer's performance.

4.48   The ABE guidance also includes specific advice and guidance about the following topics:

- using drawings, pictures, photographs, symbols, dolls, figures and props with children;

- witness support and preparation;

- interviewing disabled children and children with communication difficulties;

- interviewing very young or psychologically disturbed children;

- truth and lies – specific examples intended to explore the difference between truth and lies;

- the enhanced cognitive interview;

- national standards for child witness preparation;

- national standards for the child witness supporter in the live link room;

- technical guidance; and

- guidance on the completion of a record of video interview (ROVI).

Checklist for analysing interviews

4.49 In *Re TW*,[11] it was held that a finding that a relative (TW) had sexually abused a child aged 4 and a half (LR) should be set aside given the deficiencies in the child's ABE interview, and the manner in which the judge dealt with them. The trial judge's analysis of the child's police interview as 'significantly flawed' was endorsed by the Court of Appeal.

4.50 The principal question considered on appeal was whether the extent and implication of the unreliability of the ABE interview were properly taken into account by the trial judge. The Court of Appeal held that, given the deficiencies in the ABE interview and the manner in which the judge dealt with them, there was no doubt that permission to appeal should be granted. It was held that the principal basis upon which the judge reached her finding of fact about whether LR was abused by TW was LR's ABE interview. Analysis of interviews should focus on the four key phases as outlined above:

4.51

Before the interview

- Who conducted the interview?

- Was the interviewer sufficiently and adequately trained?

- How was it decided who should conduct the interview?

- How was it decided if anybody else should be in the interview?

- Was it clear that the interviewer kept an open mind?

4.52

Planning and preparation

- What pre-interview planning took place?

- Was sufficient time allowed for planning?

- Who was involved in planning?

- Were the objectives for the interview clearly defined?

- Were the techniques to be used during the interview clearly identified?

---

[11] [2011] EWCA Civ 17.

- Did the planning of the interview take account of the child's stage of development?

- Who accompanied the child to the interview?

- What conversations took place with the child between the child's first statement or indication about concerns, and the actual interview (eg: discussions with foster carers, teachers, contact supervisors, escorts)?

- Where was the child during such conversations?

- Are there any contemporaneous notes of such conversations?

- What consideration was given to the location, timing and duration of the interview (including pace, breaks and the possibility of more than one session)?

- What planning was there about what should happen after the interview?

4.53

Conduct of the interview

- Who operated the equipment and were they present throughout?

- Was a phased approach taken during the interview?

- Were each of the phases clearly distinguished?

- What types of question were used?

- How directive were the questions used? Were forced-choice or leading questions used?

- Were multiple questions used?

- Did the interview commence with open-ended questions and then proceed, if necessary, to specific-closed questions?

- Was the child allowed enough time to complete their answers before being asked further questions?

- Did the interviewer fill pauses by asking additional questions or making irrelevant comments?

- Did the interviewer interrupt the child when still speaking suggesting that only short answers were required?

- Did the interviewer switch questioning to a new topic without advance warning?

- Were questions simple?

- Did questions contain only one point per question?

- Did questions contain abstract words or double negatives?

- Did questions contain jargon?

- Did the interviewer check that the child understood by asking them to convey back what was said?

- Did the questioning take account of the child's stage of development?

- What happened during any breaks in the interview?

4.54

After the interview

- How did the interview end?

- Was there any informal discussion with the child at the end of the interview?

- If the child was subsequently interviewed again, what happened between the interviews?

SECTION 5 – OTHER INVESTIGATIONS

4.55 During the s 47 assessment the social worker aims to build a picture of the child's situation on the basis of information from many sources. The social worker's main focus during this stage of the investigation process will be to make direct enquiries of a number of relevant individuals. This work should include:

- interviews with parents and/or caregivers;

- observation of the interactions between parents and child(ren);

- interviews with those who are personally and professionally connected with the child, including members of the extended family;

- specific examinations or assessments of the child by other professionals (for example, medical, educational or developmental checks, assessment of emotional or psychological state);

- interviews with those who are personally and professionally connected with the child's parents and/or caregivers;

- direct work with the child including ascertaining their wishes and feelings.

4.56 Individuals should always be enabled to participate fully in the enquiry process. Where a child or parent is disabled, it may be necessary to provide help with communication to enable the child or parent to express himself to the best of his or her ability. Where a child or parent speaks a language other than that spoken by the interviewer, there should be an interpreter provided.

4.57

Analysing the s 47 assessment

- Was the s 47 assessment authorised by a relevant manager?

- Was there any unreasonable delay in completion of the s 47 assessment?

- Was the s 47 assessment conducted by a suitably qualified and experienced social worker?

- Were any interviews with the child conducted by professionals with specialist training and experience (police and/or social workers) and in accordance with the guidance in *Achieving Best Evidence?*

- If children were too young (or otherwise unable) to be directly interviewed, were appropriate observations of them carried out by social workers?

- Was it necessary and reasonable to conduct any interviews with children without their parents' knowledge?

- Did the social worker interview the child's parents, carers or other relevant family members?

- Did the social worker observe the interactions between the child and parents (or other relevant family members)?

- Did the social worker interview other professionals or people connected with the child?

- Did the social worker interview other professionals or people connected with the child's parents or family?

- Was the child examined by an appropriate practitioner (medical, developmental or psychological)?

SECTION 6 – WORKING IN PARTNERSHIP

4.58 The local authority's investigation and consultation process should also involve the child's parents as a matter of course. In *Venema v the Netherlands*[12] (applying *P, C and S v UK*),[13] it was held that:

> '... it is essential that a parent be placed in a position where he or she may obtain access to information which is relied upon by authorities in taking measures of protective care or in taking decisions relevant to care and custody of a child. Otherwise the parent will be unable to participate effectively in the decision-making process or put forward in a fair or adequate manner those matters militating in favour of his or her ability to provide the child with proper care and attention.'

4.59 In *Re L (Care: Assessment: Fair Trial)*,[14] it was held that:

> 'The state, in the form of the local authority, assumed a heavy burden when it sought to take a child into care, and part of that burden was the need, in the interests not merely of the parent but also of the child, for a transparent and transparently fair procedure at all stages of the process ... both in and out of the court ... documents must be made openly available and crucial meetings at which a family's future was being decided must be conducted openly and with the parents, if they wished, either present or represented. Otherwise there is unacceptable scope for unfairness and injustice, not just to the parents but also to the children.'

4.60 The procedures and timescales set out in *Working Together* should also be followed when there are concerns about the welfare of an unborn child.

4.61 In *Birmingham City Council v AG and A*,[15] it was held that the consent of parents was not required before enquiries could be made of third parties on an initial assessment, although parents were asked to consent and co-operate with such assessments.

4.62 Section 47 enquiries should always be carried out in such a way as to minimise distress to the child, and to ensure that families are treated sensitively and with respect. Social workers should explain the purpose and outcome of s 47 enquiries to the parents and child (having regard to age and understanding) and be prepared to answer questions openly, unless to do so would affect the safety and welfare of the child. It is particularly helpful for families if social workers provide written information about the purpose, process and potential outcomes of s 47 enquiries. The information should be both general and specific to the particular circumstances under enquiry. It should include information about how advice, advocacy and support may be obtained from independent sources.

---

[12] [2003] 1 FLR 552.
[13] [2002] 2 FLR 631.
[14] [2002] 2 FLR 730 at [151].
[15] [2010] 2 FLR 580.

4.63 Essential principles to be followed by social workers in working with families, particularly during the investigation and assessment part of their work, are helpfully listed in *Re L (Care: Assessment: Fair Trial)*:[16]

- Social workers should (as soon as possible and practicable):

  - notify parents of material criticisms of and deficits in their parenting or behaviour;
  - notify parents of the expectations of them;
  - advise parents about how they may remedy or improve their parenting or behaviour.

- All the professionals involved (including social workers, social work assistants, children's guardians, expert witnesses) should at all times keep clear, accurate, full and balanced notes of all relevant conversations and meetings between themselves and/or with parents, other family members and others involved with the family.

- The local authority should at an early stage of court proceedings make full and frank disclosure to the other parties of all key documents in its possession or available to it, including contact recordings, attendance notes of meetings and conversations, minutes of child protection conferences, core group meetings and similar meetings.[17]

- Social workers (and guardians) should routinely exhibit to their reports and statements notes of relevant meetings, conversations and incidents.

4.64 In the great majority of cases children remain with their families following s 47 enquiries, even where concerns about abuse or neglect are substantiated. As far as possible, s 47 enquiries should be conducted in a way that allows for future constructive working relationships with families. The way in which a case is handled initially can affect the entire subsequent process. Where handled well and sensitively, there can be a positive effect on the eventual outcome for the child.

---

[16] [2002] 2 FLR 730 at [154].
[17] The local authority should notify the other parties of any objection to the disclosure of inspection of these documents at the earliest possible stage in the court proceedings and should raise the matter with the court without delay.

4.65

Analysing the local authority's partnership with the family

- Did the s 47 investigation involve the parents (or child's family) in discussion and consultation?

- Were the parents (or child's family) given the information relied upon by the local authority in making decisions about the child during the s 47 investigation?

- Were the parents notified of strengths, criticisms and deficits in their parenting or behaviour?

- Were the parents informed of the local authority's expectations of them?

- Were the parents given advice about how they may remedy or improve their parenting or behaviour?

- Were the child and family treated sensitively and with respect?

- Did the social worker explain the purpose and outcome of the s 47 investigation to the parents (and child if appropriate)?

- Is there evidence that the social worker answered the family's questions openly?

- Were the parents provided with written information about the purpose, process and potential outcomes of the s 47 investigation?

- Was the s 47 investigation handled in a way that allowed for future constructive working relationships with the family?

SECTION 7 – THE OUTCOME OF THE SECTION 47 INVESTIGATION

4.66 The local authority should decide how to proceed following the s 47 investigation after discussion between all those who have conducted, or been significantly involved in those enquiries, including relevant professionals and agencies, as well as foster carers where involved, and the child and parents themselves. Where the agencies most involved with a child judge that the child may continue to suffer, or to be at risk of suffering significant harm, the local authority should convene a child protection conference.

4.67 At the conclusion of the s 47 investigation the social worker should record the outcome in the Outcome of the s 47 Enquiries Record. Parents (and children of sufficient age and appropriate level of understanding) should receive a copy of this record, in particular in advance of any initial child protection conference that is convened. This information should be put into an appropriate format for younger children and for people whose preferred language is not English.

4.68 Professionals and agencies who have been significantly involved during the investigation should also be given a copy of this record.

4.69 At the conclusion of the s 47 investigation the social worker should consider whether the core assessment has been completed or what further work is required before it is completed.

4.70 The s 47 investigation may result in no further action being taken by the local authority. Lawyers should include consideration of previous investigations within the overall analysis of the case, and in particular whether previous investigations resulted in no further action being taken and/or the case being closed by the local authority. In cases where it appears that little has changed since previous investigations, it may be possible to argue that the local authority is being unreasonable in seeking to take action now. Conversely, the local authority may seek to argue that there is a longstanding history of neglect and chronic failure to improve in such cases; in those circumstances, a pattern of past investigations (regardless of outcome) may lend weight to such arguments.

SECTION 8 – UNSUBSTANTIATED CONCERNS

4.71 Section 47 enquiries may not substantiate the original concerns about the child being at risk of, or suffering, significant harm. However, in such cases it is still important that the social worker completes the core assessment in respect of the child.

4.72 It may be decided that, once the core assessment has been completed, no further action is necessary. In these circumstances, the local authority and other relevant agencies should always consider with the family what support and/or services may be helpful and how the child and family might be provided with these services, if they wish it and by whom (perhaps via the CAF process). The focus of s 47 enquiries is the welfare of the child, and the assessment may well reveal a range of needs. The provision of services to these children and their families should not be dependent on the presence of abuse and neglect. Help and support to children in need and their families may prevent problems escalating to a point where a child is abused or neglected. Again, the overall analysis of the case may reveal previous recommendations for help or support for families which were never offered by the local authority, or which were offered but never taken up by families.

4.73 In some cases, there may remain concerns about significant harm, despite there being no real evidence. In these cases it may be appropriate for the local authority to put in place arrangements to monitor the child's welfare, either directly by social workers or by other agencies (such as health visitors, schools or nurseries). However, monitoring should never be used as a means of deferring or avoiding difficult decisions. The purpose of monitoring should always be clear, that is, what is being monitored and why, in what way and by whom. It will also be important to inform parents about the nature of any ongoing concern. There should be a time set for reviewing the monitoring arrangements through the holding of a further discussion or meeting.

4.74

Analysing the outcome of the s 47 investigation

- Did the social worker complete the core assessment in respect of the child (regardless of the outcome of the investigation)?

- Were the parents given advice about how they may remedy or improve their parenting or behaviour?

- Did the social worker discuss with the family (and with other agencies if relevant) what support and/or services might be helpful to them?

- What consideration was given to convening a family group conference as a means of making plans and providing support for the child?[18]

- Did the social worker discuss with the family how such support and/or services might be provided to them?

- Did the social worker formulate a plan with the family to help prevent problems occurring or escalating again in the future?

- Did the local authority make appropriate arrangements to monitor the child's welfare (by social workers and/or other agencies)?

- Was the purpose of any monitoring arrangement made clear to other agencies?

- Was the purpose of any monitoring arrangement clearly explained to the family?

- Was the family informed of the nature of any ongoing concerns?

- Was a time and mechanism for reviewing any monitoring arrangements made with other agencies and the family?

---

[18] See Chapter 2.

SECTION 9 – CARE PROCEEDINGS

4.75 In some cases the s 47 investigation will lead to a decision by the local authority to issue care proceedings in relation to a child.

The duties of the local authority before issuing care proceedings

4.76 The duties of the local authority before issuing care proceedings were previously set out in the Public Law Outline Practice Direction (April 2008), were revised and replaced by the *Practice Direction Public Law Proceedings Guide to Case Management* (in force from 6 April 2010), and are now incorporated into the Family Procedure Rules at *Practice Direction 12A: Public Law Proceedings Guide to Case Management* which came into force on 6 April 2011.

4.77 Guidance for professionals working with children and families where care proceedings are being considered or applied for is found in the non-statutory guidance *Preparing for Care and Supervision Proceedings.*[19] This is a best practice guide for use by all professionals involved with children and families pre-proceedings and in preparation for applications made under s 31 of the CA 1989 ('Best Practice Guide').

4.78 The term pre-proceedings is used to indicate the several stages of interaction between the child, family and the local authority which occur prior to a court application being issued for a s 31 CA 1989 order. It is not always easy to ascertain where the pre-proceedings stages begin. It could be assumed that all stages of involvement prior to an application being made could be termed 'pre-proceedings'. However, for the purposes of the recent reforms the use of the term pre-proceedings is rather precise and denotes the stages from the point that the local authority is considering making an application to court to protect the child but the risk of harm to the child is manageable if an application is not made immediately. Effectively, the local authority's approach will be to attempt further engagement with the parent(s) in order to put an agreement in place which reduces the risk of significant harm to the child to a manageable level at that stage.

4.79 The point at which pre-proceedings stages nominally commence in view of the recent reforms is where the legal gateway/planning meeting has been held and the local authority makes the decision to send a letter before proceedings (LBP).

The legal gateway or planning meeting

4.80 The purpose of a legal gateway or planning meeting is for the local authority to seek legal advice about a particular case. These meetings should be attended by the child's social worker and managers, together with the lawyer

---

[19] Ministry of Justice, August 2009.

advising the local authority. The social work team will usually set out the facts of the case, their concerns and explain what has been done to work with the child and the family. The ultimate question will be 'are the threshold criteria in s 31 of the Children Act 1989 met and are court proceedings necessary at this stage?'

4.81   In those cases where it is agreed that it will be necessary to initiate care proceedings the local authority will consider if it is appropriate to write to the parent to inform him or her that an application to court will be made shortly and to explain that he or she should seek legal advice. A template letter is found at Annex A in the Best Practice Guide.

4.82   The Best Practice Guide notes two important points about sending such a letter to parents:

• The letter is not intended to be a letter before proceedings and therefore may not act as the trigger letter for Family Help Lower (level 2) publicly funded advice and assistance. However, the parent may still be eligible for means-tested advice under Legal Help from a solicitor. Parents should be advised to seek further guidance from a solicitor on this point.

• It will not be appropriate to send this letter in all cases where immediate issue of proceedings is decided. Whether or not to send the letter requires very careful assessment of the situation by the local authority. For example, there may be concerns that if a parent knows that the local authority is going to apply for a court order allowing removal of the child from his or her care, then they may leave or seek to leave the area.

4.83

Analysing the legal gateway or planning meeting

• Did the local authority hold a legal gateway or planning meeting?

• Was the legal gateway or planning meeting attended by the social worker with relevant knowledge of the child and family?

• If the social worker attended, can or should relevant parts of minutes of the legal gateway or planning meeting be disclosed (ie those parts not subject to legal privilege)?

• Did the legal gateway or planning meeting explicitly consider the s 31 threshold criteria and whether court proceedings were necessary at that stage?

The letter before proceedings (LBP)

4.84 If following a legal gateway or planning meeting it is decided that there is time to work with the family to avoid proceedings, and the short term safety and welfare of the child permits, an LBP should be issued. The LBP allows social workers to structure their work with the child and family and to consider alternative options and services which could be provided to the family. The Family Justice Review Final Report (November 2011) considered and encouraged the use of the LBP, noting that the aim of such letters is to head off the need for proceedings by giving families clear warning, or at least to narrow and focus the issues of concern.

4.85 Once the LBP inviting a parent to a pre-proceedings meeting (PPM) is sent out, the local authority has an opportunity to work with the family and to explore all options prior to making an application to court.

4.86 In deciding the timing about when best to send the LBP, the local authority should first have considered and sought legal advice about whether it should make an application to the court. If it makes an 'in principle' decision that it would be appropriate to apply for an order but also concludes that the risk can be managed without an immediate application, the local authority is effectively concluding that it can see a window of opportunity to try to continue to work with the family to maintain their children safely with their parents. The LBP should be sent at this point.

4.87 Once the LBP is sent the local authority should utilise this opportunity to secure a plan or agreement to protect the child safely at home and work towards reducing the risk of significant harm to the child.

4.88 Where a local authority judges that there is not a window of opportunity to work with the family to continue to maintain the child at home, given its assessment of the safeguarding concerns in the case, the local authority will need to apply immediately to court even on short notice for a s 31 CA 1989 order. Where this is the case local authorities should consider using the immediate issue template letter at Annex A in the Best Practice Guide.

4.89 The LBP is an important letter and should be carefully drafted. The LBP should subsequently be filed with the court and needs to be concise, clear and focused. It is important that the LBP can be understood by the recipient. It should be written in plain English, should be jargon free, and if necessary should be translated into the language of the parent or carer. The Best Practice Guide makes it clear that there should be no surprises in the LBP. Although the parent should already have had notice or knowledge of the local authority's concerns, the purpose of the LBP is to be clear, within a single document, about the concerns and what the parent needs to change or improve in order to reduce those concerns. Finally, the LBP acts as a formal notification that the parent should seek legal advice, together with a final warning that court proceedings may follow if the situation fails to improve.

4.90   The LBP should state what concerns need to be addressed by the parent and what support will be provided by the local authority to help. These issues will be reflected in the existing child in need plan, child protection plan or care plan. The local authority should update the plan accordingly and send it to the parent as a draft plan (ideally within the LBP) which he or she should then be asked to agree to at the PPM.

4.91   The Family Justice Review Final Report (November 2011) recommended that research be undertaken about the impact and effectiveness of LBPs on the reduction of delay in care proceedings and to establish why the use of such letters remains variable between different local authorities. Concerns about the use and efficacy of LBPs as indicated in the existing research (due to be published in full in 2012) were highlighted as follows:[20]

> 'The pre-proceedings process has some advantages – lawyers appear to help parents feel less vulnerable, their presence may make it easier for parents to participate in a meeting to agree care arrangements. Involving local authority lawyers can ensure that threshold and evidence have been considered long before proceedings are issued. Some parents will make positive use of this "last chance". However, there are also disadvantages. Applications to court may be delayed to the detriment of children; the creation of a new step towards proceedings may slow progress of cases to the court even where efforts to engage parents have proved futile. Starting the pre-proceedings process may give a false impression to social workers and managers that the case is progressing, leading to further drift and delay.'

4.92   The Family Justice Review Final Report (November 2011) therefore recommends that the operation of the pre-proceedings process will need to be reviewed once the full research is available, and that this will need to form part of the discussions around remodelling the PLO. However, it is noted that, given the potential of the process to support parents as well as providing the courts with better prepared cases, the use of the pre-proceedings process should be encouraged in the interim.

---

[20]   J Masson *Families on the edge of care proceedings – interim report on the use of the pre-proceedings process* (2011) unpublished, prepared for and supplied to Family Justice Review Panel, August 2011 and cited in the Family Justice Review Final Report (November 2011) at para 3.108.

4.93

Analysing the letter before proceedings (LBP)

- If the decision was taken to issue care proceedings, did the local authority write to parents to inform that an application to court would be made and advising them to seek legal advice?

- If no LBP was sent to parents, was it appropriate in all the circumstances of the case?

- Was the LBP sent to parents inviting them to attend PPM at specified date, time and venue?

- Was the LBP sent at the right time?

- If no LBP was sent, was it appropriate for the local authority to judge that there was no opportunity to work with family to continue to maintain the child at home?

- If no LBP was sent, did the local authority apply immediately for a s 31 order?

- Did the LBP follow Best Practice Guide guidance? Was the LBP written in plain English? Was it jargon free? Was it translated if necessary?

- Did the LBP set out the local authority's concerns clearly and include changes or improvements required by parents in order to reduce concerns?

- Did the LBP contain any surprises or did parents already know about the nature and extent of the local authority's concerns?

- Did the LBP include reference to support to be provided by the local authority to help the family?

- Did the LBP include a draft plan to which the parents would be asked to agree at the PPM? Did the LBP include formal notification to parents to seek legal advice, with a final warning that court proceedings may follow if the situation fails to improve?

The pre-proceedings meeting (PPM)

4.94 The LBP also invites the parent to a pre-proceedings meeting (PPM) to discuss matters and hopefully finalise a plan or agreement. The LBP needs to be sent in sufficient time in order to allow the recipient to make changes in the situation balanced against any risk to the child. The recipient needs to be given enough time to receive and consider the letter, and to seek legal advice in advance of the PPM. Social workers should consider these factors when proposing the date and time of the PPM in the LBP.

4.95   The Best Practice Guide makes it clear that the PPM will work best where both the local authority and the parent have had a good opportunity to prepare. This means that the parent must be able to consider the LBP and to understand the plan which he or she is being asked to agree to. Parents should be able to understand the details of the concerns about the child's developmental needs, including the need for safeguarding and the plan to meet them in order to know what is required of them, and how they can fulfil the requirements or discuss the issues if they feel unable to make a meaningful change. Nothing in the proposed plan should be new or a surprise to the parent because the concerns will have continuously been referred to during meetings, case conferences, documents or correspondence between the local authority and the parent. Alternatively, the parent should be in a position to suggest factual corrections or amendments to the proposed plan through the negotiation that will take place during the PPM.

4.96   The LBP should state a date, time and venue for the PPM. Consideration should be given to rescheduling when requested by the parents so long as this not does affect the child's safety and welfare.

4.97   The aim of the PPM is to reach an agreement on the proposed plan between the family and the local authority and to track and monitor progress to implementing the plan.

4.98   The plan for the child might be that the child will be accommodated by the local authority. This is a key option for the child even if only as a temporary measure. If it is agreed that the child should be looked after under s 20 of the CA 1989 the local authority must comply with all statutory duties in relation to looked-after children (see Chapter 7).

4.99   Where the child is not a looked-after child because he or she will remain in the care of the family or be subject to a private fostering arrangement between the parent and a third person (such as a family friend or more distant relative) it is likely that the child will remain a child in need for the requisite period. The local authority will however be responsible for checking and supervising any private fostering arrangements. If the arrangements are brokered by the local authority then the child becomes a looked-after child under a s 23 placement (see Chapter 7).

4.100   Although agreement may not be able to be reached in all cases or about all areas of the plan, the Best Practice Guide encourages a conciliatory approach between the participants and their lawyers. The PPM is a social work led meeting which is not intended to be adversarial in nature. Neither is the PPM a forum for disputed facts to be determined, such as in a fact finding hearing. If there are disputed facts or issues, the participants can through negotiation agree facts or narrow issues down voluntarily. The PPM will not however, decide on anything which fundamentally remains contested or disputed. No participant should feel pressured to agree to anything that he or she does not want to. Legal advice during the meeting should assist the parent with this. It is vital for the parent to understand that the proposed plan being put forward by the local authority warrants careful thought so that the parent is aware of what is likely to happen in the event that an agreement to the plan or amended plan cannot be secured.

4.101 Many local authorities have formulated an outline agenda for use at the PPM. Outline agendas can be helpful as they formalises the meeting, ensure that everything is covered and demonstrate to the participants that the PPM is of a more serious nature than perhaps other routine meetings between a parent and the local authority. A suggested outline agenda is set out in Annex C of the Best Practice Guide. However, it remains for each local authority to decide how it wishes to conduct the meetings and whether it chooses to create its own agenda using some or all of the suggestions contained in Annex C.

4.102 It is good practice for minutes to be taken of the PPM which should then be approved by the local authority and circulated to the parent as quickly as possible. The parent will then have the opportunity to suggest corrections or additions which the local authority can then consider. The plan and any agreement which has been reached during the meeting will be a material document and it is important that it is accurate, and comprehensive.

4.103 If parents attend the PPM with their lawyer the local authority lawyer should also attend. The local authority might reconsider at this point use of a family group conference which might assist identification of wider family support. However, the PPM is not a multidisciplinary meeting or forum and it is not appropriate for other agencies to attend.

4.104 The Best Practice Guide recommends that it is preferable that a PPM be chaired by someone with no prior direct involvement with the child and family. It is recommended that this should increase the chances of a productive meeting as the parent will hopefully look to the chair as someone who is fresh to the case, be less likely to have preconceived ideas about the child or family, perhaps be more impartial than the child's social worker, and is sufficiently distanced to have a wider perspective on the issues. It is recommended that if the chair is able to gain the trust of the participants in the meeting, the meeting will proceed more effectively.

4.105

Analysing the pre-proceedings meeting (PPM)

- Was consideration given to rescheduling the PPM if requested by parents?

- Was the PPM a social work led meeting which applied a conciliatory approach?

- Was it appropriate for all PPM attendees to have been invited?

- Were parents able to participate fairly, properly and without pressure?

- Were the parents consulted about the participation of the child at the PPM?

- Did parents understand the local authority's proposed plan and were they aware of what could happen in event that the plan or amended plan not agreed?

- Was an outline agenda prepared for use at the PPM?

- Was the PPM chaired by someone with no prior direct involvement with the child and family?

- Was proper attention paid during the PPM to requirements of parents with special needs? Was immediate and urgent referral made to the relevant adult team if necessary following assessment?

- Were suitable arrangements made for an independent interpreter?

- Was the child notified about the PPM? Did the social worker make the child's views clear at the PPM?

- What consideration was given, if any, to invite the child to (at least part of) the PPM?

- Were accurate and comprehensive minutes taken of the PPM?

- Were the PPM minutes circulated to parents as quickly as possible to enable corrections or additions to be made?

- Were any discussions held about joint instruction for specialist assessments, if required?

People with special needs

4.106 Given the nature, sensitivity and seriousness of the issues to be discussed at the PPM, it is crucial that the participants understand and are able to follow the discussions.

4.107 Some of the issues which come within the remit of the pre-proceedings stages are just as important as some of those that arise within proceedings. Where a person lacks the capacity to follow the litigation within proceedings, it is likely that he or she would also find it difficult to understand everything that is being said and asked of him or her pre-proceedings. Where an informal assessment suggests a parent may struggle to follow the pre-proceedings discussions or otherwise may have a learning disability or mental health problems which affect the parent's ability to follow the issues, then an immediate and urgent referral must be made to the Adults with Learning Disability Team/Community Learning Disability Team (ALDT/CLDT) or local authority equivalent.

4.108 Lord Justice Wall's comments in *P v Nottingham City Council and the Official Solicitor*[21] have clarified expectations of the court in such cases:

'It is, I think, inevitable that in its pre-proceedings work with a child's family, the local authority will gain information about the capacity of the child's parents. The critical question is what it does with that information, particularly in a case where the social workers form the view that the parent in question may have learning difficulties.' [175]

'At this point, in many cases, the local authority will be working with the child's parents in an attempt to keep the family together. In my judgment, the practical answer in these circumstances is likely to be that the parent in question should be referred to the local authority's adult learning disability team (or its equivalent) for help and advice. If that team thinks that further investigations are required, it can undertake them: it should, moreover, have the necessary contacts and resources to commission a report so that as soon as the pre-proceedings letter is written, and proceedings are issued, the legal advisers for the parent can be in a position, with public funding, to address the question of a litigation friend. It is, I think, important that judgments on capacity are not made by the social workers from the child protection team.' [176]

'In the pre-proceedings phase local authorities should feel free to do whatever is necessary in social work terms to assist parents who may become protected parties. My view, however, is that this is best achieved by members of the adult learning disabilities team who do not have responsibility for the children concerned.' [181]

4.109 On a practical level the adult teams must be asked to assess the parent and to make recommendations as to the parent's capacity to understand the information being discussed and shared at the PPM. It may be that the parent can properly engage during pre-proceedings if supported by a social worker from the specialist adult team. Alternatively, a voluntary sector organisation may be able to provide an advocate who is experienced in working with those with learning disabilities. If those options fail then the local authority may wish to consider inviting a close family member or friend to support the parent during the PPM. Ultimately, if the social worker or the lawyer for the parent

---

21   [2008] EWCA Civ 462.

believes that the parent is unable to understand and follow the subject matter properly in order to then give considered instructions to the solicitor, it may be the case that the local authority will have to issue an application to court so that the Official Solicitor can be invited to act for the parent within the proceedings.

4.110 Language barriers must also be considered where a parent's capacity to understand is clearly limited and the local authority should make arrangements for a suitable independent interpreter and not rely on a family member or friend.

Participation of the child

4.111 So far as it is reasonably practicable and consistent with the child's welfare, every child should be notified in age appropriate language by the local authority that a PPM is to be held, with an explanation that the purpose is to help parents to keep them safe. The child should then be given the chance to make representations, including written presentations, to the PPM. The social worker has an ongoing duty to ascertain the wishes and feelings of the child and should be in a position to feed those wishes and feelings into the PPM. The Best Practice Guide makes it clear that acting in the best interests of the child will be the responsibility which pervades everything the social worker does in a particular case. The social worker is therefore in a position to make clear the child's views at the PPM.

4.112 Additionally, the local authority must decide in each individual case whether to invite the child to the PPM. In considering the matter, there will be a variety of factors which will be taken into account including:

• the child's age;

• the child's level of understanding as to what is involved;

• the child's coping skills; and

• whether it is appropriate for the child to be present for all or for part of the PPM.

4.113 If the child is invited and attends the meeting, the local authority should review agenda items accordingly, as there may be information that could be difficult for a child to manage within this forum. The social worker should also inform the chair of the PPM that the child will be attending.

4.114 If it is felt inappropriate to invite the child to attend the PPM or the child rejects the invitation, the social worker must consider how the child's wishes and feelings could be heard at the PPM.

4.115 The local authority should ascertain the parent's views towards the child's attendance at the meeting. If the parents oppose the child's attendance at the meeting it must be remembered that the local authority does not have parental responsibility at this stage.

4.116 If parents do not wish the child to attend, the child should be informed about the local authority's complaints procedure. In such circumstances the local authority should consider other methods of ensuring that the child's voice is heard, such as:

- the child making representations (via writing, audio or video) for the meeting;

- the social worker having a meeting with the child; or

- the child being referred to a local advocacy service able to support the child.

4.117 If the child does not attend the PPM the social worker should explain the plan to the child and take account of their wishes and feelings.

Specialist assessments (pre-proceedings)

4.118 The key question for the local authority to consider is whether there is an element or aspect of the core assessment process which cannot be completed pre-proceedings because specialist expertise is required. Specialist assessments are those assessments which the local authority believe are required when for example there is a particular aspect of the child's or family's circumstances which require a specialist assessment from a professional other than a social worker such as an adult mental health assessment. The specialist assessment should only address that specific aspect and should feed into the core assessment (see Chapter 5).

4.119 Where a specialist assessment is thought to be required, the decision to commission such an assessment should be made as soon as possible to avoid introducing unnecessary delay into resolution of the proceedings. Consideration should also be given to the joint instruction of experts, and the PPM can be used for this purpose.

4.120 Any specialist assessments commissioned pre-proceedings should be presented by the local authority in any subsequent proceedings, and it is therefore suggested within the Best Practice Guide that the local authority should consider the requirements of the Experts Practice Direction 2008 (and reiterated in the new Practice Direction 25A introduced by the Family Procedure Rules from 6 April 2011), particularly those that relate to pre-proceedings assessments.

4.121

Analysing pre-proceedings specialist assessments

- Was there a part of the core assessment process which could not be completed pre-proceedings because specialist expertise was required?

- Was the decision to commission any specialist assessment made as soon as possible?

- Were the parents consulted about the need for and possibility of, joint instructions?

- Did the local authority follow requirements of the Experts Practice Direction in commissioning any specialist assessment?

- Did the local authority consider the use of family group conference at the appropriate stage?

The pre-proceedings checklist

4.122 The local authority must state in any application form in care or supervision proceedings all information concerning significant steps in the child's life that are likely to take place during the proceedings. The local authority is responsible for updating this information regularly and giving it to the court. The local authority is required to obtain information about these significant steps and any variations and additions to them from others involved in the child's life such as other parties, members of the child's family, the person who is caring for the child, the child's guardian and the child's key social worker. When the other people involved in the child's life become aware of a significant step in the child's life or a variation of an existing one, that information should be given to the local authority as soon as possible.

4.123 It is clear that the local authority should prepare the case properly before proceedings are issued. In care and supervision proceedings the local authority should use the pre-proceedings checklist.[22] This checklist contains the documents which are specified in the Annex to the Application Form. The rules require those documents which are known as the 'Annex Documents' to be filed with the application form where available.

4.124 The Annex Documents are as follows:

- social work chronology;

- initial social work statement;

- initial and core assessments;

---

[22] Public Law Proceedings Guide to Case Management PD12A: April 2010, para 11.1.

- letters before proceedings;

- schedule of proposed findings;

- minutes of family group conferences (FGCs), if held; and

- care plan.

4.125 In addition, the pre-proceedings checklist contains examples of documents other than the Annex Documents which will normally be on the local authority file at the start of proceedings. These documents are known as the 'other checklist documents' and are not to be filed with the court at the start of the proceedings but should be disclosed to the parties normally before the day of the First Appointment or in accordance with the court's directions and to be filed with the court only as directed by the court.

4.126 It is recognised in the rules that in some cases the circumstances are such that the safety and welfare of the child may be jeopardised if the start of proceedings is delayed until all of the documents appropriate to the case and referred to in the pre-proceedings checklist are available. The safety and welfare of the child should never be put in jeopardy because of lack of documentation. The court recognises that the preparation by the local authority may need to be varied to suit the circumstances of the case. In cases where any of the Annex Documents required to be attached to the application form are not available at the time of issue of the application, the court will consider making directions on issue about when any missing documentation is to be filed. The expectation is that there will be a good reason why one or more of the documents are not available. Further directions relating to any missing documentation are likely to be made at the First Appointment hearing. The court also recognises that some documents on the pre-proceedings checklist may not exist and may never exist (for example, a s 37 report) and that in urgent proceedings no LBP may have been sent.

4.127 The revised PLO requires the following checklist documentation by the First Appointment:

- previous court orders, judgments, and reasons;

- any relevant assessment materials;

- initial and core assessments;

- s 7 and s 37 reports;

- relatives and friends materials (eg a genogram);

- single, joint or interagency materials (eg Health and Education or Home Office and Immigration documents);

- records of discussions with the family;

- key local authority minutes and records for the child (including the Strategy Discussion Record); and

- pre-existing care plans (eg child in need plan, looked-after child plan and child protection plan).

4.128

Analysing the local authority application

- Has the local authority provided all relevant information in accordance with the pre-proceedings checklist?

Chapter 5

ASSESSMENT

SECTION 1 – DEFINITION OF TERMS

Abuse and neglect

5.1   Abuse and neglect are forms of maltreatment of a child. Somebody may abuse or neglect a child by inflicting harm, or by failing to act to prevent harm. Children may be abused in a family or in an institutional or community setting, by those known to them or, more rarely, by a stranger. They may be abused by an adult or adults, or another child or children. Munro cautions that:[1]

> '... since the subject matter is intentional human behaviour, it is not possible to specify abuse just in behavioural terms. It also includes some comparison with a standard of acceptable parenting and some comment on what was going on in the mind of the abuser.'

5.2   There is no universal consensus as to what constitutes abuse and neglect, except at the most general level. In the UK, definitions are provided in *Working Together to Safeguard Children.*[2]

Physical abuse

5.3   Physical abuse may involve hitting, shaking, throwing, poisoning, burning or scalding, drowning, suffocating, or otherwise causing physical harm to a child. Physical harm may also be caused when a parent or carer fabricates the symptoms of, or deliberately induces, illness in a child. Factitious or induced illness may also constitute physical abuse, whereby a parent or carer feigns the symptoms of, or deliberately causes ill health in a child.

Emotional abuse

5.4   Emotional abuse is the persistent emotional maltreatment of a child such as to cause severe and persistent adverse effects on the child's emotional development. It may involve conveying to children that they are worthless or unloved, inadequate, or valued only insofar as they meet the needs of another person. It may feature age or developmentally inappropriate expectations being imposed on children. These may include interactions that are beyond the child's

---

[1]   Professor Eileen Munro *Effective Child Protection* (Sage Publishing, 2nd edn, 2008).

[2]   Department for Children, Schools and Families (DCSF) (now DfE) *Working Together to Safeguard Children – A Guide to Inter-agency Working to Safeguard and Promote the Welfare of Children* ('*Working Together*') (TSO, 4th edn, 2010).

developmental capability, as well as overprotection and limitation of exploration and learning, or preventing the child participating in normal social interaction. It may involve seeing or hearing the ill-treatment of another. It may involve serious bullying, causing children frequently to feel frightened or in danger, or the exploitation or corruption of children. Some level of emotional abuse is involved in all types of maltreatment of a child, though it may occur alone.

Sexual abuse

5.5   Sexual abuse involves forcing or enticing a child or young person to take part in sexual activities, including prostitution, whether or not the child is aware of what is happening. The activities may involve physical contact, including penetrative (eg rape, anal or oral sex) or non-penetrative acts. They may include non-contact activities, such as involving children in the production of, or in looking at, sexual online images, watching sexual activities, or encouraging children to behave in sexually inappropriate ways.

Neglect

5.6   Neglect is the persistent failure to meet a child's basic physical and/or psychological needs, likely to result in the serious impairment of the child's health or development. Neglect may occur during pregnancy as a result of maternal substance abuse. Once a child is born, neglect may involve a parent or carer failing to:

- provide adequate food, clothing and shelter (including exclusion from home or abandonment);

- protect a child from physical and emotional harm or danger;

- ensure adequate supervision (including the use of inadequate caregivers);

- ensure access to appropriate medical care or treatment.

5.7   It may also include neglect of, or unresponsiveness to, a child's basic emotional needs.

Children in need

5.8   Children who are defined as being 'in need', under the Children Act 1989 (CA 1989), s 17, are those whose vulnerability is such that they are unlikely to reach or maintain a satisfactory level of health or development, or whose health and development will be significantly impaired, without the provision of services,[3] plus those who are disabled. The critical factors to be taken into account in deciding whether a child is in need in accordance with s 17 of the CA 1989 are:

- What will happen to a child's health or development without services being provided?

- What is the likely effect the services will have on the child's standard of health and development?

5.9 Local authorities have a duty to safeguard and promote the welfare of children in need.

The concept of significant harm

5.10 Some children are in need because they are suffering, or likely to suffer, significant harm. The Children Act 1989 introduced the concept of significant harm as the threshold that justifies compulsory intervention in family life in the best interests of children, and gives local authorities a duty to make enquiries to decide whether they should take action to safeguard or promote the welfare of a child who is suffering, or likely to suffer, significant harm.

5.11 There are no absolute criteria on which to rely when judging what constitutes significant harm. Consideration of the severity of ill-treatment may include the degree and the extent of physical harm, the duration and frequency of abuse and neglect, the extent of premeditation, and the presence or degree of threat, coercion, sadism and bizarre or unusual elements. Each of these elements has been associated with more severe effects on the child, and/or relatively greater difficulty in helping the child overcome the adverse impact of the maltreatment.

5.12 Sometimes, a single traumatic event may constitute significant harm, e g a violent assault, suffocation or poisoning. More often, significant harm is a combination of significant events, both acute and long-standing, which interrupt, change or damage the child's physical and psychological development. Some children live in family and social circumstances where their health and development are neglected. For them, it is the corrosiveness of long-term emotional, physical or sexual abuse that causes impairment to the extent of constituting significant harm. In each case, it is necessary to consider any maltreatment alongside the family's strengths and supports.

5.13 There is an important distinction to be made between *significant harm* and *abuse* (although the two may coexist). Abuse describes acts and/or omissions, whereas significant harm describes the *effect* on the child.

---

[3]   Children Act 1989, s 17(10).

5.14   Section 31(9) of the CA 1989[4] provides the following definitions:

- 'harm' means ill-treatment or the impairment of health or development, including, for example, impairment suffered from seeing or hearing the ill-treatment of another;

- 'development' means physical, intellectual, emotional, social or behavioural development;

- 'health' means physical or mental health;

- 'ill-treatment' includes sexual abuse and forms of ill-treatment which are not physical.

5.15   Section 31(10) of the CA 1989[5] provides the following definitions:[6]

'Where the question of whether harm suffered by a child is significant turns on the child's health and development, his health or development shall be compared with that which could reasonably be expected of a similar child.'

The social work assessment

5.16   Children have varying needs that change over time. Judgments on how best to intervene when there are concerns about harm to a child will often, and unavoidably, entail an element of risk – at the extreme, of leaving a child for too long in a dangerous situation or of removing a child unnecessarily from his or her family. The guidance in *Working Together* makes it clear that the way to proceed in the face of uncertainty is through competent professional judgments, based on a sound assessment of the child's needs and the parents' capacity to respond to these (including their capacity to keep the child safe from significant harm) and the wider family circumstances.[7]

5.17   The purpose of an assessment of a child is to identify the child's needs within their family context and to use this understanding to decide how best to address these needs. It is essential that the plan for the child is constructed on the basis of the findings from the assessment, and that this plan is reviewed and refined over time to ensure the agreed case objectives are achieved.

5.18   Assessment is therefore a key task in social work practice. It is essential that childcare lawyers have a thorough knowledge of what makes a good assessment, how assessments are conducted and some of the difficulties that can arise when social workers are carrying out assessments. Assessment is defined by the Oxford English Dictionary as 'judging or valuing the worth of

---

[4]   As amended by the Adoption and Children Act 2002.
[5]   As amended by the Adoption and Children Act 2002.
[6]   See also M Adcock and R White *Significant Harm: its management and outcome* (Significant Publications, 1998).
[7]   *Working Together*, para 1.10.

something'; in other words, the term assessment implies a skilled activity by someone qualified to evaluate and judge between things of different value and the use of standards against which something can be appraised.[8]

5.19 The Family Justice Review final report reiterates the importance of good assessment in addressing the unwillingness of courts to rely on local authority assessments rather than on independent experts to undertake assessments. The report confirms that assessments and reports need to be appropriately detailed, evidence based and clear in their arguments, and recommends improved training in court presentation skills for social workers.[9]

> 'Effective social care interventions follow careful assessment and planning. Assessments need to be completed quickly with a focus on the critical question: is this child safe to stay in their current circumstances? Rigorous assessments must be completed regardless of whether the family courts will be involved or not because careful planning has been shown to improve outcomes for children. Assessments should include thorough analysis of the accumulating risks of children being harmed. Good quality social and family history taking is essential, including accurate chronologies and historical information about parents' childhood relationships and behavioural backgrounds. Professionals need to avoid the 'start again' syndrome with parents where all previous history is ignored, including the removal of other children. The child's right to a safe and nurturing home must not be overridden by the parents' human rights.'[10]

5.20 The importance of carrying out assessments properly has been addressed in two judicial review cases which nonetheless make it clear that it is *substance* rather than *form* that is the relevant factor to be considered when evaluating core assessments.

- In *R (AB and SB) v Nottingham City Council*,[11] claims were brought for judicial review of the way the local authority had failed to carry out a core assessment in accordance with the guidance in the *Framework for Assessment*.[12] It was held that there should be a systematic assessment of needs which took into account the three domains (the child's developmental needs, parenting capacity, and family and environmental factors) and involved collaboration between all relevant agencies so as to achieve a full understanding of the child in his or her family and community context. It was held that where a local authority followed a path that did not involve the preparation of a core assessment as such, it must nevertheless adopt a similarly systematic approach with a view to

---

8   See J Parker and G Bradley *Social Work Practice: Assessment, Planning, Intervention and Review* (Learning Matters, 2003).
9   Family Justice Review Final Report (March 2011), para 3.103.
10   D Maskell-Graham et al *Safeguarding Children Across Services: Messages from research on identifying and responding to child maltreatment: Messages for professionals working in children's social care* (Department for Education, 2011).
11   [2001] EWHC 235 (Admin).
12   Department of Health *Framework for the Assessment of Children in Need and Their Families* ('*Framework*') (TSO, 2000).

achievement of the same objectives. It was held that failure to do so without good cause would constitute an impermissible departure from the guidance.

- In *R (EW and BW) v Nottinghamshire County Council*,[13] two children sought judicial review of the way the local authority had conducted assessments. It was claimed that the core assessments had failed properly to assess the children's needs or to identify how those needs should be met, and specifically that the assessments had failed to comply with the guidance given in the *Framework for Assessment*. The local authority did not acknowledge that the core assessments had been flawed, but conducted fresh assessments in any event. It was held that the original core assessments had plainly been deficient. They gave the appearance of having been prepared either quickly or without much care, being little more than a very brief narrative of information and containing little, if any, analysis of the children's precise needs, or of how those needs were to be met. However, it was also held that while it was true that the core assessment was a critical part of the process in deciding how a child in need could be helped, in an appropriate case it was possible for shortcomings in a core assessment to be neutralised by other action that properly identified the child's needs and how they were to be met:

  > 'One should guard against setting Elysian standards for local authorities, or setting the bar too high. What was important was whether the outcome of the local authority process included a proper analysis of the children's needs, and a clear identification of how those needs were to be met, including by whom and when.'

5.21 Definitions of assessment are fluid but broadly include elements of the following:

- An analytical process by which decisions are made and a basis for planning what needs to be done to maintain or improve a person's situation.

- Gathering and interpreting information in order to:

  – understand a person and their circumstances or situation;
  – identify areas for potential change;
  – establish the desirability and feasibility of change; and
  – identify the services and resources which are necessary to effect change in the future.

- Making judgments based on information.

---

[13]   [2009] EWHC 915 (Admin), [2009] 2 FLR 974.

5.22 Assessment is also part of a continual process which links with planning, intervention and review. The ASPIRE model describes this continual process perfectly:

AS Assessment

P Planning

I Intervention

RE Review and Evaluation

5.23 If assessment is effective then it makes it more likely that intervention will succeed. Conversely, when assessments are carried out without adequate preparation and without a clear sense of purpose and direction they are unlikely to produce useful material to assist in planning. Assessments are critical to social work intervention and its effectiveness.

5.24 Assessments should lead to the identification of:

- the family's strength and needs;

- goals for change; and

- the actions and means for achieving these goals within agreed timescales.

5.25 The purpose of assessment in social work is to acquire and study information about people in their environment to decide upon an identified problem and to plan effective solutions to resolve that problem. Good assessments should not simply be fact-finding exercises but should also represent a collaborative construction of the individual or family's narrative or story. Assessment covers a spectrum of activities, from observation and judgments made within the context of an initial encounter through to more formal and complex frameworks of assessment.

5.26 It is only after social workers understand and identify relevant factors in any situation, that they can formulate appropriate and relevant plans.

Characteristics of good assessments[14]

5.27 Preparation and planning requires:

- identification of the key people to be interviewed;

- the creation of a schedule for data collection and interviews; and

---

[14] See J Parker and G Bradley *Social Work Practice: Assessment, Planning, Intervention and Review* (Learning Matters, 2003), at p 17.

- production of a statement of intent including the purpose and system of the assessment.

5.28 Information gathering requires:

- summary of verbal data and reporting;

- distinction between facts and opinions;

- comparing accounts with direct observations of relationships; and

- consideration of other sources of information including evidence from other agencies or expert sources.

5.29 Preliminary analysis of the data involves:

- identification of persistent themes or patterns;

- consideration of the seriousness of the situation and how well the person is functioning;

- clustering themes and ranking in order of importance;

- keeping an open mind and checking for inconsistencies;

- identifying strengths as well as gaps; and

- identifying people to help and further people to be consulted.

5.30 Testing the data (deep analysis) includes:

- developing hypotheses and identifying goals;

- developing tentative explanations; and

- testing explanations by interviews with the key people involved and check the data again.

5.31 Use the data to create an action plan by:

- identifying what help is needed and by whom;

- listing the outcomes to be achieved and the consequences to avoid;

- explaining how outcomes can be measured;

- preparing a plan of intervention within agreed timescales;

- developing an independent mechanism to monitor outcomes (eg supervision, multi-agency forum such as Core Group or LAC review).

- preparing a report listing sources of information, analysis, initial judgment; and

- obtaining feedback on the report and adjust accordingly to prepare final report.

Reflective assessments

5.32 Respect for individual differences during the assessment process is essential if the aim of the process is to enhance an individual's strengths and coping abilities. By the very nature of the task, assessments are rarely, if ever, value free. Social workers' individual perspectives are inevitably likely to affect the conduct and analysis of an assessment. Research has found that assessments are more likely to offset bias when social workers are reflective, ie when they identify and question their own biases and ensure that assessments are interactive and collaborative. In other words, an assessment needs to be considered as a process completed *with* an individual, rather than as a process done *to* them.

5.33 Social work assessments, therefore, combine the judgment or evaluation of a person, a situation or an event with an explicit acknowledgement of values, diversity and the views of others.

The aim of social work assessments

5.34 Social work assessments should identify:

- the strengths and needs in the family (adults and children);

- the nature and level of risk to the child;

- the ways in which the child can be protected;

- the parents' and family's capacity to change; and

- any services that may be appropriate to meet the needs of the child.

Phases of assessment

5.35 The social work assessment should include clearly defined and readily discernible phases as follows:

- Clarify the source of the referral and reason for it.

- Gather the existing information.

- Explore the differences between the family, child and professional understandings and feelings.

- Produce an analysis of needs within the family and local community context.

Different types of social work assessment

5.36 Social work assessments can be divided into various types. However, the complex nature of assessment means that the different types may overlap each other. Each social work assessment may include elements of every type of assessment.

Ongoing and fluid assessments

5.37 In this type of work, assessment is generally regarded as a continuous process. In other words it is acknowledged that changes and developments in people occur throughout the assessment process as they respond to ideas or situations that are presented to them. This process is dynamic, continues over time and is not simply a single event:[15]

> 'The process of assessment ... continues throughout the planned change process; while the initial assessment serves as a blueprint it will be modified as ideas are tested out and new data and information are gathered. The worker continually reassesses the nature of the problem, the need for supporting data and the effectiveness of the approaches chosen to cope with it.'

Single event or time-specific assessments

5.38 Social workers do not always need to continue the assessment throughout a planned piece of work. A time-specific assessment may lead to the production of a report after a time-limited period of assessment has taken place (eg a court report, a report for a child protection conference). The nature of this type of assessment is that it may only provide a 'snapshot' of an individual or a family at a particular moment in time and may not provide a full or accurate picture of a person in different circumstances.

5.39 This type of assessment may identify needs and services for a specific period of time after which no further action is necessary (eg a child may need to be accommodated for a short period of time while the caregiver requires short-term hospital treatment).

Risk assessments

5.40 There is no agreed or clear definition of assessment of risk. However, introducing the term 'risk' shifts the emphasis in social work practice from the

---

[15]   A Pincus and A Minahan *Social Work Practice: Model and Method* (Peacock, 1973).

immediate situation, to the future. A risk assessment enables the social worker to make a prediction about what might happen to the child in the future. Once the risk has been assessed, the task for the social worker is to manage it and to plan how to intervene to reduce such risk.[16]

> '… a risk assessment aims to predict the probability of a child's suffering from abuse if the situation continues unaltered.'

5.41   Assessment of risk in relation to children therefore usually refers to the capacity of a carer to ensure that the child is safe and protected. While the term risk suggests negative elements of danger or harm, any assessment of risk to a child must also identify the positive elements, namely the ways in which the child is being or can be protected and kept safe.

5.42   The distinction between immediate and ongoing risk depends to some degree on the type of abuse. Serious physical and sexual abuse may carry a greater and clearer risk of immediate harm, but psychological abuse and most types of neglect may present not immediate or urgent problems but cumulatively concerning damage to the child's development:[17]

> 'Long-term problems occur when the parenting style fails to compensate for the inevitable deficiencies that become manifest in the course of the 20 years or so it takes to bring up a child. During this period, occasional neglect, unnecessary or severe punishment or some form of family discord can be expected … If parenting is entirely negative, it will be damaging; if negative events are interspersed with positive experiences, outcomes will be better … In families low on warmth and high on criticism, negative incidents accumulate as if to remind a child that he or she is unloved.'

5.43   Munro suggests that, notwithstanding the damaging long-term effects of neglect, it is the assessment of immediate risk that has become dominant in social work practice in the last 20 or 30 years; this is attributed to the combination of the sharp increase in allegations of abuse with the limited resources available to local authorities which has required social workers to make difficult decisions about priorities.[18]

5.44   The Munro review final report[19] identified four major drivers of developments in child protection practice in recent times:

- The importance that members of the public attach to children and young people's safety and welfare and, consequently, the strength of reaction when a child is killed or suffers serious harm.

---

[16]   Prof Eileen Munro *Effective Child Protection* (Sage Publishing, 2nd edn, 2008), at p 60.
[17]   Department of Health *Messages from Research* (HMSO, 1995).
[18]   Prof Eileen Munro *Effective Child Protection* (Sage Publishing, 2nd edn, 2008), at p 61.
[19]   *The Munro Review of Child Protection: Final Report – A Child-Centred System*, Cm 8062 (2011).

- The sometimes limited understanding amongst the public and policy makers of the unavoidable degree of uncertainty involved in making child protection decisions, and the impossibility of eradicating that uncertainty.

- The tendency of the analyses of inquiries into child abuse deaths to invoke human error too readily, rather than taking a broader view when drawing lessons. This has led to recommendations that focus on prescribing what professionals should do without examining well enough the obstacles to doing so.

- The demands of the audit and inspection system for transparency and accountability that has contributed to undue weight being given to readily measured aspects of practice.

5.45 The Munro Final Report concludes that these four drivers have led to reforms and developments in the child protection system that, while having some value, have had the unintended, cumulative effect of creating obstacles to good practice. Consequently, it is often cases of physical and sexual abuse (the forms of abuse often carrying immediate danger) that are prioritised above cases of long-term emotional abuse or neglect. If social workers focus predominantly on the assessment of immediate risk, then the consequence inevitably will be that the families in which children are at immediate risk will get resources. This confirmed the findings in the Department of Health 1995 research which found that many of the families who were assessed appeared to experience significant long-term problems in caring for their children adequately but were offered no services unless there was also immediate risk.[20]

---

[20]   Department of Health *Messages from Research* (HMSO, 1995).

5.46 There are three elements in risk assessments which are associated with the stage in the process at which they are undertaken:[21]

	When?	What are the key questions to ask?	What are the possible problems?
Preventive risk assessment	Before any intervention is carried out with the individual and/or family	Should anything be done?	This type of risk assessment often relies on research evidence which is equivocal
Investigative risk assessment	Initial contact and assessment stage	What is happening here?	This type of risk assessment relies heavily on procedures, guidelines and checklists which may be interpreted too prescriptively or mechanically
Continuation risk assessment	Continuing involvement with the individual and/or family	Has the identified risk reduced?	This type of risk assessment requires a difficult balance between the risk of intervening and the risk of *not* intervening.

SECTION 2 – THE *FRAMEWORK FOR ASSESSMENT*

The context

5.47 All assessments undertaken by the local authority should adhere to the statutory guidance within the *Framework for the Assessment of Children in Need and their Families* (commonly known as the '*Framework for Assessment*' or the 'Lilac Book'). The *Framework for Assessment* was published by the Department of Health in April 2000 and provides a conceptual framework for practitioners that takes a developmental/ecological approach to assessing the child's needs, including the need for protection. It was developed in response to the finding that professionals had become so focused on investigating alleged incidents of abuse or neglect that they were paying too little attention to the overall quality of care that the child was receiving. While the majority of child protection enquiries concluded that the alleged incident did not warrant further action, many of the parents were experiencing problems, such as domestic violence or mental ill health, which were having an impact on their standard of care but they were not offered any help.

5.48 It is designed to enable social workers and managers to take a systematic approach to an assessment but one which is tailored to the needs of the

---

[21] V Coulshed and J Orme *Social Work Practice: An Introduction* (Palgrave Macmillan, 2006).

individual child and/or family in accordance with the CA 1989, s 47. The emphasis on systematic and evidence-based assessment is clear throughout the *Framework for Assessment*. The social worker's role is to plan the assessment carefully and in partnership with the child and family, and to gather and record information in a systematic and precise way, checking information with the child and family throughout. Differences in accounts or types of information should be recorded and the assessment should acknowledge strengths as well as needs.

5.49   The guidance builds on and supersedes the earlier Department of Health Guidance *Protecting Children: A Guide for Social Workers Undertaking a Comprehensive Assessment* (1988) (commonly known as 'the Orange Book').[22]

5.50   The guidance is intended to be used when an assessment of a child and family is undertaken whether assessing a child in need *or* in the context of a child protection enquiry.

Scope of the guidance

5.51   The *Framework for Assessment* provides a systematic way of analysing, understanding and recording what is happening to children and young people within their families and the wider context of the community in which they live. Such an understanding should then enable clear professional judgments to be made, including:

- whether the child being assessed is in need;

- whether the child is suffering or is likely to suffer significant harm;

- what actions must be taken; and

- which services would best meet the needs of this particular child and family.

5.52   Chapter 3 of the *Framework for Assessment* sets out the detail of the assessment process.

5.53   Accompanying the guidance is *The Family Assessment Pack of Questionnaires and Scales*[23] which includes:

- strengths and difficulties questionnaire;

- parenting daily hassles scale;

- adult well-being scale;

---

[22]   Department of Health *Messages from Research* (HMSO, 1995).
[23]   Department of Health, A Cox and A Bentovim *The Family Assessment Pack of Questionnaires and Scales* (TSO, 2000).

- home conditions scale;

- adolescent well-being scale;

- family activity scales (in age bands); and

- recent life events questionnaire.

5.54 The *Framework for Assessment* uses an evidence-based approach drawn from a wide range of research studies and theories across a number of disciplines and from the accumulated experience of policy and practice. The *Framework* is grounded in knowledge which is defined as:[24]

'... theory, research findings and practice experience in which confidence can be placed to assist in the gathering of information, its analysis and the choice of intervention in formulating the child's plan.'

5.55 The *Framework* encompasses many theories from a range of disciplines which contribute to the understanding of human growth and development, and the interaction between internal and external factors which have an impact on the lives of individuals. The interrelation between these factors is a fundamental theme running through the *Framework*:[25]

'Social workers need a framework for understanding and helping children and families which takes into account the inner world of the self and the outer world of the environment, both in terms of relationships and in terms of practicalities such as housing.'

5.56 The interaction between the three domains relating to children and the way they influence each other must be carefully analysed in order to gain a complete picture of a child's needs, and how best to respond to those needs which are unmet.

5.57 The three domains described in the *Framework* take account of this inner world of the self and the outer world of the environment:

5.58 The three domains are:

- the child's individual and developmental needs;

- parenting capacity; and

- family and environmental factors.

---

[24] Department of Health *Assessing Children in Need and their Families: Practice Guidance* ('*Framework Practice Guidance*') (TSO, 2000), para 1.1.

[25] Department of Health *Assessing Children in Need and their Families: Practice Guidance* (TSO, 2000), para 1.3 (citing G Schofield 'Inner and outer worlds: a psychosocial framework for child and family social work' (1998) 3 *Child and Family Social Work* 57–67).

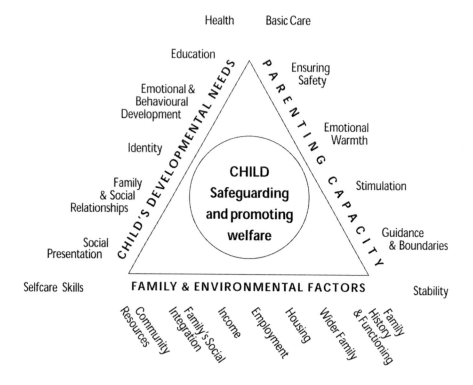

The first domain – the child's developmental needs

5.59 It is well established that children develop along several dimensions, often simultaneously, and need to reach a series of milestones along each dimension if they are to achieve their optimal outcomes. Different aspects of development will have more or less weight at different stages of a child's life.

Examples of age-related developmental tasks[26]

- *Infancy to pre-school children*:

    - attachment to caregiver(s);
    - language;
    - differentiation of self from the environment;
    - self-control and compliance.

- *Middle childhood*:

    - school adjustment (attendance, appropriate conduct);
    - academic achievement (eg learning to read);

---

[26]   A Masten and D Coatsworth 'Development of Competence in Favourable and Unfavourable Environments' (1998) 53 *American Psychologist* 205–220 and Brigid Daniel and Sally Wassell *Assessing and Promoting Resilience in Vulnerable Children I and II* (Jessica Kingsley Publishers, 2002).

- good relationships with peers (making friends, social acceptance);
- rule-governed conduct (following social rules for behaviour);
- quality of attachment to caregiver.

- *Adolescence*:

  - successful transition to secondary schooling;
  - academic achievement (learning the skills necessary for higher education and/or work);
  - involvement in extracurricular activities – talents and interests;
  - forming close relationship within and across gender;
  - forming a cohesive sense of self-identity and resilience;
  - developing a value base.

5.60 The *Framework* identifies seven dimensions along which children develop:

- health;

- education;

- emotional and behavioural development;

- identity;

- family and social relationships;

- social presentation; and

- self-care skills.

5.61 These seven dimensions are influenced by many factors. Key among them are the concepts of attachment and resilience. The two concepts are interactive and impact on each other.

Attachment

5.62 An attachment is a tie or bond based on the need of the infant child for safety, security and protection from their primary caregiver who is also known as their primary attachment figure. The role of the attachment figure, usually the parent, is to provide a secure base from which the child can explore, and a safe haven to which the child can retreat when threatened.[27]

5.63 Attachment theory is defined as:[28]

---

[27]   Vivien Prior and Danya Glaser *Understanding Attachment and Attachment Disorders: Theory, Evidence and Practice* (Jessica Kingsley Publishers, 2006).
[28]   J Bowlby *Attachment and Loss* (Hogarth Press, 1969), vol 1: Attachment; J Bowlby *Attachment*

'... a theory of normal development that offers explanations for some types of atypical development.'

5.64 The foundation of later development is determined by what happens to children in the first years of life. Children who are securely attached to significant adults in early childhood have been shown to be able to develop appropriate peer relationships, and to cope well with problems that confront them. It is also well established that children who have had good attachment experiences will be able to use these in their relationships with their own children in later life. This is why secure attachments for children are so important in the early years.

5.65 Approximately 65% of all patterns of attachment are secure. However, there are three other patterns of insecure attachments which are classified as:

- insecure-avoidant;

- insecure-resistant/ambivalent; and

- insecure-disorganised.

5.66 International research has identified that the four different patterns of attachment are consistent across cultures.

5.67 Secure attachment organisation is determined by the nature of caregiving which the child receives. Carers of securely attached children are sensitively responsive. However, the carers of children with attachment difficulties have been found to demonstrate a different range of behaviours:

- insecure-avoidant children tend to have rejecting or intrusive carers;

- insecure-resistant/ambivalent children tend to have carers who are under involved and unpredictable in their responses to the child; and

- insecure-disorganised children tend to have frightening or abusive caregivers.

5.68 Within the attachment theory model, the child develops an attachment with their caregiver while the caregiver bonds with the child. Such attachment and bonding are crucial, intense emotions and relationships.

5.69 The ability of social workers to identify attachment and bonding between parents and children has important implications for social work planning and intervention. A good working knowledge of attachment theory is therefore essential for social workers because it:

---

and Loss (Basic Books, 1973), vol 2: Separation: Anxiety and Anger; J Bowlby *Attachment and Loss* (Basic Books, 1980), vol 3: Loss: Sadness and Depressions.

- informs the working hypothesis about the relationships between the parent and the child;

- requires an emphasis on the parent's personal history and the nature of previous relationships;

- requires information about the parent's current relationship with the child;

- places great importance of observations of the relationship between the parent and the child in everyday settings;

- informs matching and the need for foster care support; and

- informs the nature of the most appropriate service and support to the child and/or parents.

Secure attachment

5.70

Signs of secure attachment in infants

- The caregiver is used by the infant as a secure base for exploration

- Infant readily separates from the caregiver to play

- The infant accepts stranger in the caregiver's presence

- The infant accepts comfort when distressed, and is able to return to play

- The infant actively seeks contact with the caregiver upon reunion

- Contact between the infant and the caregiver terminates the infant's distress

- The infant feels confident, worthy and secure

5.71

Signs of secure attachment in children of school age

- The child demonstrates positive affect and enthusiasm

- The child appears co-operative

- The child presents socially competent

- The child demonstrates perseverance

- The child has resilience

Insecure-avoidant attachment

5.72

Signs of insecure-avoidant attachment in infants

- Giving up by the infant

- The infant carries out little sharing or checking with the caregiver

- The infant shows little distress at separation from the caregiver

- The infant appears self-contained

- The infant shows little preference for the caregiver over a stranger

- The infant avoids and turns away from the caregiver upon reunion

- The infant demonstrates an absence of spontaneity and pleasure during separation from the caregiver and during play

- The infant is insecure and views the caregiver as being unavailable or unhelpful

---

5.73

Signs of insecure-avoidant attachment in children of school age

- The child is disobedient, aggressive or withdrawn

- The child demonstrates a lack of empathy for his or her peers

- The child demonstrates a lack of motivation

- The child shows behaviour problems

Insecure-resistant/ambivalent attachment

5.74

Signs of resistant/ambivalent attachment in infants

- The infant is distressed at separation but then resists being settled by the caregiver on return

- The infant demonstrates an inability to be calmed – angrily crying or passively whining in order to get the caregiver to be available even then it may not be clear how helpful the carer will be

- The infant becomes anxious, especially in new situations

- The infant demonstrates a preoccupation with contact with the caregiver

- The infant demonstrates a mixture of passivity and resistance (eg hitting, kicking)

5.75

Signs of resistant/ambivalent attachment in children of school age

- The child is over-dependent on teachers

- The child has a lack of confidence

- The child presents with low self-esteem

- The child displays a lack of social skills

- The child is often victimised, bullied or bullying

Insecure-disorganised attachment

5.76

Signs of insecure-disorganised attachment in infants

- The infant does not know how to behave to get the carer to be available and will demonstrate avoidance or resistance

- The infant may prefer a stranger to the caregiver

- The infant displays self-protection behaviour such as covering face, frozen posture

- The infant appears confused and apprehensive

5.77

Signs of insecure-disorganised attachment in children of school age

- The child appears resentful and hostile

- The child presents with a conduct disorder

- The child does not participate and refuses to respond

- The child displays poor impulse control

Secure caregiving

5.78

Characteristics of secure caregiving or parenting

- Caregivers are consistent, responsive and sensitive

- Caregivers show an acceptance of positives and negatives in the child and themselves

- Caregivers demonstrate warmth, involvement and responsiveness

- Caregivers offer structure and guidance

- Caregivers manage a two-way relationship with the infant or child which is flexible according to the needs of the child

- The caring or parenting adapts with increased age and autonomy of the child

---

Avoidant caregiving

5.79

Characteristics of avoidant caregiving or parenting

•   Caregivers are chronically unresponsive and neglectful

•   Children are seen as a chore and as demanding

•   Caregivers have difficulties with drug addiction and/or alcoholism

•   Caregivers are uncomfortable with emotions and are emotionally distant, dismissing and rejecting

•   Caregivers are intrusive and controlling to suit their own needs

•   Caregivers are able to acknowledge intellectually the importance of being a 'good parent'

•   Caregivers maintain a denial of attachment issues

Ambivalent/resistant parenting

5.80

Characteristics of ambivalent/resistant parenting

•   Caregivers offer inconsistent and unpredictable care

•   Caregivers are preoccupied with one extreme or another – everything is wonderful or everyone is hateful

•   Caregivers are attention-seeking and need to be at the centre for everyone

•   Caregivers are emotionally demanding

•   Households are disorganised and always in crisis

•   Caregivers need to know everyone's business

•   Caregivers maintain a lack of routines and structures

Disorganised parenting

5.81

Characteristics of disorganised parenting

- Caregivers are abusive with unresolved traumas

- Caregivers are vulnerable to psychiatric diagnosis, including depression

- Caregivers are likely to misuse drugs and/or alcohol

- Power, control, rejection and conflict are re-occurring themes in caregivers' relationships

- Caregivers express or demonstrate dissatisfaction with their children's behaviour, abilities or achievements

- Caregivers demonstrate a limited capacity to change

- Caregivers respond unpredictably or inconsistently to children's behaviour

---

Protective factors and resilience

5.82 Other factors within individual children will influence the way they are likely to react to experiences of their families and the environment in which they are growing up. These factors can include temperament, personality and gender. Children vary widely in the ways in which they may respond to a set of circumstances – some children may do well even in the most adverse circumstances while others appear to have limited capacity to deal with small amounts of stress. It is therefore crucial for the assessing social worker to understand what may be protective factors in children's lives and what may be stressors or vulnerabilities for particular children. Resilience is defined as 'the phenomenon of overcoming stress or adversity'.[29]

5.83 Resilience, like attachment, is a broadly based and complex concept. This means that there must be a careful analysis of the child which focuses not just on the individual or the family, but on the relevant stresses and adversities in the child and family's social context. The ability of the social worker to analyse resilience and to differentiate the vulnerabilities and strengths of children at different ages and stages of development is critical in any assessment of the child's needs.

5.84 A resilient child would be able to state and apply the following concepts about themselves:

---

[29] M Rutter 'Resilience concepts and findings: implications for family therapy' (1999) 21 *Journal of Family Therapy* 119–144, 159–160.

- **A secure base (I HAVE).** This means the resilient child can say:

    – *Trusting relationships:* I have people around me I trust and who love me, no matter what (family and friends);
    – *Structure and rules:* I have people who set limits for me so I know when to stop before there is danger or trouble;
    – *Role models:* I have people who show me how to do things right by the way they do things;
    – *Encouragement to be autonomous:* I have people who want me to learn to do things on my own;
    – *Access to education, health, welfare and security services:* I have people who help me when I am sick, in danger or need to learn.

- **Good self-esteem (I AM).** This means the resilient child can say:

    – *Lovable and appealing:* I am a person that people can like and love;
    – *Loving and empathic:* I am able to do nice things for others and show my concern;
    – *Proud of myself:* I am respectful of myself and others;
    – *Autonomous and responsible:* I am willing to be responsible for what I do;
    – *Filled with hope, faith and trust:* I am sure things will be all right.

- **Master and Control (I CAN).** This means the resilient child can say:

    – *Communicate:* I can talk to others about things that frighten me or bother me;
    – *Problem solve*: I can find ways to solve problems that I face;
    – *Manage my feelings:* I can control myself when I feel like doing something not right or dangerous;
    – *Gauge the temperament of myself and others:* I can figure out when it is a good time to talk to someone or to take action;
    – *Seek trusting relationships*: I can find someone to help me when I need it.

5.85   A resilient child does not need to have all of these features to be resilient, but a single feature is not enough. Resilience results from a combination of these features.

5.86   A child may be loved (I HAVE), but if he or she has no inner strength (I AM) or social, interpersonal skills (I CAN), there can be no resilience. A child may have a great deal of self-esteem (I AM), but if he or she does not know how to communicate with others or solve problems (I CAN), and has no one to help him or her (I HAVE), the child is not resilient.

5.87   Alternatively a child may be very verbal and speak well (I CAN), but if he or she has no empathy (I AM) or does not learn from role models (I HAVE), there is no resilience.

5.88 Social workers are required to gain an understanding about the development of attachment and resilience. However, they are not trained to carry out assessments of attachment disorders. This work should only be done by child psychologists and child psychiatrists. Lawyers should consider and analyse carefully the qualifications and experience of professionals who assess attachment and resilience in children, and, where necessary, consider the instruction of relevant experts to provide information about these issues.

The second domain – parenting capacity

5.89 The positive role of parents or caregivers will clearly affect the chances of optimal development for children from birth to adulthood. It is well established that there can be a diversity of family styles and that although some basic needs are universal, there can be a variety of ways of meeting them. Patterns of family life will differ according to culture, class and community, and there is no one perfect way to bring up children. Care must therefore be taken by social workers carrying out assessments of children and families to avoid value judgments and stereotyping (this is particularly pertinent in relation to black children and children from minority ethnic groups).

5.90 Children's chances of achieving optimal outcomes will depend, to a significant degree, on their parents' capacities to respond appropriately to their needs at different stages of their lives. There are many factors within parents that may affect and inhibit their responses to their children and prevent them providing parenting that is adequate to promote optimal outcomes in their children.

5.91 The *Framework* identifies six dimensions of parenting capacity:

- basic care;

- ensuring safety;

- emotional warmth;

- stimulation;

- guidance and boundaries; and

- stability.

5.92 Many factors may inhibit parents' ability to provide adequate parenting in accordance with these dimensions, including parents' own life experiences as adults and in childhood. It is important for social workers carrying out assessments to understand the nature of the adversity that parents may have experienced in early or adult life, and to understand the level of any protective factors to help overcome adversity which can build resilience in adult life (for example, it is well established that the presence of a supportive partner in adulthood could help counteract negative experiences of growing up in care).[30] It is also important for social workers to understand and analyse what may inhibit parents from responding appropriately to their children and what the consequences of that inappropriate response may be for children of different ages. Not all children are vulnerable to the adverse consequences of parental problems (for example, a 2-year-old may be at risk of significant harm from a parent whose practical caring skills are diminished by alcohol misuse, but a 16-year-old in a similar situation may be able to remain relatively unharmed). It is vital that social workers are able to understand the interaction between parents' responses and capabilities, and children's needs – this is a key principle underpinning effective social work assessment and intervention.

5.93 Problems likely to affect parenting are mental illness, alcohol and/or drug misuse, and domestic violence. Research suggests that children are less likely to be adversely affected when parental problems:

- are mild and of short duration;

- are not associated with family violence, conflict and disorganisation;

- do not result in the family breaking up.

5.94 Parents' views about their contact with social workers and other professionals have been well documented, particularly where there have been child protection concerns. Parents often have a strong sense of losing control once child protection agencies are involved. The things that parents value from social work agencies include:

- open, honest, timely and informative communication;

- social workers who listen, give feedback, provide information and advice, and who are reliable;

- practical and accessible services which are tailored to particular needs;

- a social work approach which is empathetic, reinforces strengths and does not undermine their parenting capacity.

5.95 The interaction between the family and the social worker is one of the most significant indicators of quality of parental care. For example, families who withdraw from contact, fail to keep many appointments or demonstrate disguised compliance can indicate danger to the child.[31]

---

[30]   M Rutter and M Rutter *Developing Minds: Challenging and Continuity across the Life Span* (Penguin, 1992).
[31]   P Reder, S Duncan and M Gray *Beyond Blame: Child Abuse Tragedies Revisited* (Routledge, 1993).

5.96 The *Framework Practice Guidance*[32] also reminds social workers not to confuse theory with ideology. Ideological approaches such as all children should be kept in family-based care because residential care is bad for them or siblings should be kept together at all costs should never get in the way of ethical and professional social work practice which deals effectively with the developmental needs of a particular child.

Interviews with parents

5.97 In any child protection investigation it cannot be assumed that all those with parental responsibility or all carers of the child are involved in causing harm. The investigation and assessment should establish whether there is a parent or carer able to protect the child during the investigation process and beyond.

5.98 It is important for social workers to demonstrate that the purpose and process of any investigation and assessment is clearly explained, and that parents' views about any concerns or injuries are taken into account. Social workers should keep an open mind and not make assumptions about parents' knowledge (or lack of) and/or about their capacity to care for their children. This is particularly important in cases of investigating allegations about sexual abuse when it could well be that the parent(s) have no knowledge of the concerns. Social workers should not conclude that having no prior knowledge of the concerns is necessarily a factor in failing to protect a child.

5.99 Social workers should also recognise that the position of the parent may change over time. This applies especially in the case of allegations about sexual abuse when it is not uncommon to have initial feelings of denial.

5.100 In assessing whether a parent has the capacity to care and protect their child in cases of sexual abuse, the following factors should be considered by the social worker:

- **Belief**

    - Does the parent believe the possibility that their child may have been sexually abused? If not, social workers should establish the extent of the parent's beliefs and the level of changes required.
    - Does the parent completely deny the allegations and put the child under pressure to retract?
    - Alternatively, is this a case of minimisation and disbelief, and the parent needs more time to shift to a position of belief?

- **Attitude**

---

[32] Department of Health *Assessing Children in Need and their Families: Practice Guidance* ('*Framework Practice Guidance*') (TSO, 2000).

- How does the parent feel towards the child following the allegation being made?
- Is the child being cared for, ignored or scapegoated?

- **Role**

  - How did the parent come to know about the allegations of sexual abuse?
  - Did the parent bring the concerns to the attention of others or did the parent delay in bringing their concerns to the attention of others?
  - Or did the parent explicitly conceal concerns from others?

- **Responsibility**

  - Who does the parent perceive as having responsibility for the alleged abuse?
  - Does the parent perceive the alleged perpetrator as being responsible?
  - Does the parent see the child as contributing to their own abuse or even being responsible for their abuse?

- **Co-operation**

  - Does the parent demonstrate active co-operation with the investigative process?
  - Does the parent have good reasons to avoid co-operating?
  - Does the parent demonstrate compliance or refusal to co-operate without giving any explanation?

- **Openness**

  - How open is the parent about discussing allegations and concerns with immediate and extended family members, and significant others?
  - Are the discussions open and age appropriate, or are the allegations and concerns kept private and unclear?

- **Dependency**

  - How dependent is the parent on the alleged perpetrator?
  - Is the parent independent with their own support networks?
  - Alternatively, is the parent isolated but able to form new support?
  - Is the parent completely dependent on the alleged perpetrator?

- **History of abuse**

  - Does the parent have a previous experience of abuse and how was it dealt with?

- Was any previous experience of abuse openly discussed and resolved towards protection?
- Are there still unresolved issues or is the abuse denied and contact with alleged abuser ongoing?

The third domain – family and environmental factors

5.101 It is widely recognised that there is a significant number of external factors which may affect children. The *Framework* identifies such factors along seven dimensions:

- family history and functioning;

- wider family;

- housing;

- employment;

- income;

- family's social integration; and

- community resources.

5.102 The wider family can be a significant source of support for children and families. Conversely, extended families may not always be supportive, and in some cases may be positively harmful or detrimental.

5.103 A social work analysis of the role and function of the wider family is a fundamental part of a good assessment. Similarly, the contribution of the wider community in providing practical and emotional support to the immediate family also needs to be understood and considered. It may be necessary for the social worker to chart families' interrelationships over time as well as in terms of their present living arrangements. There are a number of activities and tools that can be used with children and/or families to gather and represent the data social workers may collect in order to complete assessments (initial and ongoing). These tools include genograms and ecomaps.

Genograms

5.104 A genogram is a type of family tree which provides an immediate visual representation of the individual or family being assessed; it is a commonly used method of work in family therapy. It is also a 'snapshot' of how that person or family is structured and regarded at a particular moment in time. A genogram can be a useful tool for social workers by:

- highlighting areas that may cause concern;

- identifying information that is required but lacking;

- identifying historical patterns within families which may influence the way the family still operates;

- identifying areas or themes for further exploration with the family.

5.105 Genograms are not used solely for the benefit of gathering information by social workers. They are used with families in a collaborative and participatory way that can encourage the formation of good working relationships with service users. Using genograms can help facilitate discussion about difficult or painful issues (for example, divorce, separation, miscarriage or still births, adoption, previous abuse). However, social workers should remember that this means the process will necessarily take time and cannot be rushed. People need time to assimilate information about themselves and their families.

Ecomaps

5.106 An ecomap looks at the networks available in the environment in which the service user lives, unlike genograms, which identify a family's connections across and between generations. Such networks may represent individuals, organisations or agencies.

5.107 An ecomap seeks to show how family members act and react to each other, and how the family as a whole relates to other families, groups and organisations in society. It can show the different levels at which individuals and families interact on an everyday basis and can consider the reciprocal influences between them.

5.108 Ecomaps (like genograms) can also be very helpful in strengthening the working relationships between families and social workers. They can encourage discussion about difficult issues and debate about beliefs and disagreements between family members.

Cultural diversity

5.109 In using tools such as ecomaps and genograms it is essential that social workers include a consideration and analysis of the meaning and impact of culture in the lives of individuals and families being assessed. It is particularly important to develop such practice with people who are refugees or asylum seekers.

5.110 There are ten important factors in relation to culture and diversity about which information is gathered when completing assessments:

- the reasons for immigration;

- length of time in the community;

- legal or undocumented status;

- age at time of immigration;

- language spoken at home and in the community;

- contact with cultural institutions;

- health beliefs;

- holidays and special events;

- the impact of crisis and significant events; and

- values held about family, education and work.

5.111 Parents who are socially isolated (through an absence of physical and emotional support) will often experience a sense of a lack of well-being and control over their lives. Where social isolation is combined with fears for personal safety (for example, because of a violent partner or a hostile community), cumulative negative factors can have an impact on parents' mental and physical heath.

5.112 There is also considerable evidence about the detrimental impact of the environment on parenting capacity. The impact on families' health and well-being of living on a low income is well documented, and research studies have demonstrated the strong association between economic disadvantage and living conditions and the chances that children will fail to thrive. However, environmental considerations are often omitted from the social work assessment process.[33] It is therefore vital that social workers consider and analyse the effects on the health and educational development of children of growing up and living in areas of deprivation.

5.113 The relationship between disability and disadvantage is also important yet is not always clearly analysed or understood. Research has established that families with more than one disabled child are (among other things) less likely to be in work, more likely to be in semi-skilled or unskilled work, more likely to be dependent on benefits and more likely to report housing as unsuitable.

5.114 In summary, the evidence suggests that the families of many children in need who are most disadvantaged are those living in poverty, in poor housing, lacking adequate social support and in hostile neighbourhoods in areas of great deprivation. Such families will clearly face multiple stresses which are interlinked.

---

[33] See for example, O Stevenson *Neglected Children: Issues and Dilemmas* (Blackwell, 1998).

The importance of context

5.115 A single event or chain of events may set off a cycle or chain of interaction for families. This event or chain of events may interact with the child's needs and the surrounding vulnerabilities (or stressors) and protective factors within the family. The importance of *context* is therefore critical in understanding the relationship between outcomes and those events which may act as stressors. Social workers should bear in mind that the context of an event (or chain of events) often gives meaning to behaviour. Consideration of an incident without analysis of the context will clearly represent a deficient analysis.

Principles of assessment

5.116 Important principles underpinning the approach to assessing children and families are outlined in the *Framework Practice Guidance*. They are important in understanding how an assessment should be carried out. Clarity about aims is fundamental to all assessments. The general intention must be to gather a range of relevant information in a manner that promotes or sustains a positive working relationship with those being assessed. Information will usually be of limited use if collaboration with those being assessed has broken down.

Assessments are a tool for planning

5.117 The *Framework Practice Guidance* places great emphasis on social workers using evidence-based practice as the model for their assessment work. This means that social workers should not only think about evidence as part of the judicial process, but should consider evidence throughout the whole of their work with children and families:[34]

> 'The whole child care service, from strategic planning to monitoring of individual outcomes, is permeated by questions of evidence. Gathering, testing, recording and weighing evidence are tasks basic to professional competence ... decisions can only be as good as the evidence on which they are based.'

5.118 Evidence-based practice is defined in the *Framework* as the ability to:[35]

> '... use knowledge critically from research and practice about the needs of children and families and the outcomes of services and interventions to inform their assessment and planning.'

5.119 An evidence-based assessment is therefore the process whereby social workers gather relevant information about what is happening to a child and use their knowledge critically from research findings, theoretical ideas and practical

---

[34]   Department of Health *Patterns and Outcomes in Child Placement* (HMSO, 1991).
[35]   Department of Health *Framework for the Assessment of Children in Need and Their Families* (TSO, 2000), para 1.58.

experience to achieve a greater understanding of a particular child and family's experiences or problems. In evidence-based assessments social workers are therefore expected to:

- record and update information systematically, distinguishing sources of information (for example, direct observation, other agency records or interviews with family members);

- evaluate continuously whether the intervention is effective in responding to the needs of an individual child and family and modifying their interventions accordingly.

5.120 Evidence-based social work requires the careful use of knowledge during work with a child and family to undertake the task of determining what is most relevant in a family's situation, what is most significant for the child, the impact of current or past intervention, and the judgment or decision about when more or less action is required in the child's best interests. The *Framework Practice Guidance* quotes from Reder and Duncan (1999) as follows:[36]

'... assessment comes before action and the impact of actions needs to be monitored ... Assessment should be an evolving process in which thought and action are reciprocal. Actions are guided by thought and the consequences of action are noted, considered and fed back to influence further action.'

5.121 It is the combination of evidence-based practice grounded in knowledge with finely balanced professional judgment which is 'the foundation for effective practice with children and families'.[37]

Assessments should be child-centred

5.122 Fundamental to an assessment of a child's needs is the principle that the approach must be child-centred. This means that the child is at the centre of the assessment, and that account is always taken of the child's perspective. It is easy in complex situations for attention to be diverted from the child to other issues being faced by the family; this can result in the child becoming lost during the assessment and the impact of the family and environmental circumstances on the child not being clearly identified and understood. The significance of seeing and observing the child throughout any assessment cannot be overstated.

Assessments should ascertain children's wishes and feelings

5.123 The wishes and feelings of the child must be sought, and can only be ascertained by talking with the child according to their maturity and level of understanding. It is therefore necessary for social workers to have experience

---

[36] P Reder and S Duncan *Lost Innocents* (Routledge, 1999).
[37] Department of Health *Framework for the Assessment of Children in Need and Their Families* (TSO, 2000), para 1.59.

and skills in communicating with children in different ways – verbally, through play, and by observation. Communication with children should be based on sound knowledge of child development within their ethnic, cultural, religious and linguistic context. In cases where the child has disabilities it may be necessary to involve someone who is skilled in communicating with the child in order to ascertain their wishes and feelings.

Assessments should be rooted in child development

5.124 Children have a range of different and complex developmental needs which must be met during different stages of childhood if optimal outcomes are to be achieved. A thorough understanding of child development is essential for social workers undertaking assessments of children. Children who come to the attention of local authorities are frequently very vulnerable and may have missed the opportunity to fulfil their full potential. It is therefore crucial for social workers to know about the importance of developmental milestones that children need to reach, if they are to be healthy and achieve their full potential.

5.125 Social workers should understand the consequences of variations in these developmental stages for children of different ages, some of whom may have special educational needs or profound difficulties. Social workers also need to be aware of the significance of timing in children's lives, especially in cases where children may not be getting what they need at a crucial stage in their development and when time is passing.

5.126 Plans and interventions should be based on a clear assessment of the developmental progress and difficulties a child may be experiencing. Social workers should ensure that planned action is timely and appropriate in terms of the child's developmental needs.

Assessments should be ecological in their approach

5.127 An understanding of the child must be located within the context of the child's family (defined as the child's parents and/or other carers) and of the community and culture in which he or she is growing up.

Assessments should ensure equality of opportunity

5.128 Ensuring equality of opportunity does not mean that all children are treated the same. It means understanding and working sensitively and knowledgeably with diversity to identify the particular issues for a child within their family, taking account of personal experiences and family context.

5.129 A child's racial, cultural and ethnic background, religious persuasion and language are central to the formation of his or her self-identity. Social workers should recognise the need to challenge and eliminate stereotypes and they should have an understanding about how power relationships and the impact of violence, or threat of it, are crucial when evaluating information and observed responses.

5.130 Families affected by disability must be able to participate fully, both by ensuring suitable accessible venues and by communicating in the user's chosen language, including sign language and Braille. Understanding the impact on families of caring for a disabled child is a prerequisite for effective working.

Assessments should build on strengths as well as identify needs

5.131 Good assessments aim to achieve a full understanding of what is happening to a child in the context of his or her family and the wider community. Therefore social workers should examine carefully the nature of the interactions between the child, family and environmental factors, and should identify both positive and negative influences on these interactions. These will vary for each child. Nothing can be assumed – the facts must be sought, the meaning attached to them explored and weighed up with the family. Working with a child or family's strengths may be an important part of the plan to resolve difficulties; a realistic and informed appraisal of the strengths and resources in each family can be mobilised to safeguard and promote the child's welfare.

5.132 Social workers should recognise that:

- families are more widely defined than parents and include any significant others who are not necessarily blood related;

- children are best looked after within their families. It is essential that support, advice and assistance, including financial assistance, is provided to families to enable them to protect and promote the welfare of children;

- children should not be removed from the care of their families without clear evidence of the children suffering significant harm and/or likely significant harm.

Assessments should be interagency in their approach to assessment and the provision of services

5.133 Effective communication and collaboration with other agencies and professionals is central to the investigative and assessment process. Omissions and/or conflicts among professionals should be addressed to ensure children are protected.

Assessments should be a continuing process, not a single event

5.134 Although an assessment has many uses, it should generally be therapeutic. The assessment should inform the identification of current needs as well as future work, and evaluate the progress and effectiveness of interventions. The way in which the assessment is conducted is vital. The assessment should enable those involved to gain fresh perspectives on their family situation, which are in themselves helpful and assist in taking the work forward.

Assessments should be transparent

5.135 Work with families should be respectful, open and honest. The purpose and process of assessments should be fully explained and understood by families, and each member of the family be given the opportunity to have access to information held about them.

Assessments do not take place in a vacuum

5.136 Assessments benefit from multiple sources of information and multiple methods. Any single source of information used in isolation is likely to provide only a limited or unbalanced view. This applies to all the main approaches of interviewing, observation and the use of standardised tests and questionnaires. Limitations should be recognised. Contrasting data from different methods and/or sources are vital to developing a deeper and more balanced understanding of the child and family's situation.

Principles for the use of materials to assist assessment

5.137 The *Framework Practice Guidance* provides useful guidance for social workers about the choice of materials and tools in their assessment work with children and families.

5.138 Various practice materials are available for use by social workers in their assessment work.

Assessment records

5.139 The Department of Health has designed various assessment records for use by social workers in their assessment work with children and families – the Referral and Initial Information Record (RIIR), the Initial Assessment Record (IAR) and the Core Assessment Record (CAR).

5.140 The assessment records can provide checklists for structuring what social workers observe or discuss in their assessment work. They can also help in the precise recording and systematic assembly of information for analysis. They are intended to complement, but *not* to replace, the information gathered through interviews and observations. The gathering of information is intended to help explain what is happening to children and their families. It is the analysis and the making sense of that information that is the key task in the assessment process. The materials recommended within the *Framework Practice Guidance* are useful tools in helping to structure the social worker's thinking about families, assisting them to record systematically and consistently what they have seen and heard, and aiding their analysis and formulation of appropriate plans – 'Good tools cannot substitute for good practice, but good practice and good tools together can achieve excellence'.[38]

Questionnaires and scales

5.141 There is a wide range of questionnaires and instruments available for use when assessing children and families. In particular, eight questionnaires and scales are identified in the *Framework Practice Guidance* as particularly easy to incorporate in social work practice. The questionnaires are contained within *The Family Assessment Pack of Questionnaires and Scales*[39] which is a companion pack accompanying the *Framework*. It sets out how the questionnaires and scales can be used by social workers when assessing children and their families. These tools are designed to assist social workers by providing a clear evidence base for the judgments and recommendations made regarding a child and by informing the child care plan.

5.142 They can be used by social workers following a process of familiarisation with the materials but do not require any formal training.

5.143 *Strengths and Difficulties Questionnaires* – these scales are a modification of the widely used instruments to screen for emotional and behavioural problems in children and adolescents. There are two versions of the questionnaire for use with children aged 11–16 and for adult caregivers (or teachers) of children aged 3–16. The questionnaires are suitable for use with disabled children and their carers (and teachers) and are available in 40 languages.

- *Parenting Daily Hassles Scale* – this scale aims to assess the frequency and intensity or impact of 20 potential parenting daily 'hassles' experienced by adults caring for children. It has been widely evaluated and research shows that parents generally like completing this form because it touches on many aspects of parenting that are important to them.

- *Home Conditions Assessment* – this scale addresses various aspects of the home environment. The total score for this scale has been found to correlate highly with indices of children's development.

- *Adult Well-being Scale* – this scale considers how adults are feeling in terms of depression, anxiety and irritability.

---

[38] Department of Health *Framework for the Assessment of Children in Need and Their Families* (TSO, 2000), para 4.2.
[39] Department of Health, A Cox and A Bentovim *The Family Assessment Pack of Questionnaires and Scales* (TSO, 2000).

- *Adolescent Well-being Scale* – this scale is validated for children between 7 and 16. It is intended to enable social workers to gain more insight and understanding about how adolescents feel about their lives.

- *Recent Life Events Questionnaire* – this scale focuses on recent life events (ie those occurring in the last 12 months), although it could be used over a longer timescale. It is intended to help in the compilation of a social history (for individuals or for families) and respondents are asked to identify which (if any) of these events still affect them. The scale can contribute to a greater contextual understanding of the family's current situation, help social workers explore how particular recent life events have affected the family, and in some situations identify life events which family members have not reported earlier.

- *Family Activity Scales (in two age bands)* – these scales provide an opportunity to explore with parents or carers the environment that is provided for their children through joint activities and support for independent activities. This includes information about the cultural and ideological environment in which children live, as well as how their parents respond to their children's actions. These scales are designed to be used independent of socio-economic resources. There are two separate scales – one for children aged 2–6, and one for children aged 7–12.

- *Alcohol Scale* – this scale is designed to identify not necessarily the amount of alcohol consumed by a parent or carer, but the way in which alcohol impacts on the individual and, in particular, on their role as a parent. The questionnaire has been found to be effective in detecting individuals with alcohol disorders and those with dangerous drinking habits.

5.144   These questionnaires and scales are intended to assist social workers by providing a clear evidence base for judgments and recommendations. They provide a useful way of understanding families' or individual members' needs, and can also help social workers in understanding the extent of current shared knowledge of the family's predicament. Although questionnaires and scales are sometimes thought to be limited, judgmental and superficial, the *Framework Practice Guidance* clearly recommends that, with careful use, they can often elicit more frank responses than interviews. The vital issue is how and when they are used. Although most of the questionnaires are designed to be completed by respondents, rather than assessors, they can be used in other ways, for example, as mental checklists for the assessor (either regarding what they observe or what they discuss with the respondent).

5.145   The use of questionnaires and scales requires careful preparation and introduction to families by social workers and a clear explanation about how they fit into the initial or core assessment. They can be administered verbally, or can be used to provide prompts that are the basis for further discussion between the social worker and the respondent. It is not appropriate for the social worker simply to pick up a completed questionnaire and leave, or to ask the questions and just note the answers. Unless the questionnaire has been used simply as a mental checklist, it should be discussed with the respondent. Discussion should cover the respondent's overall thoughts and feelings about completing the questionnaire, and individual items which raise possible issues or indicate improvements. Discussion is probably best at the completion of the questionnaire, but there will be times when it is important to pick up on individual items during completion if they are of immediate significance (for example, questions relating to self-harm within the Adult Well-being Scale). Social workers need to be prepared to take up issues that arise, whether indicators of needs or progress.

5.146 Each questionnaire or scale should be used for the purpose for which it was developed. They are intended to contribute to the overall assessment and should be applied sensitively. The eight questionnaires and scales have all been well evaluated, but although widely used in psychology and psychiatry are not commonly used by social workers. The *Framework Practice Guidance* lists the following benefits of using these questionnaires and scales in social work practice:

- strengthens the voice of the family and child in the assessment process;

- strengthens the relationship between the social worker and the family;

- clarifies the nature and extent of need;

- provides a focus for assessment;

- provides a structure for a plan of intervention;

- provides a method of structuring discussions with families about issues they may feel reluctant or unable to discuss;

- provides an evidence base for social work reports; and

- enables social workers to monitor progress over time and allows a clear analysis between professionals and families of areas in which particular changes are planned or required.

5.147 The questionnaires have been evaluated by the Department of Health as being helpful in both initial and core assessments, as well as in reviewing progress.

Timescales for assessments

5.148 The timescales for completing the various elements of an assessment are clearly stated in the *Framework for Assessment*.

5.149

What are the timescales for assessments?

- WITHIN 1 WORKING DAY – there should be a response from a referral to the local authority

- WITHIN 7 WORKING DAYS – an initial assessment should be undertaken and completed

- WITHIN 35 WORKING DAYS – a core assessment should be undertaken and completed

---

5.150   These are *maximum* timescales for completing an analysis of the needs of children and the parenting capacity to respond to those needs. The needs of some children (particularly those who require emergency intervention) may mean that the initial assessment stage is brief. It may also be brief where the needs of the child can be determined in a period of less than seven working days. The same considerations apply to the minimum and maximum timescales for core assessments.

5.151   *Working Together* requires that within 42 days of beginning the initial assessment the local authority should have completed a core assessment in respect of every child who is the subject of a Child Protection Plan (see Chapter 6). Where a child is not the subject of a Child Protection Plan but meets the criteria for a core assessment, then this too should take place within the same timescale (provided that the parents wish the assessment to take place).

5.152   The *Framework* led to the production of the Referral and Initial Information Record (RIIR). The RIIR begins the process of systematic information gathering about children in need and their families. This process is continued in the Initial Assessment and Core Assessment Records. The records have been designed to provide an integrated framework for the process of recording and analysing information in line with the *Framework Practice Guidance*.

SECTION 3 – INITIAL ASSESSMENT

5.153   The initial assessment is a brief assessment of each child referred to the local authority where it is necessary to determine whether the child is in need, the nature of any services required, and whether a further, more detailed core assessment should be undertaken.

5.154   The purpose of the initial assessment is to decide whether the child is a child in need, the nature of any services required, from where and within what timescales, and whether a more detailed core assessment should be carried out.

The fact that a decision is made to carry out a core assessment should not prevent a child or family from receiving services which are necessary to support them.

5.155 An initial assessment is deemed to have commenced at the point of referral to the local authority, or when new information on an open case indicates that an initial assessment should be repeated. An initial assessment may include some or all of the following (as appropriate):

- interviews with child and family members;

- involvement of other agencies in gathering and providing information;

- consultation with supervisor or manager;

- record of initial analysis;

- decisions on further action or no action;

- record of decisions or rationale with family or agencies;

- informing other agencies of the decisions;

- statement to the family of decisions made.

5.156 The initial assessment should be completed by the local authority, working with colleagues, within a maximum of 7 working days of the date of referral. The initial assessment period may be very brief if the criteria for initiating s 47 enquiries are met.

5.157 Where a common assessment has been completed (in accordance with the Common Assessment Framework (CAF)) this information should be used to inform the initial assessment (see Chapter 2).

5.158 Information should be gathered and analysed within the three domains of the Assessment Framework, namely:

- the child's developmental needs;

- the parents' or caregivers' capacity to respond appropriately to those needs; and

- the wider family and environmental factors.

5.159 The initial assessment should be led by a qualified and experienced social worker. It should be carefully planned, with clarity about who is doing what, when, and how information is to be shared with the parents. The planning process and decisions about the timing of the different assessment activities should be undertaken in collaboration with all those involved with the child and family.

5.160 The process of initial assessment should involve:

- seeing and speaking to the child (according to age and understanding) and family members as appropriate;

- drawing together and analysing available information from a range of sources (including existing records);

- involving and obtaining relevant information from professionals and others who have current (or previous) contact with the child and family.

5.161 All relevant information (including historical information) should be taken into account. External agencies outside the local authority should be consulted and involved as appropriate as a fundamental part of the initial assessment. Permission to contact other relevant agencies should be obtained from parents except in cases where the safety of the child would be jeopardised. Social workers will need to clarify at this stage whether other professionals will agree to information they provide being shared with the family. Agencies contacted or involved in the initial assessment should be recorded by a tick on the Initial Information Record completed by the social worker. The name and address of any agency contacted or involved in the initial assessment not already recorded on the RIIR should be added to the Initial Information Record.

5.162 During the initial assessment the child should be seen within a timescale that is appropriate to the nature of concerns expressed at the time of the referral, according to the agreed plan (which may include seeing the child without his or her caregivers present). This includes observing and communicating with the child in a manner appropriate to his or her age, maturity and understanding.

5.163 During the initial assessment it will not necessarily be clear whether a criminal offence has been committed, which means that even initial discussions with the child should be undertaken in a way that minimises distress to them and maximises the likelihood that the child will provide accurate and complete information, avoiding leading or suggestive questions.

5.164 Interviews with family members (which may include the child) should also be undertaken in their preferred language and where appropriate for some people by using non-verbal communication methods.

5.165 In the course of an initial assessment, the local authority should ascertain:

- is this a child in need?;[40] or

- is there reasonable cause to suspect that this child is suffering, or is likely to suffer, significant harm?[41]

5.166 The focus of the initial assessment should be the welfare of the child. It is important to remember that even if the reason for a referral was a concern about abuse or neglect that is not subsequently substantiated, a family may still benefit from support and practical help to promote a child's health and development.

5.167 If the child's needs and circumstances are complex, a more in-depth core assessment will be required in order to decide what other types of services are necessary to assist the child and family.

5.168 Following an initial assessment, the local authority should decide on the next course of action, following discussion with the child and family, unless such a discussion may place a child at increased risk of significant harm. If there are concerns about a parent's ability to protect a child from harm, careful consideration should be given to what the parents should be told, when and by whom, taking account of the child's welfare. All decisions will have to take account of the child's safety and whether permission has been obtained from other agencies to share information. In some cases it will not be appropriate to include all the initial information (for example, where a neighbour has made a referral but wishes to remain anonymous).

The Initial Assessment Record

5.169 Whatever decisions are taken, they should be endorsed at a managerial level agreed within the local authority and recorded in writing in the Initial Assessment Record (IAR). The IAR continues the process of systematic information gathering that was commenced in the RIIR, and develops the analysis of this material. This process of assessment is continued still further if a core assessment is subsequently undertaken.

5.170 The main headings of the IAR are organised according to the *Framework for Assessment* domains and dimensions. The initial assessment therefore covers the following areas:

- *The child's developmental needs* – these are as set out in the seven dimensions described in the *Framework*. However, as this is an initial assessment some dimensions which are interrelated have been placed together (for example, Identity and Social Presentation). The child's strengths and current needs should be recorded under each of the

---

[40] CA 1989, s 17.
[41] CA 1989, s 47.

developmental dimensions listed. *For example, Daniel (aged 18 months) was born profoundly deaf. In areas other than speech, Daniel's development is at the expected level.*[42]

- *Parents' (or carers') capacities to respond appropriately to the child's needs* – it is vital that parents' strengths as well as any areas of difficulty that they are experiencing are recorded. This part of the Initial Assessment includes key issues which research has shown affect parents' abilities to respond appropriately to their child's needs; for example, problems with mental health, domestic violence, drug and alcohol misuse, a history of childhood abuse or being a perpetrator of child abuse are all likely to affect parenting capacity. It is important to record not just that an issue is present, but to whom it refers and its effect on parenting capacity. *For example:*

  - *Basic care: Mrs Smith is at times unable to care for Daniel. However, Mr Smith is able to respond to Daniel's needs.*
  - *Physical/mental illness: Mrs Smith has suffered from postnatal depression since the birth of Daniel earlier this year. Mrs Smith is receiving medication for this.*

  It is also important to record in this section details about any adult who is deemed to pose a risk of significant harm to the child (for example, relatives who are Schedule 1 offenders or parents who are violent to their partners). The social worker will need to decide which is the most appropriate category (or categories) in which to record this information within this part of the initial assessment.

- *Family and environmental factors which have an impact on the family* – the Initial Assessment expects an analysis by social workers that the environment within which children and families live can play an important role in reducing or increasing the stresses on families, depending on the support available to them. In this section it is important to record factors that support families as well as those that increase stress; for example, extended family members may offer a great deal of support to a young couple caring for a new baby, alternatively they may compound the family's difficulties. It is also important to note how family and environmental factors may be impacting on the child and family. *For example:*

  - *Housing: the Smith family live on the 19th floor of a tower block of flats. The exterior of the building is in poor condition. However, Mr and Mrs Smith keep the inside of their flat in very good condition.*

5.171 The Initial Assessment Record should also include the reasons for social work decisions and future action to be taken:

---

[42] Examples stated in the Department of Health *Framework for Assessment: Guidance notes and glossary for Referral and Initial Information Record, Initial Assessment Record and Core Assessment Record* (TSO, 2000).

- *Immediate action* – this section should be used to record any actions taken during or on completion of the initial assessment. More than one box may be completed; for example, a family may be allocated a nursery place for their baby in addition to a referral being made to another agency such as Home Start and a strategy discussion. It is important to remember that if a core assessment is planned, the family should still receive services as appropriate.

- *Further action* – professional judgment will be required to determine whether a core assessment is appropriate or required. In some cases it will be immediately clear that more specialist assessments are necessary (for example, a psychological assessment of a parent's cognitive or intellectual functioning) and such assessments should be commissioned or arranged by the local authority at this stage.

5.172 The social worker who has completed the initial assessment should always sign and date the form which should then be passed to the relevant manager to confirm the action recommended. A copy of the completed initial assessment should then be sent to appropriate family members.

5.173 The family, the original referrer, and other professionals and services involved in the assessment, should as far as possible be told what action has been and will be taken, consistent with respecting the confidentiality of the child and family concerned, and not jeopardising further action in respect of concerns about harm (which may include police investigations). This information should be confirmed in writing to the agencies and the family.

5.174 *Working Together* identifies ten common pitfalls often encountered during initial assessments and provides guidance as to how these can be avoided.

5.175

Analysis of initial assessments

• Was enough weight given to information from family, friends and neighbours?

• Was enough attention paid to what children say, how they look and how they behave?

• Was attention focused on most visible or pressing problems while other warning signs were not appreciated?

• Did pressures from high status referrers or the press, with fears that a child may die, lead to over-precipitate action?

• Did professionals think that when they have explained something as clearly as they can, the other person will have understood it?

• Did assumptions and prejudgments about families lead to observations being ignored or misinterpreted?

• Was parents' behaviour, whether co-operative or unco-operative, misinterpreted?

• If the initial enquiry shows that child not at risk of significant harm, was family referred to other services which were needed to prevent longer-term problems?

• When faced with an aggressive or frightening family, were professionals reluctant to discuss fears for their own safety and ask for help?

• Was information taken at point of referral adequately recorded? Were facts checked and reasons for decisions noted?

5.176   Where a child is suspected to be suffering, or likely to suffer, significant harm, the local authority is required by the CA 1989, s 47 to make enquiries, to enable it to decide whether it should take any action to safeguard and promote the welfare of the child.

5.177   Where there is a risk to the life of a child or a likelihood of serious immediate harm, the local authority or the police should act quickly to secure the immediate safety of the child. Emergency action might be necessary as soon as a referral is received, or at any point in involvement with children and families. The need for emergency action may become apparent only over time as more is learned about the circumstances of a child or children. Neglect, as well as abuse, can pose such a risk of significant harm to a child that urgent protective action is needed.

5.178 When considering whether emergency action is required, an agency should always consider whether action is also required to safeguard and promote the welfare of other children in the same household, the household of an alleged perpetrator, or elsewhere.

5.179 Planned emergency action will normally take place following an immediate strategy discussion between police, the local authority, and other agencies as appropriate. Where a single agency has to act immediately to protect a child, a strategy discussion should take place as soon as possible after such action to plan the next steps (see Chapter 6).

5.180 Emergency action addresses only the immediate circumstances of the child. It should be followed quickly by s 47 enquiries as necessary. The agencies primarily involved with the child and family should then assess the needs and circumstances of the child and family, and agree action to safeguard and promote the welfare of the child in the longer term.

SECTION 4 – CORE ASSESSMENT

5.181 The core assessment is a holistic assessment of the child (social workers or other professionals sometimes refer to a core assessment of a parent – this demonstrates a lack of clear understanding about the function, purpose and nature of a core assessment). In order to complete the core assessment the social worker will draw on information from a variety of sources including the child, parent or carers and other professionals. A core assessment should also draw upon existing reports and specialist assessments concerning the child and family (having obtained the necessary permission to use such information).

5.182 Completion of the core assessment, within 35 working days, should include an analysis of the child's developmental needs and the parents' capacity to respond to those needs, including parents' capacity to ensure that the child is safe from harm. It may be necessary to commission specialist assessments (e g from child and adolescent mental health services) that cannot be completed within this time period. This should not delay the drawing together of the core assessment findings at this point.

5.183 The analysis of the child's needs should provide evidence on which to base judgments and decisions on how best to safeguard and promote the welfare of a child and support parents in achieving this aim. Decisions based on analysis of the child's developmental needs should then be used to develop the child protection plan.

The core assessment record

5.184 The core assessment records are intended to assist social workers undertaking a core assessment by providing a framework to record information systematically across all domains and dimensions in a manner that facilitates analysis and planning. However, it is important to remember that the core assessment record is only a tool which requires the skills, knowledge and professional judgment of the social worker to be used effectively.

5.185 The records are designed for use with children of all abilities and an assessment of a disabled child should consider the same domains and dimensions as an assessment of a non-disabled child. However, the needs of disabled children may be very complex in one dimension and it is important for social workers to ensure that all areas of a disabled child's needs are given attention during a core assessment.

5.186 The structure of each core assessment record is the same. Each record has two parts:

- information gathering; and

- analysis and planning.

5.187 There are five different core assessment records for use with children of different ages:

- 0–2 years;

- 3–4 years;

- 5–9 years;

- 10–14 years; and

- 15 years and over.

5.188 Social workers should use the record which relates to the child or young person's chronological age. However, this may result in some sections of the core assessment record being inappropriate to the needs of a disabled child, and it is important that social workers complete the records with a full consideration of the child's abilities and achievements.

Information gathering

5.189 The information gathering part of the core assessment record should assist social workers and their supervisors in quickly identifying the key factors in an assessment. However, it is not sufficient simply to tick the boxes. It is important that further information is included to provide the context for the information which is recorded. There is only limited space within the core assessment record to record this information, but the *Framework Practice Guidance* states that this is not to encourage practitioners to be brief, but to be relevant. For example, *Mrs Smith's depression means that at times she has no energy to play games with Daniel. However, Mr Smith regularly plays with him and reads to him each evening.*

- *Sources of information* – this section is used to record the sources of information and methods used to gather information during the core assessment. It should include a list of the agencies involved, all meetings with family members and details of any questionnaires and scales used. The *Framework Practice Guidance* recommends that this page should be completed as the assessment progresses.

- *Details concerning the core assessment* – this records the background details to the core assessment. This will include the reason for the assessment and details of any specific matters (including disability) which affect the child. This section should be completed before the core assessment begins and should draw on the information already known about the child and family from the initial assessment or the local authority's existing records.

- *Child's developmental needs* – this section records information about the child's developmental needs. These needs reflect the seven areas defined in the child's developmental needs domain of the *Framework* and are categorised as:

  - health;
  - education;
  - emotional and behavioural development;
  - identity;
  - family and social relationships;
  - social presentation (combined with identity for children under five); and
  - self-care skills (combined with emotional and behavioural development for children under five).

- *Parenting capacity* – this section records information about the parents' capacities to respond to their child's identified needs appropriately. These capacities reflect the six areas defined in the parenting capacity domain of the *Framework* and are categorised as:

  - basic care;
  - ensuring safety;
  - emotional warmth;
  - stimulation;
  - guidance and boundaries; and
  - stability.

  As already mentioned, it is vital that social workers record the strengths as well as the weaknesses of parents. It is also important that if any of the identified key areas are not considered relevant then they should not simply be left blank; reasons why they are not considered relevant should be recorded.

Within the summary section at the end of each of the key areas the social worker should consider the impact on the child's health and development of any needs which are not responded to appropriately.

- *Family and environmental factors* – this forms the final section in the information gathering part of the core assessment; the layout of this section is similar to the section dealing with the child's developmental needs.

Summary, analysis and plan

5.190 The second part of the core assessment record is concerned with analysis and planning. The analysis and planning part of an assessment is frequently the weakest (as identified by research, the findings of inquiry reports and Social Services Inspectorate (SSI) inspections). Social workers tend to pour most of their energies into the information gathering part of the assessment which results in an assessment that is mostly *descriptive* about what is happening. Less attention is often given to the *analysis* of the information gathered.

5.191 Analysis takes the assessment process beyond the surface considerations and seeks to identify:

- why particular strengths and difficulties are present;

- why the relationship between parents' shows particular strengths and difficulties and their implications for the child and other family members; and

- what types of services would best help the child and family members.

5.192 The core assessment record provides room for social workers to carry out analysis in detail:

- *Summary* – the second part of the core assessment record begins with a summary of the needs, strengths and difficulties identified in each of the three domains. Parents and young people should be asked for their views and asked, if possible, to record these in writing for inclusion in the core assessment.

- *Analysis* – the core assessment record then requires social workers to analyse the significance and consequences of the needs, strengths and difficulties identified in the assessment. This is a *key stage in the assessment process*. Social workers should consider the interrelationship between each of the three domains. For example, *a child's difficult and demanding behaviour may be a major contributory factor to a parent's depression, which may in turn lead to the home environment being neglected.* Social workers should list the key protective and stress factors in each domain and indicate how they relate to those identified in the other domains. Once again, it is vital that strengths as well as weaknesses are identified. Strengths should be used to inform the plan. Social workers should also seek to evaluate the impact on the child and family of any services already provided.

- *Objectives and plans* – the final part of the core assessment record provides for a description of the objectives and the actions which are to be achieved to ensure that all the child's identified needs are responded to appropriately. The *objectives* of the plan should be:

  - specific;
  - measurable; and
  - have clear timescales.

  The *actions* defined in the plan should include those to be taken by the child and family members, the local authority and all other relevant agencies.

5.193 One consequence of completing a core assessment record may be that the need for a more specialist assessment is then identified. It is important that any further assessment is fully discussed with the child or young person and their parents or carers.

5.194 It is vital that family members (and the child, if appropriate) are fully involved in agreeing the objectives and actions to be taken and that they are given sufficient opportunity to be able to comment on the plan. This will enable the plan to serve as a written agreement between the local authority and the family.

SECTION 5 – TIME FOR CHANGE

5.195 The Munro Review Final Report (May 2011) carried out a major critical analysis and review of current child protection practice in the UK. A significant part of the Review's remit was to remove unnecessary bureaucracy and guidance. The Review considered the current focus on compliance with guidance and performance management criteria, rather than on using these as a framework to guide the provision of effective help to children. The Review concluded that the statutory guidance needs to be revised and the inspection process modified so that they enable and encourage professionals to keep a clearer focus on children's needs and to exercise their judgment on how to provide services to children and families.

5.196 The Review considered the positive benefits of professional practice procedures:

- Enables professionals to work together effectively by allowing them to predict what each other will do, and setting out basic rules about roles and tasks.

- Provides an effective way of formulating best practice in carrying out specific tasks.

- Allows good practice wisdom to be disseminated effectively throughout an organisation.

- Provides effective training tools for novice workers, and valuable as a checklist for more experienced workers.

5.197 However, the Review also highlighted a number of weaknesses about procedures in general:

- They can lead to people *just* following procedures and not seeking to understand them or trying to become more effective in their complex tasks.

- Procedures are inevitably always incomplete and require skill and the use of judgment to implement them.

- Procedures may be followed in a way that is technically correct but is so inexpert that the desired result is not achieved.

- The inclusion of advice about good practice within the guidance may have contributed to the de-professionalisation of child protection, as those working in the field feel increasingly obliged to do things 'by the book' rather than use their professional judgment about children's needs.

5.198 The Munro Review endorses and praises the ten underpinning principles in the Framework guidance as 'excellent'. However, the Review expresses concern about the fact that the principles have become linked with specific theories, recording forms and processes which have subsequently become the subject of performance targets. Evidence to the Review clearly indicated that professionals too often feel they must complete a form before a child is eligible to receive support, instead of responding to obvious or urgent needs while carrying out the assessment process. The Review found that the division between initial and core assessments seems to have resulted in a distinct division of the assessment process in many local authorities, with different social workers often undertaking each assessment and the second one frequently starting the whole process again rather than building on a common assessment submitted by another agency or the initial assessment.

5.199 The Review also found that the importance of making a proportionate assessment seems to be neglected:[43]

> 'For some children, a brief assessment is all that is required prior to offering services and for others the assessment needs to be more in-depth, broader in scope, and take longer in order to get a sufficiently accurate understanding of the child's needs and circumstances to inform effective planning. A decision about the depth and breadth of an assessment should be made at a local level rather than having to follow a centrally prescribed formula. The rationale for undertaking these assessments – getting help to children and families quickly and proportionately – at present seems to be overshadowed by process demands.'

Recommendations for the future

5.200 The Review recommends that the approach taken in the *Framework for Assessment* guidance needs to be revised and reissued to present the ten underpinning principles only, but give professionals themselves the responsibility for deciding how they can be implemented in practice.

5.201 The Review also recommends that *Working Together* should be revised to distinguish more clearly between rules and professional guidance.

5.202 The Review makes a series of specific recommendations about the nature of the revisions to the statutory guidance in both the *Framework for Assessment* and *Working Together* (and their associated policies). These include recommendations to:

- distinguish the rules that are essential for effective working together from guidance that informs professional judgment;

- set out the key principles underpinning the guidance;

- remove the distinction between initial and core assessments and the associated timescales in respect of these assessments, replacing them with the decisions that are required to be made by qualified social workers when developing an understanding of children's needs and making and implementing a plan to safeguard and promote their welfare;

- give local areas the responsibility to draw on research and theoretical models to inform local practice; and

- remove constraints to local innovation and professional judgment that are created by prescribing or endorsing particular approaches (e g nationally designed assessment forms, national performance indicators associated with assessment, or nationally prescribed approaches to IT systems).

---

[43]   The Munro Review Final report (May 2011) at para 3.9.

SECTION 6 – PLANNING AND INTERVENTION FOLLOWING ASSESSMENT

Planning

5.203 Once information is gathered and analysed at the conclusion of the assessment process, social workers will need to make plans to determine what action is to be taken with an individual and/or family. A social work plan should present a detailed picture of a situation, those involved, what action might be taken and by whom in order to meet the identified needs.

5.204 The SMART model applies to core elements involved in planning:

- **S**pecific aims, objectives and tasks to be undertaken.

- **M**easurable outcomes and goals that are agreed upon.

- **A**chievable goals and outcomes so that those involved are likely to succeed.

- **R**ealistic and **R**elevant outcomes that maintain a focus on the core issues.

- **T**imely and **T**ime-limited in addressing current issues and planning for review.

5.205 There are some general principles about plans for working with children and families, whatever the circumstances in which they have been drawn up. Wherever possible, plans should be drawn up in agreement with the child and key family members, and their commitment to the plan should have been secured. However, the professionals responsible for the plan need to ensure that objectives are reasonable and timescales are not too short or unachievable, and that plans should not be dependent on resources which are known to be scarce or unavailable. The plan must also maintain a focus on the child, even though help may be provided to a number of family members as part of the plan.

5.206 There are five types of plan that social workers may complete following social work assessments:

- *Children in Need Plan* – negotiated with the child, family and contributing agencies;

- *Child Protection Plan* – completed following a child protection conference and the CA 1989, s 47 assessment;

- *Care Plan* – prepared during care proceedings for approval by the court before a child can be made subject of a care or supervision order;

- *Care Plan for Looked After Children* – completed for children who are either subject of care orders or who are accommodated (CA 1989, s 20);

- *Pathway Plan* – completed for a young person in care in preparation for leaving care.

5.207 It is essential that plans are constructed on the basis of findings from the assessment, and that the plans are reviewed and refined over time to ensure that the agreed case objectives are achieved. Plans should include specific outcomes (expressed in terms of the child's health and development) which can be measured. These outcomes provide objective evidence against which to evaluate whether the child and family have been provided with appropriate services.

5.208 The child or young person (rather than the family) must be the focus of every type of plan.

Characteristics of effective plans for children and families

5.209 The *Framework Practice Guidance* recommends that the following should be included as a matter of course within all plans for children:

- the objectives of the plan;

- what services will be provided and by whom;

- timing and nature of the contact between professionals and families;

- the purpose of services and professional contact;

- the commitments to be met by the family;

- the commitments to be met by professionals (including attending to matters of diversity and equal opportunities);

- details of which parts of the plan can or cannot be renegotiated;

- what needs to change and what goals need to be achieved;

- what is unacceptable care; and

- what sanctions will be used if the child is placed in danger.

5.210 All plans should include a statement noting the timing of its review and how this review will take place.

5.211   In completing plans, social workers need to be:

- honest about the reasons for the plan;

- open about who does what and what 'comebacks' there might be;

- simple in their use of language;

- explicit about their concerns; and

- clear in their written language.

Intervention

5.212   Decisions about how to intervene, including what services to offer, should be based on evidence about what is likely to work best to bring about good outcomes for the child. A number of aspects of intervention should be considered in the context of:

- the child protection plan;

- the evidence from assessment of the child's developmental needs;

- the parents' capacity to respond appropriately to the child's needs; and

- the wider family circumstances.

5.213   It is important that services are provided to give the child and family the best chance of achieving the required changes. If a child cannot be cared for safely by his or her caregiver(s) he or she will have to be placed elsewhere while work is being undertaken with the child and family. Irrespective of where the child is living, interventions should specifically address:

- the developmental needs of the child;

- the child's understanding of what has happened to him or her;

- the abusing caregiver/child relationship and parental capacity to respond to the child's needs;

- the relationship between the adult caregivers both as adults and parents;

- family relationships; and

- possible changes to the family's social and environmental circumstances.

5.214 Intervention may have a number of interrelated components:

- action to make a child safe;

- action to help promote a child's health and development (ie welfare);

- action to help a parent(s)/caregiver(s) in safeguarding a child and promoting his or her welfare;

- therapy for an abused child; and

- support or therapy for a perpetrator of abuse.

5.215 The development by the child of a secure attachment to the parent is critical to his or her healthy development. The quality and nature of the attachment will be a key issue to be considered in decision-making, especially if decisions are being made about moving a child from one setting to another, reuniting a child with his or her birth family, or considering a permanent placement away from the child's family. If the plan is to assess whether the child can be reunited with the caregiver(s) responsible for the maltreatment, very detailed work is required to help the caregiver(s) develop the necessary parenting skills.

5.216 A key issue in deciding on suitable interventions is whether the child's developmental needs can be responded to within his or her family context and *within timescales that are appropriate for the child.* These timescales may not be compatible with those for the caregiver(s) who is receiving therapeutic help. The process of decision-making and planning should be as open as possible, from an ethical as well as a practical point of view. Where the family situation is not improving or changing fast enough to respond to the child's needs, decisions are necessary about the long-term future of the child. In the longer term it may be in the best interests of the child to be placed in an alternative family context. Key to these considerations is what is in the child's best interests, informed by the child's wishes and feelings.

5.217 Children who have suffered significant harm may continue to experience the consequences of this abuse irrespective of where they are living: whether remaining with or being reunited with their families, or alternatively being placed in new families. This relates particularly to their behavioural and emotional development. Therapeutic work with the child should continue, therefore, irrespective of where the child is placed, in order to ensure the needs of the child are responded to appropriately.

Reviews

5.218 The commitment of all parties involved in the work is fundamental to plans and intervention following assessment. Plans should be signed by parents (or carers) and those who have lead responsibility for ensuring that the plans are to be carried forward (this should include the team manager as well as the social worker). There should also be a clear recorded statement on the plan about when and how it will be reviewed.

5.219   Reviewing the child's progress and the effectiveness of services and other interventions is a continuous part of the process of work with children and families. The timescales and procedures for reviewing plans for children in need (which are also part of other guidance, regulations and legislation) are already prescribed.

5.220   For children in need (CIN) plans, where work is being undertaken to support children and families in the community, it is good practice to review the plan with family members at least every 6 months, and to record such review formally in writing and at a meeting. Key professionals should also be involved in the review process and in constructing the revised plan.

Chapter 6

CHILD PROTECTION PLANNING

SECTION 1 – THE CHILD PROTECTION CONFERENCE

6.1   Child protection conferences (CPCs) have been in general use since the 1970s with the emergence of the child protection register. Their operation has been prescribed by a series of departmental circulars since 1974. Guidance about the procedure relating to CPCs is contained in *Working Together*.[1]

6.2   A CPC is a multi-agency meeting to discuss the case of a particular child that is convened at the request of either the local authority or any other agency involved, but chaired by a local authority officer.

6.3   The decision of the CPC is not binding upon the local authority, but is a recommendation to the local authority or to a particular agency for action.

The type of child protection conference

6.4   There are three types of CPCs:

- initial child protection conference;

- review child protection conference; and

- pre-birth child protection conference.

6.5   Although the local authority has the lead role in convening and arranging CPCs, the key point about CPCs is that they are *multi-agency* meetings. The context of multi-agency working in relation to children and families is described in Chapter 1, but it is worth highlighting the benefits of this approach specifically in the context of CPCs. Multi-agency working has the following benefits:

- It allows relevant information about the child and family to be shared with the local authority.

- It ensures that all relevant agencies involved with the child and family share the responsibility for safeguarding and promoting the welfare of the child.

---

[1]   Department for Children, Schools and Families (DCSF) (now DfE) *Working Together to Safeguard Children* (TSO, 4th edn, 2010).

- It prevents vital information about the child and family from being lost or allowed to 'slip through the net' when formulating an effective child protection plan for the child.

- It prevents the local authority from becoming too fixed, subjective or single-minded in its approach to working with the child and family.

- It enables all agencies working with the child and family to contribute to and participate in an effective child protection plan to protect the child.

6.6   The aim of a child protection conference is to:

- enable professionals most involved with the child and family to assess all relevant information in making decisions about whether the child is at continuing risk of significant harm;

- enable professionals to make an interagency plan about how to safeguard the child and promote welfare if the child is at continuing risk of significant harm; and

- involve the child's family in assessing and planning how to protect the child.

6.7   The local authority is responsible for arranging the CPC, but there will be an independent chair with special skill and experience in child protection social work.[2]

SECTION 2 – PARTNERSHIP AND CHILD PROTECTION CONFERENCES

6.8   Until the early 1990s it was highly unusual for parents (or children where appropriate) to be invited to attend CPCs. Social workers and other professionals attended CPCs in private to discuss their concerns about the child and to formulate a child protection plan without the involvement of the family. The plan would then be explained to the family by the social worker after the meeting.

6.9   The emphasis on working in partnership embodied in the Children Act 1989 and the accompanying guidance, combined with research findings and the campaigning by organisations such as the Family Rights Group and the NSPCC, has now ended the universal practice of parents being excluded from CPCs as a matter of course: 'exclusion should be kept to a minimum and needs to be especially justified'.[3]

---

[2]   Historically an NSPCC worker, but now most local authorities will provide or utilise a specialist independent reviewing and chairing service.
[3]   *Working Together*, para 6.15.

6.10 Local Safeguarding Children Board (LSCB) procedures should set out criteria for excluding a parent or caregiver, including the evidence required. A strong risk of violence or intimidation by a family member at or subsequent to the conference, towards a child or anybody else, might be one reason for exclusion. The possibility that a parent or caregiver may be prosecuted for an offence against a child is not in itself a reason for exclusion although in these circumstances the chair should take advice from the police about any implications arising from an alleged perpetrator's attendance. If criminal proceedings have been instigated, the view of the Crown Prosecution Service should be taken into account. The decision to exclude a parent or caregiver from the child protection conference rests with the chair of the conference, acting within LSCB procedures. If the parents are excluded, or are unable or unwilling to attend a child protection conference, they should be enabled to communicate their views to the conference by another means.

6.11 Including parents and other relevant family members (and children if appropriate) in the discussions, planning and decision-making at CPCs requires particular sensitivity, thought and preparation by the allocated social worker, the chair of the conference, and by the other professionals attending. With strong leadership from the chair and the commitment of all professionals to be open and honest, parents can participate in CPCs and assist in effective decision-making.[4] Inclusion of parents enables both professionals and families:

- to be clear about the allegation of abuse;

- to be directly informed about the findings of the professionals; and

- to join in decision-making about further work (including the nature and extent of future partnership).

6.12 Preparation for attendance at CPCs is essential and requires work by the social worker and the chair, as well as work to prepare the family. It may not be possible for all family participants to remain in the meeting throughout the discussions. There may be conflicts of interest between participants and these may necessitate partial withdrawal of some people at some stages. For example, some young people will decline to be in the room with an alleged abuser or will be unable to speak in front of a parent or relative, but might necessarily want the opportunity to speak with professionals without the presence of those adults. Many adults and children will find it helpful to have a supporter at the CPC, but the nature and extent of the supporter's role should always be examined and clarified. It will certainly help adults (and children) to contribute more effectively to CPCs if they are assisted beforehand to think through their own interpretations of the events which are causing concern.

---

[4] See Department of Health *The Challenge of Partnership in Child Protection: A Practice Guide* (HMSO, 1995).

6.13   Before a conference is held, the purpose of a conference, who will attend, and the way in which it will operate, should always be explained to a child of sufficient age and understanding, and to the parents and involved family members. Where the child or family members do not speak English well enough to understand the discussions and express their views, an interpreter should be used. The parents (including absent parents) should normally be invited to attend the conference and helped to participate fully. Social workers should give parents information about local advice and advocacy agencies, and explain that they may bring an advocate, friend or supporter. The child, subject to consideration about age and understanding, should be invited to attend, and to bring an advocate, friend or supporter if he or she wishes. Where the child's attendance is neither desired by him or her nor appropriate, the social worker (or other professional) who is working most closely with the child should ascertain what his or her wishes and feelings are, and make these known to the conference.

Exclusion of family members from the CPC

6.14   The involvement of family members at a CPC should be planned carefully. It may not always be possible to involve all family members at all times in the conference, for example, if one parent is the alleged abuser or if there is a high level of conflict between family members. Adults and any children who wish to make representations to the conference may not wish to speak in front of one another. Exceptionally, it may be necessary to exclude one or more family members from a conference, in whole or in part. The conference is primarily about the child, and while the presence of the family is normally welcome, those professionals attending must be able to share information in a safe and non-threatening environment. Professionals may themselves have concerns about violence or intimidation, which should be communicated in advance to the conference chair. The following table highlights the preparation work that should be completed before a CPC.

Preparation by the chair	*Preparation by social workers*	*Preparation with families*
Ensure that family is aware of the CPC and that appropriate family members were invited.	Ensure that no other work commitments prevent social worker attending CPC throughout.	Encourage families to make constructive contributions by helping them prepare information to present to the CPC.

Preparation by the chair	Preparation by social workers	Preparation with families
Ensure that family has received all relevant information about CPCs in understandable form.	Set aside time for work with family before and after CPC.	Spend time with family discussing their worries and concerns, and explaining the CPC process.
Ensure that sufficient time is set aside for CPC to enable family and invited professionals to contribute fully.	Ensure that family is given a copy of social work report before CPC and has opportunity to comment on content or recommendations of report.	Make practical arrangements for attendance which are suitable and convenient.
Ensure that CPC is arranged at a time convenient (as far as possible) to enable family members to attend.	Make contact with chair to discuss any practical difficulties relating to timing or venue of CPC.	Discuss which family members will attend the CPC.
Ensure that all relevant professionals with knowledge of family are invited to attend.	Prepare for any potential difficulties in advance by discussions with chair, family or other professionals.	Explain the circumstances in which some or all family members may be excluded from the CPC.
Ensure that any special requirements of family are met (such as provision of interpreters or access for people with disabilities).		Discuss whether the family will want to bring a suitable supporter to the CPC and discuss the extent of their role.

Preparation by the chair	Preparation by social workers	Preparation with families
Ensure that written reports from invited professionals are available at CPC and have been shared wherever possible with family in advance by person preparing each report.		Advise the family to seek legal advice or representation if they have not already done so.
Ensure that agenda is available to all those attending the CPC.		Chair meets with family members to discuss process of meeting in advance and to enable them to raise issues of concern in private.

6.15

Analysis of the local authority's partnership with the family arising from the CPC

- Did the social worker carry out work in advance to prepare the family to attend the CPC?

- Did the social worker spend time with the family explaining the purpose of the CPC and the concerns of the local authority and other professionals?

- Was the CPC arranged at a suitable time and venue to enable the family to attend?

- Were the family advised about the benefits of bringing a supporter to the CPC?

- Did the social worker advise the family about seeking legal advice prior to the CPC?

- Was the family given a copy of the social worker's report in sufficient time before the CPC?

- Did the social worker discuss the content of the report and the recommendations with the family in sufficient time before the CPC?

- Were written reports from invited professionals shared if possible with the family in advance by the authors of each report?

- Was the family given all relevant information about CPCs in an understandable form in sufficient time before the CPC?

- Were any special requirements of the family met (for example, the provision of interpreters or access for people with disabilities)?

- Was the family excluded from any part of the CPC and, if so, was it for a good and clearly documented reason?

The social work report to the CPC

6.16 The local authority should provide a written report summarising and analysing the information from the assessment. The local authority will also usually request written reports from other professionals.

6.17 The written report should summarise and analyse the information obtained by the local authority during the initial assessment. Reports should include as much information as possible to enable the CPC to devise an effective child protection plan for the child. Information in the social worker's report should include:

- a chronology of significant events;

- information about the child's health and development in all domains;[5]

- information about the capacity of the parents and other family members to protect the child from harm and to promote the child's development;

- the wishes and feelings of the child, parents and other family members about the protection plan;

- analysis of the implications of the information obtained for the child's future safety;

- a clear recommendation about future planning for the child.

6.18 It is good practice for parents to be provided with a copy of the social worker's report in advance and for them to have been given an opportunity to discuss the contents and recommendations of the report with the social worker.

---

[5]   See Chapter 5.

6.19

Analysis of the social work report to the CPC

- Does the report contain a clear chronology of events leading to the current referral?

- Does the report indicate that the social worker has conducted a thorough initial or core assessment in respect of the child (including direct interviews with the child where appropriate)?

- Does the report contain detailed information about the child's health and development?

- Does the report contain information and analysis about the capacity of *all* relevant family members (not just the parents) to protect the child?

- Does the report indicate that the social worker discussed the recommendations with the family (and child if appropriate) before submitting it to the CPC?

- Does the report refer to the wishes and feelings of the child, parents and other family members?

- Does the report analyse the information gained during the initial or core assessment in terms of the future safety of the child and the need for any child protection plan?

- Does the report make a clear proposal about the nature of a child protection plan to protect the child?

Attendance at the CPC

6.20 A policy of refusing to allow a solicitor for the parents to attend a CPC is unlawful. A policy of refusing to provide parents with the minutes of a CPC is also unlawful.[6]

6.21 It is good practice to invite solicitors or representatives from the firm representing parents and the child to attend the CPC.[7]

6.22 Those attending conferences should be there because they have a significant contribution to make, arising from professional expertise, knowledge of the child or family or both. The local authority should consider whether to seek advice from, or have present, a medical professional who can present the medical information in a manner that can be understood by conference attendees and enable such information to be evaluated from a sound

---

[6]   *R v Cornwall County Council, ex parte LH* [2000] 1 FLR 236.
[7]   Guidance document produced by the Law Society's Family Law Committee (in consultation with the Professional Ethics Division) (1997).

evidence base. There should be sufficient information and expertise available –
through personal representation and written reports – to enable the conference
to make an informed decision about what action is necessary to safeguard and
promote the welfare of the child, and to make realistic and workable proposals
for taking that action forward. At the same time, a conference that is larger
than it needs to be can inhibit discussion and intimidate the child and family
members. Those who have a relevant contribution to make may include:

- the child, or the child's representative;

- family members (including the wider family);

- local authority staff who have led and been involved in an assessment of
  the child and family;

- foster carers (current or former);

- residential care staff;

- professionals involved with the child (for example, health visitors, midwife,
  school nurse, children's guardian, paediatrician, school or nursery staff,
  GP);

- professionals involved with the parents or other family members (for
  example, family support services, adult mental health services, probation,
  GP);

- professionals with expertise in the particular type of harm suffered by the
  child or in the child's particular condition, for example, a disability or
  long-term illness;

- professionals involved in investigations (for example, the police);

- local authority legal services (childcare);

- NSPCC or other involved voluntary organisations;

- a representative of the armed services, in cases where there is a Service
  connection.

Quorum

6.23 The relevant LSCB protocol should specify a required quorum for
attendance, and list those who should be invited to attend, provided that they
have a relevant contribution to make. As a minimum, at every CPC there
should be attendance by the local authority and at least two other professional
groups or agencies that have had direct contact with the child who is the subject
of the CPC. In addition, attendees may also include those whose contribution

relates to their professional expertise or responsibility for relevant services. In exceptional cases, where a child has not had relevant contact with three agencies (that is, the local authority and two others), this minimum quorum may be breached.

6.24 Professionals and agencies who are invited but are unable to attend should submit a written report.

SECTION 3 – THE INITIAL CHILD PROTECTION CONFERENCE

Timing

6.25 However, the timing of an initial child protection conference will depend on the urgency of the case and on the time needed to obtain relevant information about the child and family. If the CPC is to reach well-informed decisions based on evidence, it should take place following adequate preparation and assessment. Cases where children are at risk of significant harm should not be allowed to drift.

6.26 Initial child protection conferences should take place within 15 working days of the strategy discussion.

Purpose

6.27 The purpose of the initial child protection conference is to formulate a multi-agency outline child protection plan in as much detail as possible. The CPC should decide whether the child's name needs to be placed on the child protection register and under which category.

6.28 The tasks of the initial child protection conference will be to:

- appoint a key worker (usually the social worker);

- identify members of the core group of professionals and family members who will develop and implement the child protection plan;

- establish how parents, children and the family should be involved in the planning process;

- establish timescales for meetings of the core group, production of the child protection plan and for child protection review meetings;

- identify in outline what further core and specialist assessments are required;

- outline the child protection plan, including specific details of what needs to change;

- consider the need for a contingency plan; and

- clarify the purpose of the initial child protection conference, the core group and the review child protection conference.

6.29 The outline child protection plan should:

- identify the risks of significant harm to the child and ways in which the child can be protected through an interagency plan based on assessment findings;

- establish short-term and longer-term aims and objectives that are clearly linked to reducing the risk of harm to the child and promoting the child's welfare;

- be clear about who will have responsibility for what actions (including actions by family members) within what specified timescales; and

- outline ways of monitoring and evaluating progress against the plan.

6.30 The initial child protection conference should agree a date for the first review child protection conference, and under what circumstances it might be necessary to convene the review child protection conference before that date.

Outcome

6.31 The CPC should consider the following question when determining whether the child should be the subject of a child protection plan:

Is the child at continuing risk of significant harm?

6.32 The test in considering this question is two-fold:

- Can the child be shown to have suffered ill-treatment or impairment of health or development as a result of physical, emotional, or sexual abuse or neglect, and is it the judgment of the professionals that further ill treatment or impairment are likely? or

- Is it the judgment of the professionals (substantiated by the findings of enquiries in this individual case or by research evidence), that the child is likely to suffer ill-treatment or the impairment of health or development as a result of physical, emotional, or sexual abuse or neglect?

6.33 If the CPC decides that the child is at continuing risk of significant harm, it will automatically be the case that safeguarding the child requires interagency help. In these circumstances intervention with the family will need to be delivered through a formal child protection plan.

6.34 Conference participants should base their judgments on:

• all the available evidence obtained through existing records;

• the initial assessment; and

• the in-depth core assessment undertaken following the initiation of s 47 enquiries.

6.35 The method of reaching a decision within the CPC on whether the child should be the subject of a child protection plan should be set out in the relevant LSCB protocol. The decision-making process should be based on the views of all agencies represented at the conference, and also take into account any written contributions that have been made.

6.36 The decision of the conference and, where appropriate, details of the category of abuse or neglect, the name of the key worker, the lead professional and the core group membership should be recorded in a manner that is consistent with the initial child protection conference report and circulated to all those invited to the conference within one working day.

Record

6.37 All child protection conferences, both initial and review should have a dedicated person to take notes and produce a record of the meeting. The record of the CPC is a crucial working document for all relevant professionals and the family. It should include:

• the essential facts of the case;

• a summary of discussion at the conference, which accurately reflects contributions made;

• all decisions reached, with information outlining the reasons for decisions; and

• a translation of decisions into an outline or revised child protection plan enabling everyone to be clear about their tasks.

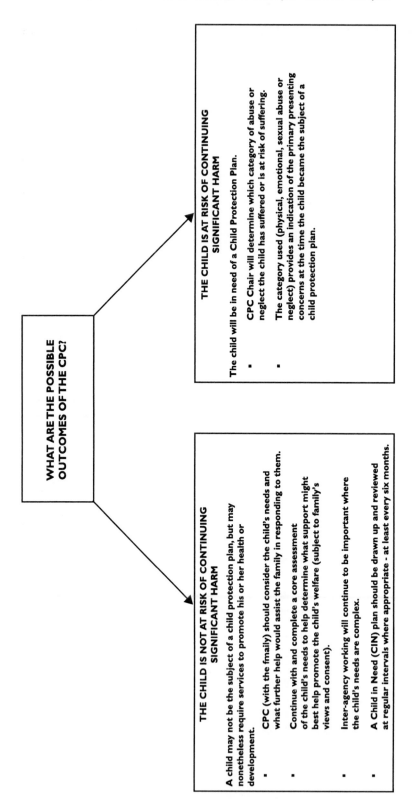

WHAT ARE THE POSSIBLE OUTCOMES OF THE CPC?

THE CHILD IS AT RISK OF CONTINUING SIGNIFICANT HARM

The child will be in need of a Child Protection Plan.

- CPC Chair will determine which category of abuse or neglect the child has suffered or is at risk of suffering.

- The category used (physical, emotional, sexual abuse or neglect) provides an indication of the primary presenting concerns at the time the child became the subject of a child protection plan.

THE CHILD IS NOT AT RISK OF CONTINUING SIGNIFICANT HARM

A child may not be the subject of a child protection plan, but may nonetheless require services to promote his or her health or development.

- CPC (with the fmaily) should consider the child's needs and what further help would assist the family in responding to them.

- Continue with and complete a core assessment of the child's needs to help determine what support might best help promote the child's welfare (subject to family's views and consent).

- Inter-agency working will continue to be important where the child's needs are complex.

- A Child in Need (CIN) plan should be drawn up and reviewed at regular intervals where appropriate - at least every six months.

6.38 In *Re X (Emergency Protection Orders)*,[8] McFarlane J reiterated the guidance in *Working Together* and set out some basic requirements in respect of the recording of confidential information shared during CPCs:

- if the circumstances are sufficient to justify the exclusion of the parents from part of a CPC (or the parents are otherwise absent), a full minute should nevertheless be taken of everything that is said during the CPC;

- if it is considered necessary to treat part of what is minuted as confidential from the parents, that part of the minutes should be disclosed for approval to the professionals who attended the CPC, but that part of the approved minutes should be maintained separately from the body of the minutes, which are sent to the parents;

- the non-confidential section of the minutes should expressly record at the appropriate stage that confidential information was disclosed or discussed;

- the need for continued confidentiality with respect to confidential sections of the minutes should be kept under review by the CPC chair, with confidentiality only being maintained if it continues to be necessary.

6.39 A copy of the CPC record should be sent as soon as possible after the conference to all those who attended or were invited to attend, including family members, except for any part of the conference from which they were excluded. This is in addition to sharing the main decisions within one working day of the conference.

6.40 The CPC record is confidential and should not be passed by professionals to third parties without the consent of either the CPC chair or the key worker. However, in cases of criminal proceedings, the police may reveal the existence of the notes to the Crown Prosecution Service (CPS) in accordance with the Criminal Procedure and Investigation Act 1996. The record of the decisions of the CPC should be retained by the recipient agencies and professionals in accordance with their record retention policies.

---

[8]   [2006] 2 FLR 701 at [29].

6.41

Analysis of the CPC record

- Was the CPC quorate and attended by appropriate professionals with knowledge or professional experience of the child and family?

- Were all relevant family members invited and encouraged to attend the CPC? Were they accompanied by an appropriate supporter?

- Were the family members excluded from any part of the CPC? If so, were the reasons for exclusion reasonable and clearly explained?

- Was the summary of background and concerns relating to the child and family accurate and substantiated by clear evidence?

- Are the recorded contributions of the invited professionals consistent with their written reports and the other evidence in the case?

- Were the recorded contributions of the family consistent with other evidence in the case?

- Were the contributions of the invited professionals unanimous or were they finely divided?

- Were clear decisions reached supported by reasons?

- Were the decisions translated into a clear and specific Child Protection Plan?

Pre-birth child protection conferences

6.42   Where the s 47 enquiry raises concern that an unborn child may be at future risk of significant harm, the local authority may need to convene an initial child protection conference prior to the child's birth. Such a conference should have the same status, and proceed in the same way, as other initial child protection conferences, including decisions about registration.

SECTION 4 – ACTIONS AFTER THE CHILD PROTECTION CONFERENCE

6.43   After the initial child protection conference the following actions should be implemented:

- a key worker will be appointed (this will normally be the social worker acting as the lead professional);

- members of a core group will be appointed and meetings of the core group arranged and coordinated by the key worker or the lead professional; and

- a child protection plan will be formulated and implemented.

The key worker (or lead professional)

6.44 When a CPC decides that a child should be the subject of a child protection plan, the local authority should carry future childcare responsibility for the case and designate a qualified and experienced social worker to be the key worker/lead professional.

6.45 It is important that the role of the key worker is fully explained at the initial child protection conference and at subsequent core group meetings.

6.46

The responsibilities of the key worker

- To ensure that the outline child protection plan is developed into a more detailed interagency plan

- To complete the core assessment of the child, securing contributions from core group members and others as necessary

- To act as the lead professional for the interagency work with the child and family

- To coordinate the contribution of family members and other agencies to planning the actions which need to be taken

- To put the child protection plan into effect

- To review progress against the planned outcomes set out in the child protection plan

- To regularly ascertain the child's wishes and feelings

- To keep the child and family up to date with the child protection plan and any developments or changes

The core group

6.47 The core group is responsible for developing the child protection plan as a detailed working tool, and implementing it within the outline plan agreed at the initial child protection conference. Although the key worker has the lead role, all members of the core group are jointly responsible for the formulation and implementation of the child protection plan, refining the plan as needed, and monitoring progress against the planned outcomes set out in the plan.

6.48

Who should be the members of the core group?

- The key worker (who leads the core group)

- The child (if appropriate)

- Family members

- Foster carers (if appropriate)

- Professionals who will have direct contact with the family, such as:

  - health visitor
  - nursery staff
  - social work assistant
  - school nurse
  - teacher

6.49 The core group is an important forum for working with parents, wider family members, and children of sufficient age and understanding.

6.50 It can often be difficult for parents to agree to a Child Protection Plan within the confines of a formal CPC. Their agreement may be gained later when details of the plan are worked out in the core group. Sometimes there may be conflicts of interest between family members who have a relevant interest in the work of the core group. The child's best interests should always take precedence over the interests of other family members.

6.51

Core group meetings

- First meeting within 10 working days of the initial child protection conference to:

  - flesh out the child protection plan
  - decide what steps need to be taken by whom to complete the core assessment on time

- Subsequent meetings to be held sufficiently regularly to:

  - facilitate interagency working with the child and family
  - monitor actions and outcomes against the child protection plan
  - make any necessary alterations as circumstances change

6.52 There should be a written note recording the decisions taken and actions agreed at core group meetings. The child protection plan should be updated as necessary.

6.53

Analysis of the core group activity

•   Did the key worker arrange the first meeting of the core group within 10 working days of the initial child protection conference?

•   Were all relevant family members included as members of the core group?

•   Were all relevant professionals with ongoing involvement with the child and family included as members of the core group?

•   Was the child protection plan refined and expanded at the first core group meeting?

•   Was it clear what steps needed to be taken by whom to complete the core assessment on time?

•   Is there clear evidence of inter-agency working with the child and family?

•   Did the key worker arrange subsequent core group meetings regularly?

•   Did all members of the core group attend subsequent core group meetings?

•   Did the core group monitor actions and outcomes against the child protection plan at subsequent core group meetings?

•   Did the core group make any necessary alterations or amendments to the child protection plan as the child and family's circumstances changed?

•   Was a clear record made of all core group meetings?

SECTION 5 – THE REVIEW CHILD PROTECTION CONFERENCE

Timing

6.54 The first review child protection conference should take place within 3 months of the initial child protection conference and further reviews should be held at intervals of no more than 6 months for as long as the child remains the subject of a child protection plan. This is to ensure that momentum is maintained in the process of safeguarding the registered child.

6.55 The core group should provide reports for the review child protection conferences.

Purpose

6.56 The purpose of the review child protection conference is to:

- review the safety, health and development of the child against intended outcomes set out in the child protection plan;

- ensure that the child continues adequately to be safeguarded; and

- consider whether the child protection plan should continue in place or should be changed.

6.57 Every review child protection conference should consider explicitly whether the child continues to be at risk of significant harm, and therefore whether the child's welfare should continue to be safeguarded through the provision and implementation of a child protection plan. If not, then the child will no longer need to remain the subject of a child protection plan.

SECTION 6 – CHILD PROTECTION PLANS

The transition from the Child Protection Register

6.58 The 3rd edition of *Working Together* (2006) required that the maintenance of a separate Child Protection Register by local authorities was to be phased out by 1 April 2008. Following these changes all local authorities have now moved from the Child Protection Register to the Integrated Children's System (ICS) and, more specifically, through the existence of a child protection plan. Local authorities have been required to ensure that their local ICS could use data from the ICS child protection plans since 1 April 2008.

6.59 Children whose names were previously on the Child Protection Register are now the subjects of child protection plans. When a child is no longer at risk of harm his or her child protection plan will come to an end. It may be replaced with a child in need (CIN) plan or no further action by the local authority.

The child protection plan

6.60 The initial child protection conference is responsible for agreeing an outline child protection plan. Professionals and parents or caregivers should develop the details of the plan in the core group.

6.61 The child protection plan should be based on the findings from the assessment and follow the dimensions relating to the child's developmental needs, parenting capacity and family and environmental factors, drawing on knowledge about effective interventions.

6.62   The aim of the child protection plan is:

- to ensure the child is safe and to prevent the child from suffering further harm;

- to promote the child's welfare, health and development; and

- to support the family and wider family members to safeguard and promote the welfare of their child (provided it is in the best interests of the child).

6.63   The child protection plan should set out what work needs to be done, why, when and by whom.

6.64   The child protection plan should contain:

- a description of the identified developmental needs of the child, and what therapeutic services are required;

- specific, achievable, child-focused outcomes intended to safeguard and promote the welfare of the child;

- realistic strategies and specific actions to achieve the planned outcomes;

- a contingency plan to be followed if circumstances change significantly and require prompt action;

- clearly defined roles and responsibilities of professionals and family members, including the nature and frequency of contact by professionals with children and family members;

- clearly defined points at which progress will be reviewed, and the means by which progress will be judged; and

- clearly defined roles and responsibilities of professionals who will have routine contact with the child and professionals who will provide specialist or targeted support to the child and family.

Partnership and the child protection plan

6.65   The child protection plan should take into consideration the wishes and feelings of the child, and the views of the parents, insofar as they are consistent with the child's welfare. The key worker should make every effort to ensure that the children and parents have a clear understanding of the planned outcomes, that they accept the child protection plan and are willing to work to it.

6.66   The child protection plan should be constructed with the family in their preferred language and they should receive a written copy in this language. If family members' preferences are not accepted about how best to safeguard and promote the welfare of the child, the reasons for this should be explained within the child protection plan. Families should be told about their right to complain and make representations, and how to do so.

6.67 The child protection plan should be explained to and agreed with the child in a manner appropriate to their age and understanding. An interpreter should be used if the child's level of English means that he or she is not able to participate fully in these discussions unless they are conducted in his or her own language. The child should be given a copy of the plan written at a level appropriate to his or her age and understanding, and in his or her preferred language.

6.68 Parents should be clear about the evidence of significant harm that resulted in the child becoming the subject of a child protection plan, about what needs to change, and what is expected of them as part of the plan for safeguarding and promoting the child's welfare. All parties should be clear about the respective roles and responsibilities of family members and different agencies in implementing the plan. The parents should receive a written copy of the plan so that they are clear about who is doing what, when and the planned outcomes for the child.

6.69

Analysis of the child protection plan

- Has the family been given a written copy of the child protection plan?

- Was the family present at the CPC when the outline child protection plan was formulated?

- Was the family present at the core group meetings when the child protection plan was expanded and refined?

- Did the key worker ensure that the child protection plan has been properly explained to the family?

- Are the developmental needs of the child identified? Are any therapeutic services required, and if so by whom?

- Are the outcomes intended to safeguard and promote the welfare of the child SMART and child-centred?

  - **S**pecific
  - **M**easurable
  - **A**chievable
  - **R**ealistic
  - (with) **T**imescales

- Are there defined and realistic strategies and specific actions to achieve the planned outcomes?

- Is there a clear contingency plan to be followed if circumstances change significantly and require prompt action? Is the family aware of the circumstances in which the contingency plan may need to be implemented?

- Are the roles and responsibilities of professionals clearly identified, including the nature and frequency of contact by professionals with children and family members?

- Are the roles and responsibilities of family members clearly identified? Is the family aware of the consequences of non-compliance with the child protection plan?

- Are there clearly defined points at which progress will be reviewed?

- Is the method of evaluation of progress clearly identified?

- Are the roles and responsibilities of professionals providing specialist or targeted support to the child and family clearly defined?

Chapter 7

LOOKED-AFTER CHILDREN

INTRODUCTION

7.1 It is the right of all children to grow up belonging to a family who will nurture them during childhood, enabling them to develop their full potential and to have a positive sense of their own identity. Children are best looked after within their birth families. Local authorities must make every reasonable effort to enable and support the child's own birth family to provide a permanent home for the child when it is safe and appropriate to do so.[1]

7.2 When birth parents are unable or unwilling to care for their children, every effort must then be made to enable those children to be brought up within their extended families. The definition of extended families includes 'friends, neighbours and community members if they are considered part of the child's family'.[2]

7.3 Social workers should therefore regard accommodation or care arrangements for children as arrangements of last resort (unless accommodation is provided as part of a package of family support, for example, respite care for disabled children). Priority should be given to placing children with their extended family members (also known as connected persons in the family and friends regulations), if birth parents are unable or unwilling to care for their children.

7.4 Local authorities will not normally consider looking after a child in foster care unless:

- an initial and/or core assessment has been completed and concluded that neither the parents or anyone within the family is able or willing to care for the child;

- the merits of entry to the care system has been fully explored and evaluated and alternatives have been exhausted;

- a legal planning meeting has been convened in cases where parents do not give consent for the child to be accommodated;

---

[1]   Children Act 1989, Pt III generally (in particular, s 17).
[2]   Department for Children, Schools and Families (DCSF) (now DfE) *Working Together to Safeguard Children – A Guide to Inter-agency Working to Safeguard and Promote the Welfare of Children* ('*Working Together*') (TSO, 4th edn, 2010).

- a family group conference has at least been discussed if not convened with the family – see Chapter 2.

SECTION 1 – WHAT DOES IT MEAN TO BE LOOKED AFTER?

7.5   Children placed with foster carers should expect to be looked after like any other child, and their parents should be fully involved in decision-making about them.

7.6   Parental consent must be sought regarding all matters pertaining to children's welfare. This includes:

- *consent in key matters* – such as religious upbringing, medical treatment, trips abroad, and school choices;

- *consent in relation to any activity for which one would expect consent from any resident parent* – such as consent for hair cuts (for young children), school activities (swimming, trips etc), ear piercing and so on.

SECTION 2 – ROUTES INTO THE CARE SYSTEM

7.7   There are several routes into care for children:

- Voluntary care under the Children Act 1989 (CA 1989), s 20 at the request of the parent(s); for example:

    - babies relinquished for adoption;
    - parents in need of accommodation for their children while requiring hospital treatment;
    - young people (16+) requesting accommodation.

- Police Protection Order, Emergency Protection order, interim care order and full care order.

- Children and young people remanded into care by the criminal courts.

SECTION 3 – THE DUTIES OF THE LOCAL AUTHORITY WHEN MAKING PLACEMENTS

7.8   The local authority does not acquire parental responsibility for children who are accommodated (under the CA 1989, s 20 or s 17(6)).

7.9   Parents share parental responsibility with the local authority when their children are looked after under an interim care order or a care order.

7.10 In either case, parents are to be regarded as individuals with needs of their own. The local authority's development of a working partnership with parents is usually the most effective route to providing effective supplementary or substitute care for their children. Parents should therefore be enabled to retain their responsibilities and to remain as closely involved as is consistent with their child's and young person's welfare, even if that child or young person cannot live at home either temporarily or permanently.

7.11

The local authority's duties towards families and children when arranging placements

- To consult parents about placement options for their children.

- To make every effort to place children with foster carers who are local to their family home, and who reflect their ethnicity and religious needs. When this is not possible, the national minimum standards specify such a placement should be sought within a period of 6 weeks.[3] Placement with foster carers of similar ethnic origin, culture and religion is very often the best way to meet their needs as fully as possible. A foster carer who reflects the child or young person's heritage can be a resource for empowering a child with skills of coping with discrimination, including racism and is more likely to provide a child or young person with:

  - positive attachment figures
  - an environment for promoting the child's heritage and identity needs
  - the potential for positive role models.

- To give children and families choices in placement options.

Children and young people's wishes and feelings must be sought and taken seriously. Their age, level of understanding and maturity as well as any disabilities must be taken into account in deciding the most appropriate way to seek their views.

- To make every effort to place siblings together (as long as this accords with their best interests). It should be assumed that sibling relationships have the potential for long lasting and close relationships; separation should therefore be sought only when there is evidence to the contrary. The reasons for separation must be clearly recorded. In the event of separation of siblings, contact should be promoted to enable the relationships to be sustained for the duration of their childhood and beyond if at all possible.

- To keep children and young people informed about what is happening in their lives while they are looked after.

- To enable children and young people to participate in any decision-making processes about them (according to their level of understanding and maturity).

- To consult parents about contact arrangements for their children. ➡

---

[3]   The amendments in s 22C(8) of the CA 1989 introduced by the Children Act 2008 were intended to strengthen this provision and now place a duty on the local authority to place children in their home area, unless this is not consistent with the child's welfare.

> • To actively maintain and promote family links when children are in care by arranging and promoting visits and other forms of contact (to parents, siblings and/or grandparents as well as any other significant person in the child or young person's life).[4]

SECTION 4 – TYPES OF PLANNING

The care planning process

7.12 Part 2 of the Care Planning, Placement and Case Review (England) Regulations 2010 ('the 2010 Regulations')[5] sets out the arrangements which the responsible authority must make for looking after a child. The making of a care plan is central to these requirements. The care plan will contain information about how the child's current developmental needs will be met as well as the arrangements for the current and longer term care for the child. It ensures that there is a long term plan for the child's upbringing (referred to as 'the permanence plan') to which everyone is working, including the team around the child, the child and, where appropriate, the family.[6] There should be clarity in the care plan, particularly about the desired outcomes for the child and those expected from services and other actions identified. This clarity will support effective reviews of the child's case to monitor the progress made towards meeting the short and long term goals for the child and his or her family and the child's carers.

7.13 Care planning is a core element of the assessment, planning, intervention and review cycle which underpins social work with children and families. The primary focus of the legislation about children in need, which includes children looked after by the local authority, is how well they are progressing and whether their health or development will be impaired without the provision of services by the authority in accordance with s 17(10) of the CA 1989. The cycle of assessment, planning, intervention and review must therefore focus on the child's developmental progress, including his or her health, and the desired outcomes for the child, taking account of the wide range of influences which affect a child's development both positively and negatively.

7.14 The conceptual framework whereby the multiple influences on a child's development can be understood and assessed, services planned and delivered, and their impact reviewed is set out in guidance in the *Framework for the Assessment of Children in Need and Their Families* ('*Framework for Assessment*').[7] The Assessment Framework describes how a child's developmental needs, parental capacity and wider family and environmental factors are assessed, enabling the desired outcomes to be identified and planned for.

---

4   CA 1989, s 34.
5   SI 2010/959.
6   The 2010 Regulations, reg 5(a).
7   Department of Health *Framework for the Assessment of Children in Need and Their Families* (TSO, 2000).

7.15   The purpose of care planning and case review is about bringing together children who are looked after, their families, the child's carers and professionals, in order to plan for the care of the child and to review that plan on a regular basis. Assessing the needs of children and deciding how best to meet those needs is a fundamental part of social work with looked-after children. To do this effectively not only requires an understanding of the importance of planning, but also the conceptual and practice framework for planning. The purpose of such a framework is threefold:

- to ensure that children and their families and the child's carers are treated with openness and honesty and understand the decisions that are made;

- to provide clarity about the allocation of responsibilities and tasks, in the context of shared parenting between parents, the child's carers and the corporate parents and ensure that actions lead to improved outcomes; and

- to demonstrate accountability in the way in which the functions of local authorities under the 1989 Act are exercised.

7.16   The independent reviewing officer (IRO) appointed for the child is responsible for monitoring the performance of the responsible authority functions in relation to the child's case in accordance with s 25A(1) of the CA 1989. The intention is to enable the IRO to have an effective and independent oversight of the child's case to ensure that the care plan represents an effective response to the assessed needs of the child and that progress is being made towards achieving the identified outcomes.

7.17   The care plan often overlaps and is linked with other plans in place for the child.

The care plan, health plan and personal education plan

7.18   The child's care plan provides the overarching vehicle for bringing together information from the assessment across the seven dimensions of the child's developmental needs[8] and from any other assessments of the child and his or her family. The health and education dimensions of the care plan are populated by the health plan[9] and the personal education plan (PEP).[10]

The care plan and placement plan

7.19   When a suitable placement has been identified for the child the placement plan will set out in detail how the placement is intended to contribute to meeting the child's needs The placement plan is concerned both with what may need to happen in the placement to achieve the permanence

---

[8]   The 2010 Regulations, reg 5.
[9]   The 2010 Regulations, reg 7.
[10]   The 2010 Regulations, reg 5(b)(ii).

plan – for example promoting positive contact to support a return to home or helping the child move to an adoptive family – and with the way in which a child's needs will be met on a day-to-day basis and it is therefore integral to the care plan. It is essential that the placement plan is developed in partnership with the child (where appropriate), the child's carer and the parent as well as the social worker to ensure that the contribution required of all parties for the success of the placement is clearly recorded.

The care plan and pathway plan

7.20 At the point at which a young person becomes an eligible child and it is envisaged that he or she will be leaving care, the pathway plan must be prepared which must include the child's care plan. This is in order to capture the actions which will be necessary from the responsible authority, the young person's carer, young person, parent and other identified parties in order for the young person to make a successful transition from care to independence.

The care plan and child protection plan

7.21 In most cases where a child who is the subject of a child protection plan becomes looked after it will no longer be necessary to maintain the child protection plan. There are however a relatively few cases where safeguarding issues will remain and a looked-after child should also have a child protection plan. These cases are likely to be where a local authority obtains an interim care order in family proceedings but the child who is the subject of a child protection plan remains at home, pending the outcome of the final hearing, or where a young person's behaviour is likely to result in significant harm to themselves or others.

7.22 Where a looked-after child remains the subject of a child protection plan it is expected that there will be a single planning and reviewing process, led by the IRO, which meets the requirements of both the 2010 Regulations and guidance and *Working Together*.

7.23 The systems and processes for reviewing child protection plans and plans for looked-after children should be carefully evaluated by the local authority and consideration given to how best to ensure the child protection aspects of the care plan are reviewed as part of the overall reviewing process leading to the development of a single plan. Given that a review is a process and not a single meeting, both reviewing systems should be aligned in an unbureaucratic way to enable the full range of the child's needs to be considered in the looked-after child's care planning and reviewing processes.

7.24 It is recognised that there are different requirements for the independence of the IRO function compared to the chair of the child protection conference. In addition, it is important to note that the child protection conference is required to be a multi-agency forum, while children for the most part want as few external people as possible at a review meeting where they are present.

However, it will not be possible for the IRO to carry out his or her statutory function without considering the child's safety in the context of the care planning process. In this context consideration should be given to the IRO chairing the child protection conference where a looked-after child remains subject to a child protection plan. Where this is not possible it will be expected that the IRO will attend the child protection review conference.

7.25   This means that the timing of the review of the child protection aspects of the care plan should be the same as the review under Part 6 of the 2010 Regulations, to ensure that up-to-date information in relation to the child's welfare and safety is considered within the review meeting and informs the overall care planning process. The looked-after child's review, when reviewing the child protection aspects of the plan, should also consider whether the criteria continue to be met for the child to remain the subject of a child protection plan. Significant changes to the care plan can only be made at the looked-after child's review.

Reunification

7.26   A child's first review should confirm the assessment plan and clarify what further work will be needed in order for the child to return to the care of his or her parents. A permanence plan should be drawn up at the second review if the child is still in care, and even where the plan is for the child to return home. The plan should identify the support services to be provided, if any, and who should be responsible for implementation.

Parallel/twin-track planning

7.27   In some cases it will not be clear whether reunification is likely to be achievable within reasonable timescales for the child or it may not yet be known whether reunification is in the best interests of the child. In such cases the social worker should continue working with the child and their family towards reunification while *at the same time* taking steps towards making other permanent plans, in case the child cannot return home. This parallel or twin-track planning will normally include assessments and approval by the Adoption and Permanence Panel of other family members or friends and completion of the child's permanence report (CPR) identifying the child's needs in all domain. It will *not* include presenting the child to the adoption and permanency panel for a recommendation about permanent placement for a child until the conclusion of the assessment of birth parents. Birth parents must be informed that the two plans (reunification and alternative permanence) are being made to meet the child's needs and avoid unnecessary delay. The primacy of the reunification plan should be stressed. Retaining the co-operation, understanding and involvement of the birth parent(s) is essential to successful parallel planning.

Concurrent planning

7.28 This is a specific twin-track plan where the child is placed with foster carers who are also approved as adoptive applicants. The capacity of the birth parents or wider birth family to parent the child is assessed, while at the same time the child is placed with foster carers who (if the birth family cannot parent) become the adopters. It is fairly rare approach and is usually implemented in care proceedings in relation to newly born babies. There are few projects of this nature in the country.[11]

Contingency planning

7.29 Contingency planning should exist for any type of planning. In this type of plan a firmly fixed plan is being pursued but the plan considers what will happen if this fails by determining what type of placement will be sought and what support will need to be in put in place.

---

[11] These include the Goodman project in Manchester and the Coram project in London.

7.30

Questions to consider in analysis of the care planning process

- Did the *first review* confirm the assessment plan and clarify what further work will be needed in order for the child to return to the care of his or her parents?

- Was a permanence plan drawn up at the *second review* if the child is still in care?

- Was a permanence plan drawn up at the *second review* even where the plan is for the child to return home?

- Did the plan identify the support services to be provided, if any?

- Did the plan identify who should be responsible for implementation?

- In a case where it was not yet clear whether reunification was likely to be achievable did the social worker continue working with the child and their family towards reunification while *at the same time* taking steps towards making other permanent plans, in case the child cannot return home?

- Did the parallel or twin-track plan include assessments and approval by the Fostering Panel (of other family members or friends) and/or Adoption and Permanence Panel for a recommendation as to whether the child should be placed for adoption (ie completion of the child's permanence report (CPR) identifying the child's needs)?

- Were the birth parents informed that the two plans (reunification and alternative permanence) were being made to meet the child's needs and avoid unnecessary delay?

- Was the primacy of the reunification plan stressed to the parents?

- Was every effort made to retain the co-operation, understanding and involvement of the birth parent(s) required for successful parallel planning?

- Was a contingency plan in place to consider what will happen if the firmly fixed plan failed?

- Did the contingency plan determine what type of placement would be sought and what support would be needed to implement such a plan?

- Were the child's wishes and feelings taken into account in the planning making process and if not are the reasons recorded?

SECTION 5 – PLACEMENTS WITH PARENTS

7.31 The 2010 Regulations set out the requirements to be followed when a child subject to a care order is being placed back with a parent.[12]

7.32 The circumstances for placing a child with his or her parents could arise when:

- the child has remained at home pending court proceedings and remained there after the granting of an interim care order;

- a child has been returned home directly after a court order.

In all such cases the 2010 Regulations will apply and all the requirements of the regulations must be complied with.[13]

7.33 The responsible authority may not place a child back with a parent under the 2010 Regulations if to do so would be incompatible with any order made by the court under s 34 of the CA 1989.

7.34 Responsible local authorities are required to consider carefully whether a placement in accordance with the 2010 Regulations is the most appropriate way to discharge their responsibilities under s 22C(2) of the CA 1989. Where it is decided that such a placement is the most appropriate way to discharge their duty under s 22, the responsible local authority should reconsider whether the care order is still required.

7.35 It may be that the responsible local authority and the parent agree that an application to discharge the care order is appropriate. In those circumstances such an agreement must include:

- the level of support and supervision by the responsible local authority;

- the expected co-operation by the parent; and

- commitment from all involved to working together in the child's best interests.

If such agreement can be reached and the court makes an order to discharge the care order then the child will no longer be looked after and the 2010 Regulations will not apply.

7.36 In many cases a placement in accordance with the regulations will be part of the planned progress towards discharge of the care order. The management of the placement should aim to enhance the parent's role and support the family relationships with that aim in mind.

---

[12]   The 2010 Regulations, Part 4, regs 15–20.
[13]   The 2010 Regulations, reg 2.

7.37   However, even in those cases where the discharge of the care order is not a foreseeable option, the possibility should be constantly reviewed and the aim should be to build a genuine working partnership with the parent.

7.38   All such placements with parents will be subject to the requirement for a placement plan[14] and the case is required to be reviewed in accordance with the 2010 Regulations.[15]

Assessment of parents' suitability to care for the child

7.39   A care order cannot be made under the CA 1989 unless the court is satisfied that a child is suffering or is likely to suffer significant harm, and that this is attributable to the care given, or likely to be given, to him or her not being what it would be reasonable to expect a parent to give; or the child being beyond parental control. It is therefore important to be especially careful to ascertain how far those factors that were identified as grounds for the current care order have been addressed before deciding whether a child can be placed back with parents.

Parenting capacity

7.40   Before deciding to place the child with his or her parent the responsible local authority must assess the suitability of the parent to care for the child,[16] taking into account the suitability of the proposed accommodation and of other people in that accommodation.[17] The matters to be taken into account when assessing the suitability of the parent to care for the child are set out in the 2010 Regulations and use the framework of the core assessment.[18]

7.41   Factors to be given particular weight in assessing the parenting capacity of the parent include:

- Adequate protective factors in place. Domestic violence, parental alcohol or substance abuse, uncontrolled mental health problems and severe learning disabilities can have an adverse impact on the parent's capacity to safeguard and promote the child's welfare.

- The parent's previous experiences of looking after children. Where the parent has other children of their own who are subject to care or adoption orders, earlier case records should be explored to ascertain the circumstances which led to social work involvement with these children, and any indications that the capacity of the parents to bring up children has changed.

---

[14]   The 2010 Regulations, reg 9.
[15]   Part 6.
[16]   The 2010 Regulations, reg 17.
[17]   The 2010 Regulations, reg 17(a)(i) and (ii).
[18]   Schedule 3.

- Parental and family history and wider family functioning of a new partner, if there is one, as well as the relationship between the child and the new partner.

- Suitability of all members of the household who are aged 18 or over. While it is only possible to obtain Criminal Records Bureau (CRB) checks on young people over the age of 18, the assessment should address the history and current lifestyle of the other young people in the household who are under 18.

- The quality of the relationships between the parent with whom the child will live, and other adults who have a significant role in the child's life, such as other persons who may provide care to the child and other adults such as grandparents.

7.42   The 2010 Regulations require a decision to place the child back with a parent to be approved by a nominated officer of the responsible authority before it is put into effect.[19] Before granting this approval the nominated officer must be satisfied that:

- the child's wishes and feelings have been ascertained;

- the assessment as to the suitability of the parent has been carried out;[20]

- the placement will safeguard and promote the child's welfare; and

- the IRO has been consulted.

Immediate placements with parents

7.43   In some cases, the responsible local authority will consider that it is in the best interest of the child to make a placement back with the child's parents before the assessment under reg 17 is complete.[21] For example, in the case of an unforeseen breakdown of a foster placement requiring the child's immediate removal and where the permanence plan is for the child to return to his or her parent, the least traumatic move for the child may be to place him or her back with a parent rather than in another short-term placement. It is not expected, however, that these placements will happen frequently.

7.44   When an immediate placement is proposed,[22] the following checks must be carried out before the placement which must be approved by a nominated officer of the responsible authority:

---

[19]   The 2010 Regulations, reg 18.
[20]   The 2010 Regulations, reg 17.
[21]   The 2010 Regulations, reg 19.
[22]   The 2010 Regulations, reg 19.

- An interview should be held with the parent to obtain as much of the information specified in Sch 3 as possible.

- Practitioners should also seek to meet with all other members of the household in order to have a complete understanding of the household composition and relationships before placing the child. This is particularly relevant to identifying issues such as domestic violence and substance misuse which may impact on the child's safety.

- The assessment of the parent in accordance with reg 17 and a review of the child's case must be undertaken within 10 working days of the child being allowed to live with the parent. This will enable early identification of any difficulties, including whether any adults in the household have a relevant conviction or caution or there are other unsuitable adults in the household. An early review will enable the parent, social worker and other practitioners involved with the child's case to share information about progress and any difficulties which may impact on the child's welfare.

- Within 10 working days of the completion of the assessment a decision must be taken as to whether the placement should be confirmed or not in accordance with reg 19 (ie 20 working days from the date the child goes to live with the parent).

- If the child is to remain with the parent, the placement plan will need to be reviewed. As much of the placement plan as possible should be developed and shared with the parents when the child goes to live with them. If the placement is subsequently confirmed, the placement plan must be reviewed and, if necessary, amended.[23] If the decision is not to confirm the placement, it must be terminated.[24]

Support and services

7.45 Following the assessment of the parent's capacity to meet the child's needs, the responsible local authority must identify and set out in the child's care plan the services and other support which will be provided to the parent and child to meet the identified needs.[25] The effectiveness of these services and any other support in addressing the needs of the child, parenting capacity and wider family and environmental factors will be considered as part of the review of the child's case.

---

[23]   The 2010 Regulations, reg 19(c)(i).
[24]   The 2010 Regulations, reg 19(c)(ii).
[25]   The 2010 Regulations, reg 20.

7.46

Questions to consider in analysis of the placement with parents process

- Were all the requirements of the 2010 Regulations complied with before the placement was made except in the circumstances outlined in the guidance where the placement could be made at short notice?

- Did the local authority consider carefully whether a placement in accordance with the 2010 Regulations was the most appropriate way to discharge their responsibilities under s 22C(2) of the CA 1989?

- Where it was decided that a placement with parents was the most appropriate way to proceed, did the local authority reconsider whether the care order was still required?

- If the local authority and the parent agreed that an application to discharge the care order was appropriate, did such an agreement include the level of support and supervision by the local authority and co-operation by the parent?

- If discharge of the care order was not a foreseeable option, is there evidence that the possibility was constantly reviewed with the aim of building a genuine working partnership with the parent?

- Did the local authority's assessment of the parent take account of the suitability of accommodation and of other people in that accommodation?

- Did the assessment include the parent's physical, mental and emotional health and their age?

- Did the assessment consider whether the parent had had sufficient support in addressing issues of concern before the child could return home?

- Did the assessment include available information about the parent's previous experiences of looking after children?

- Did the assessment explore earlier case records to ascertain the circumstances which led to social work involvement with previous children, and any indications that the capacity of the parents to bring up children has changed?

- Did the assessment take account of any new parental partner and children, including the parental and family history and wider family functioning of the new partner as well as the relationship between the child and the new partner?

- Was a formal assessment of suitability undertaken for all members of the household who are aged 18 or over? ➡

- • Were the wishes and feelings of the child sought and given due weight?

- • Did the assessment explore the relationships between the parent with whom the child will live, and other adults who have a significant role in the child's life, such as other persons who may provide care to the child and other adults such as grandparents?

- • Was the decision to place the child back with a parent approved by a nominated officer of the responsible authority before it was put into effect?

- • If an immediate placement under reg 19 was made, were the appropriate timescales for assessment and review followed?

- • Did the local authority identify and set out in the care plan the services and other support to be provided to the parent and child to meet the identified needs?

SECTION 6 – PERMANENCY PLANNING

7.47

The legal framework

- • The *Children Act 1989 Guidance and Regulations: Volume 2: Care Planning, Placement and Case Review* (HMSO, 2010)

- • The *Children Act 1989 Guidance and Regulations: Volume 3: Planning Transition to Adulthood for Care Leavers* (HMSO, 2010)[26]

Permanency planning

7.48 Local authorities are required to make all reasonable efforts to rehabilitate looked-after children with their families whenever possible unless it is clear that the child can no longer live with his or her family and the authority has evidence that further attempts at rehabilitation or reunification are unlikely to succeed. Where it is clear that a child can no longer live with his or her parents, and that reunification is not possible, decisions about placing children with alternative permanent families need to be made as a matter of priority, and within 4 months of the child being looked after. In those situations the local authority will seek alternative, permanent placements for children.

---

[26] See also Department of Health *Looking after children: good parenting: good outcomes: reader* (HMSO, 1996) – this guidance applies to all looked-after children (within the meaning of the Children Act 1989) and all children placed for adoption under the Adoption Agencies Regulations 2005, SI 2005/389 (the principles outlined should be taken to apply to both types of placement unless specifically stated otherwise).

7.49 Permanence is the framework of:

- emotional permanence (attachment);

- physical permanence (stability); and

- legal permanence (the carer has parental responsibility for the child).

7.50 Permanence gives a child a sense of security, continuity, commitment and identity. The objective of planning for permanence is therefore to ensure that children have a secure, stable and loving family to support them through childhood and beyond. Permanence provides an underpinning framework for all social work with children and families from family support through to adoption.[27] One of the key functions of the care plan is to ensure that each child has a plan for permanence by the time of the second review, as set out in the statutory guidance to the Adoption and Children Act 2002.

7.51 Achieving permanence for a child will be a key consideration from the day the child becomes looked after.

7.52 The purpose of the Children Act 2008 has been to extend the statutory framework for children in care in England and Wales and to ensure that such young people receive high quality care and services which are focused on and tailored to their needs.

7.53 The 2008 Act aimed to improve the stability of placements and improve the educational experience and attainment of young people in local authority care or those about to leave care. In particular, the 2008 Act aimed to enable children entering the care system to achieve the aspirations all parents have for their children, and to reduce the gap in outcomes between children in care and their peers (with particular emphasis on educational attainment). The Act also aimed to improve placement stability and ensure more consistency for children in care. The implications for local authorities are far reaching in terms of their developing appropriate policies, but most importantly in the implementation of their plans. For the good intentions of the Act to be achieved, it is beyond question that additional financial and human resources will be needed.

7.54 Planning for permanence is a process that should begin as soon as a child comes into the care of the local authority. Care planning and reviewing should not be viewed as static events, but rather as a process of continuous monitoring and reassessment. Local authorities must adhere to timescales for reviewing the plans made for a child in accordance with the regulations specifying who should be involved in making the plans, how plans should be conducted and when they are to be reviewed.

---

[27] The *Children Act 1989 Guidance and Regulations: Volume 2: Care Planning, Placement and Case Review* (HMSO, 2010), para 2.3.

7.55 Planning for permanency should ensure that children have a secure, stable and caring environment to enable them to achieve their full potential in all domains during childhood and beyond. The aim of the planning process is to identify:

- which placement option is most likely to meet the needs of the individual child; and

- what services should be put in place to sustain the most suitable option chosen.

7.56

Analysis of a plan for permanency

- Who was party to the formulation of the plan? (All consultations should be recorded including any disagreements)

- What are the aims and objectives of the plan?

- What are the clearly identified timescales for achieving these objectives?

- What are the identified key tasks?

- Who is named as being responsible for implementation of the key tasks?

- Are the needs of the child outlined in all domains?

- Who is named as being responsible for meeting the child's identified needs?

- What contingency plan is proposed should anything go wrong?

- What are the identified wishes and feelings of the child and his or her knowledge about making complaints?

- What is the date for review?

7.57 The options for permanence are:

- *Return to birth family* – for many children this is the best permanence option when it has been possible to address the factors in family life which led to the child becoming looked after.

- An alternative *family and friends placement* – this route to permanence, may be most suitable for some children particularly where such care can be supported by a legal order such as a residence order, special guardianship order or, in a few cases, adoption.

- *Long-term foster care* – this is another important route to permanence where attachments have been formed and it has been agreed through the care planning and review process that this is where the child or young person will remain until adulthood.

- *Adoption* – this may be the permanence route for children who are unable to return to their birth or wider family. Adoption offers a lifelong and legally permanent new family. Twin-track or parallel planning, including concurrent planning, may provide a means to securing permanence at an early stage for some children.

7.58 The planning process, informed by multi-agency contributions, will identify which option is most likely to meet the needs of the individual child and take account of his or her wishes and feelings. The child's care plan will set out details of this plan and the arrangements for implementing it.

7.59 It is also important to think about the needs of older children and young people in relation to achieving permanence in their lives. They may not be able to live with birth parents for a variety of reasons nor wish to be in a foster home or to be adopted but prefer to live in a children's home. Nevertheless the care planning process must identify adults such as wider family and friends or other connected people who can provide emotional support and a long-term trusting relationship which will provide continuing support, particularly during periods of transition. Good quality work with families can help the young person build bridges back to his or her parents or other family members who may be able to provide that support even though it is not possible for the young person to live at home.

7.60 In considering the options and making a decision about the most appropriate permanent placement for a child, the local authority should not begin the permanency planning process with any preference for a particular option, other than prioritising a placement with birth family or friends, if at all possible. It is the needs of an individual child that should determine whether a child and/or young person is to be placed for adoption, remain in foster care, or be placed in a residential setting.

7.61

Analysis of the permanency planning process

- Is there evidence that the local authority made all reasonable efforts to rehabilitate the child with his or her family whenever possible?

- If not, was it clear that the child could no longer live with his or her family?

- Did the local authority have evidence that further attempts at rehabilitation or reunification were unlikely to succeed?

- Was any decision about placing the child with an alternative permanent family made as a matter of priority, and within 4 months of the child being looked after?

- Was the permanency planning process begun as soon as the child came into the local authority's care?

- Was the care planning and reviewing process subject to continuous monitoring and reassessment?

- Did the planning process clearly identify which placement option was most likely to meet the needs of the individual child, taking account of his or her wishes and feelings, and what services should be put in place to sustain the most suitable option chosen?

- Was the planning process informed by multi-agency contributions?

- Did the care plan set out details of the plan and the arrangements for implementing it?

- Was there evidence of the local authority's work with the child's family to help the child build bridges back to his or her parents or other family members who may be able to provide support even if it was not possible for the young person to live at home?

- Is it clear that the local authority did not begin the permanency planning process with any preference for a particular option, other than prioritising a placement with birth family or friends, if at all possible?

SECTION 7 – REVIEWS

Purpose of reviews

7.62 The review of the care plan is the fourth component in the cycle of assessment, planning, intervention and review. The purpose of a review is to contribute to a continuous process of planning and reconsideration of the plan for the child.[28] Review meetings are an essential element of the planning process in that they provide a forum in which to:

- review care plans;

- ensure that everyone who has an interest in the child is consulted; and

- ensure that the views of those people are given due weight in accordance with their level of understanding and maturity.

7.63 Reviews take place in order to ensure that the child's welfare continues to be safeguarded and promoted in the most effective way throughout the period that he or she is looked after.

Local authority policy on reviews

7.64 The responsible local authority has a statutory duty to review the case of a looked-after child.[29] The responsible local authority is required to have a written policy regarding the manner in which they will conduct reviews of children's cases under the 2010 Regulations.[30] Copies of the local authority's policy must be given to the child (if appropriate), the child's parents, anyone with parental responsibility and anyone else considered to be relevant (eg the child's carer).

7.65 Responsible local authorities must ensure that their system of review provides for:

- a structured, coordinated approach to the conduct of a review;

- the full participation of both child and parents in the decision-making process where possible and appropriate; and

- the full participation of the child's carers, subject to the wishes and feelings of the child where age appropriate.

Timing of reviews

7.66 The guidance sets out the required timing of a child's reviews and the maximum intervals that may separate them.[31] The specified frequency of reviews is a *minimum standard*, and the guidance makes it clear that a review should take place as often as the circumstances of the individual case require.

---

[28] The Care Planning, Placement and Case Review (England) Regulations 2010.
[29] The 2010 Regulations, reg 32.
[30] The 2010 Regulations, reg 34(1).
[31] The 2010 Regulations, reg 33.

7.67

Timescales for reviews

- Every child in care must have his or her case reviewed within *20 days* of being looked after

- The second review must take place within *3 months* of the first review

- The third and subsequent reviews must take place no more than at *6 monthly* intervals

---

Changes of plan

7.68 Where there is a need for significant changes to the care plan, then the date of the review should be brought forward. No significant change to the care plan can be made unless it has been considered first at a review, unless this is not reasonably practicable. The functions of the IRO are set out in s 25B(1) of the CA 1989 and reg 45 of the 2010 Regulations. Between reviews, if the care plan continues to meet the needs of the child, there may be no need for any communication between the IRO and the social worker or the child.

7.69 However, in the event of a significant change or event in the child's life, the social worker must inform the IRO. Such changes include:

- a proposed change of care plan for example arising at short notice in the course of proceedings following directions from the court;

- where agreed decisions from the review are not carried out within the specified timescale;

- major change to the contact arrangements;

- changes of allocated social worker;

- any safeguarding concerns involving the child, which may lead to enquiries being made under s 47 of the CA 1989 ('child protection enquiries') and outcomes of child protection conferences, or other meetings that are not attended by the IRO;

- complaints from or on behalf of the child, parent or carer;

- unexpected changes in the child's placement provision which may significantly impact on placement stability or safeguarding arrangements;

- significant changes in birth family circumstances for example births, marriages or deaths which may have a particular impact on the child;

- if the child is charged with any offence leading to referral to youth offending services, pending criminal proceedings and any convictions or sentences as a result of such proceedings;

- if the child is excluded from school;

- if the child has run away or is missing from an approved placement;

- significant health, medical events, diagnoses, illnesses, hospitalisations, or serious accidents; and

- panel recommendations in relation to permanency.

This list is by no means exhaustive and there may be many other circumstances in which the IRO may request that a review be convened. Parents and children should also be consulted about the need for an additional review.

Links with other reviews

7.70   The review of the care plan may be carried out at the same time as other reviews, for example reviews within the youth justice system.[32]

7.71   Where a looked-after child is subject to a child protection plan, the timing of a child protection review conference should be the same as the review under the 2010 Regulations, to ensure that information in relation to the child's safety is considered within the review meeting, and informs the overall care planning process. Consideration must be given to ensuring that the multi-agency contribution to the review of the child protection plan is addressed within the review of the care plan.

Preparation for reviews

7.72   The social worker responsible for the child's case, in discussion with the line manager and the child (subject to age and understanding), should identify who should be invited to the review meeting.

7.73   The social worker should discuss with the IRO:

- the proposed invitees;

- the progress of the case since the last review;

- the content of any written reports that will be available to the review meeting; and

- any other relevant information.

---

[32]   The 2010 Regulations, reg 32(3).

The IRO must attend and chair the meeting so far as reasonably practicable.[33]

Conduct of the review

7.74   A review is made up of a number of elements[34] including:

• preparation;

• consultation;

• gathering information;

• assessments;

• consideration of the information at the review meeting; and

• evaluating progress and/or revising the care plan.

7.75   Through this process the social worker should be in a position to report on:

• the progress made in implementing the plan and achieving the specified outcomes for the child;

• any changes required to the provision of services; and

• any change required to the legal status of the child (this may include the need for care proceedings or for discharge of the care order).

7.76   The formal element of the review will usually involve a meeting or a series of meetings. Other meetings, perhaps solely involving professionals concerned with the child's care, will be held about the child as part of the continuous monitoring of the child's case but these will not form part of the review process.

7.77   It is important to remember that a review is not a reconsideration after a complaint, or part of line management supervision of a decision. Multidisciplinary meetings to consider a case are not part of the review process but information gathered at such meetings may be considered at a review.

Consultation and information gathering

7.78   As with planning, it is essential that there is full consultation with all the relevant individuals before the review meeting. Appropriate provision should be made for children and parents with communication difficulties or whose first

---

[33]   The 2010 Regulations, reg 36(1)(a).
[34]   The 2010 Regulations, regs 4–6.

language is not English. The responsible authority should obtain and take account of the wishes and feelings of the following people about the plan and the progress made since the last review:[35]

- the child (subject to age and understanding);

- his or her parents;

- any person who is not a parent but who has parental responsibility; and

- any other person thought to be relevant, for example:

  - the current carer (foster carer or residential social worker);
  - relevant health care professionals;
  - the child's GP;
  - the appropriate local authority where it is proposed (or it is the case already) that the child will be looked after in their area;
  - the appropriate local authority officer with lead responsibility for implementing the authority's duty to promote the educational achievement of its looked-after children;
  - the most appropriate teacher at the child's current and/or new school which, where appropriate, should be the designated teacher for looked-after children; and
  - the independent visitor (if one has been appointed); and
  - the children's guardian appointed by the Children and Families Court Advisory and Support Service (CAFCASS) in cases where there are court proceedings.

7.79 Where it is considered that written views or reports will be adequate, these should be sought and obtained in time to be considered as part of the review meeting. All relevant written information should be provided to the IRO in advance and circulated to others who will be attending the meeting, as appropriate.

7.80 It should be clear that there is a process already in place to ensure the continuous collection of information about the child's progress as part of the overall care planning process, rather than a separate one-off exercise for the review meeting alone.

Attendance at the review meeting

7.81 The review must be child-centred and discussion should take place between the social worker and the child at least 20 working days before the meeting about who the child would like to attend the meeting and about where the meeting will be held. This will allow time for subsequent discussion about attendance and venue between the IRO and the social worker and for written

---

[35] CA 1989, s 22(4).

invitations to be sent out. The involvement of the child will be subject to his or her age, understanding and welfare. The possibility of a child being accompanied to a review meeting by an advocate should be considered.

7.82 It is expected that *the parents* and *the child* (if he or she is of sufficient age and understanding) will be present at the whole of the review, but this will depend on the circumstances of each individual case.

7.83 In exceptional circumstances the social worker, in consultation with the IRO may decide that the attendance of the child or parent (if this would not be in the interests of the child) at all, or part of, the review meeting will not be appropriate or practicable. This may be the case if there is a clear conflict of interests. However, the anxieties of professionals should not be the sole reason for excluding a child or his or her parent from a review. Alternative arrangements should be considered. If a parent or child is excluded from a review, a written explanation of the reasons should be given. Other arrangements should be made for their involvement in the review process, and details of this should be placed on the child's case record.

7.84 In addition to the parent and child, the *child's carer* should be invited. The carer provides day-to-day parenting for the child and cannot do this effectively and deliver the actions set out in the placement plan if he or she is not part of the care planning and decision-making process.

7.85 *Other people with a legitimate interest in the child* should also be invited if they have a contribution in the discussions at the review meeting. The attendance of such people should always be discussed with the child before invitations are made and his or her views on their attendance obtained. It may be appropriate where the contribution from such people is strictly factual for the information to be provided in writing or at a separate meeting.

7.86 Where a long-term plan is in place, a small group (those consistently and constantly involved with the child) should be identified as essential attendees at the next and subsequent review meetings. In the majority of cases, the group will consist of the social worker, the child, parents, the IRO and the carer (if different from the parent). This will vary according to the circumstances of the individual case.

7.87 The child, parents and carers should always be consulted about the timing and venue for the review to ensure maximum participation. Meetings should always be arranged at a place and time to meet the needs of the child. Children should not be required to miss school or essential health appointments in order to attend their review. Parents may need financial or other support to enable them to attend.

Matters for consideration at the review meeting

7.88 The aim of the review is to assess how far the care plan is addressing the child's needs and whether any changes are required to achieve this. The focus of the first review meeting will be on examining and confirming the plan. Subsequent reviews will be occasions for monitoring progress against the plan and making decisions to amend the plan as necessary, to reflect new knowledge and changed circumstances.

7.89 The 2010 Regulations provide a checklist of matters for consideration at the review.[36] This is not comprehensive or exclusive but sets the minimum requirements. In addition, the review must consider matters specified in the CA 1989 relating to the child's welfare. Other matters will arise in individual cases which it is not possible to cover in a list of general applications.

7.90 The matters covered by Sch 7 and the relevant statutory provisions are:

- the effect of any change in the child's circumstances since the last review;

- whether decisions taken at the last review have been successfully implemented, and if not the reasons for lack of implementation;

- whether the responsible local authority should seek any change in the child's legal status;

- whether there is a plan for permanence;

- the current arrangements for contact and whether there is a need to change these arrangements to promote contact between the child and his or her family or other relevant people;

- whether the placement continues to be appropriate and is meeting the needs of the child;

- the child's educational needs, including consideration of:

  - the child's most recent assessment of progress and development;
  - whether the arrangements that are in place are meeting the child's educational needs;
  - whether any changes are, or are likely to become, necessary or desirable before the child's next review; and
  - whether the child has a PEP and also whether its content provides a clear framework for promoting the child's educational achievement;

- the child's leisure interests and activities and whether the current arrangements are meeting the child's needs;

---

[36] Schedule 7.

- the child's health, including consideration of:

    - the child's most recent health assessment (to include physical and emotional health needs);
    - whether the arrangements that are in place are meeting the child's health needs;
    - whether any changes are, or are likely to become, necessary or desirable before the child's next review; and
    - whether the content of the health plan provides a clear framework for promoting the child's health;

- whether the identity needs of the child are being met and whether any changes are needed, having regard to the child's religious persuasion, racial origin and cultural background;

- whether the child understands any arrangements made to provide advice, support and assistance and whether these arrangements continue to meet his or her needs;[37]

- the child's wishes and feelings about the care plan including in relation to any changes or proposed changes to the care plan (having regard to his or her age and understanding);

- the views of the child's IRO about any aspect of the case and the care plan;

- whether the plan fulfils the responsible authority's duty to safeguard and promote the child's welfare;[38] and

- whether it would be in the child's interests for an independent visitor to be appointed.[39]

7.91 The responsible local authority is required to have arrangements in place for implementing decisions made in the course of or as a result of the review. These arrangements must include a process for informing the IRO of any failure to implement the decisions within the agreed timescale. Health authorities, local authorities, local housing authorities and other social services departments have a duty to comply with a request from a children's services department for help in the exercise of their functions.[40]

7.92 The responsible local authority is required to inform the IRO if they fail to implement decisions made in the course of the review.[41]

---

[37]   The 2010 Regulations, reg 31.
[38]   CA 1989, s 22(3).
[39]   CA 1989, s 23ZB(1)(b).
[40]   CA 1989, s 27.
[41]   The 2010 Regulations, reg 37(b).

Updating and amending the care plan

7.93 The responsible authority must give a copy of any revised, amended, care plan to the child, parent and the IRO.[42] The following people should also be given a copy of the care plan:

- where the child is placed with a foster carer, the fostering service provider who approved the foster carer;

- where the child is placed in a children's home, the person registered under Part 2 of the Care Standards Act 2000 in respect of that home; and

- where the child is placed in accordance with other arrangements under s 22C(6)(d), the person who will be responsible for the child at that accommodation.

Record of the review

7.94 A written record of each review should be completed and placed on the child's case record.[43] The record should contain a list of those who attended. In circumstances where the child or parents do not attend, the reasons for this should be noted. The record should contain an accurate and comprehensive note of the meeting, or meetings, which constituted the review, and of the views of all those who attended or were consulted as part of the review process.

7.95 The review record should be an important document for enabling the social worker to confirm how it was agreed to update the care plan.

7.96 The IRO is responsible for completing the record of the review on behalf of the responsible authority. This should include:

- an assessment of the extent to which the care plan is meeting the needs of the child;

- the identification of any changes that are necessary in the light of information presented at the review, and the intended outcomes of any changes;

- a list of the decisions made;

- the name of the person responsible for implementing each decision; and

- the relevant timescales.

The guidance makes it clear that high quality recording of information obtained in the course of the review and of the decisions arising from the

---

[42] The 2010 Regulations, reg 6(3).
[43] The 2010 Regulations, reg 38.

review is essential to enable practitioners involved with the child's case to understand the actions for which they are responsible in order to meet the needs of the child, the family where appropriate, and the carer.[44]

7.97

Analysis of the review process

- Was a copy of the local authority's policy about reviews given to the child (if appropriate), parents, or anyone with parental responsibility and anyone else considered to be relevant if requested?

- Were reviews held in accordance with the appropriate timescales?

- Was the review brought forward if there was a need for significant changes to the care plan?

- Was any significant change to the care plan made having first been considered at a review, unless not reasonably practicable?

- In the event of a significant change or event in the child's life did the social worker inform the IRO?

- Were the child and parents consulted about the need for any additional review?

- Was the review of the care plan carried out at the same time as other necessary reviews?

- Was the timing of any child protection review conference the same as the review under the 2010 Regulations? Was information in relation to the child's safety considered within the review meeting? Did information about the child's safety inform the overall care-planning process? Was consideration given to ensuring that the multi-agency contribution to the review of the child protection plan was addressed within the review of the care plan?

- Did the social worker discuss the proposed invitees, the progress of the case and any other relevant information with the IRO before the review?

- Did the IRO attend and chair the meeting?

- Did the IRO meet the child on their own to ascertain their wishes and feelings, and if not are the reasons recorded?

- Was there full consultation with all the relevant individuals before the review meeting?   ➡

---

[44] Reviews in relation to children in adoptive placements are discussed in Chapter 11 (dealing with adoption).

- Were written reports sought, obtained and circulated in time for the review?

- Did discussion take place between the social worker and the child at least 20 working days before the review about who the child would like to attend the meeting and about where the meeting will be held? Was the possibility of the child being accompanied by an advocate considered?

- Were the relevant people invited to the review and consulted about the timing and venue?

- Were the relevant matters in Sch 7 considered and discussed at the review?

- Did the local authority inform the IRO of any failures to implement decisions made in the course of the review?

- Was a copy of any revised, amended, care plan given by the local authority to the child, parent, the IRO and any relevant carer?

- Was a written record of each review completed? Does the record contain an accurate and comprehensive note of the meeting, or meetings, which constituted the review, and of the views of all those who attended or were consulted?

- Does the review record enable the social worker to confirm how it was agreed to update the care plan?

SECTION 8 – INDEPENDENT REVIEWING OFFICERS (IROS)

7.98 Detailed guidance about the role of the IRO is found in the Care Planning, Placement and Case Review (England) Regulations 2010 and in the guidance within *The IRO Handbook: Statutory guidance for independent reviewing officers and local authorities on their functions in relation to case management and review for looked after children.*[45]

7.99 IROs were introduced on a statutory basis in 2004. The government's commitment to IROs as a key element in improving care planning and securing better outcomes for looked-after children is clearly stated within the guidance. As such the role of IROs is to provide a quality assurance role within the care planning and review process.

7.100 The IRO's responsibilities have now been extended from monitoring the performance by the local authority of their functions in relation to a child's

---

[45] DCSF, 2010. Issued under s 25B(2)(b) of the CA 1989 (as amended by the Children and Young Persons Act 2008 which created a new power for the Secretary of State to issue statutory guidance to IROs) and s 7 of the Local Authority Social Services Act 1970.

review, to monitoring the performance by the local authority of their functions in relation to a child's *case*. The intention of such changes is stated in the guidance as being to enable the IRO to have an effective independent oversight of the child's case and to ensure that the child's interests are protected throughout the care planning process.

7.101 The IRO's primary focus is

- to quality assure the care planning and review process for each child; and

- to ensure that his or her current wishes and feelings are given full consideration.

The guidance also states that every IRO should feel confident in his or her role and personal authority and understand his or her responsibilities to monitor and review the child's case and, where necessary, to challenge poor practice. The guidance recognises that it is not the responsibility of the IRO to manage the case, supervise the social worker or devise the care plan, and that although it is important for the IRO to develop a consistent relationship with the child, this should not undermine or replace the relationship between the social worker and the child.

7.102 The IRO should chair all review meetings of looked-after children and ensure that:

- the child's views are understood and taken into account;

- the persons responsible for implementing any decision taken in consequence of the review are identified; and

- any poor practice and/or failure to review the case in accordance with Regulations is brought to the attention of persons at an appropriate level of seniority within the responsible authority.

As a last resort the IRO has the power to refer a case to CAFCASS, which will be able to refer the case to court if they consider it appropriate to do so.

7.103 The duties of the IRO in the review process include:

- Speaking to the child in private in advance of the meeting(s) about the matters to be considered, unless the child refuses to do so or the IRO considers it inappropriate, having taken into account the child's age and understanding.[46]

---

[46]   The 2010 Regulations, reg 36.

- Reviewing the child's needs and whether the placement continues to be the most suitable to meet the totality of the child's needs and enabling him or her to achieve the five outcomes specified in *Every Child Matters*.[47]

- Ensuring at the meeting(s) that a named person is identified as having responsibility for the implementation of each decision made at the review, within an agreed timescale.

- Framing the decisions of the meeting in such a way that the identified needs and planned outcomes are clear.

- Ensuring that the person responsible for implementing the decision and the timescale for implementation is recorded.

7.104 Following the review, the IRO must advise staff at an appropriate level of seniority of any failure to review the case in accordance with the 2010 Regulations or of a failure to implement any decisions.

7.105 Under the Care Planning, Placement and Case Review (England) Regulations 2010, the IRO now has the power to adjourn reviews if he or she is not satisfied that sufficient information has been provided by the responsible authority to review the child's care plan in accordance with Sch 7.[48] For example:

- the IRO is not satisfied that the local authority has complied adequately with all the requirements relating to reviews (eg the duty to consult the child, the child's parents and others before taking decisions with respect to the child, or appropriate planning and paperwork being available) and considers that such omissions will adversely affect the efficacy of the review; or

- the IRO is not satisfied that the child has been properly prepared for the meeting.

7.106 However, the guidance recommends that careful consideration should be given before taking such action and the wishes and feelings of the child, the carer and, where appropriate, the parents should be sought before any decision is made. The IRO should consider the effects on the child of delaying a meeting for which he or she has been prepared and will need to weigh up the benefits between proceeding with the meeting on limited information and the delay in decision-making as a result of adjournment. However, responsibility for deciding whether or not a review should be adjourned rests solely with the nominated IRO for the child concerned. In such circumstances the review may be adjourned once but should be completed within 20 working days of the original scheduled date.

---

[47] Cm 5860 (2003).
[48] The 2010 Regulations, reg 36(2).

7.107 Where disagreements or differences in opinion arise in the course of the review process between those present, every effort should be made to resolve the matter on an informal basis. Where agreement cannot be reached, the responsible local authority should ensure that the child, parents, carers and others involved with the child are aware of the representations procedure they are required to have in place.

7.108 The IRO is under a duty to advise the child of his or her right to make a complaint and of the availability of an advocate to assist the child in making a complaint.

7.109 Where the IRO is of the view that the responsible local authority:

- has failed to address the needs of the child set out in the revised plan; and/or

- has failed to review the case in accordance with the regulations; and/or

- has failed to implement effectively any decision made at a review; or

- is otherwise in breach of its duties to the child in any significant way,

the IRO must advise staff at an appropriate level of seniority of this failure. It will be important that senior managers then work to resolve the failure within a timescale that meets the needs of the individual child.

7.110 The IRO has the statutory power to refer a case to CAFCASS (or a Welsh family proceedings officer) if the IRO considers it appropriate to do so.[49] The IRO will encounter a wide range of situations in which there are concerns about the plan for the child or the service that is being provided. In most cases it will be possible to address these through:

- discussion with the local authority, including access to the dispute resolution procedure;

- use of the complaints procedure, either by the child directly or by an adult who is authorised to act on the child's behalf; or

- application to the court for an order under the CA 1989, either by the child or by an appropriate adult who is able and willing to act.

7.111 When considering whether to make a referral to CAFCASS, the IRO should consider the impact that a referral would have for the child. In some cases, there will be time available first to pursue the full dispute resolution procedure within the local authority. In other situations, the matter will be of sufficient urgency that the dispute resolution process needs to be curtailed. It is

---

[49] CA 1989, s 25B(3).

the responsibility of the IRO to make the decision about whether and when a referral is necessary, based on the timetable for the child.

SECTION 9 – SOCIAL WORK CASE RECORDS

7.112 Guidance is provided about the need for good case recording within *Volume 2: Care Planning, Placement and Case Review*.[50] Effective case recording is important to demonstrate the accountability of staff working in looked-after children's services to those who use those services. It helps to focus the work of staff and it supports effective partnerships with service users and carers. It ensures there is a documented account of the responsible authority's involvement with individual service users, families and carers and assists with continuity when workers are unavailable or change.

Establishing the child's record

7.113 The responsible authority is required to establish and maintain the child's written case record.[51] This is an individual case record for each child looked after by them. Records are the basis for a clear and common understanding of the plan for the child, the arrangements made, the agreements reached, the decisions taken and the reasons for them. Careful recording of information which pertains to a child's plan, placement and progress, enables the case to be monitored effectively and kept under review.

7.114 The case record must include:[52]

- documents created as part of the assessment process (including health care and education documents);

- any court order relating to the child such as the care order or order relating to contact;

- the first care plan, any changes made to that plan and any subsequent plans (to include the health plan, the placement plan and the PEP); and

- details of any arrangements for the responsible authority's functions to be discharged by an independent fostering provider or provider of social work services.

These should be regarded as the minimum requirements for the case record. For some children and particularly those who are placed permanently away from their family it provides an important narrative of their childhood which is too frequently lost.

---

[50] The *Children Act 1989 Guidance and Regulations: Volume 2: Care Planning, Placement and Case Review* (HMSO, 2010).
[51] The 2010 Regulations, reg 49.
[52] The 2010 Regulations, reg 49(2).

7.115   Records should also include:

• details of arrangements for contact;

• copies of reports provided during court proceedings such as guardian's reports and specialist assessments;

• additional information about educational progress;

• copies of all the documents used to seek information, provide information or record views given to the authority in the course of planning and reviewing the child's case and review reports;

• records of visits; and

• other correspondence which relates to the child.

7.116   It is also recommended that any contribution the child may wish to make such as written material, photographs, school certificates and similar items should be included. However, care must be taken to ensure that the child retains either originals or copies of information which will form part of his or her own progress file to keep with him or her.

7.117   The responsible local authority's records are an important source of information for the child who is looked after away from his or her family. They provide information about the sequence of events and the reasons why important decisions in the child's life were made. For some children they will provide a means to trace relatives with whom they may have lost contact, such as brothers and sisters.

7.118   The record should be maintained in such a way that it is easy to trace the process of decision-making and in particular so that the views of the child and his or her parents can be easily found and related to the sequence of decisions taken and arrangements made. In addition, any papers temporarily placed in the record which are the property of the child should be identified as such and marked for return at the appropriate time.

7.119   The child's record should be separate from other records, such as those relating to a foster carer or the registered children's home which are not solely concerned with the individual child. Where some information on one of these other records is relevant to the child a duplicate entry should appear in the child's record. Records should not be amalgamated even in the case of siblings, although a degree of cross-reference and duplicate entry will be necessary.

Retention and safekeeping

7.120 The child's case record must be kept until the 75th anniversary of his or her date of birth, or 15 years from the date of death in the case of a child who dies before reaching the age of 18.[53]

7.121 Responsible local authorities must secure the safekeeping of records and must take any necessary steps to ensure they are treated as confidential. This requires not only arrangements for the physical security of the records but effective procedures to restrict access to records to those who are properly authorised and require access because of their duties in relation to a case.[54]

Access and confidentiality

7.122 The CA 1989 requires local authorities to give access to records to persons duly authorised by the Secretary of State and to guardians appointed by the court.

7.123 Access to records by the local commissioner is provided for in the Local Government Act 1974. The other relevant piece of legislation is the Data Protection Act 1998. This gives individuals rights of access to certain information about themselves. The Data Protection Act 1998 applies to all records, including social work records. The Act provides for certain information (such as adoption records) to be exempted in prescribed circumstances from the right of access.

Electronic records

7.124 The Data Protection Act 1998 applies to both paper/manual records and records held electronically. Responsible local authorities should therefore ensure that their electronic recording systems comply with all the requirements of the legislation. It is also important, however, that electronic recording systems comply with the requirements for children and their families to easily find their story in a logical narrative.

7.125 Responsible local authorities should act in accordance with the above guidance and with their own legal advice in matters relating to the disclosure of information held in the records. It is good practice that information held about an individual should be shared with him or her unless there are special reasons for withholding it, covered by the legislation and guidance mentioned.

The Integrated Children's System (ICS)

7.126 Looked-after children (LAC) materials were introduced in 1995 to assist the planning and review process for social workers, children and families. These materials have been gradually replaced by the Integrated Children's System

---

[53] The 2010 Regulations, reg 50(1).
[54] The 2010 Regulations, reg 50(2).

(ICS) (operational since 2007), and social workers' practice and case record keeping is now supported by information technology that is designed to handle a large amount of information on individual children.

7.127   The use of information required for recording the facts and events of children's lives, for assessing the needs of children and monitoring their developmental progress, is fundamental to good, safe practice and better outcomes. Central to many of the shortcomings in social work practice relating to children has been the failure to record, retrieve and understand the significance of information about children.

7.128   With this in mind, the ICS was developed by the government to improve outcomes for children defined as being in need in accordance with the CA 1989. All local authorities were required to have the new fully operational systems in place by 1 January 2007. The ICS was intended to provide a conceptual framework, a method of practice and a business process to support social workers and managers in undertaking the key tasks of assessment, planning, intervention and review. It is based on an understanding of children's developmental needs in the context of parental capacity and wider family and environmental factors. Because the work with children in need requires skilled use of detailed and complex information, the ICS is designed to be supported by an electronic case record system. A key aim of the ICS is to provide frontline staff and their managers with the necessary help, through information communication technology (ICT), to record, collate, analyse and output the information required.

7.129   The ICS was developed over several years in response to the findings of inspections, research and inquiries. These findings have demonstrated the need for conceptual systemisation in working with children in need which was considered in detailed by the Munro Review of Child Protection. In 2010 the government commissioned Professor Eileen Munro to conduct an independent review of child protection in England.[55]

7.130   The Munro Review was highly critical of the increase in recent years of too much prescription of practice and concluded that too much prescription reduces scope for professionals to respond appropriately to each individual case and diminishes professional responsibility for judgments and decisions. This has the unintended consequence of reducing the job satisfaction, self-esteem and sense of personal responsibility experienced by child protection workers which leads to the further unintended consequence of increasing amounts of time taken off absent or sick. In addition, the large amounts of time social workers are forced to spend on the Integrated Children's System (ICS), reduces the time they can spend directly engaging with children, young people and families. Overall, the Munro Review has concluded that the increasing

---

[55]   Munro Review Report of Child Protection, *Part One: A Systems Analysis* (October 2010*), Interim Report: The Child's Journey* (February 2011) and *Final Report: A Child-Centred System* (May 2011), Department for Education.

dependence on prescriptive record keeping, of the sort included in the ICS, only serves to reduce the quality of outcomes for children and families.

7.131 At the time of writing (January 2012) government research is planned to consider whether replacing nationally prescribed timescales for assessment with timely, professional judgments can have the positive impact on practice envisaged by the Munro Review. The trials within eight local authorities about using more flexible and less prescriptive methods of social work assessment and recording have been extended until 31 March 2012; the changed flexibilities will be consulted on as part of the broader *Working Together to Safeguard Children* and the *Framework for the Assessment of Children in Need and their Families* planned for early 2012.

The ICS documents

7.132 Pending any revision of the ICS documents as indicated by the Munro Review 2011, the existing documents remain in use by all local authorities.

7.133 The *Referral and Information Record* (previously the Essential Information Record (EIR) Part 1) and the *Chronology* (previously the Essential Information Record Part 2) – these records are designed to hold important personal information about a child or young person. Part 1 provides information needed immediately by carers and should be completed *before* the child is placed. Part 2 asks for more comprehensive information about a child's background including their legal and placement history. For a planned placement, this should be completed in advance and given to carers before or when a child is placed. If this is not possible then it should be given to carers as soon as possible after the placement begins and not later than the first placement meeting which should be held within 7 days.

7.134 The *Placement Information Record and Agreements* (previously the Placement Plan Part 1) and the *Chronology* (previously the Placement Plan Part 2) – the placement information record outlines the purpose of the placement in meeting the child's identified needs. The foster carer placement agreement, which must be completed before a child is placed, should be signed by the foster carer and the child's social worker. The record provides detailed information and day-to-day arrangements about a child or young person's everyday routines with particular reference to health, education and identity needs and arrangements for contact. For a planned placement, this should be completed in advance of placement. If this is not possible then it should be completed as soon as possible after the placement begins and no later than 7 days after placement. In practice the placement information record is usually completed at the formal placement agreement meeting attended by the child, their parents and anyone else with parental responsibility, the child's social worker, foster carer and their supervising social worker. There is no requirement for this meeting to be chaired by an independent person.

The foster placement agreement

7.135 It is a statutory requirement that before placing a child with foster carers, the placing authority must make a written foster placement agreement with the foster carer relating to the care of the child or young person. The placement information record and the placement agreement must be completed in advance or at the point of placement. The information about the day-to-day arrangements should be completed at a placement agreement meeting attended by:

- the child or young person;

- the birth parent(s);

- the child's social worker;

- the foster carer;

- the foster carer's supervising social worker; and

- any other appropriate person.

Wherever possible the placement agreement meeting should take place prior to the placement commencing, or in the case of an unplanned placement within 72 hours.

The placement agreement meeting

7.136 Wherever possible the placement agreement meeting should take place prior to the placement commencing, or in the case of an unplanned placement within 72 hours. The meeting should include discussion about:

- The child's routine including details of personal care, bedtimes, mealtimes, special comfort objects, likes and dislikes.

- Household routine including the foster carer's expectations about issues such as bedtime, mealtimes, household chores, visitors, smoking.

- The extent to which day-to-day decisions on the child's care are delegated to the foster carer, eg haircuts, going out with friends.

- Confirmation of the household safe caring guidelines.

- Pocket money including details of what items the child is expected to purchase from their pocket money and what the foster carer will be responsible for, eg clothes, toiletries.

- Other financial arrangements such as payments for fares or school dinners.

- Arrangements for meeting the child's health care needs (including arrangements for child to be registered with a new GP and to see the dentist and optician, the extent to which consent to medical treatment is delegated to the foster carer, arrangements for the child's health care assessment).

- Arrangements for meeting the child's education needs (including arrangements for the child's schooling, financial support to the foster carer or child, arrangements for obtaining a school place if the child needs to change school, arrangements for the completion of the child's personal education plan, agreement as to who will attend education functions such as parent evenings or school assemblies).

- The child's needs arising from their race, culture, religion and identity (including additional support and training needed by the foster carer, arrangements for the child to practice their chosen religion, special dietary needs, additional support needed when the child's first language is not English or they have other communication difficulties, in trans-racial or trans-cultural placements, the arrangements for ensuring the child's identity needs are met).

- Arrangements for contact (including confirmation that a risk assessment has been carried out, expectations of the foster carer in supervising and/or monitoring contact, arrangements for allowing the child to stay away from the placement overnight).

- Arrangements for the child to continue and develop hobbies and leisure activities including arrangements for financial support to the foster carer or child.

- Details of the elements of matching that were taken into account when choosing the placement.

- Arrangements for meeting any of the child's needs that cannot be met in the placement.

7.137 The *Child's Initial Plan: Care Plan Part 1* (previously the Care Plan) – the care plan ensures that all looked-after children have clearly stated objectives set out for their care and a strategy for achieving them. This is completed by the child's social worker. The initial care plan will be confirmed at the child's first review and subsequent reviews will confirm or revise the plan for the child and the arrangements for meeting their needs. Most initial plans are designed to enable the child to return home as soon as possible, providing all the necessary tasks have been completed. However, plans for permanency should be made by the second child care review and after the child have been looked after for a period of 4 months.

7.138 *Consultation papers* – There are three types of consultation papers:

- for people with parental responsibility;

- for the foster carer or independent visitor; and

- for the child or young person.

These are intended to give the above people an opportunity to have their views heard and recorded *before* a statutory review.

7.139 The *Review Record* (previously the Review of Arrangements) – the review record, following proper consultation, should inform the IRO of events since the previous review and identify whether:

- the overall care plan is still appropriate; and

- the placement meets its agreed objectives and continues to meet the child's needs.

7.140 The *Assessment and Progress Records* (previously the Assessment and Action Records) – to achieve the aim of producing better outcomes for children and young people, the progress of children in care is measured along the following seven developmental dimensions (see Chapter 5):

(1) health;

(2) education;

(3) identity;

(4) family and social relationships;

(5) social presentation;

(6) emotional and behavioural development; and

(7) self-care skills.

7.141 The tool used for this purpose is the Assessment and Progress Record. The records are designed to measure an individual's progress, assess the standard of care and plan improvements. There are three age-related assessment and progress records. In records for younger children the questions are directed toward the carer. For 10- to 14-year olds and 15 years and over, questions are directed to the young people themselves.

7.142 The assessment and progress records should be used at the following frequency:

- every 6 months for children aged under 5 who experience more rapid developmental changes; and

- annually for children aged 5 and over.

7.143 The child's social worker is responsible for ensuring that the assessment and progress records are fully completed and the appropriate people are consulted about the child's development in each dimension.

The review process

7.144 The child or young person should be the central part of this process. Depending on age and maturity of the child, the child should be asked who they think should attend their review.

7.145 The following people should attend the child's review:

- the child;

- the child's parents;

- the child's carer(s);

- the child's social worker; and

- the carer's supervising social worker (usually appointed for foster carers but not all kinship carers have a supervising social worker to support them).

7.146 These people should be part of the planning and review process unless there are particularly strong reasons against this. Should it be decided to exclude parents from the planning and review meeting, the IRO should meet parents and those with parental responsibility before the review meeting to seek their views. The views of health and education should also be sought by the child's social worker in advance of the review meeting (usually health visitor and teacher). Alternatively, they can be invited to the review if this is acceptable to the child.

7.147 Subject to their age and understanding, the child will usually attend the review. Obviously it will have little meaning for a very young child but on the whole it is expected that children over the age of 4 should attend at least part of their review meeting. It is expected that the child will have been well prepared, their wishes and feelings sought before the review meeting (with the consultancy form completed) and that the IRO has met the child alone before the meeting to find out from the child key issues for discussion (or not).

7.148   Reviews will be held in the most appropriate venue for the child, which would usually be in their placement.

7.149   The review meeting should discuss and record a number of specified issues:

- the child's general progress in placement;

- the child's health needs (the child should have an annual medical examination, see the dentist 6 monthly and have an annual optician check-up);

- education needs (the review should ensure that the child's PEP is up to date. All looked-after children of statutory school age should have a PEP within 20 working days of entering care; effective communication between relevant professionals is an underlying principle of the PEP);

- identity needs;

- social presentation and self-care skills;

- emotional and behavioural development (the review should consider if there is a need for counselling or further assessment);

- family and social relations including review of contact;

- wishes and feelings;

- any complaints (the IRO should ensure that the child (and family) are aware of the complaints procedure and know how to complain should they be dissatisfied with the services provided);

- any amendments to be made to the care plan;

- a contingency plan in the event of placement breakdown; and

- whether an independent person or advocate is to be appointed for the child.

7.150   The review should also address whether an independent visitor or advocate should be appointed for the child. Local authorities are required[56] to

---

[56]   See the CA 1989, Sch 2, para 17 and the Definition of Independent Visitors (Children) Regulations 1991, SI 1991/892.

appoint 'independent visitors' for children and young people in their care who have had little or no contact with their parents for more than a year. Independent visitors are usually volunteers and are expected to make friends with children and young people, visiting them regularly and helping them participate in decisions about their future.

7.151 The child's care plan should be reviewed in light of the discussions about the child's progress in all domains of development. As already described, by the second review meeting (ie when the child has been in care for 4 months) the IRO should ensure that the permanent care plan is in place and make proposals for its implementation.

Respite reviews

7.152 Some children with disabilities have regularly planned respite care to support their care placement at home. If this amounts to more than 120 days in any one year or 20 days in a single episode the children will be considered as looked-after children. The review process for these children follows the standard format.

Changes of placement

7.153 Stability is a key principle in the support of children in public care. Stable care and school placements help to promote resilience in children and maintain self esteem. However, there are times when changes cannot be avoided due to placement breakdowns or are planned when the child moves on to a permanent placement. Most local authorities will regard a change of placement as a new episode of being looked after for purposes of reviews.[57] A review will be held within one month of the date of a new placement, 3 months after the first review, and 6 monthly thereafter.

SECTION 10 – RESOURCES OR PLACEMENT PANEL

7.154 Local authorities have established local panels (usually named resources or placement panels) to test the evidence that the threshold required to become looked after has been met under the CA 1989, s 20 (in care proceedings the threshold is tested firstly by a legal planning meeting and subsequently by the court) and also to carry out a quality assurance assessment of the subsequent care planning and placement for each looked-after child.

7.155 The core function of such panels is to monitor and review all expenditure on placements of looked-after children placed with in-house resources or in the private and voluntary sector. This function applies to both foster and residential placements and involves:

---

[57] Although it should be noted that there is no statutory duty for local authorities to regard respite placements as new placements for the purposes of reviewing a child's progress.

- scrutinising and gate keeping the plans and arrangements for placements to ensure effective assessment, care planning and decision-making is in place and that good value for money is being achieved;

- ensuring that children are not drifting in high cost placements;

- identifying those children who should be moved from private and voluntary placements back to in-house placements;

- maintaining an oversight of the financial management of the total placements budget.

7.156 The membership of the panel is usually multidisciplinary and includes managers from different sections of the local authority. The panel membership usually includes:

- a directorate member of Children and Families who would normally chair the panel;

- a special educational needs strategy manager;

- a manager for looked-after children in education;

- a fostering manager;

- a representative from in-house residential homes;

- a manager from the placements or fostering team;

- a manager from the children's social work team;

- a manager from Family Support Services;

- a manager from CAMHS Service;

- a manager from the asylum team; and

- a minute taker.

The local procedure of panels

7.157 There are no national guidance or legal requirements relating to the procedure of such panels, and the procedure below should be read as a general pro-forma which local authorities use:

- Panels meet fortnightly or monthly depending on each local authority's workload and the population of looked-after children.

- All children who become looked after or who move placements should be referred to the placements panel by the placement finding team, preferably before they are looked after, or, in an emergency, as soon afterwards as possible. Once a request for a placement has been accepted by the placements team they will be booked into the first available panel by the panel administrator, and the social worker and team manager would be expected to attend and/or submit written reports.

- Occasionally, it will be necessary for the chair of the panel to agree a placement outside of a panel meeting. In these circumstances the panel administrator will still book a place at the next panel meeting and inform the social worker and manager to attend.

- The placements panel will either agree the placement and set a review date or defer to another date for more information. In either case the decision will be minuted and signed by the chair. This will normally act as the financial agreement to the placement.

- The placements panel may decide to refer to the complex care panel for a discussion for joint funding. In this case the panel administrator will book it into the next available panel and inform the team manager and social worker.

- Every 3, 4 or 6 months (depending on local arrangements) the list of placements for all children looked after will be reviewed by the resources panel.

The complex needs panel

7.158 Children with complex needs have a number of discrete needs – relating to their health, education, welfare, development, and home environment – that require additional support from more than *one* agency. Their needs are often chronic and may be lifelong. These different needs tend to interact, exacerbating their impact on the child's development and well-being. Children with higher levels of need are often described as children with 'severe and complex needs' or children with 'significant and complex needs'.[58]

7.159 These are children and young people up to the age of 18 (or 19 for a young person with a statement of special educational needs) who may be in need of health, education and/or social care as a result of illness (congenital or acquired), degenerative disease, physical disability, sensory impairment, learning disability or significant psychological or psychiatric disturbance. Their needs may include complex care in the community, specialist residential homes, day and residential special schools, or support within a specialist health care setting such as therapeutic communities.

---

[58] The definition used by the Department for Education and Skills in *Every Child Matters*, Cm 5680 (TSO, 2003).

7.160   The range of services that may be available from the NHS includes:

- clinical care;

- primary health care support;

- NHS day care or day hospitals;

- community health services;

- assessments involving doctors, registered nurses and allied health professionals;

- rehabilitation;

- health support during short breaks or respite care;

- health care equipment;

- specialised transport services; and

- mental health services (CAMHS).

7.161   The range of services that may be available from the local authority social services department include:

- assessment and case management;

- support to carers and family members;

- children looked after away from home under the CA 1989, ss 20 and 31;

- day care support;

- respite care and short breaks;

- occupational therapy service, equipment and adaptations; and

- coordinating the safeguarding of all children.

7.162   The range of services that may be available from the education department include:

- educational psychology;

- specialist school provision;

- educational support services;

- hospital schools;

- in-school support;

- pupil referral units;

- Early Years support services;

- preschool provision; and

- safeguarding of all children.

7.163 Local authorities have a multi-agency panel for agreeing and reviewing packages of care for children and young people with complex and continuing health, social care and/or special educational needs. Panel members will normally include senior managers who have the authority to commit funds on behalf of their organisation or agency.

7.164 The local authority will fund placements only where there is agreement that the child needs to be looked after away from home, and that residential placement is the most appropriate way of meeting the child's care needs. A child will not normally become looked after purely because his or her health or educational needs cannot be met locally. However, funding may be sought from health and education in the event of the placement needs of the child requiring this.

SECTION 11 – UNACCOMPANIED ASYLUM SEEKING CHILDREN (UASC)

7.165 Unaccompanied asylum seeking children (UASC) are children or young persons under the age of 18 who have made a claim for asylum and who entered the UK without a parent, adult relative or adult household member.

The legal framework

7.166 In 2003 there were two key legal developments in relation to service provision for UASC: the *Hillingdon* judgment[59] and the subsequent Local Authority Circular LAC (2003)13[60] now expect local authorities to provide:

- support in accordance with s 20 of the CA 1989 to all UASC on arrival in their area, until an assessment has been completed;

---

[59] *R (on the application of Berhe) v Hillingdon London Borough Council* [2004] 1 FLR 439.
[60] *Guidance on accommodating children in need and their families.*

- provision of s 20 of the CA 1989 support based on an assessment of need to most UASC, including 16- and 17-year-olds. This includes entitlement to leaving care services.

7.167 Where older UASC refuse to become looked after, the local authority might, after taking account of the child's wishes as required under the CA 1989, s 20(6) decide that the child is able to look after himself and be supported under the CA 1989, s 17 and not become a looked-after child.

7.168 Section 17(6) of the CA 1989[61] now provides:

'The services provided by a local authority in the exercise of functions conferred on them by this section may include providing accommodation and giving assistance in kind or, in exceptional circumstances, in cash.'

7.169 However, the power is for local authorities to provide accommodation for families and children; and the provision of accommodation in this way does *not* make a child looked after.

7.170 A child who is accommodated under the CA 1989, s 17 is not considered to be 'looked after' and would not, therefore, be able to benefit from the provisions of the Children (Leaving Care) Act 2000. In *R (Berhe) v Hillingdon London Borough Council*,[62] it was held that s 17 can be used to accommodate UASC only in *exceptional circumstances*.

The assessment of need

7.171 LAC (2003)13 makes specific reference to supporting UASC:

'... where a child has no parent or guardian in this country, perhaps because he has arrived alone seeking asylum, the presumption should be that he would fall within the scope of section 20 and become looked after, unless the needs assessment reveals particular factors which would suggest that an alternative response would be more appropriate. While the needs assessment is being carried out, he should be cared for under section 20.'

7.172 The emphasis in LAC (2003)13 is on undertaking an assessment in accordance with the statutory guidance set out in the *Framework for the Assessment of Children in Need and their Families* (see Chapter 5) and states that the assessment should first determine whether the child meets the criteria set out in the CA 1989, s 20(1) which includes that 'there is no person who has parental responsibility for him'. Similarly, UASC are covered by the Children (Leaving Care) Act 2000 in exactly the same way as other children in this country.

---

[61] As amended by the Adoption and Children Act 2002, s 116.
[62] [2004] 1 FLR 439.

7.173 However, UASC have particular needs, the impact of which must be taken into account in their assessment. This includes:

- Immigration status – most UASC need support in relation to their application for asylum, acceptance as a refugee, and whether they are granted exceptional leave to remain or refused leave to remain.

- Their limited knowledge of the indigenous culture or services available. This is important in decision-making about whether to assist the UASC as requiring services under the CA 1989, s 17 (as amended) or as a person in need to be looked after.

- Language needs – many local authority staff may need to work with interpreters to understand unaccompanied minors whose first or chosen language may not be English.

- Their isolation from family, friends and community.

7.174

Checklist for lawyers representing UASC

- Did the local authority comply with the requirements of the *Hillingdon* judgment and LAC (2003)13?

- Was the young person who refused s 20 support services fully informed about the merits and differences between the amended s 17 and s 20 service provisions? (Given that the system is so complicated, it is important that the implications of opting for s 17 support are thoroughly explained to young people and that they are given the opportunity to reconsider at a later date, within the time limit-for them still to be entitled to access leaving care services)

- Has the local authority carried out a thorough needs assessment or was the assessment limited to an assessment of age or financial independence?

- Did the local authority address the particular needs of the child as a UASC?

- Is s 20 support provided at the level required by CA 1989 and the Children (Leaving Care) Act 2000, including the provision for each young person of:

  - an allocated social worker
  - a care plan
  - a personal education plan
  - access to leaving care services
  - regular statutory reviews?

- Do the staff have the knowledge and expertise to work with UASC? (This includes training about asylum legislation and procedures, age assessment, transition at 18, and dispelling myths about asylum seekers)

Chapter 8

FOSTERING

INTRODUCTION

8.1 Foster care is about providing alternative care when families would find this supportive, or where it is necessary either under s 20 of the Children Act 1989 (CA 1989) with the agreement of the parent(s) or as a compulsory intervention in family life in order to safeguard a child and promote their welfare.

8.2 Deciding to use foster placements can be a valuable choice for a child or young person and their family especially when providing a placement or a series of short breaks to help families under particular stress and struggling to meet the children's needs (e g for disabled children and young people).

8.3 Children are considered to be looked after when they are placed in foster care (or alternative accommodation). The local authority has responsibility to improve outcomes and actively promote the life chances of children they look after (this is referred to as 'corporate parenting'). The role of the local authority as the corporate parent is to act as the best possible parent for each child they look after and to take action by speaking out on their behalf, arranging for appropriate services to meet their needs, and standing up for them. Fostering services have a crucial role in this task, and they must ensure that the welfare, safety and individual needs of looked-after children are a central role of foster carers.

8.4 There are about 60,000 looked-after children at any one time, representing about 0.5% of the children's population in England and Wales. At 31 March 2009, 59% of looked-after children were on interim or full care orders, and 32% were voluntarily accommodated under s 20. Most of the remainder were placed under adoption agency regulations. About a third of all children and young people placed in foster care are in placements outside their local authority area.[1]

8.5 Under the sufficiency duty however, the local authority must ensure that there are sufficient foster care placements to meet the needs of looked-after children in the local area – ie specifically within the local authority boundary except where this is not consistent with the children's needs and welfare.

---

[1] Department of Education statistics.

8.6   Essentially the National Minimum Standards[2] specify that:

- the foster carer should be recognised as a core member of the team around the child with an important contribution to make in planning and decision-making about the child; and

- the central importance of the child's relationship with their foster carer should be acknowledged; and

- the work of the wider team around the child will be undertaken in a way that strengthens and supports the role of the foster carer.

SECTION 1 – TYPES OF FOSTERING ARRANGEMENTS

8.7   There are several types of fostering arrangements:

- *Foster carers*
  This includes:

  - short-term foster carers;
  - short-breaks and respite foster carers. This would include foster carers caring for disabled children as a means of supporting birth families;
  - foster carers specialising in caring for young people on remand;
  - foster carers providing parent and child placements;
  - permanent/long-term foster carers.

- *Family and Friends foster carers*
  This includes family relatives, friends or any other connected person to a specific child.[3]

- *Supportive lodgings*
  This describes accommodation for care leavers, and in some local authorities their approval is referred to the fostering panel.[4]

- *Private Fostering*
  This describes an arrangement that is essentially made privately (ie without the involvement of a local authority) for the care of a child under the age of 16 (under 18, if disabled) by someone other than a parent or close relative.[5]

---

[2]   Department for Education *Fostering Services: National Minimum Standards* (2011).
[3]   See Chapter 9 for family and friends carers.
[4]   See Chapter 13 for care leavers.
[5]   See section 13 below for duties of the local authority.

SECTION 2 – FOSTERING SERVICE PROVIDERS

8.8   Foster service providers include local authorities, as well as the voluntary, independent and private service providers. They must be registered and available for inspection by Ofsted.

8.9   Any foster service provider must meet the requirements set out in the Fostering Services (England) Regulations 2011.[6]

8.10   The requirements under reg 5(2) are that:

'(a)   the person is of integrity and good character,
(b)   the person is physically and mentally fit to carry on the fostering agency, and
(c)   full and satisfactory information is available in relation to the person in respect of each of the matters specified in Schedule 1.'

A person may not carry on a fostering agency if that person has been adjudged bankrupt (within the meaning of s 251A of the Insolvency Act 1986).

SECTION 3 – THE LEGAL FRAMEWORK

8.11   The relevant regulations and guidance are:

• the Fostering Services (England) Regulations 2011;

• the *Fostering Services: National Minimum Standards*;[7]

• *The Children Act 1989 Guidance and Regulations Volume 4: Fostering Services*;[8]

• *Short Breaks: Statutory guidance on how to safeguard and promote the welfare of disabled children using short breaks.*[9]

• *Sufficiency: Statutory guidance on securing sufficient accommodation for looked after children*;[10] and

• the Care Standards Act 2000.

What skills are foster carers expected to have?

8.12   Foster carers are expected to have a wide range of skills including:

• commitment to the fostering and caring task;

---

6   SI 2011/581.
7   Department for Education (2011).
8   HMSO, 2011.
9   Department for Children, Schools and Families (2010).
10   Department for Children, Schools and Families (2010).

- the ability to provide positive models of behaviour for children and young people;

- the ability to maintain appropriate personal boundaries and provide safe care for children;

- the ability to deal with the problems and difficulties children present;

- the ability to work constructively and openly with children, birth families and professional agencies;

- the capacity to prioritise and promote the best interests of children;

- the ability to be flexible and non-judgmental;

- the ability to negotiate and take full account of children's wishes and feelings;

- the ability to advocate on behalf of children placed in their care;

- the ability to demonstrate confidence in dealing with issues relating to gender, religion, ethnic origin, cultural background, linguistic background, nationality, disability or sexual orientation, and be able to involve external professional advice and support as necessary;

- the capacity to promote equality and to work in a way that challenges discrimination;

- the understanding and ability to empathise with children who have been neglected and/or abused;

- the understanding and ability to empathise with parents who have maltreated or been unable to protect and/or care for their children;

- the ability to care for any child placed with them as if the child was a child of the foster carer's family (reg 27(5)(b), para 2(a) of Sch 5). Foster carers should not treat the child differently to their own children;

- the capacity to maintain confidentiality.

8.13 In *R (Johns) v Derby City Council*,[11] the court considered the local authority's approach to the views of prospective foster carers about homosexuality.

8.14 It was held that the local authority is entitled to explore the extent to which prospective foster carers' beliefs may affect their *behaviour*, and their

---

[11] [2011] EWHC 375 (Admin).

treatment of a child being fostered by them. It was held that indeed if the local authority had failed to explore these matters it might very well have found itself in breach of its own guidance and of the National Minimum Standards for fostering and the statutory guidance. It was held that an examination by the local authority of the attitudes to homosexuality and same-sex relationships of a person who has applied to be a foster carer was not *Wednesbury* unreasonable, and that the attitudes of potential foster carers to sexuality are relevant when considering an application for approval.

SECTION 4 – THE ASSESSMENT OF FOSTER CARERS

8.15 Any person who is applying to become a foster carer should expect the following action from the local authority (or the fostering agency):

- To be sent an information pack about becoming a foster carer and the approval process, including details about their training needs, and complaint procedures within 5 days of making the initial enquiry.

- To be invited to an information giving meeting about the fostering and for the assessment process to be completed within a period of 8 months from the date of making the application.

- To be given a formal application form and forms giving consent for statutory checks and references, including Criminal Records Bureau (CRB) checks.

- To be considered as a potential foster carer regardless of marital status, race, religion, gender or sexual orientation. Assessment priority will be given to those applicants who are likely to reflect the needs of children and young people looked after by the local authority.

- To be invited to attend training. Preparation groups will focus on preparing applicants for the home assessment and becoming foster carers. The groups will provide applicants with an opportunity to learn as much as possible about the emotional, psychological and practical aspects of fostering and enable them to decide whether it is right for them. Training forms part of the assessment process.

- For the formal home assessment to begin within one month of completion of training and receipt of completed enhanced CRB checks.

- To be fully involved in the assessment process, and to identify, collect and organise the evidence required with the assessing social worker to prove that he or she meets the core requirements set out in National and Local Standards.

- To be fully informed of the assessment requirements and their responsibilities as foster carers, and to be supported through the evidence gathering process.

- To receive information about the local authority's policies and procedures, expected timescales for the assessment process (6 months), including details about their training needs, and be informed of the contents of reports made about them to the fostering panel.

- To receive a copy of the assessment report at least 28 days before the fostering panel and be given at least 10 working days to comment on the report.

- To be invited to attend the fostering panel considering their application and to be informed orally of the panel's recommendation within 24 hours.

- To be provided with information about decisions made about them with the reasons for the decisions made (subject to the fostering service provider's responsibility not to disclose confidential information about third parties).

- The right to seek representation against the decisions made if an applicant disagrees with the recommendation of the fostering panel, and/or the decision of agency decision-maker. Applicants should have 28 days to make representations.

Assessment reports about foster care applicants

8.16 A local authority will prioritise recruiting foster carers who live within the area of the local authority in accordance with s 22G of the CA 1989 (as inserted by s 9 of the Children and Young Persons Act 2008). This requires the local authority to take steps to secure sufficient accommodation to meet the needs of looked-after children in the local area (known as the 'sufficiency duty').[12]

8.17 No one has a right to be a foster carer,[13] and fostering decisions must focus on the interests of the child.

8.18 Assessment reports will be prepared by the assessing social worker on the basis of:

- personal interviews;

- household interviews (adults, children, and family unit as a group);

---

[12] Department for Children, Schools and Families (now DfE) *Sufficiency: Statutory guidance on securing sufficient accommodation for looked after children* (2010).
[13] See *EB v France* (2008) 47 EHRR 21.

- group preparation;

- participation in training;

- checks and at least two personal references (including health checks);

- any other external reports available to the assessing social worker (eg childminding and/or school reports and any other records and inspection reports on the applicant if he or she was previously approved but ceased to be, an approved foster carer with another foster care agency);

- checks with the local authority in whose area the applicants lives, if this is different from that of the fostering service;

- assessment of risk in relation to any family pets; and

- health and safety assessment of the house and garden.

8.19 Applicants must understand that the household as a whole is being assessed. Information as to the prospective foster parent and other members of their household and family is set out in Sch 3 of the Fostering Regulations 2011:

'1.   Full name, address and date of birth.
2.   Details of health (supported by a medical report), personality, marital status and details of current and any previous marriage, civil partnership or similar relationship.
3.   Particulars of any other adult members of the household.
4.   Particulars of the children in the family, whether or not members of the household, and any other children in the household.
5.   Particulars of their accommodation.
6.   Religious persuasion and capacity to care for a child from any particular religious persuasion.
7.   Racial origin, cultural and linguistic background and capacity to care for a child from any particular racial origin or cultural or linguistic background.
8.   Past and present employment or occupation, standard of living and leisure activities and interests.
9.   Previous experience (if any) of caring for their own and other children.
10.   Skills, competence and potential relevant to their capacity to care effectively for a child placed with them.
11.   The outcome of any request or application made by them or any other member of their household to foster or adopt children, or for registration as an early years provider or later years provider under Part 3 of the Childcare Act 2006, including particulars of any previous approval or refusal of approval relating to them or to any other member of the household.
12.   Names and addresses of two persons who will provide personal references for the prospective foster parent.
13.   In relation to the prospective foster parent and any other member of his household who is aged 18 or over, an enhanced criminal record certificate

issued under section 113B of the Police Act 1997 which includes suitability information relating to children (within the meaning of section 113BA(2) of that Act).'

8.20 Applicants should be encouraged by the assessing social worker to write about themselves, their family and social network, their lifestyle and reasons for their application. The personal records of applicants, if completed, will be presented to the panel. The absence of personal records from applicants will not affect the panel's recommendation, although the panel will expect the assessing social worker to address the applicants' decision not to write their personal record in their assessment.

8.21 Assessing social workers will prepare their assessment report (most local authorities use BAAF Form F). The reports must be typed and signed by the assessing social worker, team manager, and applicants before submission to the panel administrator, usually at least 10 working days before the panel meeting date.

8.22 The assessing social worker must verify the authenticity of all other documentation forming the assessment process. The documentation must include:

- proof of identity documentation together with photographs;

- a full employment history, together with a satisfactory written explanation of any gaps in employment;

- documentary evidence of any relevant qualification;

- enhanced CRB checks, and local authority checks;

- references (at least two personal references should be interviewed and it is helpful to interview adult children of either applicant as well as former partners);

- medical reports (the person providing the medical reports should have seen the applicant within the last 3 months of the report).

8.23 The local authority (or fostering agency) must verify that all relevant documentation was received and satisfactorily completed according to the required standards before accepting the application for consideration by the panel.

8.24 No foster carer will be approved unless he or she has been checked according to requirements and has demonstrated their ability (or potential ability by identification of transferable skills) to provide high quality parenting to children who have experienced trauma and disruptions in their early lives.

8.25 The panel must be satisfied that the reports indicate that applicants are fit enough to cope with looking after one to three children in addition to coping with any children of their own.

8.26 The National Minimum Standards 2011 reinforce the role of the foster carer as follows:

(1) As a parental figure with emphasis on:

- the 'good parent' (standard 3);
- the reasonable and responsible parent (standards 2 and 7);
- delegation of decision-making to foster carers about every day matters (standards 6 and 7, eg regarding health, contact, leisure);
- proportionate approach to risk taking (standard 4 in relation to activities and social development);
- the foster placement as a family home – to help child to feel as part of the family (standards 10 and 11).

(2) As empowering the child to be resilient and an active participant in decision-making:

- regarding consultations and information sharing (standard 2);
- in ensuring an understanding of safeguarding (standards 4 and 5), health (standard 6) and positive behaviour (standard 3);
- regarding education (standard 8).

(3) As a significant attachment figure for the child and valuing the importance of relationships. The advocacy role of the foster carer is noted in standard 6 (in relation to health) and 8 (in relation to education).

8.27 Fostering assessment reports should consider seven key areas:

- parenting capacity;

- providing a safe and caring environment;

- working with the children/young people and their families;

- working as a member of a team;

- own development;

- number of children; and

- size of the accommodation.

Parenting capacity

8.28   Assessments of parenting capacity should include:

- Capacity to provide good standard of care which promotes children's health, emotional, physical, social, sexual, and educational development.

- Understanding and knowledge of child development.

- Ability to promote identity and self esteem of children and/or young people from different backgrounds, and to promote cultural, religious, and racial identity.

- Ability to promote an anti-discriminatory approach to parenting.

- Ability to listen and communicate with children in a way that is appropriate to their level of maturity.

- Ability to provide appropriate boundaries and manage children's behaviour without using inappropriate means of discipline.

- Ability to accept the child as he or she is, and promote children's individual identities.

- Ability to promote a young person's development towards independence and adulthood.

Providing a safe and caring environment

8.29   Assessments of capacity to provide a safe and caring environment should include:

- Ability to manage children's special needs or disabilities (if appropriate).

- Ability to help children and/or young people to keep themselves safe, and know how to seek help if their safety is threatened.

- Ability to recognise the particular vulnerabilities to abuse of previously abused children and/or children with disabilities.

- Ability to provide adequate supervision, re-education and support to children who have been abused.

- Ability to work as a member of a team.

- Ability to work with other professionals, and to contribute to the care plans of children and/or young people.

- Ability to communicate effectively and keep professionals informed about any changes in their circumstances and about children or young people's welfare.

- Capacity for record keeping and maintaining confidentiality.

- Ability to promote diversity, equality and rights of children and young people.

- Ability to work with children, young people and their families.

- Commitment and ability to understand and meet children's needs in relation to their history, disability and other identity needs.

- Ability to work closely with children's families and significant others.

- Ability to work consistently and in partnership with children and their families.

- Ability to promote contact, manage children's needs and behaviour around contact.

- Ability to transfer children's attachments to their permanent placement and manage endings.

- Commitment and ability to understand and address the effects of discrimination, homophobia and racism on the development of children and young people.

Own development

8.30 Assessments of a carer's own development should include:

- Commitment and ability to use training effectively, and use what they have learned to improve their knowledge and/or skills.

- Ability to use support groups, personal and professional networks for their own support and development.

- Ability to sustain positive relationships when under stress.

Number of children

8.31 No foster carer will be approved to care for more than three children at any time (unless a sibling group).

8.32 Shared carers for disabled children are normally approved to look after no more than one child with disability at any one time, unless they are a sibling group.

Size of accommodation

8.33 Adequate accommodation arrangements to reflect child's own need for privacy and space.

8.34 The National Minimum Standards expect a child over the age of 3 to have their own bedroom, but this is not a requirement in the regulations. While many fostering service providers expect every child to have their own bedroom with a window to ensure the provision of space and privacy, the absence of a private bedroom cannot be a barrier to fostering unless this is essential for the child's welfare. Fostering agencies should undertake a risk assessment to demonstrate it is safe for a child to share bedrooms (see advice about sharing bedroom – DfE)

SECTION 5 – THE FOSTERING PANEL

8.35 A fostering service must constitute one or more fostering panels, as needed, with sufficient capacity to undertake the required duties of such panels. A fostering panel may be constituted jointly by any two or more fostering service providers, whether local authority or independent. Constitution and membership of panels are set out in regs 23 and 24 and standard 14.

8.36 Like adoption agencies, fostering services providers must produce a statement of purpose outlining aims and objectives, and facilities offered. The fostering service provider must also produce a children's guide to reflect these and include information about making complaints. There must also be a written policy and procedure for panels.

The functions of the fostering panel

8.37 Fostering panels are intended as multi-disciplinary bodies with a considerable element of independence from the fostering service. This independence means that they cannot themselves make decisions, which are the responsibility of the fostering service, but instead make recommendations in relation to their statutory functions. The functions are:

- consider applications for approval and to recommend whether or not a person is suitable to act as a foster carer, and if so the terms on which they should be approved (eg number and age of children to be placed);

- consider the first review of newly approved foster carers, and any subsequent reviews referred to it by the fostering service,

- to recommend whether or not the foster carers remain suitable and if the terms of their approval remain appropriate;

- to advise on, and monitor the effectiveness of, the procedures for undertaking reviews of foster carers; and

- to give advice and make recommendations on any other matters or cases referred to the panel by the fostering service. This could include:

  - identifying areas for further development in the knowledge and skills of applicants and/or foster carers, and make recommendations for future training;
  - considering any complaints made by foster carers, and make recommendations to the fostering service provider about the appropriate forum for investigation and/or resolution of complaints;
  - giving advice in relation to exemptions to the usual caring criteria, and to monitor and review the use of exemptions by the fostering service provider;
  - assisting the fostering service provider in improving quality of care to looked-after children, and alert the fostering service provider to any concerns brought to their attention in the course of their work;
  - informing the fostering service provider when any child and/or young person brought to their attention during a carer's annual review has no up-to-date care plan;
  - promoting equality in practice, and challenge all forms of discrimination;
  - monitoring the effectiveness and quality of the panel's recommendations annually by receiving annual reports from the fostering service provider outlining any placement breakdowns, exemptions, and complaints received over the previous year.

The members of fostering panels

8.38 There is no requirement for a fixed panel membership; however, it is recommended that panel has a core list of members. There is no limit on the number of people who may be included on the core list of panel membership. The regulations recommend that fostering services should have a pool of people with different skills, experience and qualifications to allow it to work effectively.

8.39 The central list of members should include:

- at least one social worker with a minimum of 3 years child care social work (including fostering experience) post qualifying experience;

- people with experience of fostering (could include foster carers), education, short-break care and family and friends care, be gender balanced and reflect the diversity of the local community;

- elected members; as representatives of the corporate parent they may also make a valuable contribution as panel members.

8.40 It is for the fostering service to decide how many panel members should be present at each panel meeting, subject to each meeting being quorum. There is no limit set on the number of people who may be appointed to a panel, but a panel should not be so large as to make it difficult to chair a meeting of the panel or be intimidating to prospective foster carers or anyone else attending the meeting.

8.41 The fostering agency must appoint:

- An independent chair from the pool of panel members. Independence being defined by reg 23(10)(a). In the case of a local authority fostering agency they must not be an elected member of the local authority, or someone who is employed within the fostering service or any other part of the authority in connection with making or providing placements or protection of children.
  The panel chair should have:

  - a sound understanding of the fostering process;
  - the authority and competence to chair the panel;
  - the ability to analyse and explain complex information;
  - the ability to identify key issues, problems and solutions; and
  - excellent interpersonal, oral and written communication skills.

- One or two vice chairs, being members of the fostering panel, who can act as chair if the regular chair is unable to chair a meeting or the office is vacant. There is no requirement for the vice chair to be independent of the fostering agency.

8.42 Regulation 24 prescribes a quorum of minimum five members which must be met for a fostering panel to conduct any business. The quorum must always include:

- the chair or a vice chair;

- a social worker with 3 years relevant post-qualifying experience;

- at least three other members or four in the case of a panel set up jointly by one or more service providers; and

- in the event that the chair is not present, a member (who could be one of the people listed above) who is independent of the fostering service.

8.43 A fostering panel may obtain any legal or medical advice it considers necessary in relation to its business, so far as this is reasonably practicable. This is best provided by the identification of a named medical adviser and legal adviser to the panel, who might also be shared with an adoption panel or another fostering panel. Such advisers are not required to be members of the fostering panel (although they may be) and may supply information either in writing or by attending panel meetings, as required.

The appointment of panel members

8.44 The fostering service provider is responsible for the appointment of fostering panel members. There are no stipulations about the recruitment of panel members and most are recruited through personal contacts and recommendations about individuals. Although this can work well, it can also lead to panel members being drawn from a narrow group of people already known to the fostering service provider.

8.45 Panel membership should be chosen on the basis of knowledge, experience and skills of individuals that are relevant to the functions of the panel.

8.46 The National Minimum Standards stipulate that panel members will only be appointed subject to CRB checks.

8.47 Any panel member may resign his or her office at any time by giving one month's notice in writing to the fostering service provider.

8.48 Before appointing any panel member or including them on the central list, the fostering service should inform them in writing of their performance objectives, which should include participation in induction and training, and safeguarding the confidentiality of records and information submitted to the panel. Panel members should sign an acceptance form to record their agreement to these objectives.

8.49 Each panel member's performance, including that of the chair, should be reviewed annually against agreed performance objectives.

8.50 Where the fostering service provider is of the opinion that any member of the panel is unsuitable or unable to remain in office, it may terminate his or her office at any time by giving him or her one month's notice in writing.

8.51 There is no prescribed maximum or minimum tenure, although the fostering service should plan and manage turnover in such a way that it avoids the need to replace a large proportion of the members in any one year. This may best be achieved through establishing clarity of role and reviewing appointments to the panel and those who are included on the central list regularly. Equally the fostering service will need to be mindful of the need to have a certain level of turnover to provide for a fresh perspective.

8.52

The expectations of fostering panel members

- To sign a written agreement to maintain confidentiality of information, and store all documents received concerning the panel in a safe and secure place.

- To read panel papers prior to panel meeting and prepare comments, questions and/or clarifications.

- To attend all panel meetings as required, and submit apologies at the earliest opportunity if they are unable to attend. Most fostering service providers have monthly panel meetings and also allow for some additional meetings, depending on demand. It is expected that members will attend not less then 75% of panel meetings per annum. Attendance is considered at the members' annual performance interview.

- To declare an 'interest' when having prior knowledge of any applicant brought before the panel. The panel member should not participate in discussions about applicants when their knowledge of them will prejudice their consideration.

- To inform the fostering service provider at once if they have been charged, cautioned or convicted for any criminal offence.

- To return to the administrator their numbered copy of documents at the end of every panel meeting for shredding and safe disposal.

- To attend training and business meetings as required. It is expected that training would be provided on an annual basis. Business meetings are expected to be held at 6 monthly intervals.

- New members are expected to serve the panel for 3 years.

The role of the fostering agency in relation to the work of the panel

8.53 The fostering agency must carry out a number of tasks in relation to the fostering panel:

- To coordinate and administer the panel.

- To receive reports (most use BAAF Form F's or locally designed review forms as appropriate) about applicants, and to check that *all* relevant documentation and checks have been carried out according to requirements.

- To inform assessing social worker and team manager of any omissions, and reject applications unless full, complete and signed reports are received by the due date.

- To copy and number reports, and distribute these to panel members to be received in good time (usually at least 5 working days) before the panel meeting.

- To keep written minutes of the panel's business, including the reasons for recommendations made. It is important that these are full and accurate so that the fostering service decision-maker is clear about matters discussed and the reasoning behind recommendations, as they will form the basis of decision made.

- To inform the assessing social workers of the panel's recommendation no later than 24 hours following the panel meeting.

- To reimburse panel members for the costs of travel and payment of fee (if agreed) for reading panel papers and attendance.

- To inform all other authorities and relevant agencies in cases of termination of approvals by the panel.

The role of the fostering panel chair

8.54 The fostering panel chair must carry out a number of tasks in relation to the fostering panel:

- To ensure that the panel's recommendations about approvals include any details of the criteria of approval or reasons for refusal to approve.

- To approve and sign the recommendations of the panel and ensure that applicants are provided with the terms and conditions of their approval together with information about their right to representation and/or appeal the panel's recommendation.

- To meet with applicants and/or foster carers requesting representation, and refer them for reconsideration by the panel in the event of receiving evidence suggesting that its recommendation may have been influenced by factual errors and/or discriminatory practices.

- To advise the fostering service provider about panel membership and highlight any omissions in expertise and/or community representations.

- To review members' length of service with the advisor to the panel and inform the fostering service provider when any member has served 3 years on the panel.

- To inform the fostering service provider of any childcare issues and concerns brought to attention of the panel in the course of its work.

- To attend foster carers' support groups as appropriate.

- With the assistance of the panel advisor and panel members, to prepare an annual report to the fostering service provider outlining the work of the panel and making recommendations for any operational or policy issues that need to be addressed.

Conduct of the fostering panel meeting

8.55 At least five members must be present for the panel meeting to be quorate, one of whom must be the chair or the vice chair, one of whom must be an employee of the fostering service provider, and at least two must be independent members.

8.56 Meetings are held not less than once per month. The venue and times of meetings take into account the needs of existing carers where possible.

8.57 The panel will consider applicants for approval or re-approval only when *all* relevant documentation[14] and reports have been signed by applicants. Applications to the panel may be approved, re-approved, terminated, rejected or deferred for further information. When applications are recommended for approval or rejection, the agency decision-maker has the power to overturn recommendations of the panel.

8.58 The panel administrator sends applicants an invitation to attend the panel meeting confirming the date, time and venue. Applicants will also be sent:

- procedures for conducting the panel meeting;

- profile of panel members;

- feedback evaluation form; and

- information about their right to make representations to the fostering agency provider following a decision by the agency.

8.59 Applicants should be prepared by their assessing social worker to attend the panel meeting who will provide them with a copy of the assessment report (usually BAAF Form F) for initial approval (or completed review report for re-approvals) which applicants should sign to approve distribution to panel members.

---

[14] The relevant documentation must include the application form, references, responses to all checks, medical report, information from group work/training, an assessment report (Form F or annual review form), and any other assessment tools.

8.60   As part of their assessment process, applicants are expected to attend the panel meetings considering their initial application for approval and their first re-approval meeting. They should be strongly encouraged to attend all other meetings considering their re-approval or termination, to ensure their involvement in the decision-making processes. Applications (for initial approval and first re-approval) would *not* normally be considered by the panel without the applicants being present unless they are excused from attending by the panel.

8.61   Applicants will be asked to withdraw from the meeting once representations and questions have been completed, allowing the panel members to make their recommendations, and enable the chair to inform applicants of the recommendation made immediately thereafter.

8.62   Written records will be kept of the panel's recommendations. Differences of opinion among panel members will be recorded, together with a note of any dissent from the final recommendation.

What happens following the fostering panel meeting?

8.63   The fostering panel chair will inform the applicants verbally of the panel's recommendation immediately after the meeting. If the applicants are absent, it is expected that they will be informed verbally of the panel's recommendation by their assessing social worker no later than 48 hours following the panel meeting.

8.64   Following the panel meeting, the fostering agency will pass the approved minutes, including the recommendation made by the panel, to the fostering service provider's decision-maker for a decision.

8.65   Written confirmation of the decision, together with reasons for the decision will be sent to applicants by the fostering service provider as soon as practicable.

8.66   Decisions of the fostering service provider are subject to representations by applicants who are dissatisfied with the decision-making process. In the event that the fostering service provider's decision-maker endorses the recommendations of the panel, applicants will be invited to meet with the panel chair to question the recommendations made if they so wish. The request for representation must be made within 14 days of receipt of written confirmation of the decision. The panel will then reconsider the case in light of the presentations made.

SECTION 6 – THE LOCAL AUTHORITY'S DECISIONS ABOUT FOSTERING

Recommendations v decisions

8.67 The fostering panel can only make *recommendations* regarding the cases referred to it.

8.68 The fostering service must identify a senior member of staff (usually referred to as the decision-maker) who will receive the panel's recommendations and make decisions as required. More than one decision-maker may be appointed, but they may not delegate their authority to another person. Standard 23 sets out the qualifications, knowledge and experience required of the decision-maker.

8.69 Regulation 27 requires that the decision-maker must take account of the fostering panel's recommendation before deciding whether or not to approve a person as a foster carer, and on what terms. Their decision must be made within 7 working days of receipt of the panel's recommendation via the minutes (standard 14).

8.70 In reaching a decision or making a qualifying determination, the decision-maker should:[15]

- list the material taken into account in reaching the decision;

- identify key arguments;

- consider whether they agree with the process and approach of the relevant panel(s) and are satisfied as to its fairness and that the panel(s) has properly addressed the arguments;

- consider whether any additional information now available to them that was not before the panel has an impact on its reasons or recommendation;

- identify the reasons given for the relevant recommendation that they do or do not wish to adopt; and

- state (a) the adopted reasons by cross reference or otherwise and (b) any further reasons for their decision.

The approval of foster carers

8.71 Once a foster carer is approved, they must be notified of this fact in writing and of any terms of the approval. Terms may specify, for instance, that they may foster only a specific named child or children, or may identify a maximum number of placements which may be made at any one time or an age

---

[15] See *Hofstetter v LB Barnet and IRM* [2009] EWHC 3282 (Admin).

range for children fostered. Terms may also include factors such as short-term or long-term placements, short break care, or inclusion in a particular fostering scheme. Foster carers must also enter into a foster care agreement, covering the matters set out in Sch 5 to the Regulations (reg 2 and standard 14).

8.72 Foster carers would normally be approved to care for no more than three children (Sch 7 to the CA 1989) unless:

- the foster children are all siblings in relation to each other (in which case there is no upper limit); or

- the local authority within whose area the foster carer lives exempts the foster carer from the usual fostering limit in relation to specific placements.

8.73 In considering whether to exempt a person from the usual fostering limit, a local authority must have regard, in particular, to:

- the number of children whom the person proposes to foster;

- the arrangements which the person proposes for the care and accommodation of the fostered children;

- the intended and likely relationship between the person and the fostered children;

- the period of time for which he or she proposes to foster the children; and

- whether the welfare of the fostered children (and of any other children who are or will be living in the accommodation) will be safeguarded and promoted.

8.74 The local authority should nominate an officer with delegated powers to grant exemptions from the usual fostering limit, and ensure that fostering services and agencies operating within the area are aware of the procedures to be followed in requesting such exemptions.

8.75 A child who is not looked after does not count towards the usual fostering limit. Nevertheless the needs of all children within the household must be taken into account in deciding whether to grant an exemption from the usual fostering limit. This will be pertinent, for instance, if the foster carer is also offering parent and child arrangements.

SECTION 7 – WHAT SHOULD APPROVED FOSTER CARERS EXPECT FROM THE LOCAL AUTHORITY?

8.76   Local authorities must carry out a number of actions in relation to foster carers who are approved:

- To be issued with an agreed form of identity to enable their role as foster carers to be verified.

- To be allocated a supervising social worker who will guide and support them in undertaking their task as foster carers.

- To be offered such training, advice, information and support, including support outside office hours, as appears necessary in the interests of children placed with them Incremental training courses may also be provided and ensure that, where possible, courses are linked to possible qualifications such as NVQs.

- To be provided with details about the local and national foster care association (FCA) and be encouraged to attend support groups.

- For their experience and views to be valued and to be fully involved in the planning and decision-making around the children and young people with whom they are working.

- For their practical needs relating to each placement to be addressed prior to or at the time of the placement and not in retrospect. Social workers should respect the foster carer's family life and wherever possible arrange visits at times that are convenient to them.

- To be provided with all the information they need about the child to enable them to provide appropriate care, and make sure that this information is kept up to date. This information must include the most recent version of the child's care plan provided to the fostering service provider under reg 6(3)(d) of the Care Planning, Placement and Case Review (England) Regulations 2010.[16]

- When a placement is made in an emergency, the information should be provided at the time of placement. Any missing information should be supplied as soon as possible and certainly within 5 working days of placement (regs 9(2) and 17 of the 2010 Regulations and standard 15).

- The foster carers should play an active role in agreeing the contents of the child's placement plan and must have a copy of the child's placement plan (standard 31). Sch 2 of the 2010 Regulations sets out the matters which

---

[16]   SI 2010/959 ('the 2010 Regulations').

must be included in the placement plan, and relevant statutory guidance is included in *Volume 4: Fostering Services*.[17]

- Foster carers should be given the maximum appropriate flexibility to take decisions relating to children in their care, within the framework of the agreed placement plan and the law governing parental responsibility (PR). Except where there are particular identified factors which dictate to the contrary, foster carers should be given delegated authority to make day-to-day decisions regarding health, education, leisure, etc.

- To work in partnership with professionals, and to be actively informed and consulted to ensure that every aspect of the fostering task and any policy changes are understood.

- In circumstances of an allegation being made against a foster carer, the fostering service should make support, which is independent of the fostering service, available to the person subject to the allegation and, where this is a foster carer, to their household. This support is to provide:

    – information and advice about the process;
    – emotional support; and,
    – if needed, mediation between the foster carer and the fostering service and/or advocacy (including attendance at meetings and panel hearings).

SECTION 8 – WHAT SHOULD CHILDREN EXPECT FROM THE FOSTERING SERVICE?

8.77 The local authority must carry out a number of actions in relation to children who are placed in foster care:

- Children should be matched with an appropriate foster carer capable of meeting their needs. They should feel welcomed into the foster home, treated and valued as a member of the family, and included in the everyday life of the family. They should in due course leave a placement in a planned and sensitive manner which makes them feel valued.

- Brothers and sisters should be placed together in the same placement as long as this is consistent with their welfare.

- Any placement should not disrupt the child's education or training if at all possible.[18]

---

[17] The *Children Act 1989 Guidance and Regulations: Volume 4: Fostering Services* (HMSO, 2010).
[18] CA 1989, ss 22C(7) and (8)(b).

- Having regard to the child's age and understanding, their views, wishes and feelings must be known, listened to and acted upon in all aspects of their care in the foster home, unless to do so would be contrary to their interests or adversely affects other members of the foster care household. When this is the case, it is important that children are helped to understand why decisions have been made that are contrary to their wishes and views. The views of their family and others who are significant to them should also be sought and taken into consideration.[19]

- The particular needs of children and young people with disabilities, special educational needs or complex needs must be fully recognised and taken into account when decisions are made about them, and their wishes and feelings must always be established and taken into account.

- Appropriate arrangements should be made to support children and young people for whom English is not their first language (especially refugees and asylum seekers), carefully taking into account the individual child's circumstances. Appropriate arrangements should also be made for children with disabilities which affect their ability to communicate verbally.

- All children and young people should be given information, appropriate explanations and choices about what happens to them. This requires skilled and confident foster carers.

- Every child or young person in a foster home should be able, without permission or discussing the reason why, to contact their social worker or their independent reviewing officer if they wish. They should be able to do this in private.

- Children in foster care must know how to make a complaint or representation to the local authority, be given information by their social worker about how to make a complaint, and be supported to do so if they wish by foster carers and staff of the fostering service, or by any independent person they choose to support them.

- Other than in an emergency, a child must only be placed with a foster carer whose terms of approval match the child's circumstances, although in an emergency a child may be placed for up to 6 working days with any foster carer who has been approved under the 2011 Regulations.

- Every individual child who is looked after should be cared for in a way that respects, recognises, supports and celebrates their identity and provides them all with care, support and opportunities to maximise their individual potential.

---

[19] National Minimum Standards (2011), standard 1.

- Foster carers are to give full attention to the individual child's gender, faith, ethnic origin, cultural and linguistic background, sexual orientation and any disability they might have.[20]

- Children and young people should not move to another placement, unless this is by agreement following a statutory review, it is clearly in the child or young person's best interests, the decision has taken into account the child or young person's wishes and feelings, and the move is properly planned.

- When a placement breaks down it is important not to assume that it means the child or foster carer is at fault.

- When delegating authority to foster carers, wherever practicable the child should be consulted over the issues and their views and feelings taken into account in reaching the decision. Any restrictions (eg for overnight stays with friends, visiting relatives, school trips) and the reasons for it should be fully explained to the child concerned unless, exceptionally, this would not be consistent with the child's welfare. Any restrictions should be reviewed regularly to ensure that they remain relevant.

- Subject to any court order and the contents of the placement plan, the fostering service has a duty to promote contact between a child placed with a foster carer and his parents, relatives and friends, unless such contact is not practicable or consistent with the child's welfare.

- For their welfare to be promoted by providing an environment in the foster home in which all members of the household respect each other's privacy and dignity. Children and young people should be given their own private space, and places to keep their own belongings, do homework, see friends and family, manage personal issues and feel safe.

SECTION 9 – WHAT SHOULD PARENTS EXPECT FROM THE LOCAL AUTHORITY?

8.78 The local authority must carry out a number of actions in relation to parents of children who are placed in foster care:

- To be invited to attend and/or contribute to all childcare review meetings. When appropriate to meet with the independent reviewing officer outside the review meeting.

- Parents whose child is subject to a care, interim or emergency protection order should be consulted about their child's care and their views taken into account.

---

[20] National Minimum Standards (2011), standard 2.

- For their contact with their children to be promoted and supported unless this is not consistent with the child's safeguarding and welfare needs. In circumstances of disagreement the local authority may restrict contact only under court orders and/or the child is subject to an emergency protection order, interim care order or care order.

- To have unrestricted contact with their children if they are looked after under s 20 unless this is with their agreement.

- If a child is subject to a care order, interim care order or emergency protection order, the local authority must be clear with the parents about the extent of any limits may be imposed on them in exercising their parental responsibilities to safeguard or promote their child's welfare.

- If a child is placed voluntarily under s 20 of the CA 1989, the local authority does not have PR and so agreement must be reached about what decision-making the parents will delegate to the local authority. The local authority should work with the parent(s) as far as possible to help them understand the benefits to their child of appropriate delegation to the local authority and foster carers.

- Arrangements for delegating authority from the parents to the local authority must be discussed and agreed as part of the care planning process, particularly at placement planning meetings, and agreements should be recorded in the placement plan.

- Agreements about delegation of authority should therefore be regularly reviewed through care planning and review meetings, taking into account the views of birth parent(s), the child, the foster carer and the legal status of the placement; any changes should be recorded in the placement plan.

- Each fostering service should have a designated person, who is a senior manager, responsible for managing allegations against foster carers. The designated person should keep the subject of the allegation informed of progress during and after the investigation.

SECTION 10 – INVESTIGATING ALLEGATIONS ABOUT FOSTER CARERS

8.79 In the event of an allegation being made against a foster carer, the fostering service provider will take any allegation made by a child seriously and will carry out an investigation.

8.80 The fostering service must make a clear distinction between investigations into allegations of harm and discussions over standards of care.

An investigation which finds no evidence of harm should not become a procedure to look into poor standards of care, which should be addressed separately.

8.81 Foster carers must be given appropriate information about any allegation made against them and the reasons for an unplanned removal of a child. The possible risk of harm to children posed by an accused person needs to be effectively evaluated and managed. Foster carers must not be suspended automatically or without careful thought.

8.82 The fostering agency must have clear policy and procedures. The policy and procedures should reflect the requirements of the Local Safeguarding Children Board of the area where the foster carer lives, and as far as possible those of the responsible authority.

8.83 The time taken to investigate and resolve individual cases would depend on a variety of factors (including the nature, seriousness and complexity of the allegation) but it is expected that 80% of cases should be resolved within one month, 90% within 3 months, and all but the most exceptional cases should be completed within 12 months. For those cases where it is clear immediately that the allegation is unfounded or malicious, it is expected that they should be resolved within one week.

8.84 Each fostering service should have a designated person, who is a senior manager, responsible for managing allegations against foster carers. The designated person should keep the subject of the allegation informed of progress during and after the investigation.

8.85 Child protection investigations involving foster carers should be conducted, where possible, by a worker independent of the fostering provider service. The foster carer should also be given an assigned support worker for themselves during the course of any investigation.

8.86 The fostering service should make support, which is independent of the fostering service, available to the person subject to the allegation and, where this is a foster carer, to their household. This support is to provide:

• information and advice about the process;

• emotional support; and

• if needed, mediation between the foster carer and the fostering service and/or advocacy (including attendance at meetings and panel hearings).

8.87 Each fostering service should have a designated person, who is a senior manager, responsible for managing allegations. The designated person should keep the subject of the allegation informed of progress during and after the investigation.

SECTION 11 – REVIEWS OF FOSTER CARERS

8.88   Foster carers are approved for one year and they are subject to annual reviews. The fostering panel is required to consider the first review of all foster carers.

8.89   The panel will also consider subsequent reviews as referred to it by the fostering service providers.

8.90   Other circumstances in which annual reviews may return to the panel for consideration are when:

- there have been complaints by or against the carer, including in all circumstances of s 47 investigations;

- the fostering service provider is considering changes to approval range (eg from preschool age to school age);

- there are applications for exemptions from the approval range or number of children.

8.91   The purpose of the review is to provide an appraisal of foster carers' abilities and experience of fostering over the year. The views of the children placed and their families should be sought, subject to their level of understanding, as well as the views of the foster carers' own children and family members and the social workers involved.

SECTION 12 – TERMINATION OF APPROVAL OF FOSTER CARERS

8.92   Particular requirements apply in circumstances where the fostering service considers that an applicant is unsuitable to be a foster carer or that the foster carer's terms of approval should be changed.

8.93   The applicant must be given a written determination – a notice that the decision-maker proposes not to approve them as a foster carer or to amend their terms of approval, together with the reasons for this and, where the fostering panel made a recommendation, a copy of this.[21]

8.94   The applicant must be advised that they may, within 28 days of the date of the notice, either submit written representations to the decision-maker, or apply to the Secretary of State for a review of the determination by the Independent Review Mechanism (IRM). The option to apply to the IRM does not apply if the applicant is considered unsuitable in accordance with reg 27(6).

---

[21]   This is defined as a qualifying determination by or reg 4 of the Independent Review of Determinations (Adoption and Fostering) Regulations 2009, SI 2009/395.

8.95 If within 28 days no representations are received and no application is made to the IRM, the decision-maker is free to determine whether or not to approve the applicant as a foster carer. If however representations are received, the matter must be referred back to the fostering panel, and a decision then made taking account of the panel's further recommendations.

8.96 If the application is referred to the IRM, the fostering service must, within 10 days of notification of this, supply the IRM with the documentation submitted to the fostering panel and any relevant information received subsequently, along with copies of the notices of determination (reg 29). The decision-maker must take account of the recommendation of the IRM, as well as that of the original fostering panel, in reaching a decision about approval.

SECTION 13 – PRIVATE FOSTERING ARRANGEMENTS

Legal framework

8.97 Private fostering arrangements are governed by a range of legislation:

- Children Act 1989: Pt IX and Schs 7 and 8, as amended by s 44 of the Children Act 2004;

- The Children (Private Arrangement for Fostering) Regulations 2005;[22]

- *Children Act 1989 Guidance on Private Fostering*, issued in 2005;[23]

- *National Minimum Standards for Private Fostering*;[24] and

- The Disqualification for Caring for Children (England) Regulations 2002.[25]

8.98 A private fostering arrangement is essentially one that is made privately (ie without the involvement of a local authority) for the care of a child under the age of 16 (under 18, if disabled) by someone other than a parent or close relative with the intention that the arrangement should last for 28 days or more. Private foster carers may be members of the child's extended family (eg a cousin or great aunt). However, a person who is a relative[26] (ie a grandparent, brother, sister, uncle or aunt (whether of full blood or half blood or by marriage) or step-parent) will not be a private foster carer. A private foster carer may also be a friend of the family, the parent of a friend of the child, or someone previously unknown to the child's family who is willing to privately foster a child.

---

[22] SI 2005/1533.
[23] The *Children Act 1989 Guidance and Regulations: Volume 4: Fostering Services* (HMSO, 2010).
[24] Department for Education and Skill *National Minimum Standards for Private Fostering* (TSO, 2005).
[25] SI 2002/635.
[26] As defined by the CA 1989, s 105(1).

8.99 Regulation 3 of the Children (Private Arrangements for Fostering) Regulations 2005 requires any person proposing to foster a child privately, any person involved (whether directly or not) in arranging for the child to be fostered privately, and a parent of the child or other person with parental responsibility for the child who knows that it is proposed to foster the children privately, to notify the appropriate local authority in advance of the arrangement starting. Notification by the proposed private foster carer has to be given at least 6 weeks before the private fostering arrangement is to begin, or where the arrangement is to begin within 6 weeks then immediately.

8.100 Having received a notification the local authority then has a duty to undertake an assessment (under Sch 2). A child who is privately fostered may also be assessed as a child in need, and be provided with support under s 17 of the CA 1989.

8.101 Private foster carers need not be considered by the local authority's fostering panel, although some local authorities refer private fostering arrangements to their fostering panel for recommendations about the suitability of all aspects of any proposed or existing private fostering arrangements in accordance with the Children (Private Arrangements for Fostering) Regulations 2005 and the *National Minimum Standards for Private Fostering*.

Duties relating to private fostering

8.102 The local authority has an overall duty to satisfy itself that the welfare of children who are privately fostered in their area is being satisfactorily safeguarded and promoted.[27] The local authority does not approve private fostering arrangements but it must supervise and regulate the placements.

8.103 Most local authority will have a designated worker within the fostering service dealing with private fostering arrangements, although the first visit may be carried out by the first response team.

8.104 Private fostering reports to the fostering panel will be prepared by the assessing social worker on the basis of:

- personal interviews with the private foster carer;

- personal interviews with the parents;

- personal interviews with the child; and

- interviews with all adults and children in the household.

---

[27]   CA 1989, ss 17–19, and Sch 2.

8.105 Private fostering assessment reports should address the following issues:

- whether the child's physical, intellectual, emotional, social and behavioural development is appropriate and satisfactory (once the private fostering arrangement has begun);

- the ascertainable wishes and feelings of the child about the proposed/actual private fostering arrangement;

- whether the child's needs arising from his or her religious persuasion, racial origin and cultural and linguistic background are being met (once the private fostering arrangement has begun);

- the steps taken to make arrangements for the care of the child's health (and once the private fostering arrangement has begun, that these arrangements are in place and, in particular, that the child is included on a GP's list);

- the steps taken to make arrangements for the child's education (and once the private fostering arrangement has begun, that these arrangements are in place);

- the standard of care provided for each privately fostered child;

- the contact arrangements between the child and his or her family (including with parents and siblings) and whether these will be/are satisfactory for the child;

- how decisions about the child's day-to-day care will be/are being taken;

- the financial arrangements for the care and maintenance of the child and whether these arrangements have been agreed between the parents and private foster carer (and once the private fostering arrangement has begun, that these arrangements are working satisfactorily);

- the capacity of the proposed/actual private foster carer to look after the child, and the suitability of members of their household and premises (including whether the private foster carer or anyone in the household is disqualified from privately fostering children);

- how the local authority will satisfy itself that the welfare of privately fostered child(ren) is satisfactorily safeguarded and promoted, including details about:

  - the monitoring and appointment of a responsible key worker; and
  - the support to be given to the private foster carer, child and/or parent;

- any training that may be available to private foster carers (including prospective private foster carers);

- the intended duration of the private fostering arrangement that is understood and agreed between the parent, child and the private foster carer;

- the capacity of the proposed or actual private foster carer to look after the child and the suitability of household members;

- a consideration of whether the child who is, or is proposed to be, privately fostered poses any risk of harm to children already living in the private foster carer's household, and whether those children pose a risk of harm to him, using the dimensions and domains in the *Framework for Assessment*[28] (see Chapter 5).

8.106 These reports should include:

- a clear statement of conclusions, including details of any matter for concern;

- details about whether the child was seen alone;

- reasons why the assessing social worker considered it inappropriate to see the child alone where appropriate;

- the child's wishes and feelings about the arrangement;

- comment about the child's welfare and whether the placement is satisfactory; and

- any comments about these matters made by the child or the carer.

Unsatisfactory private fostering arrangement

8.107 The local authority can prevent an individual from becoming a private foster carer according to ss 68 and 69 of the CA 1989; examples include:

- The carer had been convicted of or cautioned for any offence against a child and/or has been placed on probation or discharged absolutely or conditionally for any such offence or if this applies to any adult living in the household.

- If the carer had previously been prohibited by the local authority from being a foster carer.

---

[28]   Department of Health *Framework for the Assessment of Children in Need and Their Families* (TSO, 2000).

- If the outcome of the assessment finds the proposed carer is not suitable to privately foster a child.

- If the premises in which the child will be, or is being accommodated are found to be not suitable.

- If it is found that the care by the individual would negatively impact the child's welfare.

- The requirements being imposed by the local authority are not achievable by the carers.

8.108 Should the local authority find the placement to be unsatisfactory, the parent should be informed as soon as possible. The private foster carer should be informed in writing as to:

- the reason for the local authority's decision to find the placement unsatisfactory;

- the potential carer's right to appeal under para 8 of Sch 8 to appeal against the decision within 14 days of the date of notification.

Chapter 9

FAMILY AND FRIENDS CARE ARRANGEMENTS

INTRODUCTION

9.1　It is estimated that about 300,000 children are cared for full time by family and friends,[1] 7,000 of whom are looked-after children, placed with friends and relatives by the local authority.

9.2　The most common reasons for family members and friends taking on the care of children are those related to parental factors such as domestic violence, alcohol or substance misuse, mental or physical illness or incapacity, separation or divorce, imprisonment, or death of a parent. Child related factors such as disability or challenging behaviour may also be reasons. In many instances the characteristics and needs of children living with family and friends carers in informal arrangements are very similar to, or the same as, those of children who have become looked after.

9.3　It may be the particular circumstances giving rise to an emergency, the willingness of family members to intervene at a particular stage and/or the response of the local authority which determines whether the child goes to live with family and friends carers on an informal basis or is placed by the local authority as a looked-after child.

9.4　Family and friends often start to care for other people's children in a crisis or emergency situation. Sometimes the care will begin as a short-term measure, but gradually or subsequently become open-ended or permanent. A child may arrive in the carers' home without advance planning, sometimes in the middle of the night, in a state of confusion and without their immediate possessions. Family and friends carers may provide a series of planned short episodes of care for children, for instance whilst a parent is working away or undergoing medical treatment, or children may come and go at short notice in response to the chaotic lifestyle of their parents. Such circumstances can be very challenging for the carers, resulting in strained relationships, not just between the carers and the child's parents, but with other siblings, children of the carers, and extended family members.

---

[1]　Department for Education *Family and Friends Care: Statutory Guidance for Local Authorities* (2011).

9.5   An understanding of the circumstances leading to the placement with a relative or friend is therefore crucial in making sense of the local authority's decision-making in the event of the support being sought.

SECTION 1 – DEFINITION OF FAMILY AND FRIENDS CARERS

9.6   The term 'family and friends carer' means a relative, friend or other person with a prior connection with somebody else's child who is caring for that child full time. An individual who is a 'connected person' to a looked-after child may also be a family and friends carer. A child who is cared for by a family and friends carer may or may not be looked after by the local authority.[2]

9.7   Placements with such carers are often called *kinship placements.*

SECTION 2 – THE LEGAL FRAMEWORK

9.8   Arrangements for placing children with friends or family are governed by a range of legislation and guidance:

- Children Act 1989 (CA 1989), ss 17, 31, 38, 22C;

- Care Planning Placement and Case Review (England) Regulations 2010 ('the 2010 Regulations');[3]

- Fostering Services (England) Regulations 2011 ('the 2011 Regulations');[4]

- The National Minimum Standards (NMS) for fostering (standard 30);[5]

- Children and Young Persons Act 2008; and

- *Family and Friends Care: Statutory Guidance for Local Authorities* (England) 2011.

---

2   Department for Education *Family and Friends Care: Statutory Guidance for Local Authorities* (2011).

3   SI 2010/959.

4   SI 2011/581.

5   Department for Education *Fostering Services: National Minimum Standards* (2011).

SECTION 3 – POSSIBLE ARRANGEMENTS FOR KINSHIP PLACEMENTS

9.9   There are various possible arrangements for kinship placements.

- Informal arrangements with friends or other family members which last for a period of less than 28 days. There are no statutory responsibilities or duties under these arrangements.

- Informal arrangements with a relative or friend. This sort of arrangement was not instigated by the local authority. Financial responsibility remains with the parents although the relative may request the local authority to assess and assist by providing support under CA 1989, s 17 (or other Pt III services).

- Private fostering arrangement. This is a private arrangement whereby the child is being cared for 28 days or more (or the intention is that the arrangement will last for 28 days or more) by anyone who does not have parental responsibility, and who is not a close relative.[6] The child is not a looked-after child. The Children (Private Arrangement for Fostering) Regulations 2005 apply.[7]

- Looked-after child placed with the relative or friend approved as a foster carer. In this arrangement the child has been placed with the relative or friend by the local authority. The placement is either under s 20 with agreement of those with parental responsibility or the child is subject to an interim care order or a care order under s 31. The Statutory Guidance on Fostering Services, DfE 2011 apply.[8]

- Children living with relatives or friends under a residence order, with or without the carer receiving a residence allowance from the local authority. The order under s 8 of the CA 1989 may be granted at the conclusion of care proceedings or on an application of a carer with whom the child had resided for more than one year.

- Children living with relatives or friends under a special guardianship order (SGO) with a support plan from the local authority. The order may be granted at the conclusion of care proceedings when the child was placed with relatives by the local authority. Alternatively, relatives may apply for such an order after the child has lived with them for at least one year.

- Arrangements whereby the family and friend carer is expected to make an application for an adoption order. This could apply to children placed with a family or friend carer as looked-after children with a care plan for

---

[6]   Relative means grandparent, brother, sister, uncle or aunt (whether full blood or half blood or by marriage or civil partnership) or step-parent, as defined in s 105 of the CA 1989.

[7]   SI 2005/1533. See Chapter 8 in relation to fostering.

[8]   The *Children Act 1989 Guidance and Regulations Volume 4: Fostering Services* (HMSO, 2011).

adoption.[9] The local authority may decide that the child should be placed for adoption. They can only do so with the consent of the birth parent or under a placement order made by a court. An approved foster carer can apply for an adoption order after a year of caring for the child. Other informal carers could apply for an adoption order if the child has lived with them for a period of 3 years. The *Adoption Statutory Guidance: Adoption and Children Act 2002* revised in February 2011 applies.

SECTION 4 – THE DUTIES OF THE LOCAL AUTHORITY

9.10 The local authority has a duty to consider the most appropriate arrangement for the child in every case referred to it; however, the decision about the most appropriate arrangement will be subject to an assessment on a case-by-case basis. Where a child cannot safely remain in the care of their parents, the local authority is required to intervene to protect the child but must also take any necessary steps to promote family life for the child.

9.11 By supporting family members and friends to care for a child, the local authority is not only respecting the child's birth family connections, but also ensuring that the child belongs to a family that can:

• provide the child with a sense of permanence; and

• assist the child to maintain a sense of identity.

9.12 The usual core assessment tools should be used to inform social workers about the most appropriate level of support to be offered to a family placement. In addition the local authority should consider whether it would be appropriate to hold a family group conference to assist in forming a care plan and support to enabling a child's needs to be met within the family network.

9.13 The usual core assessment tools should be used to inform social workers about the most appropriate level of support to be offered to a family placement. Professionals must:[10]

• inform themselves about 'differing family patterns and lifestyles and child rearing patterns that vary across different racial, ethnic and cultural groups'; and

---

[9] This would be rare as it changes the biological relationship between the relative and child. Local authorities may propose this as an option when the family carer lives out of the jurisdiction and there are no other legal means to enable the child to have legal security with the relative or when it is not safe for the parents to continue to hold PR.

[10] Department for Children, Schools and Families (DCSF) (now DfE) *Working Together to Safeguard Children – A Guide to Inter-agency Working to Safeguard and Promote the Welfare of Children* ('*Working Together*') (TSO, 4th edn, 2010).

- 'work with the strengths and support systems available within families, ethnic groups and communities'.[11] A family group conference may also assist the local authority in deciding the most appropriate level of support (see Chapter 2).

9.14 The capacity of the child's family circle to compensate for deficits in parenting is a core element of the assessment:[12]

> 'The care and upbringing of children does not take place in a vacuum. All family members are influenced both positively and negatively by wider family, the neighbourhood and social networks in which they live.'

SECTION 5 – INFORMAL FAMILY ARRANGEMENTS

9.15 The local authority has a general duty under s 17 of the CA 1989 to safeguard and promote the welfare of children within their area who are in need and so far as is consistent with that duty to promote the upbringing of such children by their families in particular through the provision of family support services.

9.16 The *Family and Friends Care* guidance specifies that no child or young person should have to become a looked-after child, whether by agreement with those holding parental responsibility (CA 1989, s 20) or by virtue of a court order (CA 1989, ss 38 and 31), for the sole purpose of enabling financial, practical or other support to be provided to the child's carer.

9.17 The range and level of family support services which may be provided under s 17 is wide, and is set out in Pt 1 of Sch 2 to the CA 1989. As well as practical support, family and friends carers may need advice, guidance or counselling about how to manage issues such as those arising from contact or from caring for children with emotional or behavioural difficulties due to their earlier experiences. Such services may be provided by local authorities to support both formal and informal family and friends care arrangements. The CA 1989 does not impose a limit on the amount of support which may be provided under s 17. Section 17(6) provides that the family support services provided by a local authority may include giving assistance in kind and may also include giving financial assistance to the family.

9.18 Section 17(6) has been amended by the Children and Young Persons Act 2008 in order to remove the restriction on the local authority to provide financial assistance only 'in exceptional circumstances'. A local authority may now provide financial support on a regular basis under s 17. Local authorities providing such financial support to family and friends carers under s 17 will need to be clear that this support is provided under s 17.

---

[11] *Working Together*.
[12] The Department of Health *Framework for the Assessment of Children in Need and their Families* (TSO, 2000), para 2.13.

9.19 The local authority should have in place clear eligibility criteria in relation to the provision of support services under s 17, including financial support to children living with family and friends carers.[13]

9.20 The following principles apply in relation to the extent of the local authority's powers and duties to intervene in informal family arrangements:

- The decision for a child to go and live with anyone in the child's family/friend network rests with the parents and/or others with parental responsibility (PR) for the child.

- The local authority must not make arrangements about contact between the child and anyone in their family/friend network unless this is agreed, in writing, with the parents, others with PR and the carers.

- The child is not looked after by the local authority.

- The child will not have a care plan but there should be a child in need plan or child protection plan.

- Apart from meetings to review the support provided to the family/friend carer under s 17, any meetings arranged about the child must be at the request and permission of the child's parents and the family/friend carer.

- If there is a child protection plan a social worker should be allocated to visit the child and carers with the agreement with those with PR.

- The child must be offered access to an advocacy service where they make or intend to make representations under s 26 of the CA 1989.

- The carers will not usually have a separate social worker.

- The local authority has discretion to give financial assistance (which can be on the basis of regular payments) but there is no entitlement and family income may be taken into account since the local authority must have regard to the means of the child and parents under s 17(8) of the CA 1989.

- Child benefit and child tax credit may be payable.

- There is no entitlement to leaving care support.

- Any support offered will cease when the young person becomes 18, unless criteria are met for support from adult services (eg due to disability or ill health).

---

[13] Department for Education *Family and Friends Care: Statutory Guidance for Local Authorities* (2011).

SECTION 6 – PLACEMENT OF LOOKED-AFTER CHILDREN WITH FAMILY OR FRIENDS

The legal framework

9.21 It may not always be easy for the local authority to determine whether a child who is cared for by family or friends requires accommodation for the purposes of s 20(1) or whether that child's needs should be met by providing support under s 17 of the CA 1989. It is important to establish that the decision-making is made on the basis of the individual child and that the decision was not influenced by (lack of) general resources in the local authority.

9.22 The issue has been considered in a number of authorities,[14] but most recently and significantly in *SA and KCC*,[15] later upheld on 10 November 2011 by the Court of Appeal.[16] The case clearly illustrates the common arguments raised by this issue.

9.23 Arguments made on behalf of the family member or friend caring for the child were that:

(a) The child was a child in need, within the meaning of s 20(1) at the time of placement; and

(b) the child's parents were prevented, at that time, from providing the child with suitable accommodation and care.

(c) Therefore it followed that the local authority had a duty to provide the child with accommodation under s 20(1).

(d) If the relative carer had not been available to look after the child, the child would have had to go into local authority foster care.

(e) The placement should therefore be regulated and supported as for any looked-after child placed with approved foster carers.

9.24 Arguments on behalf of the local authority were that:

(a) The local authority were never under a duty to provide accommodation for the child under s 20(1) because, although that duty was on the verge of arising, it never actually materialised. This was because the relative in question was willing to look after the child and there was, instead, a private arrangement for the relative to provide accommodation.

---

[14] *Southwark v D* [2007] EWCA Civ 182; *Re H* [2003] EWCA Civ 1629; *CG v LD & Others* [2009] EWHC 1942 (Fam).
[15] [2010] EWHC 848 (Admin).
[16] [2011] EWCA Civ 1303.

(b)   Even if s 20(1) was found to be relevant, then in any event the local authority had discharged their duties by the arrangements being made pursuant to s 23(6).

(c)   Such an analysis was in line both with the basic legal framework of the 1989 Act and with the way in which one would intuitively view the situation where a child is living with a relative (a grandparent in the case) with the agreement of the parents and without a care order.

9.25   The court rejected the local authority's suggestion that children who are not in the care of the local authority and who go to live with relatives *always* do so under s 23(6) and never under s 23(2). Although the court concluded that this was apparently uncharted territory, nonetheless 'this all or nothing approach' seemed to ignore the enormous variation that there is in the circumstances of children and their parents and carers.

9.26   The court at first instance was not persuaded that children will be properly protected if local authorities were obliged always to overcome the s 31 threshold and the no-order principle in s 1(5) of the CA 1989 (as well as families having to go through care proceedings) before the arrangements for a child to live with a relative could be subject to regulation. Nor was the court persuaded that that such arrangements under s 23(6) would ensure sufficient support for all relatives who are caring for such children.

9.27   The decisions of the court at first instance were upheld by the Court of Appeal in November 2011.

9.28   If the local authority arranges for children to live with relatives they may do so either under s 23(2) or s 23(6). The decision as to which route is taken *depends upon the facts of the individual case*. The factors to be taken into account when analysing the nature of such an arrangement include the pattern of the local authority's involvement over time, the assessment of need for the child, and the level of discussions with the relative or friend.

9.29   In essence it therefore appears that the arrangements for the care of the child with a relative can be provided in one of two ways:

•   the local authority can make a s 23(2) placement resulting in the child being a looked-after child; or

•   the local authority can make arrangements for the child to live with a relative, friend or connection, pursuant to s 23(6) which will not result in the child being a looked-after child.

9.30   However, it is clear that the issue is far from easy to determine, and we suggest that the matter is highly likely to remain the subject of continuing legal challenge and consideration.

9.31 In any event, where the local authority has instigated the arrangement for a child to live with a friend or relative, the local authority should provide an appropriate range and level of support for those arrangements. Where a child is provided with accommodation under s 20, or is subject to a care order, the child is looked after and the duties in Part III of the 1989 Act, particularly ss 22 to 22D, and the 2010 Regulations apply.

9.32 Sections 22A to 22F of the CA 1989 (inserted by s 8 of the Children and Young Persons Act 2008) make provision in relation to the accommodation and maintenance of children who are looked after. The new s 22C is the key provision which replaces the provisions previously set out in s 23 of the CA 1989.

9.33 Section 22C sets out the ways in which looked-after children are to be accommodated and maintained. Section 22C(2) to (4) provides that a local authority must make arrangements for a child who is looked after to live with their parents, a person who is not a parent but who has parental responsibility for the child or, in a case where the child is in the care of the local authority and there was a residence order in force with respect to the child immediately before the care order was made, the person in whose favour the residence order was made.

9.34 This 'rehabilitative' duty is subject to the proviso that the arrangements must be both consistent with the child's welfare and reasonably practicable, and reflects the principle that state intervention in family life should be to keep children safe and ensure that families have the necessary support to bring up their children. For children subject to a care order the placement back with their parents must be in accordance with the 2010 Regulations.

9.35 Where a local authority is unable to make arrangements under s 22C(2) to (4), ie the 'rehabilitative' duty to place a child with their parent, then s 22C(5) applies. This requires the authority to place the child in the most appropriate placement available. Section 22C(6) to (9) sets out what those placement options are and how the local authority must determine the most appropriate placement.

9.36 The authority must 'give preference to' a placement with a person who is a relative, friend or other person connected with the child and who is also a local authority foster parent. They must have been approved as a local authority foster carer in accordance with the 2011 Regulations or have been temporarily approved as a foster carer under the 2010 Regulations. These regulations, together with the National Minimum Standards for fostering services, set out the requirements in relation to support and supervision of all foster carers including those who are family members, friends or other connected persons.

9.37 A child who is looked after and is placed with a relative, friend or other person connected with the child in accordance with s 22C(5) continues to be looked after. In the case of a child who is provided with accommodation under s 20, the child's looked-after status will end when the local authority considers that the child no longer requires accommodation under s 20(1) of the CA 1989. In the case of a child subject to a care order, the child will continue to be looked after until the order is discharged or the foster carer is granted an order which gives them parental responsibility for the child.

9.38 In relation to care proceedings, the local authorities should ensure that all the necessary steps have been completed prior to issuing proceedings to avoid unnecessary delay during the start of the court process. This includes the local authority's duty to ensure that all kinship care options have been fully explored. The local authority should ensure, when assessing the wider family within the core assessment and perhaps using the family group conference, to identify the willingness and/or capacity of the wider family to provide care for the child on a short or longer-term basis.

The extent of local authority intervention under s 20

9.39 Where the child is looked after by the local authority with consent of those with parental responsibility, the extent of the local authority's intervention is as follows:

- The child must have a care plan (including health plan and personal education plan) which will be reviewed by an independent reviewing officer (IRO). The 2010 Regulations apply.

- The child should have an allocated social worker who will visit the child and carers and oversee the child's welfare.

- The child must be offered access to an advocacy service where they make or intend to make representations under s 26 of the CA 1989.

- A supervising social worker will be appointed for the foster carers.

- A weekly fostering allowance will be paid.

- There is no entitlement to child benefit or child tax credit.

- Training and support must be offered to the foster carers.

- On leaving care the young person may be eligible for ongoing support under CA 1989.

- The local authority is able to offer continuing support (including financial support) to the carers until the young person is 21, and to support the young person in respect of education and training until they become 25.

Family and friends as foster carers

Temporary approval

9.40 All looked-after children can be placed with a connected person (relative, friend or any other person connected to the child) once this person has been approved as a local authority foster carer. Regulations 24 and 25 of the 2010 Regulations set out arrangements for the temporary approval of a connected person (as a foster carer to allow an immediate placement for a period of *up to* 16 weeks, after which a full assessment to approve the carers as foster carers is necessary).

9.41 This time period has been set to allow sufficient time for a foster carer approval process to be undertaken, including any criminal records checks required. Local authorities will need to satisfy themselves that this placement is the most appropriate way to safeguard and promote the child's welfare with what information they can ascertain as set out in Sch 4 to the 2010 Regulations.

Extension of temporary approval beyond 16 weeks

9.42 Regulation 25 of the 2010 Regulations sets out the circumstances in which, exceptionally, the period of temporary approval may be extended. Before deciding to extend temporary approval the local authority must:

• be satisfied that the placement with the connected person is still the most appropriate placement available;

• seek the views of the fostering panel established by the fostering service provider; and

• inform the IRO.

The circumstances for extending approval

9.43 There are only two circumstances in which approval may be extended:

• where the approval process has taken longer than anticipated in which case the extension is only for a further 8 weeks; or

• where the connected person has *not* been approved following the assessment process and seeks a review of the decision through the Independent Review Mechanism.[17] In these circumstances the temporary approval will continue until the outcome of the review is known.

---

[17] There is no right to review by the Independent Review Mechanism of a person who is temporarily approved under the 2010 Regulations if the fostering service decides not to undertake a full assessment under the 2011 Regulations and the child's placement is ended.

9.44 If these time periods expire and the connected person has not been approved as a foster carer in accordance with the 2011 Regulations, the local authority must arrange for an alternative placement and remove the child from the connected person in accordance with reg 25(6).

The criteria for placing a child with a temporary approved foster carer

9.45 The provisions relating to temporary approval are intended to be used exceptionally and in circumstances which could not easily have been foreseen, when it is not possible to undertake a full foster carer assessment prior to placement.[18] The power will be most useful where it is clearly in the child's interest to be placed with or remain in the care of a familiar figure in reassuring surroundings.

9.46 The local authority must nominate an officer with authority to grant temporary approval of foster carers under reg 24. The guidance suggests that it will usually be appropriate for the fostering service decision-maker to reserve the authority for granting temporary approvals.

9.47 Before giving authority to making a placement under reg 24, the local authority must:

- be satisfied that the placement with the connected person is the most appropriate placement available;

- assess the suitability of the connected person to care for the child;

- assess the suitability of the proposed accommodation;

- assess all other persons aged 18 and over who are members of the household in which it is proposed that the child would live;

- make immediate arrangements for the suitability of the connected person to be assessed as a local authority foster parent in accordance with the 2002 Regulations ('the full assessment process') before the temporary approval expires;

- make a written agreement with the temporarily approved connected person. The social worker should complete all the necessary documentation for looked-after children, including the Placement Plan Part 1: Placement Agreement. The prospective carer(s) must be prepared to comply with a written agreement with the local authority to carry out the

---

[18]   Department for Education *Family and Friends Care: Statutory Guidance for Local Authorities* (2011).

duties specified in the Fostering Regulations 2011. The social worker will therefore need to ensure that the prospective carer signs section 4 of the placement agreement.

The assessment of suitability for temporary approval

9.48 The steps to be taken by the social worker are specified in reg 24 and in the guidance. The *minimum* requirements are for the local authority to:

- Undertake an assessment of the quality of any existing relationship between the child and the proposed carer and their family members. In the event of the proposed carer not being known to the child (but to the parents), the child must be introduced to the connected person and the proposed accommodation in order for the child's wishes and feelings to be appropriately ascertained.

- Seek the views of all members of the household of the proposed connected person over 16 and take into account their wishes and feelings in relation to the proposed placement.

- Obtain consent and make an immediate application for a criminal record disclosure (CRB check) of all household members.

- Discuss with the connected person's family members their history, if any, of criminal convictions.

- Undertake local authority checks on all household members over the age of 16.

- Check and seek references from schools about any children already living in the household.

- Visit the accommodation to assess suitability before placement.

- Ascertain the child's wishes and feelings about the proposed arrangements, subject to age and understanding.

- Enable the child to visit the proposed placement before giving temporary approval if at all possible.

- Obtain the views of the parents and any other person with parental responsibility before placement.

- Visit the child in placement at least once a week until the first review and thereafter at least every 4 weeks (reg 28(6)).

- Speak to the child in private during visits unless the child, being of sufficient age and understanding, refuses or the social worker considers it to be inappropriate.

- Prepare a care plan and placement plan (to be signed by carer) in accordance with the 2010 and 2011 Regulations.

- Prepare an assessment report.

- Seek approval from the fostering panel and subsequent authorisation for temporary approval as foster carer from the nominated person of the local authority, usually the fostering service decision-maker.

- Make a referral to the fostering team for a full assessment as foster carer, or alternatively prepare a report refusing temporary approval together with reasons. In the event of refusal inform the connected person of their rights to appeal.

- Inform the IRO and children's guardian if one is appointed.

The assessment and approval process for family and friends to become foster carers for a specific child

9.49 The 'full' assessment of the connected carer as a foster carer is required if the temporary approved carer intends to care for the child for longer than 16 weeks. The assessment will normally be carried out by the fostering service most of which have a designated sub team dealing with family and friends carers. The assessment will *not* normally be done by the child's social worker who may have assessed the connected person for temporary approval.

9.50 The normal procedures for assessing any unrelated foster carer will apply (see Chapter 8), although the approval is for a specific child or children only and there is no need to consider their suitability to care for other children.

9.51 Standard 30 of the National Minimum Standards applies for assessment purposes. It clarifies that when considering whether a relative, friend or other connected person should be approved as a foster carer, account must be taken of the needs, wishes and feelings of the child whom it is proposed to place with them and the capacity of the carer to meet those particular needs. In order for the placement to be in the child's best interests, the carer will need to have the capacity to meet his or her needs for the duration of the proposed placement, whether this is short or long term. The likely length of the placement, the age of the child and if appropriate (as may be the case where the carers are older) the capacity of the wider family to contribute to the child's long-term care, should be taken into account.

Assessment reports about connected carers

9.52 Assessment reports will be prepared by the assessing social worker on the basis of:

- personal interviews;

- home visits;

- household interviews (adults, children, and family unit as a group);

- interview with the child's parents and other significant family members;

- interview with the child(ren) and ascertaining their wishes and feelings (with assistance of the child's social worker as appropriate);

- reading the child's file and discussing the case with the child's social worker;

- undertaking checks and references (including CRB, local authority and health checks); and

- reading any other external reports available to the assessing social worker (eg own children's school reports).

9.53 The connected carer must understand that the household as a whole is being assessed. This will include assessment of:

- all children and adults in the household;

- family pets; and

- health and safety assessment of the house and garden.

The assessment reports

9.54 The assessment will normally proceed on the basis of BAAF Form F although, having regard to the existing relationship between the child and the carers, the requirement for the carers to attend training/preparation groups prior to their approval will be waived.

9.55 Family and friends foster carers will usually bring with them knowledge and experience of the child they are to foster, and in many cases they will have already been providing the child with a home prior to the child become looked after. However, whether or not the prospective foster carers have direct prior knowledge of the child to be placed, the assessment should focus on the experience and strengths that they bring, and the support that they will need to enable them to provide safe care for the specific looked-after child. The assessment will need to balance the strengths of the carers arising from their position within the family network against any aspects which may make them less suitable. The needs of the child should be kept central to the process, as the assessment will of necessity also be a matching process of the child to the carer.[19]

9.56 The assessing social worker, should, give particular consideration to assessing the carers capacity in relation to the specific child. This should include an assessment of:

- the relationship between the family and friends carers and the child's parents;

- the nature and quality of any existing relationship with the child;

- the family's dynamics as a whole and how the family is able to work together (or not) in meeting the needs of the child;

- the motivation to care for the child and ability to keep the child at the centre of decision-making;

- the capacity of the carer to care for children and, in particular in relation to the child (or children) concerned and meet the totality of their needs;

- the attitude towards the assessment and working together with the local authority. Unlike unrelated foster carers who applied to be foster carers at a time of their own choosing, family and friends have responded to an emergency in the family. They have had less of an opportunity to learn about local authority procedures and their commitment to the assessment process must be established;

- the capacity to protect the child adequately from harm or danger including from any person who presents a risk of harm to the child;

- the suitability of the accommodation, location and home environment in relation to the child's age and developmental stage;

- the ability to provide a stable family environment which will promote secure attachments for the child;

- the capacity to promote positive contact with parents and other connected persons, unless this is not consistent with the child's welfare;

---

[19]   Department for Education *Family and Friends Care: Statutory Guidance for Local Authorities* (2011).

- the state of health (physical, emotional and mental), and medical history of the carers including current or past issues of domestic violence, substance misuse or mental health problems;

- family history, including their childhood and upbringing, and the strengths and difficulties of their parents or others who cared for them; their relationship with parents and siblings and each other; educational achievement and any learning difficulty/disability; chronology of significant life events; particulars of other relatives and their relationships with the child and the connected person;

- any criminal offences;

- past and present employment and other sources of income; and

- the nature of the neighbourhood and resources available in the community to support the child and the connected person.

The fostering panel

9.57 On completion, the assessment report should be booked into the first available fostering panel for approval. The panel should be attended by the child's social worker, the assessing social worker, and, wherever possible, the prospective carers. The procedure for approving the assessment via the fostering panel is the same as the procedure for the approval of all local authority approved foster carers.

9.58 The procedures relating to the review and support of the foster carers will be the same as for any approved foster carer.

The matching panel

9.59 There is no requirement for a foster carer approved for a specific child under the family and friends arrangement to be presented to a matching panel. Instead, the family and friend foster carer will be subject to reviews as any other approved foster carer.[20]

9.60 However, when the care plan is for the child to remain with their family and friends on a long-term basis and/or for the duration of their childhood, some local authorities have internal policies requiring the specific match to be presented to the adoption and permanence panel for matching.

---

[20] Some family and friends carers resent this requirement to comply with requirements that would not normally apply in family homes (e g health and safety measures to lock medicines or not smoking in house).

9.61 The social worker assessing the carers' suitability to care for the child, the child's social worker, and the carers if at all possible must attend the relevant panel meeting. The child or young person may also attend if they so wish.

9.62 The role of the panel in considering the family and friend placement is no different from the role of the panel in respect of any other foster care applicant or child brought before it.

Functions of panel in respect of a connected person placement

9.63 In these circumstances the panel's functions are as follows:

• Give advice about the most appropriate legal order, if any, which would better secure the child's stability with the proposed carers (eg SGO).

• Give advice about the quality of the reports (in particular ensuring that they are suitable for the child to read when an adult).

• Give advice about the support offered and make arrangements for the IRO to be informed of the recommendation and any advice given.

• Give an opportunity for the child to attend the panel if they so wish.

9.64 In giving its advice, the panel would normally take the following factors into account:

• the best interests of the child or young person as the paramount consideration;

• the child or young person's wishes and feelings;

• the child's and young person's need for a sense of security and stability (in particular the advantages of giving the carers legal responsibility for the child or young person placed with them);

• the attitude and views of the parents to the placement and the ability of the carers to deal with abusive or inadequate parents to whom they are related, ensuring the child's safety; and

• the child's age, level of understanding and maturity and the suitability of any court order to achieve stability and a sense of belonging to the family.

9.65 The child's social worker must complete the following reports to be submitted to the relevant panel for consideration:

• The child permanence report (CPR);

- The minutes of the adoption and permanence panel making recommendation about whether the child should (or should not) have been placed for adoption together with the decision of the agency decision–maker.

- The assessment report in respect of the family and friend approved as foster carer.

- The minutes of the fostering panel recommending approval of the connected person as a foster carer together with the decision of the fostering service decision-maker.

- The matching report (most local authorities use the adoption placement report format for this purpose).

- The proposed support plan (some local authority use the adoption support plan as the framework of identifying the support needs of the child, parent and carer).

- Up-to-date health information in relation to the child and carers.

9.66 The CPR in respect of the child should be updated and completed within 8 weeks of recommending plans for permanency at the child's second looked-after review as per any other child in care.

9.67 The CPR should explain the processes used in identifying the proposed family and friends carers as the child's family 'for life'. The report should include details about:

- the child's wishes and feelings and understanding of the permanency process, including details about contact with his or her parents and siblings, the preparation work with the child, and proposals for progressing the child's life story work;

- the views of the different members of the family, including the carers, about the proposals for permanency;

- recommendations for contact, and post placement approval support;

- the proposed legal status of the child. Specific consideration should be given as to whether the child should remain in the care of the approved family carer under a care order or whether it would be in the child's best interest to be provided with legal security to remain in placement for the duration of their childhood (eg special guardianship order);[21] and

---

[21] Some authorities maintain a policy to provide foster carers with the same financial support under an SGO as they would have provided under a care order for the duration of childhood (ie not limited to the 3 years as specified in the SGO Regulations).

• recommendations regarding any allowances and any other financial contributions, including capital expenditure and legal costs.

Financial support for a connected person placement

9.68 Once the placement is approved (as temporary approval or longer term) at the nominated person level (normally the fostering service decision-maker) under the Fostering Regulations 2011, an assessment of necessary financial support must also be carried out by the local authority. In *R (on the application of L) v Manchester City Council; R (on the application of R) v Manchester City Council*,[22] it was held that a local authority policy was unlawful under which it paid foster carers who were relatives or friends of the child at a very significantly lower rate than it paid other foster carers. The decision to pay fostering allowances at the lower rate was quashed and it was directed that the rate should be re-determined in accordance with the court's findings. Each year the Fostering Network calculates the cost of bringing up a child in its own home for the coming year and publishes a full survey of the allowances paid by each local authority. The minimum recommended rate varies according to the age of the child and whether the placement is in London or not. In addition to the basic allowance, some local authorities pay an enhanced rate for specialist foster care involving, for example, an emergency placement or a placement of a child requiring special care. Standard 28 of the NMS sets out greater levels of consistency and transparency required in the payments to foster carers

9.69 Connected carers should usually expect to receive the fostering allowance rate for the relevant age group *less* child benefit and *less* the 'reward element' given to foster carers who care for any child rather than a specific child.

Approval of people living overseas

9.70 In the event that a fostering service approves a connected person living outside of England and Wales as a foster carer, the responsible authority must take steps to ensure, as far as is practicable, that the requirements imposed on the placement mirror those that would have applied if the child or young person had been placed in England.

---

[22]   [2001] EWHC 707 (Admin), [2002] 1 FLR 43.

Chapter 10

CONTACT

INTRODUCTION

10.1 The local authority has a duty to give due consideration to contact arrangements for children with their birth family and significant others. This includes contact arrangements with parents, grandparents and other relatives, including siblings and other persons who are significant to the children.

SECTION 1 – THE LEGAL FRAMEWORK

10.2 The legal framework underpinning the arrangements for contact is dependent on the type of placement. There are various different types of placements for children who are looked after by the local authority:

- Children looked after by the local authority under the Children Act 1989 (CA 1989), ss 20 or 31 who are placed with either foster carers, children homes or with kinship carers approved as foster carers.

- Children subject to care proceedings.

- Children placed under special guardianship orders (SGOs).

- Children placed for adoption.

Contact for looked-after children under s 20, in care proceedings or under care order

- Children Act 1989, ss 34 and 8.

- Care Planning, Placement and Case Review (England) Regulations 2010.[1]

- *Fostering Services: National Minimum Standards* (2011), standard 9.

- *Children's Homes: National Minimum Standards* (2011), standard 9.

---

[1]   SI 2010/959.

Contact in special guardianship

- Special Guardianship Regulations 2005.[2]

- Special Guardianship Guidance 2005.

- Children Act 1989, s 8.

Contact in adoption

- Adoption and Children Act 2002, ss 1, 26 and 27, 46.

- Children Act 1989, s 8.

- Adoption Agencies Regulations 2005.[3]

- Adoption Support Services Regulations 2005.[4]

- Adoption and Children Act 2002 Guidance.

10.3 In addition, the court is obliged to consider the local authority's proposals for contact in various situations as follows:

In care proceedings

- Before making a final order the court must consider the proposed contact arrangements and obtain views of the parties. This includes a consideration of applications by the local authority for authority to refuse contact between the child and any person under s 34(4), or any s 8 orders.

In adoption proceedings

- Before making any adoption order the court must consider proposed contact arrangements.

- The court must therefore consider any existing arrangements, and obtain the views of parties.

- Parents retain the right to apply for s 8 order (to be heard concurrently with the adoption application).

---

[2]   SI 2005/1109.
[3]   SI 2005/389.
[4]   SI 2005/691.

SECTION 2 – TYPES OF CONTACT

10.4 Contact includes every method of maintaining links with members of the birth family and other significant people for a child. This includes:

- Direct contact by face-to-face meetings or by direct telephone exchange via landlines, Skype or other internet social network facilities (eg Facebook).

- Indirect contact involving intermediaries. This could include letters, exchanges of information by audio or video tapes, photographs and indirect links through others.

SECTION 3 – PLANNING OF CONTACT

10.5 The planning of contact is part of the overall care planning process and should not be seen as a one-off task. It is a process of assessment, subject to change and reviews. Any assessment about contact should establish:

- Why is contact important for this child and family?

- What is the purpose of contact?

- What are the practical arrangements? Who should have contact with whom, where, for how long and when?

- Does contact pose any risks and can these be alleviated with support or supervision? (see below)

- What are the arrangements for monitoring and recording the contact session, if appropriate, and for what purpose?

- What is the contingency plan in case of things going wrong?

- What are the criteria for success? What will be regarded as satisfactory contact?

- What are the mechanisms for reviewing contact?

- Is there a written agreement between the parties?

SECTION 4 – CONTACT AGREEMENTS

10.6 Contact agreements should be written clearly and in a way that can be easily understood by the parties. Contact agreements should include:

- the type of contact – direct or indirect;

- the nature of contact – supported, supervised, assessed, intervention (ie part of an assessment process of capacity to care);

- who will be involved;

- frequency, duration and timing whether direct or indirect;

- venue and transport (eg in formal supervised setting, community, placement);

- arrangements for supervision and recording sessions;

- any restraints, limits or expectations;

- tasks of who will do what before, during, after contact whether direct or indirect;

- the criteria for success;

- contingency plans – anticipating problems or difficulties;

- support arrangements for the child and family members;

- arrangements for monitoring each episode; and

- arrangements for reviewing the contact plan.

SECTION 5 – THE LOCAL AUTHORITY'S APPROACH TO CONTACT

10.7   There are various principles underpinning the local authority's approach to contact which are contained within the Children Act 1989 (CA 1989) and the guidance within *Working Together*[5] and the *Framework for Assessment*:[6]

- Contact is an integral part of care planning and must be considered at every stage of the process of planning towards permanency for the child. Contact should be compatible with the child's needs taking into account their age, wishes and feelings, ethnicity, culture, religion and disability.

- The local authority has a duty to promote contact between children in care, their families of origin and others who have played an important part in their lives unless it is not consistent with, or is detrimental to the

---

[5]   Department for Children, Schools and Families (DCSF) (now DfE) *Working Together to Safeguard Children – A Guide to Inter-agency Working to Safeguard and Promote the Welfare of Children* ('*Working Together*') (TSO, 4th edn, 2010).
[6]   Department of Health *Framework for the Assessment of Children in Need and Their Families* ('*Framework for Assessment*') (TSO, 2000).

child's welfare. The presumption in s 34 of the CA 1989 is that the local authority should make arrangements for reasonable contact between children in care and their families. The presumption of contact continues throughout the child's time in care, other than in cases where the local authority is granted authority to place a child for adoption (placement order or by consent of the parents with parental responsibility).

• For children subject to an interim care order or a full care order, the local authority can only suspend contact for a limited period (up to a maximum of 7 days) as a matter of urgency.[7] After 7 days, the local authority can only refuse to allow contact between a child and a parent upon being granted an order by the court (CA 1989, s 34(4)). However, a s 34(4) order will not be made merely to protect against the possibility that circumstances might change in the future to justify the termination of contact.[8] In the event that a s 34(4) order is made authorising the local authority to refuse to allow contact, there must then be some material change between the making of the order and any subsequent application to discharge it – the greater the change in circumstances, the stronger the likelihood of the court reconsidering the desirability of retaining such an order.[9]

• Children, young people and their family should be involved in all decisions relating to contact and their wishes and feelings taken into account.

• When the local authority has the authority to place a child for adoption, there is no presumption for or against contact between the child and their birth family. The proposals for contact are dependent on the needs of the specific child.

• Where a child is placed for adoption, the prospective adopters' views about contact should be ascertained and considered before making decisions about the child's contact with their birth family.

• When a child is adopted, the adoption support plan should adhere to the principle that links with the family of origin should not be completely severed and that the child's life-long need to know and understand their heritage is important.

• Adopted children post-18 years and their birth relatives may apply for information from the adoption agency.

10.8 In making its proposals for contact the local authority should take into account:

---

[7] CA 1989, s 34(6).
[8] *Re S (Care: Parental Contact)* [2005] 1 FLR 469.
[9] *Re T (Termination of Contact: Discharge of Order)* [1997] 1 FLR 517.

- The purpose of contact. This will inform the frequency and duration of contact. The local authority needs to establish at every stage of the planning process the purpose of contact, including:

    - Contact for the purpose of assessing the quality of the relationship between the birth family and the child.
    - The need to develop and/or maintain continuity in the parent/child relationship and attachment.
    - Reunification of child with birth parents. In the cases of babies and very young children familiarity will be essential to prepare the birth parent to become the primary attachment figure for the child whilst at the same time needing to avoid causing stress to the baby by disrupting routine or introducing strangers (eg different contact supervisors).
    - Enabling the formation of the child's identity.
    - To reduce and/or prevent feelings of rejection, separation and loss for the child.
    - To prevent unrealistic idealisation of the birth family.

- The nature of the existing relationship between child and the other person seeking contact (be it parent, sibling, grandparent or other significant person).

- The potential of developing a long lasting positive, meaningful and significant relationship in future (eg between siblings placed apart).

- The impact of contact on the child. This should include not only an assessment of the quality of contact in itself (in terms of safety, harm and/or joy) but also the impact on the child's welfare (eg with babies the need to reduce stressful circumstances such as strangeness, unfamiliarity and disruption of their routine, and in the case of older children, disruption to education and developing positive social relations).

- The level of risk and/or harm to the child during contact and whether contact needs to be supervised.

- The wishes and feelings of those involved including:

    - the child;
    - the parent, relative, sibling for whom the contact is being proposed;
    - the temporary caregiver of the child (foster carer or children's home); and
    - the future permanent carer for the child if known (adoptive parent or SGO holder).

- Evidence from research about what works and observations of contact with a child with specific members of the family or significant others seeking contact.

The complex balancing exercise

10.9 Assessing the best interests of the child, their wishes and feelings and the rights and wishes of their birth family for contact is a complex and arduous balancing task. Far too often there has been a general assumption that contact would always be positive for a child in care placed with foster carers or placed with their kin and that direct contact for the child in a adoptive placement would necessarily be negative. This assumption is reflected in the relevant statutory legislation. There is a requirement in s 34 of the CA 1989 for the local authority to promote reasonable contact between children in care and their families. This presumption of contact continues throughout the child's time in care, other than in cases where the local authority is granted authority to place a child for adoption when there is no presumption for or against contact (Adoption and Children Act 2002).

10.10 However, it is clear that the legal requirement for any contact to be reasonable and *dependent* on the paramount welfare needs of the child at times rests uneasily alongside the extent of the consideration given to the needs of the specific child. This can result in a generalised and non-specific attitude towards practice in relation to contact.

10.11 Social work knowledge and experience has changed over time in light of the increased research in relation to contact for children. The change in beliefs and attitude towards contact with the birth family is most pronounced in relation to adoption. In the early part of the twentieth century a complete break from the birth family was commonplace (in the context of a complete failure to inform adoptive children that they were in fact adopted). However, the climate has shifted in recent decades to the other side of the pendulum. Not only are adopted children informed about their adoption and biological heritage from a very early age but there now appears to be a presumption that the adopted child's contact (both direct and indirect) with their birth parents should be the norm.[10]

10.12 There now exists a significant body of research to inform practice suggesting that good quality assessments are essential for the development of contact plans which serve the best interests of the specific child and all the parties concerned. The conclusions of the current research indicate that at times life is far too complex to inform with any degree of certainty how the best interests of the child are to be served and therefore requires that each case must be judged on its own merits. The newly born baby who must be separated from her birth mother due to an identified likelihood of causing significant harm may need to have frequent contact with her mother for her to become a familiar figure with the potential of developing attachment during the assessment period. However, the disruption to the child's routine, long journeys to contact

---

[10]   Elspeth Neil and David Howe (eds) *Contact in Adoption and Permanent Foster Care* (BAAF, 2004).

and/or the use of plethora of different supervisors, all strangers to the baby are considered by the research to be a risk factor impacting on the child's future development.[11]

10.13   For some years, there have been concerns about whether the frequency and arrangements for contact between infants and parents during proceedings are in the best interests of the infant. It has become widely accepted in practice that for infants from birth to 12 months placed in foster care, frequency of contact with the mother during proceedings should be set at 5–6 days a week and that those contact visits should last for a significant length of time. Recent research has considered whether these arrangements could be better managed to safeguard the development of the infant while maintaining effective contact and supporting the possibility of reunion with the birth parents, and suggests that contact arrangements may produce high levels of stress for the infant through discontinuity of care and potentially insensitive care. The developmental needs of any infant, particularly vulnerable infants, require conditions that are quite the opposite of those that care proceedings often bring about: uncertainty, anxiety, and risk. The research is helpfully summarised in the recent article by G Schofield and J Simmonds 'Contact for infants subject to care proceedings'[12] where a number of factors are described that courts should take into account when making decisions around infant contact plans.

10.14   The assessing social worker must consider the weight to be given to each factor taken into account in assessing the contact plan in every individual case. Planning for contact requires creative and flexible thinking on the part of the social worker within the following overall approach:

•   Meet the parents and any other person with parental responsibility or connected person to establish their wishes for contact, their availability, together or apart, their cultural and religious practice, and any support they may need to travel to contact and during contact.

•   Establish the purpose for contact.

•   Ascertain the wishes and feelings of the child about contact – with whom, how and when.

---

[11]   President of the Family Division/Family Justice Council Debate: Contact for babies in care proceedings 8 December 2010. This debate centred on the arrangements for contact for babies (as set out in *Re M* [2003] 2 FLR 171), and the research by J Kenrick 'Concurrent planning: a retrospective study of the continuities and discontinuities of care, and their impact on the development of infants and young children placed for adoption by the Coram Concurrent Planning Project' (2009) 33(4) *Adoption and Fostering*, and J Kenrick 'Concurrent planning (2) "The rollercoaster of uncertainty"' (2010) 34(2) *Adoption and Fostering*. This research has demonstrated the serious negative impact on babies of high levels of contact and the debate reviewed both the legal framework and child development issues.
[12]   [2011] Fam Law 41, at 617–622.

- Ascertain the wishes of the carer about contact and assess what the carer could offer to assist in making the contact more meaningful and safe for the child (by providing venue, supervision, travel, and/or emotional support).

- Analyse the weight to be given to the child's wishes and feelings and inform the child if their wishes cannot be met together with reasons.

- Inform the parents and any other connected person wishing to have contact about their rights to advocacy and complaint procedure.

- Inform the child of their rights to advocacy and give details about the children's right officer, independent reviewing officer (IRO), children's guardian, and process for making complaints.

- Assess and analyse the risks of contact, both during contact and risks to the child's welfare caused by contact (disruption of routine, missed activities, emotional well-being before and after contact).

- Assess how and what can be done to minimise risks. This could include supervision of contact, reduction of frequency and/or duration, different times, minimise disruption to routine, local venue etc.

- Consider a family group conference or at the very least convene a family meeting as a means of enabling the family to make safe plans for contact.

- Discuss proposals with the children's guardian if one is appointed.

- Formally consult the parties about the proposals for contact (seeking legal advice where appropriate).

- Establish a written agreement about contact. Outline practical arrangements and expectations regarding behaviour during contact.

- Inform the IRO of arrangements for contact.

- Inform parents (and child if of sufficient age and understanding) of their right to make applications to the court to vary the arrangements proposed for contact.

- Ensure contact sessions, including cancellations, are recorded on case files and provide copies to the parties.

- Set dates for reviewing impact and quality of contact.

- Consider suspending or making application for authority to terminate contact (CA 1989, s 34(4)) if appropriate.

SECTION 6 – ASSESSMENT OF RISK IN CONTACT

10.15 While the local authority has the duty to promote contact for children in care with their birth family, the paramount consideration will be the child's best interests. In making plans about contact the local authority should consider any potentially adverse factors which may indicate that at the very least, direct contact could be ill advised or minimised. The factors that the local authority must consider are:

- The risk of physical and/or emotional harm to the child. When considering this issue the local authority should take account of:

  - any history of abuse or threats of abuse to the child, other carers, partners, previous children (if any) or staff;
  - previous incidents of disruption or threats to disrupt contact or failure to co-operate with conditions agreed for supervised contact;
  - previous incidents or threats of abduction;
  - previous incidents of coercion or inappropriate behaviour during contact; and
  - re-enactment of the abuse the child had suffered during contact.

- The attitude of the parents towards the placement and whether there are risks for the placement to be undermined.

- The parents' working relationship with the local authority and any previous episodes of poor co-operation.

- The extent to which maintaining ongoing relationships may create confusion or a conflict of loyalties for the child.

- The attitude of existing carers (foster carers or adopters) towards contact and the demands placed on them.

- The transient or unsettled lifestyle of parents and their difficulties in maintaining their commitment to contact.

- The impact of contact on the child's development and well-being (eg the stress and disruption caused to babies by interrupting their routine, or the impact of contact on the child's education and development of other social relations).

SECTION 7 – CONTACT RECORDS

10.16 The local authority should record the arrangements and outcomes for contact in various ways:

- the child's case records. This should include any observations made during contact, covering actions, behaviours and responses of individuals involved in contact, including time-keeping and risk management issues. Reasons for cancellation should also be recorded;

- placement plan/placement information record;

- core assessment report;

- the care plan;

- looked-after children review reports;

- court reports;

- adoption or permanence reports;

- support plans in SGO and adoption.

SECTION 8 – SUSPENSION OR TERMINATION OF CONTACT

10.17 Where it is considered that the child's contact with the parents/relatives or friends should be suspended or terminated, the local authority should seek legal advice before doing so, if at all possible.

10.18 In normal circumstances any proposal to suspend or terminate contact between the child and a significant person should be considered as part of the childcare reviews, unless the circumstances require an urgent decision to be made. When a child in subject of an emergency protection order, interim care order or care order, the suspension cannot last for more than 7 days. Any further suspensions require the authority of the courts.

10.19 Any proposal for termination or suspension of contact should be made in the context of the overall aims and objectives of the care plan. The reasons for the proposal must be explained to the parents/other relatives and to the child, and their agreement obtained if possible.

10.20 Emergency restrictions on contact can only be made by the foster carer to protect the child from significant risk and must be notified to the placing authority (child's social worker) within 24 hours.

10.21 Where the proposal is to suspend the contact for a longer period than 7 days, the length and purpose of the suspension together with the basis upon which contact will be reinstated must be made clear.

10.22 Written confirmation of the decision made, together with the reasons, must be sent to the parents/relatives, the child (depending on age) and any other relevant person (for example advocate, independent visitor or children's guardian). Staff/carers and other agencies involved with the child's care must also be informed.

Chapter 11

ADOPTION

INTRODUCTION

11.1   This chapter deals only with domestic adoptions. The involvement of the local authority in international adoptions is limited to assessing the suitability of applicants who wish to adopt a child from overseas. The assessment process is similar to that of domestic adoption, with completed prospective adopters reports submitted for approval to adoption panels. However, many local authorities have made service level agreements with voluntary adoption agencies for them to undertake assessments and approvals on their behalf.

11.2   Domestic adoption was first introduced into the UK under the terms of the Adoption of Children Act 1926. In the early days of adoption, the focus was on providing relief for unmarried mothers and to satisfy the needs of those couples unable to conceive themselves. Subsequently the Adoption Act 1976 was the main piece of legislation regulating the adoption process in the UK until the introduction of the Adoption and Children Act 2002 (ACA 2002) which was fully implemented in 2004. The focus of the new legislation has shifted from the needs of adopters to the interests and welfare of the adopted child.

11.3   Since the early 2000s adoption has become a sensitive debating issue both in the public arena and among professionals. Different governments have opened up policies, guidance, practice and procedures for adoption to scrutiny, making proposals for change with the aim of increasing the number of adoptions as the most suitable outcome for children in care in the UK.

11.4   The Labour government of the early 2000s was the first to attempt to improve adoption rates, first by increasing the pool of prospective adopters who may be eligible to adopt (for example, unmarried couples as well as gay and lesbian people became eligible to adopt for the first time) and secondly by tightening the guidance, introducing timescales and imposing adoption targets on the local authorities.

11.5   The coalition government of the 2010s has also taken a keen interest in adoption and in early 2011 appointed Martin Narey as the new Ministerial Adviser on Adoption.

11.6   Narey has called for a cultural shift in social work attitudes towards adoption. His stated task is:

- to help raise awareness of the need to increase the number of adoptions in England, where this in the child's best interests;

- to promote the identification, awareness and sharing of good practice by the whole adoption sector;

- to promote stronger collaboration between local authorities, voluntary adoption agencies and the courts;

- to visit individual local authorities who may be struggling with their adoption processes to provide advice and support on improving services so that adoption is available for all those children for whom it is in their best interests; and

- to undertake thematic studies on particular aspects of the adoption system causing concern, such as why black and minority ethnic children face particular delays in being placed for adoption.

11.7 We expect further changes in guidance (see below in relation to the assessment of adopters) following the publication of the second edition of this book. Despite the changes that have been made or changes to be introduced, it is not anticipated that the percentage of adoptions from the population of looked-after children will be increased significantly. The annual number of adoptions has remained similar over the last decade, especially when the number is combined with the number of special guardianship orders granted during the same period.

11.8 The most recent statistics[1] indicate that 65,520 children were in the care of local authorities on 31 March 2011 with 4% being placed for adoption; 2,450 children were adopted from care during the year ending 31 March 2011 (50 less from the year ending 2010 and 3,700 in year ending 2006); the average age of adoption is 3 years and 10 months; and 71% (2,170) of all adoptions for the year were children age 1–4 (this age group comprises 18% of all the looked-after children during the same period).

11.9 In 2010, 72.4% of children who were adopted during the year were placed for adoption within 12 months of the decision that they should be placed for adoption; and 91% of looked-after children who were adopted in the year ending 31 March 2010 were adopted by two people (2,900). Most adopters were married couples (82%), 6% of adopters were an unmarried couple (different gender), 2% were an unmarried couple (same gender) and 2% were civil partners; and 9% of looked-after children who were adopted in the year ending 31 March 2010 were adopted by a single adopter (of these single adopters, 93% were female, which was slightly lower than in 2009). The number of children who ceased to be looked after due to special guardianship orders is

---

[1]   See www.adoptionuk.org/information/103152/e_factsandfigs.

1,200. Special guardianship orders were introduced in 2005. The number of these has increased by 2% from 2009 and by 68% from 2007.

SECTION 1 – WHAT IS ADOPTION?

11.10   Adoption is one way of providing permanency to a child unable to live with their birth family. Other options include:

- long-term fostering;

- permanency under a residence order; and

- permanency under a special guardianship order.

11.11   Adoption is a distinct service from other permanency options in that although the child and members of the birth family may maintain some contact or communication, no legal ties remain. The birth parents do not retain parental responsibility, which is conferred under the adoption order on the adoptive parent(s).

11.12   The needs of the child should inform the most suitable permanency outcome, although the current government position is that adoption is the most successful way in which those children who need an alternative permanent placement can best achieve stability, love and support.[2]

The values underpinning adoption[3]

11.13   The values underpinning adoption are clearly set out in the National Minimum Standards (NMS) 2011 in relation to children, adoptive adults and birth relatives.

Children

- The child's welfare, safety and needs are at the centre of the adoption process.

- Adopted children should have an enjoyable childhood, and benefit from excellent parenting and education, enjoying a wide range of opportunities to develop their talents and skills leading to a successful adult life.

- Children are entitled to grow up as part of a loving family that can meet their developmental needs during childhood and beyond.

---

[2]   Tim Loughton, MP Parliamentary Under-Secretary of State for Children in foreword to the guidance (22 February 2011).
[3]   See Department for Education *Adoption: National Minimum Standards* (2011).

- Children's wishes and feelings are important and will be actively sought and fully taken into account at all stages of the adoption process.

- Delays should be avoided as they can have a severe impact on the health and development of the children waiting to be adopted.

- A sense of identity is important to a child's well-being. To help children develop this, their ethnic origin, cultural background, religion, language and sexuality need to be properly recognised and positively valued and promoted.

- The particular needs of disabled children and children with complex needs will be fully recognised and taken into account.

- Where a child cannot be cared for in a suitable manner in their own country, intercountry adoption may be considered as an alternative means of providing a permanent family.

- Children, birth parents/guardians and families and adoptive parents and families will be valued and respected.

- A genuine partnership between all those involved in adoption is essential for the NMS to deliver the best outcomes for children; this includes the government, local government, other statutory agencies, voluntary adoption agencies and adoption support agencies.

Adopted adults and birth relatives

- Adoption is an evolving lifelong process for all those involved – adopted adults, and birth and adoptive relatives. The fundamental issues raised by adoption may reverberate and resurface at different times and stages throughout an individual's life.

- Adopted people should have access to information and services to enable them to address adoption related matters throughout their life.

- Agencies have a duty to provide services that consider the welfare of all parties involved, including the implications of their decisions and actions.

- Agencies should seek to work in partnership with all parties involved, taking account of their views and wishes in decision-making.

- Agencies should acknowledge differences in people's circumstances and establish policies that provide non-discriminatory services.

- Adopted adults have their adoptive identity safeguarded and the right to decide whether to be involved in contact or communication with birth family members.

SECTION 2 – THE LEGAL FRAMEWORK

11.14 Adoption is governed by a range of legislation and guidance:

- Adoption and Children Act 2002;

- Care Standards Act 2000;

- Adoption Agencies Regulations 2005;[4]

- Adoption and Children Act 2002 – Statutory Guidance amended 2011; and

- *Adoption National Minimum Standards* (2011).

SECTION 3 – THE ADOPTION AGENCY

11.15 An adoption agency is an approved agency that makes provision for the:

- recruitment;

- preparation;

- assessment;

- approval; and

- support,

in respect of people wishing to adopt children, and for placing children with them.

11.16 Adoption agencies can be local authorities, voluntary bodies, charities or private organisations. Voluntary organisations acting as an adoption society/agency must be registered under Part 2 of the Care Standards Act 2000. Most local authorities operate an adoption agency. Examples of adoption agencies operated by the private and voluntary agencies are:

- Coram Family;

- Family Futures;

- Barnado's; and

- NCH.

---

4   SI 2005/389.

11.17 All adoption agencies must comply with the Adoption Agencies Regulations 2005,[5] (whether local authorities or the voluntary sector). All adoption agencies are subject to inspection by Ofsted at least once every 3 years.

11.18 The task of an adoption agency is to deliver a comprehensive service to meet the needs of children who cannot be cared for by their birth parents or birth family and for whom adoption is the most suitable means of providing them with a family for life. An adoption agency will have an adoption and permanency team of social workers as part of its placement service. This team will normally be responsible for:

- the recruitment, training and assessment of prospective adopters;

- providing assistance in family finding and matching with a specific child waiting for adoption; and

- providing and/or commissioning post-adoption support services.

Tasks for adoption agencies

Statement of purpose

11.19 The Local Authority Adoption Service (England) Regulations 2003,[6] and the *Adoption National Minimum Standards*[7] require all adoption agencies to draw up a statement of purpose covering the matters listed in Sch 1 of the Regulations. These are:

- the aims and objectives of the agency;

- the name, address and telephone number of the registered service provider, and the responsible manager;

- the relevant qualifications and experience of the manager;

- the number, relevant qualifications and experience of the staff working for the agency;

- the organisational structure of the agency;

- the system in place to monitor and evaluate the provision of services to ensure that the services provided by the agency are effective and the quality of those services is of an appropriate standard;

---

[5] SI 2005/389.
[6] SI 2003/370.
[7] The Department for Education *Adoption: National Minimum Standards* (2011) issued under the Care Standards Act 2000, ss 23(1), 49(1).

- the procedures for recruiting, preparing, assessing, approving and supporting prospective adopters; and

- a summary of the complaints procedure.

11.20 A copy of the adoption agency's statement of purpose must be provided upon request for inspection to:

- any person working for the purposes of the agency;

- children who may be adopted, their parents and guardians;

- persons wishing to adopt a child;

- adopted persons, their adoptive parents, natural parents and former guardians; and

- any local authority.

11.21 The statement of purpose must be kept under review and updated and modified where necessary, at least once per annum.

Children's guide to adoption

11.22 Adoption agencies must also produce a children's guide to adoption. This should be given to every child for whom adoption is the plan.[8] The children's guide must:

- include a summary of what happens at each stage of the care and adoption process;

- inform the child about how long each stage of the adoption process is likely to take;

- contain information about access to an independent advocate;

- contain information about how to make a complaint; and

- contain information about how to contact the Children's Rights Director or the Children's Commissioner for England and Wales, as appropriate.

11.23 If necessary the guide is to be in different formats and languages to meet the needs of different groups of children.

---

[8] Department for Education *Adoption: National Minimum Standards* (2011).

SECTION 4 – THE ADOPTION PANEL

11.24 Every adoption agency must have access to an adoption panel (or an adoption and permanency panel) to assist it in meeting its requirements under the Adoption Agencies Regulations 2005.[9] The adoption panel (or adoption and permanency panel) has a central role within the adoption agency in terms of contributing to an effective adoption service.

11.25 Adoption panels must not be the 'bottleneck' in the adoption decision-making process. They must meet frequently and be able to meet at short notice before the next scheduled meeting to deal with urgent cases to avoid delay.[10]

The functions of the adoption panel

11.26 The adoption panel has five key areas of responsibility:

- recommending whether a specific child should be placed for adoption;

- recommending the approval of adoptive applicants (and in the case of some adoption and permanency panels, approving and/or matching long-term foster carers or kinship carers with a specific child);

- recommending the matching of a child in need of an adoptive family with the most suitable approved applicants;

- giving advice about:

  – contact of the adopted child with his or her birth family, and
  – post-adoption support services;

- monitoring, evaluating and undertaking a quality assurance role in relation to the adoption agency's functions.

11.27 The functions of the adoption panel are:

- to recommend whether a specific child should be placed for adoption;

- to give advice to the adoption agency about the arrangements for contact between the child and any person, usually birth family and any significant others;

- to hold an adoption panel meeting urgently when necessary (eg for a newly born infant whose parent(s) request that the child is placed for adoption);

---

[9]   SI 2005/389.
[10]   The Family Justice Council guidance 2008.

- to receive regular reports from the professional adviser regarding the progress of all children whose cases have been before the adoption panel; and

- to recall cases to the adoption panel for the purpose of:

  - matching the child with an adoptive family; or
  - reviewing the progress made (and if necessary reconsidering the decision that the child should be placed for adoption) in the event that an adoptive family has not been identified for a child within a period of 6 months.

11.28 The primary function of an adoption panel is to assist the adoption agency in making decisions about a child for whom adoption is the most suitable care plan. However, some local authorities expand the remit of the adoption panel to include:

- making other permanency recommendations;

- requesting that the panel assist and make recommendations about the approval and/or matching of children with permanent carers where the most suitable outcome may be:

  - long-term fostering (with long-term foster carers or kinship carers);[11] or
  - a special guardianship order.[12]

11.29 It is rare for an adoption and permanency panel to be asked to assist local authorities in the decision-making process relating to residence orders as in these cases the local authority has no duty to assess and provide support beyond the requirements of assessment and support available to any other child.

11.30 Where the adoption panel's remit has been expanded to include other permanent options, the panel will normally be known as the adoption and permanency panel. In doing so, the membership of the panel is slightly altered to include a member who is (or was in the previous two years) a foster carer for another local authority or private and voluntary fostering agency.

11.31 Most local authorities hold no less than one adoption panel meeting per month. The venue and times of meetings take into account the availability of applicants, and needs of children awaiting permanent planning.

11.32 The adoption panel may recommend to the adoption agency decision-maker whether applications should be approved or rejected. The

---

[11] The Fostering Services (England) Regulations 2011, SI 2011/581 apply.
[12] The Special Guardianship Regulations 2005, SI 2005/1109 apply.

adoption panel may also defer an application for further information to be reconsidered at the next adoption panel meeting, subject to the additional information being provided.

11.33 Written records should be kept of the adoption panel's discussions together with recommendations made. Differences of opinion among panel members should be recorded, together with any dissent from the final decision.

11.34 Adoption case records[13] must be stored safely for a minimum period of 100 years.[14]

11.35 Lawyers may find it helpful to seek disclosure of:

• the social worker's report to the adoption panel;

• the report of the adoption panel medical adviser;

• the minutes of the adoption panel relating to decisions (particularly where the decision was finely balanced or not unanimous); and

• any written record of the agency decision-maker relating to the adoption panel's recommendations (particularly where the adoption panel's decision was finely balanced or not unanimous).

11.36 The adoption agency may assert public interest immunity (PII) in respect of such records – in these circumstances; lawyers should consider whether such decisions can be legally challenged.

Members of adoption panels

11.37 Members of adoption and permanency panels are appointed in accordance with the Statutory Adoption Guidance as amended (2011).

11.38 Each agency must maintain a list of persons whom it considers suitable to be a member of an adoption panel. There is no limit on the number of people who may be included on the central list. Having a pool of people with different skills, experience and qualifications allows for the most appropriate members to be drawn upon to consider individual cases and reduces the likelihood of panel meetings having to be postponed, whilst retaining knowledgeable and experienced members without the need to wait for a vacancy to occur to appoint a new member to the list.

11.39 Before including an individual on the central list, the agency should inform them in writing of their performance objectives, which should include participation in induction and training, and safeguarding the confidentiality of

---

[13]   As identified in the Adoption and Children Act 2002, s 56.

[14]   The Disclosure of Adoption Information (Post-Commencement Adoptions) Regulations 2005, SI 2005/888, reg 6.

records and information submitted to the panel. The individual members should sign an acceptance form to record their agreement to these objectives.

11.40 The central list must include individuals with the qualifications, experience and qualities needed for the constitution of adoption panels:

- At least one independent person to chair the adoption panel. The most significant qualities that a panel chair should have are:

  - a sound understanding of the adoption process;
  - the authority and competence to chair a panel;
  - the ability to analyse and explain complex information;
  - the ability to identify key issues, problems and solutions; and
  - excellent interpersonal, oral and written communication skills.

- Up to two vice chairs. The vice chair should have the skills and experience necessary to deputise for the chair. These should be similar to the qualities for the panel chair. Unlike the panel chair, there is no requirement for the vice chair to be independent of the agency though this would be preferable where feasible.

- One or more social workers with at least three years' relevant post qualifying experience. Relevant experience should be in childcare social work, including direct experience in adoption work. These social workers do not need to be employed by the agency.

- The agency's medical adviser. Where the agency has more than one medical adviser they may all be included on the central list.

- Other persons. These will include individuals who are not employed by the agency and whose appointment would help reflect the independent nature of the panel. (Suitable members could include specialists in education, child and adolescent mental health, race and culture; and also those who have personal experience of adoption).

11.41 In addition, the following people are members to assist the adoption panel:

- legal adviser;

- panel adviser (usually the adoption team manager); and

- panel administrator who will take minutes of the meeting.

11.42 It is the responsibility of the adoption agency (usually in consultation with the chair of the adoption panel) to select and appoint new adoption panel members.

11.43 There is no requirement to recruit adoption panel members by an open recruitment process. However, the adoption agency should ensure that a diverse membership is chosen on the basis of relevant knowledge, experience and skills of prospective members.

11.44 Panel members will only be appointed subject to normal Criminal Bureau Records (CRB) checks which must be renewed every 3 years. Once appointed the adoption agency must maintain a 'personal file' on each panel member. The file should include the member's qualifications and experience, CRB checks and possibly two references. Any training undertaken as well as any complaints made against a member should also be included. A signed confidentiality agreement should also be maintained on file. Each new panel member will normally observe at least one panel meeting before becoming a full member and they will be expected to have received induction training (within 10 weeks of appointment).

Performance reviews

11.45 To ensure that the chair and the individuals on the central list remain suitable to remain on that list their performance must be reviewed annually against agreed performance objectives. The agency's decision-maker should review the performance of the panel chair, and for this purpose may attend a proportion of panel meetings but only as an observer.

11.46 Views about the chair's performance should be sought from other panel members, and from those who attend panel meetings, such as prospective adopters and social workers.

11.47 The agency adviser to the panel and the panel chair should conduct the performance review of those individuals on the central list.

11.48 Where an agency identifies that the chair or an individual on the central list is not performing to the required standard, perhaps as part of the review process, it should ensure that this is discussed promptly with the individual with the aim of addressing any development needs through advice and training. If, however, their performance remains below the required standard and the agency considers they should not remain on the central list, they should be informed that their services are no longer required. The individual must be given one month's notice of the agency's intention to remove their name from the central list. The notice should be in writing and include the reasons for the decision.

11.49 Once appointed to an adoption panel the appointment of the chair or an individual can only be terminated if they are unsuitable or unable to consider the case. This action may be taken when, for example, the individual becomes unavailable through illness or business commitments, when a previously unidentified conflict of interest arises (eg the individual knows the prospective adopters), etc. Terminating the individual's appointment to the panel is not the same as removing their name from the central list. The agency can continue to appoint the individual to another panel for as long as it considers that individual suitable.

11.50 The expectations of adoption panel members are:

- to sign a written agreement to maintain confidentiality of information, and store all documents received concerning the adoption panel in a safe and secure place;

- to read adoption panel papers prior to adoption panel meetings and prepare comments, questions and/or clarifications;

- to attend all adoption panel meetings as required, and submit apologies at the earliest opportunity if they are unable to attend;

- to declare an 'interest' when having prior knowledge of any applicant or child brought before the adoption panel;

- to return to the adoption panel administrator the numbered copy of documents at the end of every adoption panel meeting for shredding;

- to attend training and additional meetings as required (it is expected that training will be provided on an annual basis);

- to attend business meetings to review the panel's work and performance; and

- to attend annual performance review meetings.

The adoption panel quorum

11.51 The panel's business can only be conducted if at least five members (six for joint panels) are present, including the chair or vice chair and a social worker with at least 3 years' relevant post-qualifying experience. Where the vice chair has to chair the meeting, and is not an independent member, at least one independent member will need to be present for the panel to be quorum.

11.52 Independent members of the adoption panel may be paid a fee and reasonable expenses to attend all meetings. The fee can cover reading time as well as attendance, and usually the chair of the adoption panel is paid a higher fee to reflect their additional responsibilities.

11.53 An adoption panel member who has a personal interest in any application should state the nature of the interest to the meeting and not take part in the discussion. Similarly, if an adoption panel member has prior knowledge of a particular application presented to panel, that information should also be brought to the attention of the chair of the adoption panel before the discussions begin. In the event of the information being confidential, the adoption panel member should not participate in the discussion.

11.54   The role of the adoption panel administrator is:

- to coordinate and administer the adoption panel;

- to receive reports and all other necessary information about the child and applicants within 4 weeks of the completion of the assessment:

  - prospective adopters reports (PAR) in relation to suitability of prospective adopters;
  - child permanency report (CPR) in relation to children for whom recommendation should be made about potential placements for adoption; and
  - adoption placement report (APR) for matching a child with a specific adoptive family;

- to check that all relevant documentation including CRB checks and references have been carried out according to legal requirements;

- to inform the assessing social worker and team manager of any omissions, and return applications unless full, complete and signed reports are received by the due date;

- to copy and number reports, and distribute these to adoption panel members to be *received* at least 2 weeks before the adoption panel meeting;

- to take minutes and record discussions and recommendations of the adoption panel and pass these for immediate approval by panel members before sending the final version to the adoption agency decision-maker for his or her decision and signature. If the adoption panel cannot reach a consensus on its recommendation, the minutes should clearly set out the reasons;

- to make arrangements for copies of the adoption panel minutes to be kept and stored securely and to send copies of the relevant minutes to the appropriate social workers;

- to inform the assessing social workers of the adoption panel's decision no later than 24 hours following the panel meeting;

- to inform all other authorities and relevant agencies in cases of refusal to approve by the adoption panel; and

- to distribute agency decision-maker's decision in writing to the relevant parties (eg adoptive applicants, birth parents).

11.55   The role of the chair of the adoption panel is:

- to ensure that the adoption panel's recommendations are carried out consistently and in accordance with Regulations and National Standards;

- to enable and encourage all adoption panel members to contribute to the discussions and ensure dissenting views are recorded with reasons;

- to have a second casting vote in the event of the panel being unable to reach a consensus;

- to ensure the accuracy of the panel's recommendations, reasons and, following agreement with panel members, the minutes;

- to approve and sign recommendations of the adoption panel and ensure that proper arrangements have been made to inform the applicants (in cases of approvals) verbally of the recommendations no later then 24 hours after they were made;

- to inform applicants and social workers that the adoption panel only makes recommendations and that the final decision is made by the adoption agency decision-maker within 7 working days of the adoption panel recommendation being made;

- to advise the adoption agency decision-maker about adoption panel membership and highlight any omissions in expertise and/or community representations;

- to inform the adoption agency decision-maker of any childcare issues and concerns brought to the attention of the adoption panel in the course of its work;

- to review members' performance annually (with the panel adviser); and

- to assist in the preparation of an annual report to the adoption agency outlining the work of the panel and making recommendations for any operational or policy issues that need to be addressed (with the assistance of the adoption panel adviser and members).

11.56   The role of the adoption panel medical adviser is:

- to bring a broad range of experience in child health and development;

- to consider the prescribed medical reports relating to children, and other relevant medical information about the birth family likely to impact on the child's future health and development;

- to have direct contact with the child (and the birth family where appropriate) and other professionals;

- to meet with prospective adopters wishing to discuss the health and development needs of a specific child they are considering to adopt;

- to direct further reports as necessary to ensure that full information is available to the adoption panel;

- to write a summary report about the child's health which forms part of the child permanence report (CPR);

- to give additional verbal guidance and advice to the adoption panel about the child's health and development needs (and any implications for the adoptive family, including necessary support services likely to be required); and

- to give guidance with regards to health issues of adoptive applicants and prospective adopters in matching with a specific child.

11.57   The role of the adoption panel adviser is:

- to advise the adoption panel about matters of adoption agency policy, practice and procedure, and to liaise with social workers preparing reports;

- to provide a professional overview of the quality of the reports prepared by social workers, and to give advice as necessary;

- to assist the adoption agency with the appointment (and re-appointment), termination and review of appointment of members of the adoption panel;

- to be responsible for the induction and training of members of the adoption panel;

- to be responsible for liaison between the adoption agency and the adoption panel;

- to monitor the performance of members of the adoption panel and the administration of the adoption panel;

- to prepare the agenda for every adoption panel meeting;

- to give general advice or such advice as the adoption panel may request in relation to any case; and

- to report back to the adoption agency any concerns raised by adoption panel.

The professional adviser is *not* a panel member. The adviser must be a social worker with at least 5 years post-qualification experience and with relevant management experience as determined by the local authority.

11.58 The role of the adoption panel legal adviser is:

- to provide legal advice to the adoption panel; and

- to attend adoption panel meetings if at all possible to advise on legal matters in relation to each case, as appropriate. The advice may be given verbally at the meeting and in writing.

The legal adviser need not be an adoption panel member, but most adoption panels include the legal adviser at every meeting to give legal advice and answer questions arising from discussions by adoption panel members.

Conduct of the adoption panel meetings

11.59 The adoption panel administrator will send applicants and/or social workers an invitation to attend the meeting confirming the date, time and venue. The child's social worker, as well as their team manager, will normally attend the adoption panel meeting to present their reports, and clarify matters for the adoption panel.

11.60 Prospective adopter applicants will be invited to attend the adoption panel meeting discussing their application to adopt.[15] Applicants should normally be sent the following documentation beforehand:

- procedures for conducting the adoption panel meeting;

- profile of adoption panel members;

- feedback evaluation form to be completed following attendance; and

- information about their rights to apply to the Independent Review Mechanism (IRM) to review their case. This is an independent review system which is currently managed by BAAF under contract to the Department for Education.

11.61 Adoptive applicants should be prepared by their assessing social worker to attend the adoption panel meeting. The assessing social worker should provide them with a copy of their assessment report (Form F), which applicants should sign to approve distribution to adoption panel members.

---

[15]   The Adoption Agencies Regulations 2005, SI 2005/389, reg 26(4).

11.62 Local authorities have developed their own individual styles for conducting adoption panel meetings, but by and large the process is as follows:

- On arrival at the meeting place, adoptive applicants will be met and escorted by their assessing social worker to a waiting room.

- The chair of the adoption panel will normally meet adoptive applicants and/or social workers in the waiting room to discuss the conduct of the meeting, to remind applicants that the role of the adoption panel is to make *recommendations* to the adoption agency and that the panel has no power to make decisions.

- The assessing social worker will be invited to join the adoption panel meeting in advance of the applicant(s) to clarify any matters raised by the adoption panel from the assessment reports read in advance of the meeting. The applicants will then be invited by the chair to join the adoption panel meeting.

- The chair of the adoption panel will ask the applicants whether there is anything they wish to add in support of their application.

- Panel members will have prepared a list of questions on matters arising from their earlier discussions about the written assessments and documentation received. These will be put to the applicants by different members of the adoption panel for clarification. The assessing social worker may assist with any questions raised but is not expected to answer questions on behalf of applicants.

- Applicants should then be given the opportunity to ask questions of the adoption panel.

- At the end of the meeting, applicants will be asked to withdraw (after representations and questions have been completed), allowing the adoption panel members to make recommendations, if not by consent then by majority vote.

- Applicants may be asked to complete the feedback evaluation form about their experiences of attending the adoption panel meeting to enable the panel to learn and improve the way it functions.

- Immediately after the adoption panel meeting the chair of the adoption panel will normally inform the assessing social worker and/or adoptive applicants of the panel's recommendation.[16]

---

[16] Applicants who decide not to attend the adoption panel meeting should be informed verbally of the adoption panel's recommendation/decision by their assessing social worker no later than 24 hours following the adoption panel meeting.

- The adoption panel administrator will pass the recommendation made by the adoption panel to the agency decision-maker for a decision.

- Written confirmation of the decision (with reasons for the decisions) will be sent to applicants by the agency decision-maker within 7 working days, if at all possible.

- Decisions of the agency decision-maker are subject to review by the IRM where applicants have a right to challenge the decision of the agency.

Minutes of panel meetings

11.63 The minutes of the panel must record the names of panel members attending the meeting, and the names and roles of any other people present at the meeting. The minutes must accurately reflect the discussion and cover the key issues, rather than be a verbatim record of the meeting.

11.64 Where panel members have serious reservations, the panel chair must ensure these are recorded in the minutes and are attached to the panel's recommendation. If the panel cannot reach a consensus on its recommendation after the chair and other members of the panel have voted, the panel chair has a second vote, ie the casting vote.

11.65 The panel's minutes should clearly set out the reasons why the panel chair had to use the casting vote. The final minutes must be produced promptly and agreed by the panel members and then sent to the agency's decision-maker to allow the decision to be made within 7 working days of receipt of the panel's recommendation and final set of panel minutes.

11.66 Arrangements should be made by the agency adviser to the panel for the safekeeping of the minutes and the record. Panel minutes, like other parts of adoption case records, are exempt from the subject access provisions of the Data Protection Act 1998.

SECTION 5 – MAKING THE DECISION ABOUT ADOPTION

11.67 The decision-making process in adoption and permanency is complex and requires the involvement of various professionals within the adoption agency, the adoption panel and the agency decision-maker.

Timescales

11.68 There are various timescales that must be complied with by the local authority in relation to planning for adoption:

- the child's need for a permanent home should be addressed and a permanence plan made at the 4 month review;

- the adoption panel should receive all necessary information from the agency within 6 weeks of the completion of the child's permanence report (CPR); and

- the adoption panel's recommendation on whether the child should be placed for adoption should be made within 2 months of a review where adoption has been identified as the permanence plan.

11.69 Where the agency is unable to comply with a timescale or decides not to, it should record the reasons on the child's case record.

11.70 The agency should monitor its performance against these timescales and make this information available in its 6-monthly reports under the National Minimum Standards.

The child permanence report

11.71 Most authorities use the child permanence report (CPR) format produced by BAAF for the purpose of recommending whether a child should be placed for adoption.

11.72

What should child permanence reports include?

- The child's profile and welfare together with a chart showing the child's movements throughout life

- A description of the child prepared by his or her current carer(s)

- A summary of the child's medical report prepared by the adoption agency medical adviser

- Information in relation to the health of the child's birth family

- Current and future support needs of the child and birth family, including the offer of counselling to birth parents

- An analysis of the options that have been considered by the agency for the future care of the child, and the reasons why adoption is considered the preferred option

---

11.73 When considering whether to recommend that a child should be placed for adoption, the adoption panel must have regard to:

- its principles and values underpinning adoption;

- the child's need for a permanent placement outside the birth family;

- the capacity of any family member to care for the child;

- the suitability of adoption to meet the child's long-term care needs;

- the welfare check list;[17] and

- the likelihood of finding a suitable adoptive family for the individual child within a reasonable timescale.

11.74 In *SB v a County Council, Re P*,[18] the Court of Appeal confirmed that it is permissible for the agency to pursue a dual or parallel plan. This enables the agency, where it considers the child should be placed for adoption, to start seeking adoptive and foster parents at the same time.[19] In these circumstances the adoption panel will recommend that the child should be placed for adoption while, at the same time, acknowledging that the fostering plan may be pursued.

---

[17] As set out in the Adoption and Children Act 2002, s 1(4).
[18] [2008] EWCA Civ 535.
[19] In circumstances when it is believed that finding an adoptive family may be difficult (eg for an older child or a child with complex special needs).

11.75   Issues to be considered by the adoption panel in making the decision about adoption are:

- the likelihood of finding adoptive parents for this child within a timescale that addresses the child's need for permanency and continuity. The adoption panel should include consideration of:

  - the child's age and level of maturity;
  - the child's ethnicity and cultural background;
  - the child's religious persuasion; and
  - the wishes and views of the child;

- any other means (apart from adoption) of securing permanency for the child;

- the child's history, particularly its likely impact on the child's ability to make attachments. The adoption panel should include consideration of:

  - possible impact of trauma and/or abuse;
  - developmental needs including identified and anticipated developmental delay;
  - health needs including any diagnosed or anticipated disability; and
  - educational needs (current and anticipated);

- the wishes and views of the birth family about the proposed adoption and their wishes regarding the child's religious upbringing;

- present and future connections for the child including direct and indirect contact with the birth parents and other family members;

- the views of the children's guardian if one is appointed; and

- the capacity of the parents and any other connected person to care for the child.

11.76   When in court proceedings, this must include expert reports which have been filed and served in care proceedings and which address the present and future needs of the subject child (including, but not exclusively, dealing with placement issues).

11.77   Where such reports are voluminous, as a minimum those sections of the reports setting out the experts' opinion, conclusions and/or recommendations should be provided to panel members and to the decision-maker.

11.78   A summary of the expert(s)' opinions should only be provided to the panel members and the decision-maker in substitution for the reports if:

- the summary is in writing;

- all parties to the care proceedings agree in writing that the summary is fair and accurate and should be provided to the panel and the decision-maker in substitution for the reports; and

- copies of the reports are available at the meeting for the members of the panel and the decision-maker to consult if desired.

11.79 If the adoption panel does recommend that the child should be placed for adoption, it must also consider and may give advice to the agency about:

- the arrangements that the agency proposes in respect of contact; and

- whether an application should be made for a placement order (where the agency is a local authority).

Placement order applications

11.80 When the adoption panel recommends that a child should be placed for adoption, it must also recommend as to whether an application should be made for a placement order in cases where the parents do not agree with the adoption plan. An application for a placement order is normally made concurrently with or soon after the making of a care order. A placement order permits the local authority to place a child with adoptive parent(s) and extinguishes the parental responsibility of the birth parents. Parental responsibility for the child is passed to the adoption agency.

Adoption Register

11.81 Agencies are required to refer children to the Adoption Register when they are not actively considering a local match for the child. Referrals can be made either when the agency's decision-maker has decided that the child should be placed for adoption or after 3 months of that decision during which the agency had unsuccessfully sought a local or consortium match.

11.82 If legal proceedings are ongoing at this stage, and the child is subject to an interim care order, referral to the Adoption Register can be made provided the necessary consents and the court's agreement have been obtained. See *Re K (Child) (Adoption: Permission to Advertise)*.[20]

Consent to placement for adoption

11.83 Section 19 of ACA 2002 provides that a parent may consent to the placement for adoption of their child, and that this consent may be to placement with any prospective adopter chosen by the agency, or to a specific prospective adopter.

---

[20] [2007] EWHC 544 (Fam).

11.84 Section 20 of ACA 2002 provides that a parent, who gives consent to the child being placed for adoption, may also give their advance consent to the making of an adoption order. At the same time they will have the option of making a statement that they do not wish to be informed of any application for an adoption order (although they may retract such a statement later).

11.85 The adoption agency must explain to the parent the consequences of giving consent to placement, in particular the fact that a withdrawal of their consent will be ineffective once an application has been made for an adoption order (which could be made any time after the child has lived with the prospective adopter for 10 weeks). They should also ensure that the parent understands the position about contact and the provisions of s 26 of the ACA 2002.

11.86 The agency should explain to the parent the procedure for the formal witnessing of consent. The agency should provide the parent with contact details for the social worker and any support worker to enable the parent to get in touch if they have any queries, or if they are considering withdrawing their consent. The agency should also emphasise to the parents the importance of their keeping the agency informed about their own whereabouts. This will benefit not only the parent receiving information about their child's progress, but also the child as it will help avoid possible delays in notifying the parent when the adoption application is made to court.

11.87 Consent is given on one of the forms A100 to A104 issued under the Family Procedure Rules 2010 and must be witnessed in accordance with those rules. A reporting officer from CAFCASS will witness consent prior to court proceedings.

11.88 The appointment and duties of the reporting officer in adoption proceedings are set out in detail in rr 16.30–16.32 of the Family Procedure Rules 2010. The role of the reporting officer is to ensure that the consent of the birth parents and any guardian to the making of the adoption order, is given unconditionally and with a full understanding of the nature and effect of the order, and to witness the giving of that consent.

11.89 The reporting officer should investigate all the circumstances relevant to the parents or guardians giving consent to ensure their rights are protected.[21]

11.90 The reporting officer will then need to witness the formal signing by the parent or guardian of the consent to placement form, sign the form themselves and then notify the agency in writing, including the consent form with the notification. The reporting officer must keep a copy of the original form.

---

[21]   This piece of work is one of the few instances where it is not necessary for CAFCASS to see the child.

11.91 Where the reporting officer is not satisfied that the parents wish to give their full consent, or has doubts that they fully understand its implications, or considers that they are not competent to give consent, they will be directed by CAFCASS guidance to notify the agency. In these circumstances consent cannot be given, and it will be necessary to make an application for a placement order.

'Consent' where the child is under 6 weeks old

11.92 Section 52(3) of the ACA 2002 makes it clear that any consent to adoption given by a mother before her child is 6 weeks old is ineffective.

11.93 Special provision is therefore made for those cases where it is desirable to place a child as soon as possible, but formal consent to adoption must not be sought before the child is 6 weeks old (eg concurrent placement is sought and the child placed with foster carers under s 20 who are also approved as adopters).

11.94 If the parent asks for the child to be returned, the child must be returned by the agency unless any of the following orders are applied for:

- an emergency protection order or a care order under the CA 1989; or

- a placement order or an adoption order under ACA 2002.

SECTION 6 – APPROVAL OF PROSPECTIVE ADOPTIVE APPLICANTS

11.95 On 22 December 2011 the government announced that the assessment process for prospective adopters is to be overhauled. A group of experts has been appointed to draw up a new process to recruit, train and assess people as adoptive parents.

11.96 The government's stated belief is that the current system as described below is slow and unnecessarily bureaucratic. The government stated that potentially suitable adopters are often turned away because they may not be the right ethnic match, may be overweight or may have smoked. Adoptive parents can wait up to a year or more to be approved, which leaves thousands of children in care waiting months, and even years, for a family.

11.97 The new expert panel is made up of representatives from across the adoption sector, including the Consortium of Voluntary Adoption Agencies, British Association of Adoption and Fostering, Adoption UK, and the Association of Directors of Children's Services. The group will work with Martin Narey, the government's Adoption Adviser, and provide recommendations in March 2012 about a new, more efficient process to be introduced later in 2012.

11.98   The group has been asked to:

- Consider arrangements for an improved recruitment process for adopters and ensure those who do come forward are not lost to the system.

- Streamline the training and assessment process, building on existing good practice.

- Remove bureaucracy and over-prescription regarding the information to be collected about prospective adopters.

- Provide set timescales for training and assessing the suitability of adopters, along with a new national assessment form based on a concise but robust analysis of capacity to care for a child in need of adoption.

- Suggest what, if any, new monitoring and evaluation mechanisms would need to be put in place to measure the success of the new system.

11.99   It is therefore anticipated that this section of the book is likely to require revision by the end of 2012 and should be read with this in mind.

The role of the adoption panel in approving prospective adopters

11.100   The adoption panel has responsibility for carrying out various functions in respect of the approval of prospective adoptive applicants:

- Ensuring that the assessment of adoptive applicants is based on relevant, reliable, current and sufficient information, enabling decisions to be made in accordance with legal requirements, national and local standards.

- Making recommendations to the adoption agency decision-maker about approval or rejection in a consistent manner. The adoption agency decision-maker will make a decision within 7 days of the adoption panel's recommendation.

- Making arrangements for adoption panel recommendations to be conveyed orally to applicants on the same day of the decision being made, if practicable.

- Considering any representations made by applicants if asked to do so by the adoption agency decision-maker in cases where applicants have sought representation.

- Making recommendations in relation to brief reports prepared when the local authority has decided an adoptive applicant is unsuitable to adopt but the applicant has refused to withdraw their application.

Timescales

11.101 There are clear timescales governing the progress of assessment and approval of adoptive placements:

- adoptive applicants should be given written information about the adoption process within 5 working days of making their initial enquiry;

- the enquirers should be invited to an adoption information meeting or be offered an individual interview by the agency within two months of their enquiry;

- the adoption panel should receive all necessary information about the prospective adopter from the agency within six weeks of the completion of the prospective adopter's report; and

- the adoption panel's recommendation about the suitability of the prospective adopter to adopt a child should be made within eight months of the receipt of their formal application.

11.102 Where the agency is unable to comply with a timescale, or decides not to, it should record the reasons on the prospective adopter's case record.

Prospective adoption reports (PAR)

11.103 Reports on prospective adoptive applicants will be prepared for adoption panel on the basis of:

- personal interviews;

- group preparation and training;

- references received and reports of checks carried out by the adoption agency – these should include:

  - CRB checks;
  - health reports;
  - local authority checks; and
  - at least three personal referees, not more than one of whom may be a relative. It assists the adoption panel if external references span a long period of time of knowing each applicant, and includes ex-partners and/or adult children of the applicant if any.

11.104 Reports are normally completed using the prospective adoption report (PAR) format established by BAAF.

11.105 Reports may be accompanied by a written second opinion of a co-worker from the adoption agency's adoption team or another specialist worker involved with the family. On completion of the assessing social worker's draft report, a second opinion visit will usually be made by another adoption social worker (or the team manager of the adoption team). The purpose of the second opinion visit is to give further consideration to any difficulties or sensitive issues that have arisen during the course of the assessment. The second opinion visit is of particular use where the social worker has doubts about the applicants' suitability as prospective adopters. A brief, separate report must be completed by the worker who carried out the second opinion visit and presented to the adoption panel with the Form F.

11.106 Reports must also include a summary of the health checks on applicants.

11.107 Completed, typed and signed reports must be received by the panel administrator at least 3 weeks before the panel meeting.

11.108 The information required for a full report on adoptive applicants is contained within the Adoption Agencies Regulations 2005.[22] The adoption panel will also expect assessments to demonstrate applicants' knowledge and skills in accordance with the requirements contained within the BAAF Competencies (2000).

11.109 In considering making a recommendation for approval the adoption panel will usually seek evidence from the reports to demonstrate:

•   the attitude and value base of the applicants including:

–   belief and attitudes to different family structures;
–   expectations regarding attitudes to and experience of issues of racism and discrimination;
–   attitudes and beliefs about discipline and health and safety matters including smoking; and
–   where the applicants are relatives, significant friends or existing foster carers who are seeking to adopt a child known to them, the adoption panel will also give particular consideration to family dynamics;

•   the applicants' ability to provide the child with a family for life including:

–   the health and disability of the applicants;

•   the applicants' capacity to prioritise and promote the best interests of the child including:

---

[22]   The Adoption Agencies Regulations 2005, SI 2005/389, reg 25 and Sch 4, Pt 1.

— the financial circumstances of the applicants;[23]

- the applicants' emotional capacity to make life-long commitment to a child whose history may not be fully known;

- the applicants' ability to be flexible and non-judgmental; and

- the lessons learnt from training and capacity to develop further skills.

Key Competence Skills Assessments

11.110 The PAR should provide an assessment and analysis of the capacity of applicants to adopt. This requires an assessment of the following key skills and knowledge base:

Attitudes and beliefs

- The applicants' understanding of and commitment to parenting an adopted child.

- Ability to value and promote the identity needs of a child which they may not share.

- Their capacity and skills to empathise with and meet the complex needs of children requiring permanency.

- Their attitude to informing the child about their birth origins and history and maintaining connections with the birth family and siblings.

- Their experience of and ability to deal with issues of equality and discrimination and its impact on a child's development.

- Their ability to work effectively with other agencies and to use support and health services if necessary after the child's adoption.

- The views and wishes of children already living in the adoptive family.

- Their employment arrangements and financial commitments.

Parenting capacity

- Understanding and knowledge of child development, including appreciating the impact of disruptive attachments the children have experienced.

---

[23] The adoption panel may give advice in relation to the support needs of applicants, including financial matters, in light of the agency's policy on adoption support.

- Ability to listen and communicate with children in a way that is appropriate to their level of maturity, and take into account their wishes and feelings.

- Ability to promote the identity and self esteem of the child.

- Ability to provide appropriate boundaries and manage child's behaviour taking into account their beliefs about and methods of discipline.

- Ability to accept the child as unique and promote the child's individual identity.

Providing a safe and caring environment

- Ability to ensure children are cared for in a safe environment and are free from harm and abuse.

- Ability to help children keep themselves safe, and to know how to seek help if their safety is threatened.

- Ability to recognise the particular vulnerability to abuse of previously abused children and/or children with disabilities.

Working as a member of a team

- Ability to work with other individuals and organisations.

- Ability to communicate effectively.

- Capacity to keep information confidential.

Adoption as a life-long process

- Capacity to make a life-long commitment to a child whose history may not be fully known.

- Ability to seek appropriate post-adoption support services when necessary.

- Ability to understand and promote a child's development towards adulthood.

Own development

- Insight into their own and their family's experiences.

- Insight and understanding of the impact of adoption.

- Key competencies of adoptive applicants to be considered in assessments.

- Ability to sustain positive relationships when under stress.

- Motivation to adopt (including assessment of whether and how the applicants have dealt with relevant infertility issues).

- Ability to use support and training from own personal network and/or from professional networks.

Maintaining connections between children and their birth families

- Ability to inform the child of their birth origins and history.

- Ability to maintain connections between the child and their birth parents, relatives and siblings.

- Ability to understand and commitment to meet the complex needs of children requiring permanency in relation to their history, disability and other identity needs.

The adoption panel's duties in respect of unapproved applicants

11.111 When the local authority assesses an adoptive applicant as unsuitable to adopt, it must prepare a brief report[24] for consideration by the adoption panel in the event that the applicant(s) do not agree to withdraw their application.

11.112 The assessing social worker and their manager should prepare a report giving the reasons for refusing to proceed with a full assessment. Applicants must be given a copy of the report and given 10 days to comment before it will be considered by the adoption panel.[25]

11.113 The adoption panel must consider the report and may request a full assessment of the applicants. Alternatively, the adoption panel can recommend that the applicant(s) is not suitable to adopt.

Reviews of suitability to adopt

11.114 Prospective adopters' suitability to adopt should be reviewed annually and until a child is placed with them. However, the need for an earlier review could arise, for instance, where:

---

[24] The Adoption Agencies Regulations 2005, SI 2005/389, reg 25.
[25] The Department for Education *Adoption: National Minimum Standards* (2011), para 1.55 clarifies what information can be withheld from the applicant(s).

- a child was placed with the prospective adopter and the placement disrupts;

- a child was matched with the prospective adopter, and introductions have started, but a decision is made not to proceed with the placement;

- a couple separates;

- the prospective adopter becomes pregnant or has given birth to a child;

- there are substantive changes in their health or their economic circumstances;

- concerns are raised about child welfare and safety; and

- any other matters arise which may affect their suitability to adopt.

11.115   When carrying out a review the agency must:

- make enquiries and obtain information it considers necessary in order to review whether the prospective adopter continues to be suitable to adopt;

- take into consideration minutes and recommendations of any disruption meeting held following a placement disruption; and

- ascertain and take into account the views of the prospective adopter.

11.116   The social worker conducting the review should usually be the adoption team manager but could be another social worker who did not conduct the original assessment.

11.117   Where the information gathered in the review suggests to the agency that the prospective adopter may no longer be suitable to adopt, the same original process for approval applies.

11.118

What can prospective adoptive applicants expect from the local authority?

• To receive an information pack about becoming an adoptive parent and the approval process, including details about their training needs, and complaint procedures within five days of making the initial enquiry, and to be offered an interview/information meeting within 2 months thereafter

• To be considered as potential adopters regardless of marital status, race, religion, gender or sexual orientation

• To be invited to attend preparation and training groups. Preparation groups aim to focus on preparing applicants for the home assessment and to become adoptive parents. The groups form an inherent part of the assessment process by providing applicants with an opportunity to learn as much as possible about the emotional, psychological and practical aspects of adoption and by offering an opportunity for applicants to decide whether adoption is right for them

• To be fully involved in the assessment process by identifying, collecting and organising the information with their assessing social worker

• To receive a copy of the assessment report (with the second opinion visit report) for completion and signing by them within 6 months, and at least 28 days before the adoption (or adoption and permanency) panel

• To be given at least 10 working days to comment on the report

• For the adoption panel to consider their application to adopt within 8 months of receipt of their formal application to be approved as adopters

• To be invited to attend the adoption panel considering their application and to be informed orally of the panel recommendation within 24 hours

• For the adoption agency decision-maker to inform them in writing about whether they are suitable to adopt within 7 working days of the adoption panel's recommendation

• Where the adoption agency decides not to proceed with the assessment, to be informed of the decision and reasons in writing. The adoption agency should prepare a 'brief report' about the matter in these circumstances to be sent to the adoption panel for a recommendation

• Where the adoption agency decides that the applicants are not suitable, the adoption agency decision-maker must notify the prospective adopters in writing. This is a 'qualifying determination'. The applicants must be advised they may submit any representations they wish to make to the adoption agency and/or apply to the Independent Review Mechanism for a review of the 'qualifying determination' within 40 working days

Non-agency adoption

11.119   The term non-agency adoptions applies to cases in which the child has not been placed for adoption by the local authority. It applies to:

- adoption by the partner of the child's birth or adoptive parent (ie a step-parent);

- adoption by relatives of the child;

- adoption by approved foster carers;

- adoption by private foster carers; and

- intercountry adoption.

11.120   This section only deals with approved foster carers[26] who wish to adopt the child placed with them in the absence of approval by the local authority.

Foster carers who wish to adopt

11.121   Foster carers are entitled to make a court application to adopt any child placed with them for more than 12 months,[27] even without support from the local authority. Such an application would be regarded as a non-agency adoption (ie not arranged by the local authority or any other adoption agency).

11.122   The category of non-agency adoptions also includes step-parent adoptions. In these cases the court notifies the relevant local authority of the hearing date and requests an Annex A[28] Report. The local authority would normally file the required report within a period of 6 weeks.

11.123   Non-agency adoptions are not entitled to support under the Adoption Support Regulations and Guidance. However, families may seek advice and support under s 17 of the CA 1989 as available for any other family.

11.124   Foster carers can also make a formal application to the local authority to adopt a child placed in their care. In these circumstances, the foster carer will be entitled to the same information, preparation and support as other adopters and should be assessed within 4 months.[29]

---

[26] A similar process applies to private foster carers although the child should have lived with the carer for at least 3 years.

[27] The Adoption and Children Act 2002, s 42(4). This would be in exceptional circumstances when either there is no care plan to place the child for adoption or the plan is adoption but the local authority is not supporting the foster carer's application.

[28] Application for a s 84 order. See Practice Guidance Direction Supplement 14 and r 14.11(3) of the Family Procedure Rules 2010.

[29] The Department for Education *Adoption: National Minimum Standards* (2011).

SECTION 7 – THE INDEPENDENT REVIEW MECHANISM (IRM)

11.125 Where the agency decides that prospective adopters are not suitable the agency decision-maker must notify the prospective adopters in writing together with reasons. This is a 'qualifying determination'. The agency decision-maker must also:

- send the prospective adopters a copy of the adoption panel's recommendations (if these are different); and

- advise the prospective adopters that they may apply to the IRM for a review of the 'qualifying determination' within 40 working days of receipt of the notification.

11.126 The operation of the IRM is now governed by the Independent Review of Determinations (Adoption) Regulations 2005.[30]

11.127 The following information must be sent to the IRM:

- the adoption agency's report about the prospective adopters;

- any written representations by the prospective adopters;

- any other reports or information sent to the adoption (or adoption and permanency) panel;

- the minutes of the adoption (or adoption and permanency) panel, its recommendations and the reasons for its recommendations; and

- the notification and the adoption agency's reasons for making its qualifying determination, as sent by the agency decision-maker to the prospective adopters.

11.128 The IRM review panel will then make recommendations to that adoption agency which the decision-maker must consider before reaching a final decision.

11.129 Each agency should appoint a liaison officer. Their role is to serve as the main contact between the agency and the IRM. The liaison officer sends to the IRM administrator all the appropriate documentation and ensures the case is referred to the agency's decision-maker after the IRM has made its recommendation. The liaison officer must ensure swift action is taken on requests made by the review panel, for example a request for a specialist medical report and give the IRM notification of the agency's decision.

---

[30] SI 2005/3332.

SECTION 8 – MATCHING AND PROPOSING A PLACEMENT

The adoption placement report (APR)

11.130 Matching is the term used to describe the process of placing a *particular child* with a *particular placement.*

Timescales

11.131 A proposed placement with a suitable prospective adopter should be identified and approved by the adoption panel within 6 months of the agency deciding that the child should be placed for adoption.

11.132 Where a birth parent has requested that a child aged under 6 months be placed for adoption, a proposed placement with a suitable prospective adopter should be identified and approved by the panel within 3 months of the agency deciding that the child should be placed for adoption.

The functions of the adoption panel in relation to matching

11.133 The adoption panel has a number of functions in relation to the matching process:

• to recommend whether a particular prospective adopter would be a suitable adoptive parent for a particular child;[31]

• to give advice about the nature of contact with any birth family member or any other person, post-placement and post-adoption;

• to give advice for post-adoption support for the child, adoptive family and birth family;

• to give advice as to whether the parental responsibility of the prospective adopter should be restricted and if so, the extent of the restriction; and

• to consider reports regarding any placement breakdowns, and make recommendations, if any, for the adoption panel and adoption agency practice.

---

[31]   The Adoption Agencies Regulations 2005, SI 2005/389, reg 32.

What should matching reports include?

Reports about the child

11.134 These should include:

- an up-to-date child permanence report (CPR) including recent report from the current carer and school, if relevant;

- other relevant specialist reports identifying the child's current and future development and support needs;

- a summary of a current medical report and health needs; and

- minutes of the adoption panel meeting which recommended the child should be placed for adoption.

Reports about the adoptive family

11.135 These should include:

- the assessment report on the adoptive family – PAR;

- updated CRB checks and medical information as appropriate;

- previous panel minutes approving the prospective adopters; and

- support needs of the proposed adopters.

'Matching' reports

11.136 These should include:

- The adoption placement report (APR) matching the child with the specific adoptive family. This should include information about the agency's reasons for identifying the specific family, taking into account the child's identified needs, the parenting skills of the prospective adopter, what support is required and how the prospective adopter's parenting capacities can be supported and developed alongside the child's changing needs. The guidance emphasises the need of social workers to avoid delay and to be informed by research outcomes.

- Proposals for adoption support for the child and adoptive family (including support for the purpose of contact with birth family or any other person).

Attendance at adoption panel for matching

11.137 The following professionals will normally attend an adoption panel meeting at which matching of a particular child to a particular placement is being considered:

- the child's social worker and their team manager;

- the social worker who carried out the assessment of the approved adoptive applicants; and

- the family finding social worker from the adoption team.

11.138 It is a growing practice among adoption agencies to invite the prospective adopters to the panel meeting discussing the match. This is normally for the purpose of:

- giving prospective applicants the opportunity to meet the panel making recommendations about them;

- discussing the support services offered and whether this is acceptable to the prospective adopters;

- clarifying any health issues and developmental needs of the child, although prospective adopters may have already met with the medical advisor before the panel meeting discussing the match; and

- clarifying the remits and limits for exercising of parental responsibility should approval for the match be given.

The factors considered by the adoption panel in matching

11.139 When considering whether a particular adoptive family can meet the identified and future needs of a particular child (or sibling group), the adoption panel will need to consider a range of issues, including the level of post-adoption support required to minimise the risks inherent in any adoption placement.

11.140 The core tasks for the adoption panel to consider are:

- What can the prospective adoptive family give to this child?

- What does the prospective adoptive family expect in return?

The triad factors of the child, adoptive family and birth family

11.141 There are three key factors that should be considered in adoption assessments:

(1) About the child

- The individual needs of the child.

- The resilience of the child to their past experiences and history.

- Issues identified in preparation work with the child.

- Particular behaviours of the child and in particular any attachment difficulties.

- The age of the child to be matched and the ages of children in the adoptive family, if any.

- The current medical, developmental and health needs of the child and the prognosis.

- The child's likely potential in terms of education attainments.

- The child's needs for contact and maintaining connections with their birth family including siblings.

- The child's needs and capacity to make relationships which accord with the expectations of the adoptive family.

- The identity needs of the child, including their ethnic, racial, cultural and religious needs.

(2) About the adoptive family

- The adoptive family's views about the proposed match.

- The capacity of the adoptive family to meet this child's identity needs, taking into account their ethnic, cultural and religious background.

- The adoptive family's realistic expectations of this child's capacity to make attachments, having regard to the child's history.

- The adoptive family's capacity to deal with abuse and neglect which may not yet be known about.

- The adoptive family's capacity to understand and empathise with the birth family's history, health and circumstances around the adoption.

- The adoptive family's expectations about particular behaviours of this child.

- The effect of placing a child of this age with other children (or not) in the adoptive family.

- The adoptive family's expectations regarding education attainments in terms of this child's likely potential.

- The attitudes and expectations of the adoptive parents (and any children already living in the family) towards promoting and maintaining contact with this child's birth family.

- The needs of any children already in the family in particular relation to age gaps, ethnicity and gender balance.

- The wishes and feelings of children in the adoptive family towards this child.

(3)   About the birth family

- The circumstances and views of the birth family.

- The need for any future sibling placement.

Placing a child for adoption with birth relatives

11.142   Local authorities are required by s 22 of the CA 1989 to consider a placement with relatives if the child being looked after cannot return to their birth parents. Where this solution is the right one for the child, the placement is likely to be secured under a fostering arrangement or by a residence or special guardianship order, but the appropriateness of adoption by a relative should not be automatically ruled out.

11.143   There may be some circumstances where the security provided by the irrevocability of an adoption order, and its lifelong effect, would be best for the child and outweigh the potential drawbacks of altering of biological relationships. For example, a grandparent adopting their grandchild would be legally the child's parent, which would mean the child's birth parent would, in law, be their sibling.

11.144   There is no presumption that a special guardianship order will be preferable to an adoption order if the placement is with a relative. It will be necessary to consider the particular facts of each individual case.[32] In some circumstances where the relatives who would most suitably care for the child live outside the British Islands, it may be that such a placement can best be

---

[32]   See for example *Re S (Adoption Order or Special Guardianship Order)* [2007] EWCA Civ 54, *Re AJ (Adoption Order or Special Guardianship Order)* [2007] EWCA Civ 55 and *Re M-J (Adoption Order or Special Guardianship Order)* [2007] EWCA Civ 56.

achieved by adoption. There are also the exceptional circumstances when it is considered necessary to ensure the parents do not retain parental responsibility for their child's safety.

SECTION 9 – THE ROLE OF THE ADOPTION AGENCY DECISION-MAKER

11.145 All adoption panel recommendations must be referred to the adoption agency decision-maker. The adoption agency decision-maker cannot be a member of the adoption panel and must be a senior person within the adoption agency (this is usually the assistant director of local authority children services or the director/trustee in the case of voluntary adoption agencies). The adoption agency decision-maker must take into account the recommendations of the adoption panel in making a decision about whether:

- a child should be placed for adoption;

- the prospective adopter(s) (or other carer's) are suitable to adopt a child or continues to be suitable to adopt a child;

- a child should be placed for adoption with a specific prospective adopter (the match); and

- to disclose protected information about adults under s 61 of ACA 2002 and reg 15 of the Disclosure of Adoption Information (Post-Commencement Adoptions) Regulations 2005 (AIR) when determining an application.

11.146 There may be more than one decision-maker in an agency. The decision-maker may not delegate their authority to another person.

11.147 In reaching a decision the decision-maker will need to consider:

- the exercise of powers under s 1 of the ACA 2002;

- all the information surrounding the case including the reports submitted to the adoption panel;

- that the author(s) of the reports comply with the regulations and guidance;

- the stability and permanence of the relationship of any couple under consideration (reg 4 of the Suitability of Adopters Regulations 2005);

- the recommendation and reasons of the adoption panel and the independent review panel; and

- the final minutes of the adoption panel including any minutes from adjourned panel meetings and the independent review panel.

11.148 The decision-maker must make the decision within 7 working days of the recommendation of the adoption panel or independent review panel. The child's parents or guardian and prospective adopter should be informed orally of the agency's decision within 2 working days and written confirmation should be sent to them within 5 working days. Where the independent review panel has reviewed the case, a copy of the decision must be sent to the contract manager of the Independent Review Mechanism (IRM).

11.149 In *Hofstetter v LB Barnet and IRM*,[33] the Court of Appeal set out guidance for the way in which the decision-maker should approach a case, whether it is a decision based on the agency's own panel's recommendation or one of an independent review panel's recommendation. It was held that it would be good discipline and appropriate for the decision-maker to:

- list the material taken into account in reaching the decision;

- identify key arguments;

- ask whether they agree with the process and approach of the relevant panel(s) and are satisfied as to its fairness and that the panel(s) has properly addressed the arguments;

- consider whether any additional information now available to them that was not before the panel has an impact on its reasons or recommendation;

- identify the reasons given for the relevant recommendation that they do or do not wish to adopt; and

- state (a) the adopted reasons by cross-reference or otherwise; and (b) any further reasons for their decision.

11.150 Where the decision-maker is minded not to accept the recommendation of the adoption panel or independent review panel, the decision-maker should discuss the case with another senior person in the agency who is not a member of the adoption panel or independent review panel. The outcome of that discussion, as well as the decision itself and its reasons must be recorded on the prospective adopters' case record and, in respect of a placement case, the child's case record also.

11.151 Once approved, the local authority should give the prospective adoptive family information about the National Adoption Register (including information about their ability to submit their own details to the register

---

[33] [2009] EWHC 3282 (Admin).

3 months after the approval decision is made) and a consent form to enable their details to be submitted to the National Adoption Register.[34]

SECTION 10 – CONTACT WITH BIRTH FAMILY FOR CHILD PLACED FOR ADOPTION[35]

11.152 There is no general presumption for or against contact.[36] Before making a placement order, s 27(4) of the ACA 2002 requires the court to consider the arrangements the agency has made or proposes to make for contact and to invite the parties to the proceedings to comment on those arrangements.

11.153 When the adoption order is made it also extinguishes any order under the CA 1989, and any contact order under s 26 of the ACA 2002. Section 46(6) of the ACA 2002 imposes a duty on the court, when making an adoption order, to consider the existing and proposed arrangements for contact with the child, and to seek the views of the parties to the proceedings on those arrangements. The court will be able to make a contact order under s 8 of the CA 1989 (a s 8 contact order), where it considers that to be in the best interests of the child.

11.154 At all times, the child's welfare and best interests drive any arrangements for contact. The local authority and the adoption panel when making its recommendations should ensure that the proposed contact arrangements are focused on, and shaped around, the child's needs.

11.155 Where siblings cannot be placed together with the same family, it is important to ensure that contact arrangements between them are sufficiently robust and are given very careful attention.

11.156 Contact arrangements may need to be varied as the children's relationships and need for contact change over time. Contact arrangements with a child's relatives may take the form of indirect contact, with letters and cards and some background information about the child's progress being sent via a social worker. In some cases there may be some form of direct contact.

11.157 When making a decision on the contact arrangements, the agency is required to take into account:

- the wishes and feelings of the parent or guardian of the child (including fathers without parental responsibility);

---

[34] The adoption agency must submit the details of the adopters to the National Adoption Register if it has been unable to identify a possible match between approved adopters and a child within 3 months of approval.

[35] Also see Chapter 10 on contact.

[36] Adoption Agencies Regulations 2005 (AAR), reg 45 removes the general duty in the 1989 Act to promote contact.

- any advice given by the adoption panel about the proposed contact arrangements;

- the child's welfare, throughout their life (ACA 2002, s 1(4)).

- the child's wishes and feelings, if the agency considers the child is of sufficient age and understanding; and

- the prospective adopter's views.

Variation from the terms of a contact order

11.158   A contact order may be made by the court under s 26 of the ACA 2002. The adoption agency may vary this unilaterally for a maximum of 7 days, or by agreement with all those affected.

11.159   Where the agency decides under s 27(2) of the ACA 2002 unilaterally to vary a contact order, it must inform the persons specified in the order as soon as the decision is made. The agency is also required to notify them in writing of:

- the date of the decision;

- the reasons for the decision; and

- the duration of the period.

11.160   Any agreement to vary a contact order is subject to the following steps being taken:

- ascertaining the views and agreement of the child, if of sufficient age and understanding;

- consultation with the prospective adopter; and

- forming a written confirmation with:

    –   the child, if the agency considers they are of sufficient age and understanding;
    –   the person who had provision for contact under s 26; and
    –   the prospective adopter, if the child is placed for adoption.

11.161   Once the adoption order has been made, birth parents lose their status as parents, and no longer have a right to apply for a s 8 contact order without the leave of the court. Other birth relatives, or any other person connected to the child would also need the court's leave to make an application.

11.162 In the event of an application being made after adoption, the adoption agency should assess and provide as much support as possible to minimise the risk of an adverse effect on the child's welfare. This could include mediation to avoid a dispute in court and/or counselling. Where an application for leave to apply for a s 8 contact order is made in the absence of any previous agreement for contact, it is unlikely to succeed without strong reasons. It may be unnecessary even to involve the adoptive parents, who will only need to be notified of the application.

SECTION 11 – ADOPTION SUPPORT SERVICES

11.163 The local authority has a duty to provide an assessment of support needs for all parties in the adoption process.[37] The possible support services that need to be assessed are:

In respect of the child

- Support to enable understanding the meaning of their adoption, including about connections with the birth family.

- Counselling and support throughout life.

- Support must be appropriate and sensitive to the child's development, understanding, culture, religion and background.

In respect of the birth family

- Support and counselling (using appropriate language and cultural/ethnic sensitivity) regarding feelings about the child's adoption.

- Information about procedures used for placement for adoption.

- Legal implications of giving consent now and in future.

- Counselling about wishes regarding the child's religious and cultural upbringing.

- Information and reasons for placing the child for adoption.

- Proposals and details for contact, if any.

- Must be offered access to independent support worker.

---

[37] The Adoption and Children Act 2002, s 4(1).

In respect of the adoptive family

- Financial support for which the placing authority may be responsible throughout life. This is means tested and subject to reviews.

- Assessment and provision of advice, counselling, and information to ensure continuation of adoptive relationship (duty on placing authority for 3 years).

- Support groups.

- Assistance with contact.

11.164   The local authority must also provide certain services to fathers without parental responsibility for the child who is to be adopted:

- support services must be offered;

- the local authority must ascertain his or her wishes regarding:

    - the child;
    - placement of child for adoption;
    - child's religious and cultural upbringing;
    - contact; and
    - his wish to acquire parental responsibility.

The role of adoption panel in relation to support plans

11.165   The panel has a key role in giving advice about the post-placement support plan and services which may be provided to meet the needs of the child, the adoptive family and/or the birth family.

11.166   Factors to be taken into account are:

- the support services the agency proposes and what is considered necessary;

- the services required from other agencies such as health and education;

- the support services that should be negotiated and confirmed with another authority (where the child and family live in another authority);

- the attitude of the adoptive family to using support services;

- the services proposed to support the maintenance of connections with the birth family, including contact arrangements, and whether these are sufficient; and

- the services the birth family may require.

Financial assistance and adoption allowance

11.167 The adoption panel may give advice as to whether an adoption allowance should be paid by the adoption agency. Any financial support is linked to the child's needs and is subject to means testing. The financial responsibility remains with the placing authority irrespective of where the child and adopters live. Other support services are transferred to the authority in which the adoptive family lives after 3 years.

11.168 There may be circumstances in which a capital payment may be proposed to enable a sibling group to be placed together with an adoptive family or for a child with significant disabilities. The adoption panel has no determining role in these cases, but may advise the adoption agency as it sees fit.

SECTION 12 – DISRUPTIONS TO ADOPTIVE PLACEMENTS

11.169 It is inevitable that a small number of adoptive placements (especially for children over 5) will experience such difficulties that it will not be in the child's interest for the placement to continue. Even with the most thorough assessment, matching, and preparation, some element of risk is always inherently present.

11.170 It is the task of the adoption panel to re-evaluate practice in all cases of placement disruption, and to make recommendations about:

- whether it continues to be in the best interests of the child to be placed for adoption;

- the suspension and/or termination of approval of the adoptive parents; and

- the support services to be provided for the child and adoptive parents.

11.171 In the event of a placement disruption, reports will be presented to the adoption panel, which identify the child's current and future needs. These reports will normally include:

- minutes of the disruption meeting;

- record of the sequence of events prior to and at the time of placement, and events leading to the disruption;

- the viewpoints of the parties involved and their understanding of the sequence of the events leading to disruption, including the views of the adoptive parents, their support worker, the child, their social worker and birth family;

- recommendations of the chair of the disruption meeting;

- any previous minutes of the panel including the minutes approving the applicants as adoptive parents and minutes of matching the child with them;

- if other families were considered, the panel should have a summary of the reasons for not placing the child with them.

The panel should ensure that the views of the child and the birth family are clearly presented to the panel.

11.172 The child's social worker and the supervising social worker for the adoptive family must attend the adoption panel meeting to present their reports and clarify matters for the adoption panel. The process may be slightly amended when the child placed is from a different local authority approving the adopters.

SECTION 13 – LOCAL AUTHORITY DUTIES AFTER ADOPTION PLACEMENT

11.173 Once a decision has been made that a child should be placed with a particular prospective adopter,[38] the agency will need to make a plan for the placement. The placement cannot be made unless the agency has 'authority to place' (consent under ACA 2002, s 19 or a placement order) or the child is under 6 weeks old and the birth parents have agreed in writing that the child may be placed.

11.174 If, before the child is placed, an application is made for the revocation of a placement order, the local authority cannot place the child without the leave of the court. An application for revocation can only be made if the court has granted leave under s 24(2) of the ACA 2002, and an application for leave does not in itself prohibit the local authority from placing the child. It is not, however, appropriate for a local authority to proceed with the placement when it is aware of the application for leave, and an attempt to do so in order to frustrate the birth parents' application could be challenged in court by an application for judicial review.[39]

---

[38] In accordance with reg 3 of the Adoption Agencies Regulations 2005, SI 2005/389.
[39] See *Re F (Placement Order)* [2008] EWCA Civ 439.

11.175 The agency is required to meet the prospective adopter to consider the proposed placement. A provisional draft of the adoption placement plan, should form the basis for the meeting. Contact plans should be discussed at this stage. Contact between adopted children and their birth families can be beneficial, but research has also highlighted that any form of contact needs careful planning and support, and that children's views and their need for contact may change over time so any contact plans must be kept under review.

11.176 The prospective adopter will already have received the information about the child and a copy of the adoption placement report. They should also be supplied with any relevant additional information, such as the reaction of the child and birth parents on receiving information about the proposed placement, and any advice given by the adoption panel. The agency should arrange for the child's social worker, the prospective adopter's social worker, the child's current carer and any relevant child specialists to attend the meeting with the prospective adopter. It may be helpful to involve the foster carer's social worker, if appropriate.

11.177 One of the matters to be discussed and agreed is the proposed arrangements for introducing the child and the prospective adopter. These will of course vary depending on the age of the child, and all the circumstances. As soon as possible after the planning meeting, the agency must send the prospective adopter the adoption placement plan. This will be the basis on which the prospective adopter will make their formal decision whether to accept the placement. In some cases, for example if there is any disagreement or uncertainty about the proposed adoption support arrangements, the prospective adopter may wish to take some time to consider the proposal, and take advice if necessary.

11.178 Once the prospective adopter has notified the agency that they wish to proceed with the placement, the agency may make the placement. The agency should keep the child's current carer informed of the placement arrangements and – having regard to the child's age and understanding – inform the child in an appropriate manner. Where the child is already living with the prospective adopter, such as a foster carer, the agency must notify them in writing of the date on which the child's placement with them becomes a placement for adoption. If financial support is to be paid under the adoption support plan this will be paid as from the formal 'placement' date and any fostering allowance will cease from that point.

11.179 A child who is placed for adoption remains a looked-after child and, if they are of statutory school age, will have a personal educational plan (PEP). Provision needs to be made for parental responsibility to be shared between the agency, the birth parents and with the prospective adopter. The agency has the power to determine the extent to which the exercise of parental responsibility by the birth parents and/or the prospective adopter should be restricted.

11.180 In coming to a decision on the exercise of parental responsibility, the agency should take into account the views of:

- the child, if they are of sufficient age and understanding;

- the views of the birth parents or guardian, where it is reasonably practicable to do so; and

- anybody else the agency considers relevant.

11.181 When the agency makes a decision on the exercise of parental responsibility by the birth parents, it should write to them (if their whereabouts are known). The letter should make it clear the extent to which, if at all, the agency considers it appropriate for them to exercise their parental responsibility, the fact that this will be subject to review, and that they would be notified in writing of any change.

Social work visits

11.182 The agency is required to visit the child in the adoptive placement within the first week after placement and thereafter at least once a week until the first review (4 weeks after placement). The frequency of subsequent visits is then to be decided by the placing agency at the first and each subsequent review, and noted on the adoption placement plan.

11.183 When a child is placed for adoption by a local authority, the child continues to be looked after by that local authority. It remains responsible for that child, wherever the child is living, until the adoption order is made. Once an adoption order is made, the child ceases to be looked after and the placing authority has no further responsibility towards them, except in respect of adoption support (see below).

Reviews

11.184 The review requirements for a child to be placed for adoption will continue to be governed by the Care Planning, Placement and Case Review (England) Regulations 2010 ('the 2010 Regulations') until the child is adopted.

Frequency of reviews

11.185 Where the child has not yet been placed for adoption, the first review must take place no more than 3 months after the agency obtained authorisation to place the child for adoption, and thereafter not more than 6 months after the previous review.

11.186 At this '6 month review' particular consideration must be given to establishing why the child has not yet been placed and whether the adoption plan is still appropriate. The child's details must be placed on the Adoption

Register no later than 3 months after the agency's decision-maker has decided (after considering the adoption panel's recommendation) that the child should be placed for adoption.

11.187 When the child has been placed for adoption, the first review must be held no more than 4 weeks after placement, the second no more than 3 months after this, and subsequent reviews held at 6-monthly intervals until an adoption order is made.

11.188 These provisions set out the maximum intervals between reviews. The agency may conduct additional reviews where it considers it appropriate, and should always be prepared to do so at the request of the prospective adopter or the child. In addition, if the placement disrupts and the child is returned to the agency or removed from the placement by the agency, a review must be held between 28 days and 42 days after the disruption.

Conduct of reviews

11.189 The agency should provide written information about how it intends to review a child's case to the prospective adopter, the child where the agency considers the child is of sufficient age and understanding, and to any other person the agency considers relevant, such as the child's birth parents or guardian and anyone else who has contact with the child. The independent reviewing officer (IRO) appointed by the agency would chair any meeting to review the child's case.

11.190 The 2010 guidance should be followed although there is a major difference in that once the child has been placed for adoption, the prospective adopter (who has parental responsibility for the child) will always have a major role and must be consulted, whereas the extent to which birth parents are consulted and involved will be a matter for the agency's discretion depending on the circumstances of the case. It will rarely be appropriate, for example, for birth parents to attend a review meeting once a child has been placed with prospective adopters.

Local authority duties towards children after adoption

11.191 Every child should have a named social worker who is responsible for assessing his or her needs, finding out the child's views and representing them at each stage of the adoption process, taking into account the child's age, level of maturity and understanding. Children can expect the following from the local authority:

- to be entitled to a skilled assessment of their needs, which will promote their opportunity to belong to a family and to enhance their sense of identity;

- to have their welfare, safety needs and views placed at the centre of the adoption process;

- to be prepared for adoption – before children are able to look at the future and contemplate taking risks with new relationships, they need time and help to make sense of why they are unable to live with their birth families;

- to be given the opportunity to know about their past and their heritage – children should be helped to understand (in accordance with their age, maturity and level of understanding) what has happened to them and their family and why they can't live with them;

- to be provided with counselling, explanations and written information in an appropriate manner about the adoption process, including the legal implications of adoption;

- to be provided with appropriately sensitive counselling that takes account of the child's abilities, linguistic skills, religious beliefs or other values and in an environment where the child is able to talk and ask questions in a way that enables him or her to gain an understanding of his or her situation;

- to be informed as they grow up knowing that the reports written about them (the child's permanence report) will be available for them to read as adults if they so wish;

- to be referred to the Adoption Register for family finding after 3 months of the decision made for the child to be placed for adoption, unless the adoption agency has found a suitable adoptive family;

- to be matched with an adoptive family within 6 months of the decision being made that child should be placed for adoption (where a parent has requested that a child aged under 6 months be placed for adoption, a proposed placement with a suitable prospective adopter should be identified and approved by the panel within 3 months of the agency deciding that the child should be placed for adoption);

- to be placed with the most suitable adopters, giving due consideration to all of the child's needs including the child's ethnicity, culture, religion, language and any disabilities;

- to be reassured that every effort is being made to find adoptive families where brothers and sisters can live together when this is in their best interests;

- to have their needs supported for the duration of their childhood and beyond; and

- to be provided with a later life letter explaining their history from birth. The letter should be sufficiently detailed so that in the future the adolescent child, or young adult, will have factual details about their birth family and their life before adoption, and so be able to understand why they could not live with their birth family, and why they were adopted.[40]

Ascertaining the child's wishes and feelings about adoption

11.192 Social workers must seek (or attempt to seek) children's wishes and feelings about:

- the possibility of being placed for adoption with a new family and their adoption;

- their religious and cultural upbringing; and

- their wishes for contact with their parent or guardian or other relative or with any other person the agency considers relevant.[41]

11.193 In seeking the child's views, the social worker must be wary of giving the child the impression that he or she is being asked to bear the weight of the decision that needs to be made about his or her adoption. The child should be helped to understand that their wishes and feelings will be listened to and taken into account.

11.194 The social worker must make every attempt to ascertain and record the child's views. Where the social worker is unable to ascertain the child's views, the reasons for this must be recorded on the child's case record.

Life story work

11.195 The social worker should ensure that life story work with the child begins as soon as possible after the child is no longer living in the care of his or her parents. Social workers should provide children (irrespective of age) with a life story book, which is available for when they move to their adoptive home. The book should include:

- an accurate and full account of the child's life in words, pictures, photographs and documents;

- an understanding of why the child does not live with his or her birth family including, if applicable, their experience of being abused;

---

[40] The letter should be given to the prospective adopter within 10 working days of the adoption ceremony, ie the ceremony to celebrate the making of the adoption order.

[41] The Adoption Agencies Regulations 2005, SI 2005/389, reg 13.

- a fuller picture of their identity, and pride in their ethnicity and cultural background;

- assistance in considering the reality of joining a new family, what they want and how they will fit in;

- the inclusion of short written positive memories and wishes from important people such as birth parents, relatives, carers and teachers can help promote a child's self image. Material gathered by foster carers is a vital source of information.

11.196 Life story work should never be seen as just putting together a photograph album or storybook. The process of the work is as important, if not more, than the end product.

Local authority duties towards the birth family after adoption

11.197 Social workers must make every effort to enable children to grow up in the care of their birth parents or extended family. The extended family must be considered as a first option for a child who cannot grow up in the care of one or both of their parents.

11.198 When considering adoption for a child, social workers must carry out a range of responsibilities towards the child's birth family which include:

- providing information about the adoption agency's policies and procedures about permanency planning, and alternative options for securing their child's permanent care;

- providing counselling about adoption by appropriate and experienced professionals;

- taking the wishes of the birth family into account when choosing an adoptive family, subject to the child's best interests;

- offering the birth family the opportunity to meet with adopters prior to the placement of their child unless it is not in the child's best interests;

- giving birth parents and families the opportunity (where practicable and in the child's interests) to provide continuing information for the child after the adoption order is made; this must include the possibility of face-to-face contact between the child and the birth family;

- notifying the birth family when their child has been placed for adoption.

Local authority duties towards adoptive families when making the decision about matching

11.199 The local authority must continue to provide services to adoptive families after the decision has been made to place a particular child within a particular placement including:

- arranging a meeting between the family finding social worker and the prospective adoptive family to discuss potential child(ren) to be placed;

- sending a copy of the child's permanence report (CPR) to the prospective adoptive family;

- arranging a meeting (if relevant) between the prospective adoptive family, the medical advisor and any other person with whom the child is involved, if all professionals agree that there is sufficient interest and potential for a match;

- informing or inviting the prospective adoptive family to attend the adoption panel considering a proposed match;

- giving written notice to the prospective adoptive family of the adoption agency's decision about the match within 7 days of the panel making a recommendation.

Local authority duties towards adoptive families after the matching decision

11.200 Until a child is placed with a prospective adoptive family the local authority must continue to review the prospective adoptive family annually by submitting the review assessment report (with all updated checks and references) for consideration by the adoption panel.

11.201 Once a match is approved and agreed the local authority must continue to work with the adoptive family and provide services to maintain and support the placement. This work will include:

- involving the prospective adoptive family in the plans for introductions to the child and in making plans for the move of the child to the adoptive family;

- involving the prospective adoptive family in making arrangements to meet the birth family;

- sending all relevant documentation regarding the child to the prospective adoptive family;

- writing to the adoptive family confirming their approval as adopters for the particular child;

- withdrawing the details of the prospective adopters (if registered) from the National Adoption Register;

- carrying out a social work visit within 7 working days of the placement being made, followed by weekly visits for the first 8 weeks, and monthly visits thereafter;

- holding review meetings in respect of a child subject to care order[42] within one month of placement, 3 months later and thereafter at least every 6 months until an adoption order has been granted in respect of the child;

- assisting the prospective adoptive family in making an application for an adoption order, and to enable the prospective adoptive family to participate in reviews of the child until an adoption order is made;

- involving the prospective adoptive family in the formulation of the post-adoption support plan, and assist in completion of the adoption placement report (APR), highlighting proposals for future contact with the birth family of the child (parents, grandparents and/or siblings, including any future unborn siblings); and

- providing support to the adoptive family as identified in the adoption support plan.

---

[42]   In accordance with the requirements in the Fostering Services Regulations 2011, SI 2011/581.

11.202

Information to be sent by the local authority to the prospective adoptive family about the particular child

- Child permanence report (including a chronology of events)

- Child health record

- Adoption medical information

- LAC medical reports

- Development assessments

- Foster carers' reports

- LAC review reports and other ICS (Integrated Children's System) forms

- Psychologist's reports

- School reports

- Personal education plan

- Educational statement and review reports

- Reports and statements from court proceedings (consent from the relevant court is required)

- Life story book

- Later life letter from the child's social worker

- Any letters, photos or keepsakes from the birth family and other significant people

- Birth certificate (not photocopy)

- Legal orders

- Document listing the remit for exercising parental responsibility

Assessment entitlements for support[43]

	Discussions related to adoption	Assistance in arrangements for contact	Therapeutic services	Ensuring the continuation of adoptive relationship	Assistance in cases of disruption	Counselling, advice and information	Financial support
Adoptive child	✓	✓	✓	✓	✓	✓	
Adopter(s)	✓	✓		✓	✓	✓	✓
Child of adopter(s)				✓	✓	✓	
Birth parents	✓	✓				✓	
A birth relative		✓				✓	
Intercountry adoptive child			✓	✓	✓	✓	
Intercountry adopter(s)				✓	✓	✓	
Sibling of an adoptive child		✓				✓	
Prospective adopters						✓	

43   The Adoption and Children Act 2002: Guidance (ch 9).

	Discussions related to adoption	Assistance in arrangements for contact	Therapeutic services	Ensuring the continuation of adoptive relationship	Assistance in cases of disruption	Counselling, advice and information	Financial support
Adopted adults, their parents, natural parents and a relative						√	

Chapter 12

SPECIAL GUARDIANSHIP

SECTION 1 – DEFINITION OF SPECIAL GUARDIANSHIP

12.1 A special guardianship order conveys parental responsibility to the applicant which can be exercised to the exclusion of others with parental responsibility, usually the parents. This new order in essence represents an intermediate position between an *adoption order* in which parents parental responsibility is removed and a *residence order* where parental responsibility is shared with the parents.

12.2 The intention of a special guardianship order is:

- to offer legal security for a child in a long-term fostering placement;

- to alleviate the stigma attached to the status of being a child in care; and

- to provide kinship placements with more authority for carers than that available either under a residence order (where parental responsibility is shared with the parent) or a care order (where the carer has no parental responsibility).

Who can apply for a special guardianship order?

12.3 There are clear rules about who can apply for a special guardianship order:

- Anyone[1] (over 18) with whom the child has lived for at least 3 of the last 5 years.

- A local authority foster carer with whom the child has lived for at least one year immediately preceding the application.

- With consent of the local authority any other person who cares for a child subject to a care order.

- A person who holds a residence order in respect of the child.

- A guardian for the child appointed under Children Act 1989, s 5.

---

[1]   An applicant for a special guardianship order cannot be the child's parent.

- Any other person with leave of the court (eg the child's grandparents).

12.4 The court can also make a child subject of a special guardianship order of its own motion.

12.5

The duties of the local authorities in relation to applications for special guardianship orders

- To prepare a special guardianship report in respect of the application

- To make recommendations about the making of a special guardianship order

- To prepare a support plan (similar to those applicable in cases of adoption) in the event of a special guardianship order being granted

- To make recommendations about contact in the event of a special guardianship order being granted

- In cases where the local authority decides not to provide special guardianship support services, reasons for the decision must be given

---

12.6 The local authority must prepare a report before a special guardianship order can be made.[2] Applicants must give 3 months' written notice to the local authority of their intention to apply for a special guardianship order. The court can consider making a special guardianship order of its own motion, but may not make a special guardianship order without having received and considered the report.[3]

The special guardianship report

12.7 The report should address the relevant issues as specified in the Schedule to the Special Guardianship Regulations 2005.[4]

THE CHILD	(a)	Name, sex, date and place of birth and address including local authority area.
	(b)	Physical description.
	(c)	Nationality.
	(d)	Racial origin and cultural and linguistic background.
	(e)	Religious persuasion.

---

2   The Children Act 1989, s 14A(11).
3   *A Local Authority v Y* [2006] 2 FLR 41; *Re S (Adoption Order or Special Guardianship Order)* [2007] EWCA Civ 54, [2007] 1 FLR 819; *Re S (Adoption Order and Special Guardianship Order) (No 2)* [2007] EWCA Civ 90, [2007] 1 FLR 855.
4   SI 2005/1109.

(f) Details of any siblings including dates of birth.

(g) The extent of child's contact with relatives and any other person local authority considers relevant.

(h) Whether child is or has been looked after by a local authority or is/has been provided with accommodation by a voluntary organisation and details (including dates) of placements.

(i) Whether the prospective special guardian is a local authority foster of the child.

(j) A description of the child's personality, his or her social development and his or her emotional and behavioural development and any related needs.

(k) Details of the child's interests, likes and dislikes.

(l) A health history and a description of state of child's health (including any treatment child is receiving).

(m) Names and addresses of nurseries and school attended with dates.

(n) Child's educational attainments.

(o) Whether child is subject to statement of special educational needs (Education Act 1966).

(p) Details of any court order.

THE CHILD'S FAMILY	(a) Name, date and place of birth and address including local authority area of each parent and sibling under the age of 18.
	(b) Physical description of each parent.
	(c) Nationality of each parent.
	(d) Racial origin and linguistic background of each parent.
	(e) Whether child's parents were married to each other at the time of child's birth (or have subsequently married) and whether they are divorced or separated.
	(f) Where child's parents have been previously married or formed a civil partnership, the date of marriage or civil partnership.
	(g) Where child's parents are not married, whether father has parental responsibility and, if so, how so acquired?
	(h) If identity or whereabouts of father not known, information about him that has been ascertained and from whom, and steps taken to establish paternity.
	(i) Past and present relationships of child's parents.
	(j) Where available following information in respect of each parent:

- health history including dates of any serious physical or mental illness, any hereditary disease or disorder;
- religious persuasion;
- educational history;
- employment history;
- personality and interests.

	(k)	In respect of child's siblings under 18: • person with whom sibling is living; • whether sibling is looked after by the local authority or provided with accommodation by a voluntary organisation; • details of any court order made regarding sibling, including name of the court, details of order made and date on which order made.
THE WISHES AND FEELINGS OF THE CHILD AND OTHERS	(a)	An assessment of the child's wishes and feelings (considered in light of his or her age and understanding) regarding: • special guardianship; • his religious and cultural upbringing; and • contact with his or her relatives and any other person the local authority considers relevant, and the date on which the child's wishes and feelings were ascertained.
	(b)	The wishes and feelings of each parent regarding: • special guardianship; • the child's religious and cultural upbringing; and • contact with the child, and the date on which the wishes and feelings of each parent were last ascertained.
	(c)	The wishes and feelings of any of the child's relatives, or any other person the local authority considers relevant regarding the child and the dates on which those wishes and feelings were ascertained.
THE PROSPECTIVE SPECIAL GUARDIAN (or, where two or more persons are jointly prospective special guardians, each of them)	(a)	Name, date and place of birth and address including the local authority area.
	(b)	Photograph and physical description.
	(c)	Nationality (and immigration status where appropriate).
	(d)	Racial origin and cultural and linguistic background.
	(e)	Whether prospective special guardian is married/civil partnership (with date and place of any marriage/civil partnership) or has a partner (with details of that relationship).
	(f)	Details of any previous marriage.
	(g)	Where prospective special guardians wish to apply jointly, nature of their relationship and assessment of stability of that relationship.
	(h)	If prospective special guardian is a member of a couple and is applying alone for a special guardianship order the reason for this.
	(i)	Whether prospective special guardian is relative of child.
	(j)	Prospective special guardian's relationship with child.
	(k)	Health history of prospective special guardian including details of any serious physical or mental illness, any hereditary disease or disorder or disability.

(l)   Description of how prospective special guardian relates to adults and children.

(m)   Previous experience of caring for children.

(n)   Parenting capacity to include assessment of prospective special guardian's ability and suitability to bring up child.

(o)   Relevant details of any past assessments as a prospective adopter, foster parent or special guardian.

(p)   Details of income and expenditure.

(q)   Information about prospective special guardian's home and neighbourhood.

(r)   Details of other members of household and details of any children of prospective special guardian even if not resident in the household.

(s)   Details of parents and siblings of prospective special guardian (with ages or ages of death).

(t)   Details of religious persuasion, educational history, employment history and personality and interests.

(u)   Details of any previous family court proceedings in which prospective special guardian has been involved (not been referred to elsewhere in report).

(v)   Report of each interview with three personal referees.

(w)   Whether prospective special guardian willing to follow any wishes of child or parents in respect of religious and cultural upbringing of child.

(x)   Views of other members of prospective special guardian's household and wider family in relation to proposed special guardianship order.

(y)   Assessment of child's current and future relationship with prospective special guardian's family.

(z)   Reasons for applying for special guardianship order and extent of understanding of nature and effect of special guardianship and whether prospective special guardian has discussed special guardianship with child including:

- any hopes and expectations prospective special guardian has for child's future; and

- prospective special guardian's wishes and feelings in relation to contact between the child and relatives (or any other person local authority considers relevant).

THE LOCAL AUTHORITY WHICH COMPLETED THE REPORT

(a)   Name and address.

(b)   Details of any past involvement of local authority with prospective special guardian, including any past preparation for that person to be a local authority foster parent, adoptive parent or special guardian.

(c)   Where the Children Act 1989, s 14A(7)(a) applies and prospective special guardian lives in area of another local authority, details of the local authority's enquiries of that other local authority about the prospective special guardian.

	(d) A summary of any special guardianship support services provided by the local authority for prospective special guardian, child or child's parent and the period for which those services are to be provided.
	(e) Where the local authority has decided not to provide special guardianship support services, the reason why.
MEDICAL SUMMARY	A summary prepared by the medical professional who provided the information referred to in paragraphs 1(l) and 4(k).
THE IMPLICATIONS OF THE MAKING OF A SPECIAL GUARDIANSHIP ORDER	The implication of making a special guardianship order for: • the child, • the child's parents, • the prospective special guardian and his or her family, • any other person the local authority considers relevant.
MERITS OF SPECIAL GUARDIANSHIP	The relative merits of special guardianship and other orders which may be made under the Children Act 1989 or the Adoption and Children Act 2002 with an assessment of whether the child's long-term interests would be best met by a special guardianship order.
RECOMMENDA-TION ABOUT SPECIAL GUARDIANSHIP ORDER	A recommendation as to whether or not the special guardianship order sought should be made in respect of the child and, if not, any alternative proposal in respect of the child.
RECOMMENDA-TION ABOUT CONTACT	A recommendation as to what arrangements there should be for contact between the child and his or her relatives or any person the local authority considers relevant.

SECTION 2 – THE SPECIAL GUARDIANSHIP SUPPORT PLAN

12.8   The Special Guardianship Regulations 2005, regs 12–16 also specify the contents of the support plan that the local authority is required to complete in respect of every assessment of a prospective special guardian. The support plan must include:

• counselling, advice, and information;

• financial support (ranging from toys, furniture to home improvements and legal fees);

• group meetings for child, carers and parents;

• mediation relating to contact;

- support necessary to ensure the proposed special guardianship relationship is sustained and stable;

- remuneration for foster carers who apply for a special guardianship order (foster carers will receive the same fostering allowance for a period of 2 years);

- a leaving care support package for children of 16–21 who were looked after prior to the making of the special guardianship order.

Reviews of the special guardianship support plan

12.9 The local authority must continue to monitor and review the special guardianship support plan after the order has been made.

12.10

The local authority's duties after the support plan is created

- Serve notice of the support plan on the relevant people who are affected to enable them to make representations

- Serve notice on the relevant affected people of the decisions relating to the support plan

- Nominate a person to monitor any support plan which consists of more than one off advice or payment

- Review the support plan at least annually

- Transfer the support plan (other than the financial plan) to another local authority when the special guardian lives in another local authority

---

SECTION 3 – THE ROLE OF THE PANEL

12.11 There is *no* duty on local authorities to refer special guardianship reports to the adoption and permanency panel for approval (unlike applicants who wish to adopt or become foster carers). Therefore the only way in which the reports can be scrutinised is via the court process. However, some local authorities do refer special guardianship assessments and reports to the adoption and permanency panel for the purposes of quality assurance.

Chapter 13

LEAVING CARE

SECTION 1 – THE LEGAL FRAMEWORK

13.1 A child ceases to be looked after by a local authority when:

- he or she ceases to be provided with accommodation (if he or she was provided with accommodation); or

- he or she ceases to be in care (if he or she was accommodated in care) because the care order has been discharged by a court order, by reason of his or her age or if the child becomes adopted.

13.2 If a child who was previously being accommodated is then made the subject of a care order, then he or she continues to be looked after by a local authority. If a child who was subject to a care order is no longer subject to that order, but is being provided with accommodation, then he or she continues to be looked after by a local authority.

13.3 The local authority must provide accommodation for a child in need:[1]

- for whom no one has parental responsibility; or

- who is abandoned; or

- for whom the person caring for him or her cannot provide suitable accommodation.

13.4 The local authority has a duty to provide accommodation for such a child in need who is under 18.[2] The duty therefore ceases when the child reaches that age. However, s 20(5) of the CA 1989 provides that the local authority may provide accommodation for a person between 16 and 21 in a community home if it would safeguard or promote his or her welfare. Unless a child is so provided with accommodation, on the discharge of the care order (when the child reaches the age of 18), he is no longer looked after by the local authority.

13.5 The Children and Young Persons Act 2008 amended the CA 1989 so that looked-after children must not move from accommodation regulated under the Care Standards Act 2000 to other arrangements without a statutory review of

---

[1] Children Act 1989 (CA 1989), s 20(1).
[2] CA 1989, s 20(1).

their care plan chaired by their independent reviewing officer (IRO). A move to other arrangements would include moving to accommodation, often referred to as semi-independent accommodation, which would not be subject to regulatory inspection by Ofsted. It is important to remember that children do not cease to be looked after just because they are placed in accommodation that is not regulated under the Care Standards Act.

13.6 Local authorities must now pay a higher education bursary to certain former relevant children (see chapter 5 of the revised guidance).

13.7 Care leavers under the age of 25 who wish to take up a programme of education or training will have an entitlement to resume support from a personal adviser (PA) appointed by the local authority previously responsible for providing their leaving care support.

SECTION 2 – THE DUTY OF THE LOCAL AUTHORITY TO PREPARE A CHILD FOR CEASING TO BE LOOKED AFTER

13.8 It is the duty of the local authority looking after a child to advise, assist and befriend him or her with a view to promoting his or her welfare when it ceases to look after him or her.[3] The main provisions in relation to local authority duties towards children who cease to be looked after are set out in the CA 1989 as amended by the Children (Leaving Care) Act 2000.

13.9 The main purpose of the Children (Leaving Care) Act 2000 is to improve the life chances of young people living in and leaving local authority care. The primary aims of the legislation are:

- to delay young people's discharge from care until they are prepared and ready to leave taking account of their level of maturity and readiness for independence;

- to improve the assessment, preparation and planning for leaving care;

- to provide consistency and stability of care for young people after leaving care;

- to provide better personal support for young people after leaving care;

- to improve the financial arrangements for care leavers; and

- to provide a 'safety net' and suitable contingency arrangements for young people who have left care.

---

[3]   CA 1989, Sch 2, para 19A (inserted by the Children (Leaving Care) Act 2000).

13.10 The legislation is based upon the responses to the consultation document *Me, Survive, Out There? – New Arrangements for Young People Living In and Leaving Care.*[4] It is also based upon research findings and development work by First Key and is informed by consultation with young people themselves. The Children (Leaving Care) Act 2000 amends the leaving care provisions within the CA 1989; however, the underlying principles of the CA 1989 still apply – in particular:

- taking into account the views of young people;

- consulting young people and keeping them informed;

- giving due consideration to young people's race, culture, religion and linguistic background;

- the importance of families and working with parents;

- safeguarding and promoting the welfare of young people being looked after; and

- the recognition of interagency responsibility.

SECTION 3 – CATEGORIES OF CHILDREN ENTITLED TO CARE LEAVING SUPPORT

13.11 There are five categories of young people who are entitled to care leaving support from the local authority – eligible children, relevant children, former relevant children, former relevant children pursuing education or training, and persons qualifying for advice and assistance.

13.12 These categories are set out in tabular form within the revised guidance and are summarised below.

Eligible children

13.13 An eligible child is defined in para 19B of Sch 2 to the CA 1989, and reg 40 of the Care Planning Placement and Case Review (England) Regulations 2010 ('the 2010 Regulations')[5] as a child who is:

(a) looked after;

(b) aged 16 or 17; and

4   The Department of Health (TSO, 1999).
5   SI 2010/959.

(c)   has been looked after by a local authority for a period of 13 weeks, or periods amounting in total to 13 weeks, which began after he reached 14 and ended after he reached 16.

13.14   The local authority has the same statutory obligations in relation to eligible children as they do towards other children who are looked after by them, including a duty to maintain the child's care plan, carry out regular reviews of the child's case and appoint an independent reviewing officer (IRO) for the child. In addition, the local authority must:

•   prepare an *assessment* of the eligible child's needs with a view to determining what advice, assistance and support it would be appropriate for the local authority to provide him or her (both while he or she is still looked after and after he or she stops being looked after);[6]

•   as soon as possible after the assessment of needs is completed, prepare a *pathway plan* (which includes the child's care plan);[7]

•   keep the pathway plan under *regular review*;[8] and

•   appoint a *personal adviser* for the child.[9]

Relevant children

13.15   A relevant child is defined in s 23A(2) of the CA 1989 as a child who is:

(a)   not looked after;

(b)   aged 16 or 17; and

(c)   was, before he or she last ceased to be looked after, an eligible child.

13.16   Regulation 3 of the Care Leavers (England) Regulations 2010[10] prescribes a further category of relevant child who is:

(a)   not looked after;

(b)   aged 16 or 17; and

---

[6]   CA 1989, Sch 2, para 19B(4); the requirements for carrying out the assessment are set out in reg 42 of the Care Planning Regulations 2010.

[7]   CA 1989, Sch 2, para 19B(4); the requirements for preparing the pathway plan are set out in reg 43 of the Care Planning Regulations 2010.

[8]   CA 1989, Sch 2, para 19B(5).

[9]   CA 1989, Sch 2, para 19C; the functions of the personal adviser are set out in reg 44 of the Care Planning Regulations 2010.

[10]   SI 2010/2571.

(c) at the time he or she attained the age of 16 was detained,[11] or in a hospital, and immediately before he or she was detained he or she had been looked after by a local authority for a period or periods amounting in all to at least 13 weeks which began after he or she reached the age of 14.

13.17 Regulation 3 of the Care Leavers Regulations 2010 also provides that a child who has lived for a continuous period of 6 months or more with:

(a) his or her parent;

(b) someone who is not his or her parent but who has parental responsibility for him or her; or

(c) where he or she is in care and there was a residence order in force immediately before the care order was made, a person in whose favour the residence order was made,

then that child is not a relevant child despite falling within s 23A(2) of the CA 1989. Where those living arrangements break down and the child ceases to live with the person concerned, the child is to be treated as a relevant child.

13.18 The local authority that last looked after the relevant child must:

• take reasonable steps to *keep in touch* with the relevant child;[12]

• prepare an *assessment* of the relevant child's needs with a view to determining what advice assistance and support it would be appropriate for them to provide him or her (unless they already did so when he or she was an eligible child);[13]

• as soon as possible after any assessment of needs is completed, prepare a *pathway plan*;[14]

• keep the pathway plan under *regular review*;[15]

• appoint a *personal adviser* for the child (unless they already did so when he or she was an eligible child);[16] and

---

[11] Ie detained in a remand centre, a young offender institution or a secure training centre, or any other centre pursuant to a court order.

[12] CA 1989, s 23B(1).

[13] CA 1989, s 23B(3)(a); the requirements for carrying out the assessment are set out in regs 4 and 5 of the Care Leavers Regulations 2010.

[14] CA 1989, s 23B(3)(b); the requirements for preparing the pathway plan are set out in reg 6 of the Care Leavers Regulations 2010.

[15] CA 1989, s 23E(1D); the requirements for carrying out reviews are set out in reg 7 of the Care Leavers Regulations 2010.

[16] CA 1989, s 23B(2); the functions of the personal adviser are set out in reg 8 of the Care Leavers Regulations 2010.

- safeguard and promote the relevant child's welfare by *maintaining* him or her, providing with or maintaining him or her in *suitable accommodation* and providing *assistance in order to meet his or her needs in relation to education, training or employment* as provided for in his or her pathway plan.[17]

Former relevant children

13.19   A former relevant child is defined in s 23C(1) of the CA 1989 as a young person who is:

(a)   aged 18 or above; and either

(b)   has been a relevant child and would be one if he or she were under 18, or

(c)   immediately before he or she ceased to be looked after at age 18, was an eligible child.

13.20   The local authority that last looked after the former relevant child must:

- take reasonable steps to *keep in touch* with the former relevant child, and if they lose touch with him or her, to re-establish contact;[18]

- continue to keep the *pathway plan* under *regular review*;[19]

- continue the appointment of the *personal adviser* for the child;[20]

- if his or her welfare requires it, provide *financial assistance* by contributing to the former relevant child's expenses in living near the place where he or she is, or will be, employed or seeking employment;[21]

- if his or her welfare and educational and training needs require it, provide *financial assistance* to enable him to pursue education or training;[22] and

- if the former relevant child pursues higher education in accordance with his pathway plan, to pay him the higher education bursary.[23]

---

[17]   CA 1989, s 23B(8) and reg 9 of the Care Leavers Regulations 2010; reg 9 also makes provision about the meaning of 'suitable accommodation'.

[18]   CA 1989, s 23C(2).

[19]   CA 1989, s 23C(3)(b); the requirements for carrying out reviews are set out in reg 7 of the Care Leavers Regulations 2010.

[20]   CA 1989, s 23C(3)(a); the functions of the personal adviser are set out in reg 8 of the Care Leavers Regulations 2010.

[21]   CA 1989, ss 23C(4)(a) and 24B(1).

[22]   CA 1989, ss 23C(4)(b) and 24B(2).

[23]   CA 1989, s 23C(5A) and the Children Act 1989 (Higher Education Bursary) (England) Regulations 2009, SI 2009/2274.

13.21 The duties in s 23C(2), (3) and (4)(b) continue until the former relevant child reaches 21 or, where the child's pathway plan sets out a programme of education or training which extends beyond his or her 21st birthday, they continue for so long as he or she pursues that programme.

Former relevant children pursuing further education or training

13.22 A former relevant child pursuing further education or training is defined in s 23CA(1) of the CA 1989 as a former relevant child who is:

(a) aged under 25;

(b) in relation to whom the duties in s 23C(2), (3) and (4) no longer apply; and

(c) he or she has informed the local authority that he or she wants to pursue or is pursuing a programme of education or training.

13.23 The local authority which owed duties to that former relevant child under s 23C of the CA 1989 must:

- appoint a *personal adviser* for that person;[24]

- carry out an *assessment* of the needs of that person with a view to determining what assistance (if any) it would be appropriate for them to provide him or her;[25]

- prepare a *pathway plan* for him or her;[26] and

- to the extent the person's educational or training needs require it, provide *financial assistance.*[27]

Persons qualifying for advice and assistance

13.24 A person qualifying for advice and assistance is defined in s 24 of the CA 1989 as a person who is:

(a) aged at least 16 but is under 21;

(b) with respect to whom a special guardianship order is in force (or was in force when the young person reached 18) and was looked after immediately before the making of that order; or

---

[24] CA 1989, s 23CA(2).
[25] CA 1989, s 23CA(3)(a); the requirements for carrying out the assessment are set out in regs 4 and 5 of the Care Leavers Regulations 2010.
[26] CA 1989, s 23CA(3)(b); the requirements for preparing the pathway plan are set out in reg 6 of the Care Leavers Regulations 2010.
[27] CA 1989, s 23CA(4) and (5).

(c)   at any time after reaching the age of 16 but while he or she was still a child was, but is no longer, looked after, accommodated or fostered.

13.25   The relevant local authority (as defined in s 24(5) of the CA 1989) must consider whether the person needs help of a kind the local authority can give:

- under s 24A – to advise and befriend and give assistance;

- under s 24B – to give financial assistance; or

- where the person is in full time further or higher education, is under the age of 25 and qualifies for advice and assistance, or would have done if he or she was under 21, assistance in relation to securing vacation accommodation.[28]

SECTION 4 – THE PRINCIPLES UNDERLYING PREPARATION FOR LEAVING CARE

13.26   The provisions relating to local authority duties and responsibilities for young people leaving care are contained within the Children (Leaving Care) Act 2000. The relevant parts of the powers and duties of local authorities to prepare young people for leaving care are described in paras 19A–19C of Pt II of Sch 2, and in ss 23A–23E, and 24, 24A and 24B of the CA 1989 (as amended by the Children (Leaving Care) Act 2000). The duties also apply to voluntary organisations[29] and children's homes.[30] The local authority's duties apply whether young people are in care because of a care order or are accommodated under the CA 1989, s 20. They also apply regardless of any other special status a young person may have (for example, unaccompanied asylum seeking children, children who are remanded in local authority accommodation). The legislation applies to young people until they reach the age of 21 (or if they are being helped with education or training, to the end of the agreed programme of education or training even if that extends beyond the age of 21).

13.27   The Children (Leaving Care) Act 2000 introduced new requirements on local authorities to plan for looked-after children so that they have the support they need as they make their transition to the responsibilities of adulthood. Since 2001 the trend to discharge young people from care prematurely when they are as young as 16 has been reversed and many more care leavers now live in suitable accommodation when they are no longer looked after; the numbers of care leavers in education, training and employment has also increased. However, there is still more to do as there remain too many young people expected to cope with independent living too early and without proper support.

---

[28]   CA 1989, s 24A(2) and (3), and s 24B.
[29]   CA 1989, s 61(1)(c).
[30]   CA 1989, s 64(1)(c).

The revised regulations and guidance

13.28 The new Care Leavers (England) Regulations 2010 and the revised guidance in *Volume 3: Planning Transition to Adulthood for Care Leavers* were published in October 2011 and came into force on 1 April 2011. The main aim of the revised regulations and guidance is to ensure that care leavers are provided with comprehensive personal support so that they achieve their potential as they make their transition to adulthood. The regulations and guidance are intended to ensure that care leavers are given the same level of care and support their peers would expect from a reasonable parent and that they are provided with the opportunities and chances needed to help them move successfully to adulthood. The guidance seeks to place these principles at the centre of decision-making for care leavers.

13.29 In order to improve services for care leavers and to help local authorities and key organisations design and plan their services post-implementation of the revised guidance, the Department of Education also worked with the following partnership organisations to produce good practice guidance. This includes:

- *What could make the difference? Care leavers and benefits* (March 2010)
  This report published by the National Care Advisory Service (NCAS) explores the issues that care leavers face with the benefits system and suggests some solutions.

- *Journeys to home: Care leavers' successful transition to independent accommodation*
  A good practice guide for local authorities and their partners on accommodation for young people from and in care. The guide is accompanied by a work planning tool.

- *Care leavers accommodation resources flyer*
  Details the resources produced as part of the department-funded accommodation project which ran in 2008–9.

- *National protocol: Inter-authority arrangements – second revised edition*
  This protocol provides arrangements for negotiating support for care leavers resident outside of their responsible authority.

- *Future positive: A resource guide for people working with disabled care leavers 2006*
  A resource which assists local authorities in the development of effective, joined-up services which support young disabled people up to the age of 19 leaving local authority care.

13.30 More information about care leavers and good practice in relation to the provision of leaving care services can also be obtained from the NCAS website.

The importance of dealing with transition

13.31   The revised guidance reiterates the need for professionals working with young people leaving care to deal with the transition to adulthood sensitively and appropriately. The principles associated with promoting independence and the transition to adulthood are also reiterated in *Fostering Services: National Minimum Standards* and *The Children Act 1989 Guidance and Regulations Volume 4: Fostering Services* which also came into force on 1 April 2011.

13.32   The combined guidance and National Minimum Standards makes it clear that, as part of their duties towards looked-after children under the CA 1989, local authorities, like any reasonable parent, should ensure that they support their young people as they move towards adult life and prepare to move into independence and, when the time is right, leave care. Children and young people should be cared for in a way which helps them to do this, so they can reach their potential and achieve economic well-being.

13.33   The primary expectation is that the transition into adulthood of a looked-after young person is fully supported, practically, financially and emotionally (National Minimum Standard 12). One of the ways in which some local authorities demonstrate their corporate parenting responsibility in this respect is for looked-after children to have savings accounts in the same way that many parents save for their child. Throughout their time with foster carers, children and young people should be given age appropriate opportunities to learn the skills that they need to ensure they develop self-esteem and a positive sense of their personal identity, and are prepared for adult life. As young people approach adulthood, foster carers should increasingly help to prepare them for moving into the world of work, further and higher education and training, and to develop their financial skills, capability and knowledge. They should be supported to understand how to manage the practicalities of a home and personal care, as well as understanding their sexuality and forming positive social and sexual relationships and developing responsible behaviour.

13.34   The combined guidance states that no young person under 18 should have to leave care before they feel ready to do so. When a child does leave his or her foster home for greater independence, it will usually be appropriate for the foster carer to remain in contact with him or her for a period of time and to offer appropriate support, as would a good parent. This will help the young person to feel valued and avoid feeling isolated.

13.35   For young people with a stable foster placement, continuing to live in their former foster home under a 'Staying Put' arrangement can offer a transition to independence closer to that experienced by most other young people. The combined guidance recommends that local authorities should develop Staying Put policies that provide foster carers and young people with information and guidance regarding all aspects of continuing living arrangements beyond the young person's 18th birthday, including criteria for continuing these arrangements beyond 18 and financial and support arrangements. Such arrangements are not covered by the Fostering Services Regulations 2011,[31] but the guidance recommends that local authority fostering services should have a policy covering Staying Put arrangements. The guidance also recommends that the assessment process for foster carers should prepare them for the possibility of continuing to provide support to young people beyond the age of 18. Most local authority would make the arrangements for a young person to remain in the foster placement under their 'lodgings' policies and procedures and it would be exceptional for the foster carer to continue to receive a 'fostering allowance'. The expectation would be for the young person post-18 to make a contribution towards their 'rent'.

13.36 Transition to adulthood is often a turbulent time and transitions are no longer always sequential. Young people can become adult in one area but not in others. For many young adults, their transition to adulthood can be extended and delayed until they are emotionally and financially ready and they have the qualifications they need and aspire to, so that they have the opportunity to achieve their economic potential. Young people from care may not have this option. Whilst most young people know they can call on the support of their families to help them through unforeseen difficulties, care leavers may not be able to rely on unqualified support if things do not work out as they make their journey into adulthood.

13.37 The guidance makes it clear that care leavers should expect the same level of care and support that others would expect from a reasonable parent. The local authority responsible for their care should make sure that they are provided with the opportunities they need, which will include offering them more than one chance as they grapple with taking on the responsibilities of adulthood.

Principles for transition

13.38 The guidance is founded on recent research and practice which shows that young people who have been looked after will have the best chance of success as adults if those providing transitional care and other support take the following principles into account in talking to the young person and when making any decision:

- Is this good enough for my own child?

- Providing a second chance if things don't go as expected.

- Is this tailored to their individual needs, particularly if they are more vulnerable than other young people?

---

[31]   SI 2011/581.

13.39 The guidance reiterates that no young person should be made to feel that they should 'leave care' before they are ready. The role of the young person's IRO will be crucial in making sure that the care plan considers the young person's views.

13.40 Before any move can take place, the young person's statutory review meeting, chaired by their IRO, will evaluate the quality of the assessment of the young person's readiness and preparation for any move. The young person and the professionals responsible for contributing to the plan and the review must concur that they have developed the skills necessary to manage any transition to more 'independent living' where, as a result, less support will be provided.

13.41 Finally, the guidance makes it clear that local authority provision of continuing leaving care support must ensure that throughout the period that each care leaver is provided with leaving care services, his or her needs are subject to ongoing assessment and review, so that the authority's intervention puts them on the pathway to success as they make their transition to adulthood.

13.42 Plans for transition to adulthood must be in place for all looked-after children aged 16 and 17 who have been looked after for at least 13 weeks after they reached the age of 14. The 13 weeks can be continuous or made up of separate episodes of care; they exclude short-term placements made by way of respite care, but must include a period of time (at least 24 hours) after reaching the age of 16.

13.43 Planning for transition to adulthood must take place for every looked-after child regardless of any other status that a child or young person may have. Regulation 3 of the Care Leavers Regulations defines an additional group of relevant children who would have qualified for help under the CA 1989 but for the fact that on reaching 16 they are detained – whether in a remand centre, young offender institution or a secure training centre, or any other institution ordered by a court, or in hospital.

13.44 Young people who were previously eligible and have returned home and become relevant and subsequently qualifying, will revert to being relevant if this arrangement breaks down before their 18th birthday.

13.45 Responsibilities for planning continuing support applies to all care leavers until they reach the age of 21 or, if they are being helped with education or training, to the end of the agreed programme of education or training (which can take them beyond their 25th birthday). The Children and Young Persons Act 2008 includes provision so that, where a former relevant child previously entitled to leaving care services wishes to take up additional education or training beyond the age of 21, but before the age of 25, then their responsible authority must ensure that they are allocated continuing PA support.

13.46 Where a young person is a 'qualifying child', s 24B(5) of the CA 1989 requires a local authority, where they assess there is a need, to provide either vacation accommodation or the means to secure it, to qualifying children up to the age of 24.

Qualifying children

13.47 Local authorities may give advice, guidance and assistance to certain groups of young people who 'qualify' for leaving care support. Some 'qualifying children' will be as vulnerable and have very similar needs to eligible, relevant or former relevant children.

13.48 Section 24(3) of the CA 1989 states that s 24(2)(d) applies even if the 3-month period began before the young person reached the age of 16. Section 24(4) of the CA 1989 provides that in the case of a young person formerly looked after by a local authority, the local authority which last looked after him must take such steps as they consider appropriate to keep in touch with him in order to discharge their functions under ss 24A and 24B.

13.49 Section 24(5) sets out which local authority is responsible for providing to a qualifying young person aftercare services under ss 24A and 24B. In the case of a young person formerly looked after by a local authority, the relevant authority is the one which last looked after him. In the case of someone qualifying for advice and assistance under any of the other provisions at s 24(2) the *relevant authority is the authority in whose area the person has asked for help.*

13.50 Where a qualifying child has been previously looked after, the local authority must assess their needs to establish whether they require advice and assistance. Where, following an initial assessment, the authority concludes that support will be necessary over a period of time, they should draw up a plan with the young person outlining the support that will be provided. In order to determine the extent of the support required, a core assessment may be required and the plan that follows might follow the same format as a pathway plan for a relevant or former relevant child. The plan will outline the support to be provided to the young person, including, if necessary, any financial support. The plan should be drawn up by a social worker or suitably qualified person.

13.51 A young person who was not looked after for 13 weeks may be a qualifying child. If that young person returns home, perhaps as a result of a decision made at their first statutory review as a looked-after child, then that young person should not be regarded as 'qualifying' under s 24 of the CA 1989; rather, support to the young person and his family should be provided under s 17 of the CA 1989.

13.52 The local authority should be able to provide written information, in a leaflet and available on the authority's website, to potentially qualifying young people informing them about their entitlement to an assessment and the range of services that they might expect to receive as a result. This must include clear details about how to access the authority's processes for making a complaint or representation should the young person not be satisfied with the outcomes of the assessment or any services that follow.

13.53   Children who were looked after by a local authority immediately before the making of a special guardianship order may qualify for advice and assistance under the CA 1989. Section 24(1A) provides that the child must:

- have reached the age of 16, but not the age of 21;

- if less than 18 years old, have a special guardianship order in force;

- if 18 years old or above, have had a special guardianship order in force when they reached that age; and

- have been looked after by a local authority immediately before the making of the special guardianship order.

13.54   The relevant local authority should make arrangements for young people who meet these criteria to receive advice and assistance in the same way as for any other young person who qualifies for advice and assistance under the 1989 Act. Regulation 22 of the Special Guardianship Regulations 2005[32] provides that the relevant local authority is the one that last looked after the child.

13.55   Section 26A of the CA 1989 also imposed duties on local authorities in respect of the provision of advocacy services. All looked-after children must be made aware of their entitlement to independent advocacy support and how they can access it. This entitlement is not just for when a looked-after child or care leaver wishes to complain, it includes situations where young people need to make representations about the quality of the care and support provided by their responsible authority.

13.56   Access to advocacy will be particularly important where the local authority's decision-making processes concern the child's readiness to move from their care placement. Young people may frequently require independent support to enable them to put their view across and express their wishes and feelings about the help they feel they will need for the future, so that they are enabled to reach their potential.

Working with care leavers

13.57   The key elements of successful practice in helping care leavers has been identified in and supported by a substantial body of research findings. The principles underlying preparation for leaving care should reflect good childcare practice generally, following the principles of the CA 1989. Services for young

---

[32]   SI 2005/1109.

people must take account of the lengthy process of transition from childhood to adulthood, to reflect the gradual transition of a young person from dependence to independence. The support provided should be, broadly, the support that a good parent might be expected to give. These key elements were defined in the initial guidance as follows:[33]

- Providing stable placements, continuity of carers and maintaining positive links (wherever possible) whilst young people are being looked after.

- 'Looking after' young people until they are prepared and ready to leave care.

- Promoting and maintaining relationships with carers and families (wherever possible) after young people leave care.

- Preparing young people gradually to be ready to leave care, including particular attention to:
  - practical self-care skills (health, budgeting, domestic skills); and
  - personal and relationship dimensions.

- Enabling young people leaving care to fulfil their potential in education, training and employment.

- Ensuring young people leaving care have access to a range of accommodation, and the support and skills to maintain themselves in their accommodation.

- Ensuring there is a contingency plan to support care leavers in the event of a crisis, including arrangements for respite care.

- Providing or enabling ongoing personal support.

- Ensuring that young people leaving care receive their full entitlement to any relevant welfare benefits.

- Involving young people in all assessments, planning, review and decision-making for leaving care.

- Informing young people leaving care of the available services and of their right to access their own records.

13.58 The revised guidance reiterates that all local authorities should work to meet these aims. Young people who cannot successfully return to their own families should be enabled to become as self-supporting as possible. It is vitally

---

[33] Department of Health Children (Leaving Care) Act 2000: *Regulations and Guidance* (TSO, 2010).

important that young people are properly prepared for this step and are given access to support afterwards. Local authorities need to provide great flexibility within their services for care leavers to meet a wide range of potentially differing needs and experiences.

13.59 The principles are defined in the guidance as follows:

- *Young people should be central to discussions and plans for their future* – it will be exceptional for decisions to be made without their full participation. Well before a young person leaves care, a continuing care plan should be formulated with him or her. In the case of an eligible child this should develop into the pathway plan. This should specify the type of help the young person will be receiving and from whom. For young people who will qualify for advice and assistance only under s 24(1) this continuing care plan should incorporate contingency arrangements in the event of a breakdown in the young person's living arrangements after he or she has left care. Such arrangements might include, for example, the possibility of a return to a community home or to foster care.

- *Parents should be invited to help formulate the continuing care plan* (if they are not estranged from the young person). So, too, should foster carers if the young person is leaving a foster placement (whether local authority or private). If the young person wishes it, his or her foster carer should be encouraged and enabled to play a continuing role in his or her support.

- Preparation for leaving care should help develop young people's capacity to make *satisfactory relationships*, develop their self-esteem and enable them to acquire the necessary practical skills for *independent living*.

- In helping young people to develop socially and culturally, carers must be prepared to *take some risks* and to take responsibility for doing so, to let young people take some risk, eg in attempting relationships that ultimately do not work, and to take responsibility for supporting young people through breakdowns in relationships.

- All preparation for leaving care and provision of aftercare must take account of the *religious persuasion, racial origin, cultural and linguistic background* and other needs of the young person.[34]

- Preparation for leaving care and the provision of aftercare must be *planned in conjunction with all other interested agencies*, eg education and housing authorities, the Connexions Service/Careers Service, health authorities and, where appropriate, other local authorities. These agencies should be invited to contribute to young people's continuing care plans and, as they reach 16, to their pathway plans.

---

[34] CA 1989, s 22(5)(c).

13.60 The guidance envisages that the local authority social services departments are likely to play the lead role in discharging the legal responsibilities towards care leavers, but that they will need to liaise with many other departments (both internally and externally). These departments may include, housing and education departments, health authorities, Careers Service, Benefits Agency, Employment Service, Job Centre Plus. The CA 1989, s 27 provides the right to the local authority (in effect, the social services department) to request help in its discharge of these functions from any other local authority, any local education authority, any local housing authority, any health authority, special health authority, primary care trust (PCT) or NHS Trust. Other agencies are obliged to comply with such requests by the local authority if they are compatible with their own statutory duties and obligations and do not unduly prejudice the discharge of any of their functions; in other words, such requests must be complied with by other agencies as far as possible.

SECTION 5 – THE RESPONSIBLE LOCAL AUTHORITY

13.61 *The responsible local authority* is the one which last looked after an 'eligible' or 'relevant' child or young person.[35] The local authority will retain this responsibility for a care leaver wherever the young person may be living in England or Wales. The aim of this is two-fold:

- first, to reinforce continuity of care. Research suggests that this, along with stability and the maintenance of family links, may contribute to positive outcomes for care leavers, especially in relation to their self-esteem and sense of identity; and

- secondly, to prevent disputes between local authorities over the issue of who is responsible for services.

13.62 If a young person moves to a different local authority, funding can be transferred by the responsible local authority to the local authority where the young person is living so they can provide the services under the Children (Leaving Care) Act 2000, if that is the most convenient way of proceeding.

13.63 Such arrangements are also available as a possible solution in cases where a young person's relationship with the responsible authority breaks down. Under such circumstances the authority will be able to discharge its duties through arrangements made with another authority, though it will still keep ultimate responsibility. However, it is essential that young people are provided with support services whilst new arrangements are being made and, where necessary, the funding transferred. In difficult cases this may mean use of the second authority's emergency services. It is fundamental in such

---

[35] CA 1989, s 23A(4).

circumstances that there is no delay in the provision of emergency support to the young person in order to prevent loss of housing, education or other services.

SECTION 6 – THE LOCAL AUTHORITY'S PLANNING AND POLICY ON LEAVING CARE

13.64   Each local authority should take the above principles into account in planning and developing leaving care and aftercare policies and in applying those policies to the needs of individual young people. To help ensure this, each social services department should provide a written statement of its philosophy and practice on the preparation of young people for leaving care and the provision of aftercare support.

13.65   It is a requirement of para 1(2) of Sch 2 to the CA 1989 that each local authority must publish information about services provided by them under ss 23, 23B–23D, 24A and 24B and take such steps as are reasonably practicable to ensure that those who might benefit from the services receive the relevant information. Such statements need to be placed within the framework of children's services planning required under para 1A of Sch 2 to the CA 1989. This requires councils with social services responsibilities to review their services for children in need, consult with a range of specified bodies and publish plans.

13.66   It is clear that preparation for leaving care must start well before a young person ceases to be looked after or accommodated.[36] In the case of someone who will become a relevant child, support and assistance will continue until well after he or she has done so, and where a young person qualifies for advice and assistance only under s 24(2) it is likely that it will do so.

13.67   Preparation for this process should be incorporated in the care plan for young people while they are being looked after, accommodated or privately fostered. However, the timing of the pathway planning process should take account of events happening in the young person's life and at a pace that is suitable and appropriate for each individual young person (for example, social workers should take account of exams or other school commitments). The relevant local authority, voluntary organisation or children's home will play a leading role in preparing young people for the time when they leave care, but other agencies will need to be involved. Normally, the key workers involved with a young person in care would be involved in the development of the Connexions Service, which will need to contribute. Schools will need to be consulted about the long-term educational and training needs of a young person; and the relevant health authority may need to be involved if the young person is disabled.

---

[36]   CA 1989, Sch 2, Pt II, para 19A and ss 61(1)(c), 64(1)(c).

13.68 Preparation should therefore be regarded as an integral part of the care process. A stable care relationship is, in its turn, an important basis on which to plan the preparation of a young person for leaving care.

SECTION 7 – PATHWAY PLANNING

13.69 As corporate parents, responsible local authorities should provide support to care leavers in the same way that reasonable parents provide support for their own children.

13.70 The guidance sets out the clear approach that is envisaged as good practice in the provision of such support. In particular, the participation of care leavers is considered fundamental to effective pathway planning. Young people should be central to discussions and plans for their futures and it will be exceptional for decisions about their futures to be made without their full participation. They should be seen as active participants in building their future, based on their hopes and aspirations.

13.71 The responsibilities of local authorities to prepare pathway plans and support care leavers as they make the transition to adulthood apply irrespective of any other services being provided for them, for example, because they are disabled, in custody, or because they are being looked after as they entered the country as an unaccompanied asylum seeking child (UASC). However, the guidance deals specifically with the particular needs of these groups of young people.

The link between care planning and pathway plans

13.72 Transition to adulthood for looked-after children should not just start on a child's 16th birthday; preparation for a time when they will no longer be looked after should be integral to the care planning process throughout their time in care.

13.73 The CA 1989 requires that a pathway plan must be prepared for all eligible children and continued for all relevant and former relevant children. Each young person's pathway plan will be based on and include their care plan and will set out the actions that must be taken by the responsible authority, the young person, their parents, their carers and the full range of agencies, so that each young person is provided with the services they need to enable them to achieve their aspirations and make a successful transition to adulthood. The guidance makes it clear that this plan must remain a 'live document', setting out the different services and how they will be provided to respond to the full range of the young person's needs.

13.74 All relevant and former relevant children must have a pathway plan based on an up-to-date and thorough assessment of their needs.

The content of the pathway plan

13.75   The pathway plan must address in particular:

- The young person's health and development building on the information included in the young person's health plan established within their care plan when they were looked after. The plan should support the young person's access to positive activities.

- Education, training and employment. The personal education plan (PEP) should continue to be maintained while the young person continues to receive full or part-time education. Information within the PEP should feed directly into the pathway plan. Pathway plans must have an explicit focus on career planning, taking into account the young person's aspirations, skills, and educational potential.

- Contact with the young person's parents, wider family and friends and the capacity of this network to encourage the young person and enable them to make a positive transition to adulthood.

- The young person's financial capabilities and money management capacity, along with strategies to develop the young person's skills in this area.

13.76   The assessment and pathway planning process for a care leaver must involve a measured, evidence-based analysis of the young person's continuing need for care, accommodation and support, including whether they should continue to remain looked after. Where the care plan for the young person has been maintained and kept up to date, the development of the pathway plan should build on information and services set out in the care plan, incorporating the services that will be provided to the young person to develop their resilience and equip them to make a positive transition to adulthood so that they can manage the challenges of more independent living.

13.77   Where there is any proposal for the young person to move to different accommodation, as part of the process to prepare for their transition to adulthood, then the pathway plan must include an explicit assessment of the support they need to develop the skills that they will require to be ready for this significant change. The plan must also include a thorough assessment as to the suitability of the potential accommodation for the individual young person.

Pathway plans for relevant children

13.78   A pathway plan must be prepared for each relevant child. This pathway plan should be prepared prior to the young person ceasing to be looked after (ie when they are still an 'eligible child') and considered at a statutory review chaired by the young person's IRO.

13.79 The professional preparing the pathway plan on behalf of the local authority, usually the young person's social worker, must engage constructively with the young person to define priorities and the focus of the plan. In addition they must consult with:

- the young person's parents, other adults with parental responsibility and relevant members of their wider family network;

- the young person's current carer and any prospective future provider of housing and accommodation support;

- the young person's designated teacher, college tutor or other educational professional familiar with the young person's learning needs and educational objectives;

- any independent visitor appointed for the young person;

- designated nurse for looked-after children or any other medical professional providing health care or treatment named in their health plan;

- any personal adviser (PA), already appointed to support the young person;

- the young person's IRO; and

- any advocate acting for the young person.

13.80 It is essential that discussion takes place with the young person about who will be contacted to contribute to their pathway plan. It will not always be appropriate for all those listed above to be involved in the pathway planning process, although the guidance suggests that there would need to be a compelling justification for a pathway plan to be completed without reference to the young person's carer or to professional advice about the young person's education, training and employment pathway.

13.81 The views of the young person must be recorded and incorporated into the pathway plan. The plan must also indicate how arrangements to support the young person have taken the views of the others listed above into account. Disagreements between the young person and professionals should be noted carefully.

13.82 The guidance sets out the information concerning the needs of each care leaver that must be considered in order to draw up the pathway plan, but it is a matter for each individual responsible local authority to determine the format their staff should use to record this.

13.83 Upon completion, a copy of the plan must be given to the young person. The guidance also suggests that, as a matter of good practice, where agencies are contributing to the delivery of an individual young person's pathway plan, they too should have a copy of the relevant extract from the plan relating to their contribution. This should be signed by the agency's representative, the young person and their PA, as evidence of their commitment to achieving the plan's objectives.

The role of the IRO

13.84 The IRO has a crucial role at times of transitions experienced by looked-after children and young people. The IRO should be satisfied that the local authority is making appropriate arrangements to meet the child's needs at these times. This would include:

- Ensure that the transition planning for all looked-after children with a statement of special educational needs starts at the age of 14 and be satisfied that such planning is actively being undertaken and is linked to the child's care plan.

- Ensure the pathway plan is an effective and comprehensive document which identifies the actions and services required to meet the needs and outcomes of the young person during his or her transition into adulthood and independence.

- Be satisfied that the proposed pathway plan includes the care plan and has been informed by a good quality assessment in which the young person, his or her family and professional agencies have been appropriately involved.

- Be satisfied that the pathway plan is aspirational, that it will assist the young person with the transition and that it has contingency plans in respect of health and education.

13.85 In the event that the IRO is not satisfied that the pathway plan will meet the child's identified needs he or she could:

- request additional review meetings before the young person reaches the age of 18;

- seek to resolve the issue through informal routes or if this is not successful, through the local conflict dispute resolution process;

- seek independent legal advice.

13.86 The IRO should be provided with an updated copy of the final pathway plan 20 working days before the young person's 18th birthday, whether or not a review is due to take place and should communicate directly with the young person in relation to the arrangements set out in the pathway plan. In the event that the young person or the IRO are not satisfied with the arrangements, consideration should be given to convening an additional review and/or taking other remedial action.

The IRO responsibilities when moving into independent accommodation

13.87 In addition to considering all the key areas in the care plan the IRO should ensure that consideration is given to the following:

- how the proposed move will meet the young person's needs in such a way that the young person can progress in his or her gradual journey to assuming the responsibilities of adulthood; and

- that reports provided for the review, discussion with the young person by the IRO prior to review and information provided by others during the review meeting are able to demonstrate that the young person has been properly prepared to make the move and will be able to manage in the new accommodation; and

- that the proposed move will maintain as much stability as possible for the young person, including family contact and links with the community in which he or she has been living. In particular, a young person must not be expected to make a move that will disrupt his or her plans to continue in education, participate in training or gain employment; and

- where a review concludes that it is appropriate for a looked-after young person to make the move to independent living arrangements, and such a move takes place, *this does not automatically result in the young person ceasing to be looked after*.

Pathway plans for former relevant children

13.88 Former relevant children will continue to have a pathway plan. The plan will cover the same topics and fulfil the same functions as the pathway plan for relevant children. However, the local authority will no longer be primarily responsible for the young person's financial support and maintenance. The plan should be clear about the mainstream and universal services, including accommodation that will be provided to the young person; and how these contribute to achieving positive outcomes. The plan should reflect high aspirations for the young person and allow them the chance to have more than one opportunity to succeed.

13.89 As former relevant young people mature and develop, support for them should enable and empower them to take increasing control over the pathway planning process. Empowering young people may require a PA to allow care leavers the opportunity to take risks and learn and grow, even if this means that they may not initially be successful in what they set out to achieve. This will require considerable professional skill, judgment, engagement and attention to the young person's developing and changing needs.

13.90 PAs will need to strike a balance between being 'hands off' and intervening in support of the young person. PAs must be ready to step in, and be active in making sure that young people are offered the right kind of support to enable them to succeed as they make the transition to adulthood, recognising that in order to succeed, young people may need to experience failure and a learning experience first.

13.91 If a former relevant young person is not intending to continue in an approved programme of education or training, then the pathway planning process should be brought to a conclusion in an agreed way around the time that the young person reaches the age of 21.

13.92 Depending on whether any outstanding needs have been identified for the young person, the final year of pathway planning should be focused on identifying sources of adult community-based support outside of the local authority's children's services. For care leavers whose health needs do not meet the criteria for support by adult services, their PA should ensure that all possible forms of support, including that offered by the voluntary sector, should be identified and facilitated as appropriate.

13.93

Analysis of the pathway plan

- Was the pathway plan prepared as an integral part of the care planning process throughout the young person's time in care?

- Was a pathway plan prepared in relation to all eligible children and continued for all relevant and former relevant children?

- Was the pathway plan based on and included the young person's care plan?

- Does the pathway plan set out the actions that must be taken by the responsible local authority, the young person, their parents, their carers and the full range of agencies, so that the young person is provided with the services they need?

- Is the pathway plan a 'live document', setting out the different services and how they will be provided to respond to the full range of the young person's needs?

- Is the pathway plan based on an up-to-date and thorough assessment of the young person's needs?   ➡

- Does the pathway plan include a measured, evidence-based analysis of the young person's continuing need for care, accommodation and support, including whether they should continue to remain looked after?

- Does the pathway plan take account of the young person's health and development, building on the information included in the young person's health plan established within their care plan when they were looked after? Does the plan support the young person's access to positive activities?

- Has the personal education plan (PEP) been maintained while the young person continued to receive full or part-time education? Has information from the PEP fed directly into the pathway plan?

- Does the pathway plan deal with arrangements for contact with the young person's parents, wider family and friends?

- Does the pathway plan deal with the young person's financial capabilities and money management capacity, along with strategies to develop the young person's skills in this area?

- If there is a proposal for the young person to move to different accommodation does the pathway plan include an explicit assessment of the support they need? Does the pathway plan also include a thorough assessment as to the suitability of the potential accommodation?

- Were the views of the young person recorded and incorporated into the pathway plan?

- Does the pathway plan indicate how arrangements to support the young person have taken the views of relevant others?

- Has a copy of the plan been given to the young person? Have other relevant also been given a copy of the pathway plan?

- Does the pathway plan note any disagreements between the young person and professionals?

SECTION 8 – REVIEWS OF PATHWAY PLANS

Frequency

13.94 Regulation 7 of the Care Leavers Regulations 2010 sets out the arrangements for reviewing the pathway plans of relevant and former relevant children. Regulation 7(2)(a) and (b) require the local authority to arrange a review in circumstances where it, or the PA, consider it necessary or where the relevant or former relevant child requests it. Where a relevant child moves to unregulated accommodation then the first review of the pathway plan must take place as soon as is practical after 28 days. Apart from ensuring that the pathway plan continues to respond to all the dimensions of the young person's needs, one of the essential functions of this review will be to establish that they have settled into their accommodation and that this is, in practice, suitable in the light of their needs.

13.95 In circumstances where young people move in a planned way, the first review will need to decide whether it will be necessary to review the pathway plan in a further 3 months or whether a review at 6 months is more appropriate. The decision to review sooner will depend on the PA's assessment of the vulnerability of the child or young adult concerned.

13.96 The guidance suggests that it will be good practice for reviews to take place at an early stage (usually 28 days) after any change in the young person's accommodation. This will be particularly important for any relevant child – as the local authority remains responsible for the accommodation and maintenance of this potentially very vulnerable group of young people. This first review provides a set opportunity to check that a young person has settled into new accommodation and need not be excessively formal. However, where young people are moving because of instability and uncertainty in their circumstances, then reviewing after 28 days of any move taking place provides the opportunity to bring all agencies together to scrutinise the options for bringing stability back into a young person's life.

13.97 These requirements for review describe the maximum permitted intervals between reviews, but the guidance makes it plain that reviews should always be brought forward where there is an assessed risk that a crisis may develop in a young person's life. The purpose of these meetings will be to allow all the agencies supporting the young person to meet with them and to agree strategies so that any potential crises can be averted.

Other circumstances when reviews should be held

13.98 The guidance cites the following situations as examples where, given the serious implications for a young person's future, the responsible local authority, or a relevant or former relevant young person's PA, should also ensure that a review takes place:

- where a young person has been charged with an offence and there is a possibility of their being sentenced to custody, which will risk losing their (suitable) accommodation;

- where a young person is at risk of being evicted from their accommodation or otherwise threatened with homelessness;

- where professionals are concerned about the parenting capacity of a relevant or former relevant young person, with there being a possibility that their own child may need to become the subject of a multi-agency safeguarding plan;

- where a young person asks for a review of their plan.

Involving the young person in reviews

13.99 The young person must be engaged in making the arrangements about how their pathway plan is to be reviewed. Young people may suggest that some key professionals are not invited to their review meeting, and, if so, these wishes should generally be respected. However, where professionals not invited to a review are making an important contribution to the pathway plan, they should still be consulted.

13.100 The guidance provides useful examples of the ways in which young people might be encouraged to take increasing responsibility for the review of their personal pathway plan and suggests that it will be good practice, if the young person wishes, to support them so that they chair their own pathway plan reviews with support from the chairperson, if appropriate.

Record keeping of reviews

13.101 Regulation 5(3) of the Care Leavers Regulations 2010 requires that the responsible authority keep a written record of the information obtained during an assessment; of the deliberations of any meeting held in connection with any aspect of an assessment; of the identity of the people whose views were sought for the purposes of the assessment; and the outcome of the assessment. Regulation 6(4) of the Care Leavers Regulations requires that the pathway plan must be recorded in writing; reg 4(3) requires that the responsible authority keep a written record of the child's views; and reg 7(5) requires that the results of any review are recorded in writing. Regulation 10 establishes a duty to maintain a case record which should include any assessment of needs, any pathway plan, and any review of a pathway plan.

13.102 The pathway plan, and the assessment informing it, must provide a full and accurate record of the young person's needs with explicit information about their wishes and feelings for their future. Each young person must have a copy of their personal plan and understand which professionals have access to it and the arrangements made by the local authority for secure filing and storage. Similarly, where other agencies have a copy of their contribution to the plan, then the responsible authority must assure itself that the agency understands their responsibility to maintain confidentiality and make arrangements for secure storage of documents containing personal information about care leavers. Authorities will need to satisfy themselves that they are complying with the Data Protection Act when sharing information.

13.103 Where young people have complex needs and a range of agencies is involved in supporting their pathway plan, then it may be helpful to agree arrangements for information sharing at a multi-agency meeting to confirm or to review the pathway plan.

SECTION 9 – PERSONAL ADVISERS (PAS)

13.104 Once a young person ceases to be looked after and they are a relevant child, or once they reach legal adulthood at age 18 and are a former relevant child, then the local authority will no longer be required to provide them with a social worker to plan and coordinate their care. The local authority must, however, appoint a personal adviser (PA) to support them. The PA will act as the focal point to ensure that care leavers are provided with the right kind of personal support. All care leavers should be aware of who their PA is and how to contact them, so that throughout their transition to adulthood they are able to rely on consistent support from their own key professional.

13.105 The revised guidance states that it is good practice, where possible, for the young person to maintain the same PA from the age of 18 who was allocated to support them when they were an eligible or a relevant child. However, where young people have continued to have a qualified social worker as their PA, their 18th birthday may provide the opportunity to transfer responsibility for supporting them to a PA with particular skills in working with young adults. The guidance recommends that any such transfer of support should take place in a planned and managed way; for example, the transfer of support could be timed to coincide with a scheduled review of the young person's pathway plan, or when the young person becomes more settled following a change of education/training or accommodation.

Qualifications and skills of PAs

13.106 There is no prescribed professional or occupational qualification determining which professional should carry out the PA function for any individual care leaver. However a PA should normally possess or be working towards a professional qualification.

13.107 Anyone appointed to carry out the PA function should possess a sound demonstrable understanding of human growth and development (in particular being competent in understanding the insecurities faced by looked-after children as they make their transition to adulthood). They will also need to have a working knowledge of the range of issues that care leavers might expect to face as they make their transition to adulthood and the legal framework affecting care leavers (in particular the CA 1989 and Children (Leaving Care) Act 2000 and related regulations).

13.108 PAs should work closely with doctors and nurses involved in health assessments, and the guidance recommends that they would benefit from training in how to promote both physical and mental health. They should also be capable of understanding and acting upon relevant legislation concerned with housing and homelessness. More detail about the range of knowledge and skills that a PA requires is provided at appendix A of the guidance.

13.109   In recruiting PAs, it will be ideal if the range of advisers is sufficiently wide to provide young people with a choice, bearing in mind considerations of gender and ethnicity. The responsible authority will always need to give careful consideration to any preferences expressed by the young person about who might fulfil their PA function. However, in the final analysis, the local authority must be satisfied in every case that the person acting as a young person's PA has the requisite skills and the necessary availability. For example, local authorities should ensure that a PA is familiar with a young person's way of communicating if they are disabled, eg use Makaton or other augmentative communication methods, or has access to appropriate training, interpretation or facilitation. The final decision as to who will be suitable to act as a PA for an individual care leaver rests with the responsible authority.

13.110   Where a young person has developed a trusting relationship with a carer then it should be possible for the local authority to delegate aspects of the PA function to them, as it will clearly be in young people's interests to build on the positive relationships that they have already established. However, in these circumstances the responsible authority must be clear as to the support that the carer will be providing and how any potential conflicts of interests might be managed.

13.111   It will be important that the PA is able to form a working relationship with the young person to carry forward their pathway plan. Young people will have views about the kinds of qualities that they will expect from their PA and these should be taken into account when matching an individual care leaver to a PA.

The functions of PAs

13.112   Regulation 8 of the Care Leavers Regulations 2010 sets out the seven primary functions of a PA for a relevant or a former relevant child as follows:

- Provision of advice (including practical advice) and support.

- Participation in assessment and preparation of the pathway plan.

- Participation in review of the pathway plan.

- Liaison with the responsible authority in implementation of the pathway plan.

- To coordinate the provision of services and take reasonable steps so that care leavers make use of services.

- To keep informed about care leavers' progress and well-being.

- To keep full, accurate and up–to-date records of contacts with the care leaver and services provided.

Provision of advice and support

13.113 The pathway plan should include details about the kind of support that the young person might expect their PA to provide. This might include:

- basic information and assistance to develop the practical skills the young person will need to manage the expectations placed on them as they gradually assume the responsibilities of greater independence;

- information about financial capability (including how to manage day-to-day finances, and how to take up any entitlements to benefits);

- information about the housing options potentially available to the young person and how to access accommodation and advice;

- support to the young person to develop their confidence and decision-making capacity;

- information about education, training and employment opportunities;

- support in finding and sustaining employment;

- general information about maintaining positive health and well-being; knowledge about how to access targeted and specialist health services (eg information, advice and support about mental health, or sexual health); and

- information about leisure, sporting and cultural opportunities to enable young people to enjoy and participate in community life.

The pathway plan will also need to include scope for contingencies that might be required to be followed as the relationship between the young person and the PA changes over time.

Participation in assessment and preparation of pathway plans

13.114 As already discussed, before a young person becomes a relevant child or a former relevant child at the age of 18, a pathway plan should already be in place. The PA will be the key professional responsible for coordinating each young person's support. This means that where the young person's circumstances change and it becomes necessary to revise their pathway plan, the PA may be the most suitable professional able to re-assess their needs and suggest amendments to the plan to the local authority, setting out how the young person will be supported in future. The PA should then be able to use their knowledge and skills so that the dimensions of need set out in the

Framework for Assessment of Children in Need and their Families[37] (discussed at Chapter 5) are included in the pathway plan.

13.115 Communication with young people should be at the heart of the assessment process. The PA will need to be able to establish a rapport with care leavers and take their views into account when taking forward plans for their support. However, it is important to note that, for a relevant child who has not reached legal adulthood, respecting a young person's wishes and feelings does not mean automatically agreeing with all of their views. The PA must make their own professional judgment about the child's best interests. For both relevant and for former relevant children, where young people's wishes and feelings appear to be in conflict with the PA's informed professional view of their best interests, the PA will have a responsibility to negotiate with the young person about a reasonable way forward.

Participation in review of pathway plan

13.116 The PA must make sure that the pathway plan is reviewed at the prescribed intervals (as set out above) and will also be responsible for convening additional reviews to resolve potential crises faced by the care leavers that they support. For example, where there is a risk that a young person might be evicted from their accommodation, it will be essential that the PA convenes a review involving all relevant professionals, along with the young person, to develop a plan to enable the young person to maintain their accommodation or move in a planned way, therefore preventing them from becoming homeless. However, where prompt action is required to respond to a problem faced by a care leaver, convening a review to coordinate arrangements for their professionals' support should not stop immediate and necessary action by the PA – which could involve making immediate contact with relevant agencies.

Liaison in implementation of pathway plan

13.117 Every PA needs to understand the arrangements for liaising with the responsible authority so that the pathway plan for the young people they support is implemented. The responsible authority must agree arrangements with the PA (or where the adviser is not an employee of the authority, with their agency) for their supervision and support.

Coordination of services

13.118 In carrying forward, or participating in drawing up the pathway plan the PA will need to have identified the range of services necessary to respond to each dimension of the young person's needs. The PA role will be to coordinate how services are provided for the young person, developing constructive professional relationships, in order that all agencies recognise their important investment in enabling the young person to succeed as they make their

---

[37] Department of Health (TSO, 2000).

transition to adulthood. Services will need to be provided in a timely way and each service involved with a young person will need to appreciate how they contribute to the pathway plan and understand the contribution made by other services.

13.119   It will also, of course, be essential that the PA has been able to engage and, as far as reasonably practicable, motivate the young person, so that services are accepted and used effectively. To this end, it will be important that, as far as possible, care leavers are given some choice about the services supporting them and feel that their voice is listened to, in influencing the quality and direction of the support that they receive.

Keeping informed about progress and well-being

13.120   As already identified, each care leaver must have an up-to-date and active pathway plan based on a current assessment of their needs. PAs must be in regular face-to-face contact with every care leaver that they support. The pathway plan must set out expectations for the PA to see the care leaver and, if relevant, arrangements for staying in touch in other ways. This could, for example, include expectations of regular exchanges of text messages, e-mails and phone conversations between the PA and the young person.

13.121   Regulation 8(2) of the Care Leavers Regulations 2010 requires that when a care leaver moves to new accommodation, the PA must see them at that accommodation within 7 days of the move. Subsequently they must see the care leaver at the point at which the pathway plan will be first reviewed – namely after 28 days – and then they must visit the care leavers at no less than 2-monthly intervals. However, it is important to remember that these are minimum requirements. Where care leavers develop problems as they assume the responsibilities of adulthood they should expect, and will require, much more frequent personal contact with their PA. Visits should often be scheduled to take place at the accommodation where the young person lives. On each occasion the PA must consider whether this accommodation continues to be suitable for the young person. The PA will need to observe the general state of the property and check how well the care leaver is managing in their accommodation, including that they are managing their financial commitments for rent, utilities etc. Where a young person is living in semi-independent accommodation linked to the provision of housing related support, the PA should monitor how well the accommodation, with its related support, is meeting the young person's needs. They should liaise closely with the young person and their housing support worker to identify and resolve any problems.

Keeping records of contacts and services

13.122   The PA will be responsible for keeping an up–to-date record of their involvement with each care leaver and therefore of the responsible local authority's involvement with the young person. A note should be made by the PA of each visit and on other contacts with the young person. Contact with other agencies must also be recorded. The case record can be used to establish that the plan continues to set out an effective means of supporting the young person. A properly recorded pathway plan and case file should demonstrate that the responsible local authority is meeting its statutory duties towards the care leaver concerned.

13.123 The pathway plan should be a continuously maintained and updated document (referred to in the guidance as a 'living document'). Care leavers should be given a copy of their plan and provided with regular information about the records being maintained on their behalf and where these are stored. Young people should be offered assistance so they are able to have easy access to their case files.

PAs and budget holding for the young person

13.124 The PA is responsible for coordinating the services provided to support individual care leavers. This will include provision to enable care leavers to develop financial capability and to access income maintenance services. The responsible local authority is also accountable for accommodating and maintaining care leavers who are relevant children. The way in which young people access and manage their personal finances will be a major factor determining whether they will be able to make a successful transition to adulthood.

13.125 PAs will need to discuss finance management issues with the young person and it may be desirable for PAs to have direct access to funding, for example, to provide emergency out of hours support to care leavers.

SECTION 10 – CARE LEAVERS AGED 18–24

13.126 The CA 1989 requires the responsible local authority to continue to provide various forms of advice, assistance and guidance to young people over the age of 18 making the transition from care to more independent living arrangements. These requirements apply if they have previously been eligible or relevant children, who are described as former relevant children (and may apply to qualifying children, depending on the local authority's assessment of their needs).

13.127 These duties operate primarily until the young person reaches the age of 21. However, the duties continue beyond a young person's 21st birthday where they remain engaged in education or training and continue until the end of the agreed programme as set out in their pathway plan.

13.128 Section 24B(2) gives a power to local authorities to assist with the expenses associated with education and training up to the age of 21. For the most part this will be in respect of 'qualifying' young people.

Duties

13.129   For former relevant young people, the responsible local authority will continue to:

- provide the young person with a PA;[38]

- review and revise the pathway plan regularly;[39] and

- keep in touch.[40]

13.130   Responsible local authorities' duty to provide accommodation and maintenance for care leavers ends when the young person reaches 18. However, local authority will continue to have duties to:

- provide general assistance;[41]

- provide assistance with the expenses associated with employment;[42]

- provide assistance with the expenses associated with education and training;[43]

- provide vacation accommodation (or the funds to secure it) to care leavers in higher education, or in residential further education;[44] and

- provide a bursary (£2,000) to care leavers going on to higher education.[45]

13.131   The duties outlined above should follow from the needs identified in the local authority's assessment that informs each young person's pathway plan. This assessment will have to demonstrate how, in responding to these duties, it will best meet their educational and/or welfare needs.

SECTION 11 – DISABLED CARE LEAVERS

13.132   Chapter 6 of the revised guidance deals in particular with care leavers who require additional specialist support, including:

- disabled young people making the transition to adult services;

- unaccompanied asylum seeking children and young people; and

---

[38]   CA 1989, s 23C(3)(a).
[39]   CA 1989, s 23C(3)(b).
[40]   CA 1989, s 23C(2)(a) and (b).
[41]   CA 1989, s 23C(4)(c).
[42]   CA 1989, s 23C(4)(a).
[43]   CA 1989, s 23C(4)(b).
[44]   CA 1989, s 24B(5).
[45]   CA 1989, s 23C(5A).

- care leavers in the youth justice system.

13.133 Disabled young people will face many of the same experiences and challenges as other care leavers. However, the transition to adulthood for disabled young people who are looked after may be particularly challenging. They will often experience different professional languages, styles, expectations and cultures as they make the transition from support by children's services to support from adult health and social care services. Disabled young people also have particular needs relating to their health, social care and education, and these may vary widely depending on the nature of their conditions.

13.134 The definitions in the CA 1989 and in the legislation governing provision for disabled adults often differ and have differing thresholds for eligibility for services.

13.135 Care leavers with complex needs, including those with disabilities, may transfer direct to adult services and the pathway plan will need to ensure that this transition is seamless and supported. Local authority responsibilities towards disabled care leavers are the same as for all other care leavers.[46] Because of their additional needs, some young people may draw on a number of services, receive support from several professionals and have multiple plans. The responsible local authority must ensure that these processes are streamlined as much as possible and roles and responsibilities discussed with the young person and their carer(s).

The IRO

13.136 The IRO should be rigorous in scrutinising transition plans for disabled young people from the age of 14 years on and ensuring that children's services are working closely with adult services to commence assessments in a timely manner and identify an adult placement at the earliest possible opportunity. Demand for adult placements for disabled young people is high and it is likely that there will be waiting lists for the most desirable placements. The earlier the assessment is completed and an appropriate placement identified, the more likely it is that the young person will be able to move to it at a time that will ensure a smooth transition.

13.137 The principles underpinning the involvement of children with complex communication needs are the same as for all children, however, this group of children require additional action by IROs. Essentially the requirement is for the local authority to allocate a specialist IRO with knowledge and experience of children with communication needs or an IRO with experience of the child's specific communication method.

---

[46] See Department of Health *Future Positive: National Framework for Children and Young People's Continuing Care* (2006) which provides a comprehensive resource guide for people from all agencies working with disabled care leavers.

13.138 Where specialist expertise is not available within the IRO team a presumption should be made that a child with communication needs will be supported by an independent advocate, with the child having the right to opt out or choose someone else to support him or her if he or she wishes. This support should be made available throughout the care planning and review process.

13.139 Involvement should be seen as a process and not simply measured by attendance at a review meeting. Children with communication support needs should be actively encouraged to attend review meetings that are organised to best facilitate their involvement and feedback should be provided in a format that is accessible to the individual child.

Person-centred planning

13.140 The revised guidance confirms that each disabled young person will have their own individual aspirations, hopes, needs and wants, and that whilst different services will have their own eligibility and access criteria, they must work together to adopt a holistic approach based on assessment of individual needs informed by each young person's wishes and feelings.

13.141 Person-centred planning describes the process ensuring that planning for disabled young people to make the transition to adulthood is focused on what is important to the young person for the future and what needs to be in place to ensure that they receive the support to achieve their goals.

Transition planning and joint protocols

13.142 The Children Act 2004 requires English social services authorities to divide their functions into adult services and children's services departments.

13.143 For the past 20 years there have been continuous expressions of grave concern over the failure of social services authorities to manage the transition of disabled children into adulthood; these concerns have continued and are reflected in the most recent government guidance about the provision of services for young people with disabilities who are moving from children's to adult services. Many children with disabilities experience acute problems in negotiating the transition from childcare to adult care services.

13.144 *Valuing People* identified young people moving from children's to adult services as a priority group who should benefit from a person-centred approach. The 2007 report, *Growing Up Matters: Better transition planning for young people with complex needs*,[47] called for urgent action to tackle the considerable difficulties faced by disabled young people and their families in the transition from children's to adult services, and noted that for some the process was considered to be a 'nightmare'.

---

[47] Commission for Social Care Inspection, January 2007.

13.145 Person-centred transition planning means working with young people to improve choice and control in their lives. The transition period is defined as being the period when young people are between 14 and 25 years old. The guidance in *Valuing People Now* proposed that by 2012 all relevant young people should have person-centred transition plans focusing on health, housing, jobs, friends and relationships and social inclusion. It was recognised that, in order for this to happen, young people and their families need to receive expert advice and information from age 13 or 14 about the funding streams available to support their aspirations.

13.146 Transition planning should be sufficiently flexible to enable various options to be considered in accordance with the young person's wishes and feelings. Effective transition planning requires a collaborative approach between the young person, his or her parents or carers, and all agencies involved or likely to be involved. The young person must be kept at the centre during the transition planning process with family members, carers and friends being partners in supporting the young person to achieve their potential. A shared commitment should be established to ensure that the young person's views are listened to and ways are found to remove any organisational barriers that might limit personal development and choices. It is clear that young disabled people leaving care should not simply be placed in pre-existing services and expected to adjust. Services should, in particular, be responsive to the needs and preferences of a disabled young person in relation to such issues as housing, social networks and isolation, education, employment and leisure.

13.147 PAs and others working with disabled care leavers should be given training to ensure that they are equipped to communicate effectively with them, including those with high communication needs. Trained advocates should also be available to ensure that young people's views are heard and taken into account.

13.148 In order for transition to adulthood to become a positive experience for young people and their families, it is necessary for all agencies to work together and understand each other's roles, responsibilities, professional frame of reference and legal duties within the transition process. It is therefore essential that specific protocols and agreements are drawn up in each local authority area, with the participation of all agencies. This will include children's and adult social care, children's and adult health, education, housing, youth offending, information, advice and guidance services, supported employment services and leisure services.

13.149 Local authority strategic planning approaches should be reflected at an operational level through protocols which should identify the timing and mechanisms by which key professionals come together with young people to help to identify their needs and to plan individualised support packages. In order to avoid duplication, wherever possible, such protocols will need to identify how the pathway planning process relates to other frameworks for planning the transition to adulthood for young disabled care leavers, such as those for special educational needs.

13.150 The ages at which young people transfer between services differs according to the service provider:

- transfer from child to adult health services at 16;

- transfer from child to adult social care services at 18;

- transfer from school-based education to further education between 16 and 19; and

- transfer to higher education at 18.

13.151 However, there may be exceptions to these general arrangements. Child and Adolescent Mental Health Services usually provide services up to age 18, and young people with a statement of special educational needs may not transfer to support from adult social care services until the end of school year 13, at age 19. Joint protocols must reflect the fact that age-related policies of different agencies do not fit easily with the realities of the transition process for young people leaving care, and should allow for a flexible approach which recognises the corporate responsibility towards them. Where it is likely that a care leaver will require continuing support from adult services, it will be good practice for the social work professionals working with the young person to make a formal referral as early as possible from age 16, so that eligibility for this support is established in time for the young person's 18th birthday.

13.152 Protocols should clarify roles and funding responsibilities of different agencies. The use of pooled budgets across agencies may help remove some of the barriers arising from potential differences in eligibility criteria of different services provided under different legislation.

Young people living out of area

13.153 Where disabled young people in care have been placed out of the responsible authority's area, the care authority and education authority retain responsibility for the child. The primary care trust (PCT) where the young person is registered with a general practitioner (GP) will be responsible for day-to-day health needs, but the PCT for the originating care authority will retain responsibility for commissioning any secondary health services.[48]

13.154 As care leavers living out of area turn 18, responsibility for provision of services may change. The responsible local authority will need to ensure that

---

[48]   This is set out in Department of Health guidance, *Who Pays? Establishing the Responsible Commissioner* (2007).

continued leaving care support is provided under the provision in the CA 1989 requiring responsible authorities to continue to support care leavers. However, any adult social care provision will be the responsibility of the local authority where the child is ordinarily resident within the meaning of the National Assistance Act (NAA) 1948. Where the young person's disability was the primary reason for their placement outside the area of the responsible authority, the same authority may remain responsible for the provision of adult social care services even if the young person remains living in another area. Depending on the circumstances of the individual, there may be situations in which the young person's ordinary residence will have become the local authority in which they were placed and where they have been living and settled for some years. This will primarily be affected by the young person's 'mental capacity' to make a choice regarding the area in which they live.

13.155 Relevant agencies providing health and adult social care services should have been involved in transition planning in the years leading up to the young person's 18th birthday in order to ensure a smooth transition.

Adult social care provision

13.156 Eligibility for adult social care provision is governed by the Department of Health *Guidance on Eligibility Criteria for Adult Social Care*.[49] Local authorities may provide community care services to individual adults with needs arising from physical, sensory, learning or cognitive disabilities and impairments, or from mental health difficulties. Increasingly, support is self-directed and delivered through personal budgets, following self assessment and person-centred support planning. Young people moving into adulthood and the people close to them need high quality, accessible information about personalisation from the age of 14 so that their planning can be within the context of knowing the resources that will be available for their support.

13.157 The *Guidance on Eligibility Criteria for Adult Social Care* requires local authorities to have in place arrangements to identify individuals who may need a variety of services as they move from youth to adulthood. When undertaking assessments and re-assessments, local authorities are required to ensure that marked changes in the type, level and source of support should be managed very carefully as these are usually not in the best interests of people using services.

13.158 Adult social care services have policies regarding charging arrangements and in applying these local authorities should take account of their corporate parenting responsibilities towards care leavers. Care leavers who transfer to adult social care services should be made aware of any charging policy and the impact on any financial support or arrangements.

---

[49] Department of Health *Prioritising need in the context of Putting People First: a whole system approach to eligibility for social care – Guidance on eligibility criteria for adult social care, England 2010* (2010).

13.159   Where disabled young people meet the eligibility criteria for adult placement schemes, the possibility of their former foster carers becoming their adult placement carers should be considered, so that both the young person and foster carers transfer to an adult social care service. The responsible local authority will need to ensure that they continue to provide support in accordance with the requirements of the Children (Leaving Care) Act 2000. The responsible local authority will also need to ensure that they provide support in accordance with the Carers and Disabled Children Act 2000 and Carers (Equal Opportunities) Act 2004 combined policy guidance.[50] The guidance requires local authorities to inform carers of their right to an assessment which takes into account their outside interests (work, study, leisure) and provide services to them directly and/or support carers by providing them with a direct payment to enable them to purchase carers' services for themselves.

13.160   Where it is likely that a young person leaving care will need services into adulthood, an adult services worker should contribute to pathway planning from age 16 onwards, and the change of lead worker from one service to the other should be determined within the transition planning process taking account of the young person's wishes and assessed needs.

13.161   Where disabled and vulnerable care leavers transfer to, and become the responsibility of, Adult Care Services, local authorities' leaving care teams and PAs should ensure that young people do not lose out on any leaving care entitlements. Care leavers should not be disadvantaged financially by transferring to a different service. Pathway plans and transition plans should be used to evidence young people's financial abilities and to provide a financial framework that sets out the allowances and benefits young people are entitled to, and who will assist them to manage these allowances and benefits.

SECTION 12 – CARE LEAVERS IN THE YOUTH JUSTICE SYSTEM

13.162   The looked-after status of children within the youth justice system is complex. Some children who were not previously looked after *acquire* this status through s 21 of the CA 1989. These are:

- young people where police request a transfer of detention to the local authority pending a court hearing under the Police and Criminal Evidence Act 1984 (PACE);

---

[50]   This guidance, issued under s 7(1) of the Local Authority Social Services Act 1970, sets out the government's view of the issues for local authorities in carrying out their functions under the Carers and Disabled Children Act 2000 and the Carers (Equal Opportunities) Act 2004. The Acts affect carers who provide or intend to provide a substantial amount of care on a regular basis for another individual aged 18 or over, and people with a parental responsibility for a disabled child who provide or intend to provide a substantial amount of care on a regular basis for the child.

- young people remanded to local authority accommodation under s 23(1) of the Children and Young Persons Act 1969, with or without a 'secure requirement'; and

- young people subject to a youth rehabilitation order (YRO) with a fostering or local authority residence requirement under the Criminal Justice and Immigration Act 2008 (Sch 1).

13.163 The local authority does not have parental responsibility for these young people but must care for and plan for these children in the same way as other accommodated children, and this includes the role of the IRO.

13.164 Other young people *lose* their looked-after status. These are young people looked after under s 20 or s 21 (and not young people subject to a care order unless the order is revoked) and are:

- remanded to custody or received a custodial sentence;

- placed in a young offender institution (YOI). These will be 17 year olds, or boys aged 15 or 16 and deemed not to be vulnerable;

13.165 Even where a child is no longer looked after he or she may still have an entitlement to leaving care services. If a young person is an eligible or relevant care leaver this status remains unchanged while in custody and the local authority that looked after him or her retains responsibility for providing support during his or her time in custody and on release. Some young people will achieve this status while they are in custody on attaining the age of 16: that is, those who have spent 13 weeks looked after since the age of 14 and who were looked-after children immediately prior to entering custody.[51]

13.166 Whilst local authorities have primary responsibility for care leavers, they are entitled to expect the support of partner agencies, including Youth Offending Teams (YOTs) for care leavers under the age of 18 and Probation Services for those over 18. The responsible local authority must involve the YOT and the Probation Service, and local providers of secure accommodation provision, in drawing up its written statement of policies and guides on leaving care and aftercare services. The revised guidance regards it as essential that local authority strategic and operational leaving care policies include a comprehensive response to care leavers who are involved with criminal justice services and/or in custody.

13.167 Local authority leaving care services must ensure that they establish constructive working relationships with local criminal justice services. This will help ensure that in each individual case, the right links are made between

---

[51] This is set out in the Children (Leaving Care) Act 2000.

pathway planning and plans to divert young people from offending, to support them in custody or to supervise them in the community on release from custody.

Response to offending behaviour

13.168 If a relevant care leaver is arrested, the local authority should ensure that the young person has the support of an appropriate adult and/or solicitor with the necessary knowledge and skills whilst at the police station. There will be circumstances when a care leaver is charged with an offence and it is important that they are not disadvantaged by a refusal of bail because of their status.

13.169 The court needs to have confidence that the young person will be supported to adhere to any conditions of bail and is living in suitable accommodation. Local authorities, working together with the YOT and Probation Service, should develop suitable bail support programmes and specialist accommodation schemes to ensure that there are viable alternatives to a remand to secure accommodation. It is essential that continuing leaving care support is available to relevant or former relevant children if they are convicted and sentenced to a community sentence, or imprisonment. The guidance regards this category of care leavers as young people who are especially vulnerable and who will require carefully planned and well-focused support from their responsible local authority.

13.170 If a care leaver is convicted of an offence, the PA should provide information to the worker responsible for completing the criminal justice risk assessment (Asset for under 18s, OASys for over 18s). They should also provide relevant information for the pre-sentence report (PSR) which will be used by the court to determine the appropriate sentence disposal. Explicit consideration should be given to factors that will make the young person particularly vulnerable if sentenced to custody and should be included in the report.

Care leavers in custody

13.171 Regulation 3(2) of the Care Leavers Regulations 2010 prescribes a further category of relevant child for the purposes of s 23A(3) of the CA 1989 – any child aged 16 or 17 who:

(a)   at the time *when he attains the age of 16* is detained or in hospital; and

(b)   immediately before being detained or admitted to hospital had been looked after by a local authority for a period of at least 13 weeks, which began after he reached the age of 14, is a 'relevant child' entitled to continuing leaving care support.

13.172 For the purposes of this regulation, 'detained' means detained in a secure training centre, secure children's home, young offender institution or any other institution pursuant to an order of a court.[52] Young people who have served a custodial sentence will be subject to supervision following their release. For young people under the age of 18 or those who are completing a detention and training order (DTO), this supervision will be undertaken by the YOT. For those over 18 who have served a s 90, 91, 226 or 228 sentence for a serious crime,[53] supervision will be undertaken by the Probation Service. The YOT or the Probation Service will be concerned to ensure that these young people do not re-offend. In trying to achieve this aim, they should not only address young people's offending behaviour and its consequences, but also their development into capable resilient and responsible adults.

13.173 Where a relevant or former relevant child enters custody, the guidance requires that pathway planning must continue. The young person must be visited on a regular basis and it is good practice for the first visit to take place within 10 working days of the young person being placed. This role must not be fulfilled by a YOT worker. The establishment should facilitate the visits, and PAs should be afforded the same status as legal visitors. The responsible local authority must liaise with criminal justice services to support the young person emotionally, practically and financially whilst in custody. All young people will require the responsible local authority to contribute to the plan for their resettlement on release. It will be good practice wherever possible to carry out a review of the pathway plan at least a month before release in order to give sufficient time for pre-release planning. For a relevant child, it should be exceptional for a review not to take place. Plans should be in place so that the young person is able to move into suitable accommodation, with the right kind of support, on release from custody. In *R (TG) v Lambeth LBC (ex parte Shelter)*,[54] the Court of Appeal considered the guidance which required clear links between youth justice and child protection services. The Court of Appeal also considered s 5(aa) of the Crime and Disorder Act 1998 which provided that the youth offending service (YOS) must include a nominated person with experience of social work in relation to children. In this case the YOS social worker involved in the case had the relevant experience, but had not been

---

[52] Once s 23ZA of the CA 1989 is implemented fully, the Children Act 1989 (Visits to Former Looked After Children in Detention) (England) Regulations will provide that those looked-after children who do not become 'relevant children' on entering custody and therefore will not be entitled to leaving care support (since they are children aged 16 or 17 who have been looked after for less than 13 weeks since the age of 14 or because they will leave custody before their 16th birthday), will be entitled to visits from the local authority that formerly looked after them.

[53] Section 90/91 of the Powers of the Criminal Courts (Sentencing) Act 2000 allows the Crown Court to impose longer sentences where a young person is convicted for a serious crime. If a young person is convicted of murder they will receive a mandatory life sentence under s 90 with a specified minimum term. If they are convicted of an offence for which an adult could receive at least 14 years in custody, they may be sentenced under s 91 and the length of the sentence can be anywhere up to the adult maximum for the same offence. Section 226 of the Criminal Justice Act 2003 allows young people to be detained for an indeterminate period, but at least 2 years, in order to protect the public. Section 228 of the same Act allows an extended sentence to be passed for certain violent and sexual crimes, and the minimum period of detention is 4 years.

[54] [2011] EWCA Civ 526, [2011] 2 FLR 1007.

'nominated' by any formal document. It was held that it was inaccurate to describe the guidance (which is issued under s 7 of the Local Authority Social Services Act 1970) as guidance that ought 'probably' to be followed, or as 'good practice'; it was held that in the absence of a considered decision that there was good reason to deviate from such guidance, it *must* be followed (and the case of *R v Islington LBC ex parte Rixon*[55] applied). The absence of coordination between the housing and children's services in this case was held to have been positively unlawful.

13.174   Where a care leaver is remanded or sentenced to custody, the following steps are likely to be necessary to ensure that the young person can access suitable accommodation upon their release:

- Immediate liaison with the young person's accommodation provider to inform them and discuss options.

- Liaison with the local authority's housing advice/homelessness service to obtain expert advice on the young person's options.

- If the young person is remanded or serving a short sentence, consideration should be given to retaining the young person's accommodation placement for their return on release.

- If this is not possible or appropriate, steps should be taken promptly to give up the accommodation according to the requirements in the tenancy or license agreement and collect and store the young person's possessions. This will prevent a build up of rent arrears and/or assumed abandonment by the landlord, both of which may lead to the young person's eviction in their absence, resulting in more limited housing options on their release and an amassing of debt.

- Where the young person's previous accommodation has been given up or lost, alternative accommodation should be identified and be available to the young person on release. It will only be possible to plan for care leavers' wider needs, including planning the support they'll need to divert them from further offending, if a stable base has been secured for them.

13.175   As soon as possible, and (ideally) no later than 14 days before release, a care leaver must know:

- who is collecting them;

- where they will be living;

- the reporting arrangements;

---

[55]   [1997] ELR 66.

- sources of support – including out of hours;

- arrangements for education or employment;

- arrangements for meeting continuing health needs;

- arrangements for financial support;

- when they can expect to see their PA; and

- the roles and responsibilities of the respective leaving care and youth offending staff.

It is essential that there is clarity about who is responsible for each element of the child's plan and the arrangements for communication and enforcement. The local authority should record these arrangements as part of the pathway plan and make copies available to the young person, the supervising YOT officer, the establishment and other agencies involved with supporting the young person after release, including, wherever appropriate, their family.

The role of the IRO

13.176 The IRO should be advised of any incidents where a looked-after child is arrested or charged with an offence. If the IRO considers that the child's care plan needs to be amended, he or she should request a review. This is particularly likely to be the case if the child is charged with a serious offence or his or her offending is persistent and a custodial sentence is a possibility.

13.177 The IRO should seek evidence of the following:

- Is the child's social worker working in partnership with the YOT, sharing information and actively contributing to the YOT assessment?

- Has the child been provided with expert legal representation?

- Is the social worker accompanying the child to court hearings?

- Has the social worker provided information that will assist the court in reaching an appropriate decision, including any mitigating factors, and the local authority's plans for the child?

- Is the child's placement able to support the child, including compliance with any bail conditions?

13.178 Going into custody is a significant change in the child's circumstances and a review should be held. The IRO is entitled to co-operation from the establishment, who should facilitate the review by providing a suitable room, enabling the IRO to have a private discussion with the child and enabling the attendance of key participants.

13.179   Although the child will be the subject of remand or sentence planning meetings, and there is likely to be some overlap in attendance, it is important that the review meeting is a separate event and chaired by the IRO. It will be appropriate to invite the YOT case manager and a link worker from the establishment (such as the youth offending institution social worker or the child's case supervisor), subject to the child's agreement, but the child's privacy needs to be respected. He or she may feel particularly vulnerable because of the custodial setting and a sensitive approach needs to be taken to the disclosure of personal information. This may also be the case regarding the involvement of parents.

13.180   The review has the same purpose as any review following a change in circumstances but there will be additional considerations as to how the child's needs will be met during his or her time in custody. The child's social worker should have assessed these and provided a report to the review. Specific questions to consider are:

- Is the child safe?

- Is there a risk of self harm?

- What is the child's emotional state?

- Does the child need money, clothes, books or other practical support?

- Are education staff aware of and able to meet the child's educational needs, including any special needs or abilities?

- Are the health unit and wing staff aware of, and able to meet, the child's health needs?

- Are staff aware of, and able to meet, the child's religious and cultural needs?

- Is the child worried about anything? If so, what?

- What impact has the remand/sentence had on family relationships?

- Does there need to be help with contact arrangements?

- What action is needed to provide for the child's accommodation on release?

- Are changes needed to the child's care plan/pathway plan?

13.181 Although the local authority is not responsible for the placement and cannot terminate it, there may be situations where the IRO is not satisfied that everything is being done to safeguard the child or promote his or her welfare. There are steps that the local authority can take to initiate a transfer request, and the IRO can refer to CAFCASS in the usual way if these are inadequate.

13.182 It is good practice to hold a review within the last month of the sentence to ensure that an effective plan is made for the child's release. This must be aligned with the plans being made for the child by his or her YOT case manager, who will continue to supervise him or her on release, and it should be clear who is responsible for each aspect.

Community support

13.183 The leaving care service of the responsible authority must remain a presence in the young person's life during the period of supervision by the YOT or Probation Service. Their role is different and more extensive than that of the supervising YOT or probation officer, whose involvement will be determined by the length of any order and the care leaver's offending behaviour rather than their wider needs.

13.184 Young people are vulnerable in the early days after release and will need considerable help, both emotionally and practically, to:

- readjust to living in open conditions;

- meet the requirements for reporting and surveillance;

- sort out finances;

- settle into accommodation;

- negotiate work or college;

- re-establish relationships with family and friends; and

- avoid situations where offending may occur.

13.185 The guidance recommends that it is good practice to have some joint appointments with the care leavers, supervising YOT or probation officer and the allocated PA, so that information is shared and the young person receives an integrated service. The PA and supervising YOT or probation officer should keep each other informed of significant events, including any changes in service delivery or plans.

13.186 Whilst the care leaver continues to be supervised by criminal justice services, it will be good practice to include the supervising YOT/probation officer in reviews of the pathway plan. It will be important to involve the young person in deciding who should participate in their review. However, should they decide to exclude their supervising YOT or probation officer, their PA would need to understand and agree their reasons for this, especially where the young person is a relevant child and has not yet reached legal adulthood.

SECTION 13 – UNACCOMPANIED ASYLUM SEEKING CHILDREN (UASC)

13.187 Unaccompanied asylum seeking children (UASC) are children or young people under the age of 18 who have made a claim for asylum and entered the UK without a parent, adult relative or adult household member. The duties of local authorities towards such children are considered at Chapter 7.

13.188 UASC making the transition from care to adulthood have both a leaving care status and an immigration status in addition to their placement and accommodation, education, health, financial, religious and cultural needs. Planning transition to adulthood for UASC is a particularly complex process that needs to address young people's care needs in the context of wider asylum and immigration legislation and how these needs change over time.

13.189 Pathway planning to support a UASC's transition to adulthood should cover all areas that would be addressed within all young people's plans as well as any additional needs arising from their specific immigration issues. Planning may initially have to be based around short-term achievable goals whilst entitlement to remain in the UK is being determined.

13.190 Pathway planning for the majority of UASC who do not have permanent immigration status should initially take a dual or triple planning perspective, which, over time should be refined as the young person's immigration status is resolved. Planning may be based on:

- a transitional plan during the period of uncertainty when the young person is in the UK without permanent immigration status;

- longer-term perspective plan in the UK should the young person be granted long-term permission to stay (for example through the grant of refugee status); or

- a return to their country of origin at any appropriate point or at the end of the immigration consideration process, should that be necessary because the young person decides to leave the UK or is required to do so.

13.191 Claiming asylum can be a complex process. The guidance recommends that social workers or PAs should work with the young person's legal representative and the dedicated case owner at the UK Border Agency to ensure that the young person understands the process of claiming asylum, the possible outcomes and to provide them with necessary support.

13.192 There are various possible outcomes of an asylum claim:

- The young person is granted refugee status (ie granted asylum). Leave to remain is granted for 5 years.

- The young person is refused asylum but granted humanitarian protection (HP). Leave to remain is granted for 5 years. HP is most commonly granted when the person is at some risk of 'ill-treatment' in the particular country they left but does not meet the criteria of the Refugee Convention. This is regarded as a rare category for UASC within the guidance.

- The young person is refused asylum but granted discretionary leave (DL). Discretionary leave to remain is normally granted for 3 years or until the young person reaches the age of 17½, whichever comes first. DL is granted if at the time of the decision adequate care and reception arrangements are not in place in the country of origin (ie a return cannot be effected safely).

- The young person is refused asylum with no grant of leave to remain in the UK. In this case the UASC must return to his or her country of origin.

13.193 Those UASC found to require refugee status or, more rarely humanitarian protection, are usually granted leave to remain in the UK for 5 years. Although it is not guaranteed that further leave to remain will be granted at the end of the 5-year period, the guidance suggests that it is certainly a strong likelihood and care and pathway planning should primarily focus on longer-term residence in the UK, in the same way as for any other care leaver.

13.194 Young people who are granted discretionary leave will have the opportunity to apply for an extension to this leave after 3 years or on reaching the age of 17½.

13.195 Planning for a return home for a UASC may be difficult, but care and pathway plans should include contingencies for durable and best interest plans for UASC and young people who are likely to have to return to their country of origin. Pathway plans should always consider the implications for the young person if their application to extend their leave to remain, or their appeal against refusal of that application, is dismissed. In such circumstances the person will become unlawfully present in the UK and be expected to make plans for return to the country of origin. The UK Border Agency is under a statutory duty to have regard to the need to safeguard and promote the welfare of children and relevant personal data may be shared with the Agency in order to help it discharge its duty. The management of return arrangements will require a collaborative approach with the Agency in order to ensure they take place as sensitively and humanely as possible.

Access to public funds, welfare benefits and other public funds

13.196   The guidance sets out the ways in which access to financial support should be considered for UASC who are leaving care. Financial support for looked-after UASC should reflect their needs as looked-after young people (eligible care leavers) and their immigration needs. Financial policies should highlight their entitlements and how their immigration status may impact on current and future entitlements.

13.197   Pathway plans should address funding arrangements for education and training and how a young person's immigration status may limit education, training and employment opportunities.

13.198   Pathway plans should always consider the implications for the young people if their application to extend their leave to remain is refused, or their appeal against refusal of that application is dismissed. In such circumstances the person may become ineligible for further support and assistance because of the effect of Sch 3 to the Nationality, Immigration and Asylum Act 2002.

SECTION 14 – PREPARATION FOR LEAVING CARE

What are the three aspects to preparation for leaving care?

13.199   There are three broad aspects to preparation for leaving care.

Enabling young people to build and maintain relationships with others (both general and sexual relationships)

13.200   The capacity to form satisfying relationships and achieve interdependence with others is crucial to the future well-being of young people. This skill will equip them better for the transition to adulthood and the special difficulties associated with leaving care. It is essential that the experience of being cared for provides both the opportunity for such a personal development and the attention that is required when special help is needed. The process of preparation should ensure that when young people do leave care, they have a supportive network of friends, many of whom will be from outside the care system, and that they are well equipped to enter into relationships with others.

13.201   Preparation work should be planned to cover the following points:

- Changes in care placement should be kept to the minimum consistent with the young person's welfare. This will provide continuity of care and of relationships, thereby showing young people how to relate to others.

- Social workers, residential staff and foster carers, as well as other young people who are being cared for, should be able to help a young person to relate to other people.

- A young person's friends should not all come from the care system since, if they do, he or she may be very lonely on leaving care.

- Young people who are being cared for should be encouraged to make friends with young people outside the care system (for example, through school, college, or local youth clubs and leisure activities). Disabled young people may need support and assistance to access mainstream leisure activities in order to build a wider friendship network.

- Young people who are being cared for should also be encouraged to develop friendships with suitable adults outside the care system who can provide role models. Volunteer adult befrienders who have been carefully vetted through a volunteer befriending scheme and who can stay in touch with young people after they have left care can play a very important role here. Befrienders should be 'matched' with the young person (for example, they should preferably be from the same cultural, linguistic, racial and religious background). Disabled young people may be matched with a befriender or mentor who shares their experience of impairment. It is desirable that young people themselves decide who is to act as their befriender. The befriender should be prepared to give time, to make contribution to reviews and on other occasions, if the young person so wishes. Similar considerations apply to mentors and the use of mentoring schemes.

- The foster carers of a fostered young person should be encouraged to continue to take an interest in him or her even when the fostering placement has ended.

- A young person's parents (and his or her relatives generally) should be encouraged to stay in touch with him or her unless this would not be in his or her best interests.

- Young people from ethnic minorities need to have contact with adults and young people from their own cultural backgrounds and may find it helpful to be put in touch with relevant youth groups or other voluntary organisations.

- Foster carers, parents and other important people in a disabled young person's life may need assistance or support in order to maintain their relationship, or the young person may need such assistance or support (for example, if public transport is not accessible to a young person he or she will need assistance in order to visit others).

13.202   The experience of being cared for should include the sexual education of the young person. This may be provided by the young person's school, but if it is not, the local authority or other caring agency responsible for the young person should provide sexual education for him or her. Sexual education will need to cover practical issues such as contraception. However, it must also cover the emotional aspects of sexuality, such as:

- the part that sexuality plays in the young person's sense of identity;

- the emotional implications of entering into a sexual relationship with another person;

- the need to treat sexual partners with consideration and not as objects to be used; and

- the emotional and practical implications of becoming a parent also need to be explained.

13.203   Those responsible for the sexual education of young people will need to bear in mind the particular needs of different young people (for example, the fact that disabled young people have sexual needs should be acknowledged). Young people who have been abused, or have been in touch with abused young people, may need special counselling if they are not to regard sexual feelings as a matter for shame or to regard sexual relationships as impersonal and exploitative. The needs and concerns of young lesbians and gay men must also be recognised and approached sympathetically.

13.204   A local authority, in preparing a young person for leaving care, should also take account, where appropriate, of the need to enable young people to relate better to their own family. Indeed, the local authority has a duty to make arrangements to enable a young person whom it is looking after to live with parents, relatives or friends 'unless that would not be reasonably practicable or consistent with his welfare'.[56] Even if it is proved to be impracticable or undesirable to make such arrangements, any improvement in relationships between a young person and his or her family that can be achieved is usually to be welcomed and will contribute to the young person's capacity to cope in adult life. Similarly, general contact with family and friends should be promoted where consistent with a young person's welfare.[57]

Enabling young people to develop their self-esteem

13.205   Many young people who are being, or have been, cared for, have described feelings of shame about being cared for. These are frequently

---

[56]   CA 1989, s 23(6).

[57]   CA 1989, Sch 2, para 15. Similar responsibilities are reflected in the duties of voluntary organisations and persons carrying on children's homes under the Arrangement for Placement of Children (General) Regulations 1991, SI 1991/890, reg 6 (see the Department of Health *Children Act 1989: Regulations and Guidance* (HMSO, 1991), vol 3, ch 3).

compounded by misunderstandings on the part of others (for example, that most young people being cared for have committed criminal offences, or that there is something wrong with them, or that their parents are inadequate and unable to cope).

13.206 It is therefore all the more necessary to encourage young people, from the day they begin to be cared for to:

- value themselves;

- regard their experience of being cared for without embarrassment; and

- be able to explain to other people why they are being cared for and how they feel about it.

13.207 It is particularly helpful if young people are told as much as possible about their family background and about all aspects of their cultural and individual identity (for example, race, language, culture, sex, gender, religion and any physical or mental disability). It is also helpful for young people to understand how they came to be cared for. Young people's individual identity and cultural background should be presented in a positive light. The use of life story books may be helpful in achieving this. Contact with positive role models can also be helpful.

13.208 Some young people may need considerable counselling before they do come to accept themselves. Young people who have been rejected by their parents may need a lot of help before they can accept, emotionally, that this is no reflection on their own worth. Young people with disabilities may also require counselling to enable them to accept themselves and to develop a sense of self-esteem. Young lesbians and gay men may require help to enable them to accept their sexuality and to develop their own self-esteem. Young people from minority ethnic groups may need help – preferably from someone with the same background – to help them to understand their racial, cultural, linguistic and religious background and to take a pride in themselves.

13.209 If necessary, the local authority or other caring agency may also act as an advocate for all young people leaving care in dealing with departments, organisations and people who may display prejudice.

Teaching practical and financial skills and knowledge

13.210 Some young people who are being cared for, particularly those in children's homes, do not have any opportunity of learning practical and financial skills. Young people who are being cared for should – like any other young people – start to learn these skills at a basic level when entering their teens and should be well advanced in them by the time they leave care. Disabled young people may have faced particular barriers to acquiring the skills and experiences listed above. Whatever the reason for them these barriers will need to be addressed, with the aim of increasing the young person's ability to make choices, take risks and assume responsibility. It will be important to ensure that particular needs relating to impairment are met, for example, sign language interpreters for British Sign Language users, communication aids and facilitation, information formats suitable for visually impaired people, the provision of personal assistants and so on.

13.211

What are the practical and financial skills and knowledge that should be taught to young people leaving care?

- How to shop for, prepare and cook food

- Eating a balanced diet

- Laundry, sewing and mending and other housekeeping skills

- How to carry out basic households jobs such as mending fuses (which will involve basic electrical and other knowledge)

- Safety in the home and first aid

- The cost of living

- Household budgeting, including the matching of expenditure to income, the regular payment of bills and avoidance of the excessive use of credit

- Health education, including personal hygiene

- Sexual education, including contraception and preparation for parenthood

- Applying for, and being interviewed for, a job

- The rights and responsibilities of being an employee

- The rights and responsibilities of being an employer (disabled young people may use direct payments to employ their own personal assistants)

- Applying for a course of education or training

- Applying for housing and locating and maintaining it

- Registering with a doctor and dentist

- Knowledge of emergency services (fire, police, ambulance)

- Contacting the social services department and other caring agencies

- Contacting organisations and groups set up to help young people who are, or have been, in care

- The role of agencies such as the Citizen's Advice Bureau, local councillors and MPs

- The provision of positive role models and the requirements of good citizenship

➡

- How to write letters of complaint and to obtain advice

Chapter 14

ANALYSIS

SECTION 1 – THE CHRONOLOGY

Chronology of key events

14.1 The aim for lawyers in analysing the local authority's decision-making is to achieve a comprehensive understanding of the *process* by which the local authority has arrived at its plan. An understanding of this process can then inform the lawyer's case strategy and planning. There are three key areas to consider in any analysis of the local authority's decision-making process:

- the social worker's knowledge and expertise;

- the social work assessments; and

- the case planning.

14.2 For example, it may become clear that a highly experienced social worker has managed the case throughout, that the local authority has complied fully with all statutory requirements in respect of planning and review, and that the final care plan for the child has been fully considered by a variety of professionals from a range of disciplines. In these circumstances, challenging the local authority's planning on the basis of deficient planning will probably be fruitless.

14.3 On the other hand, it may become obvious that the child's case remained unallocated for several months, that the local authority consistently failed to complete a core assessment of the child's needs, and that parents were never adequately informed about their progress during an assessment. In these circumstances, it may be possible to argue that the care plan for the child is inchoate, inadequate or disproportionately draconian because it is based on deficient assessment and planning by the local authority.

14.4 Lawyers may find it helpful to start analysing the decision-making in the case by preparing a detailed chronology – as detailed a chronology as possible within the time available. Drafting the chronology on a computer is the most time efficient way as it will enable later amendments, but there is no reason why a handwritten chronology (leaving plenty of gaps) can't work. This chronology is only for case planning purposes – no one else need ever see it – so make it as detailed as possible to develop an understanding about how the decision-making (or lack of decision-making) in the case progressed.

Key events

14.5 There should already be a social work chronology within the case papers containing a succinct summary of the significant dates and events in the child's life in chronological order. Although this may provide a useful guide as to key events and will certainly help later in the analysis of the local authority's actions, it won't necessarily be the best place to start for lawyers. Social workers invariably focus on *actions* rather than *omissions* in their own chronologies, nor do they necessarily consider it relevant to include information about key decision-making meetings such as reviews, panels or child protection conferences. Social workers' chronologies may also include subjective and unsubstantiated opinions or interpretations of behaviour by parents, children and/or other professionals, or they may omit positives and focus only on the negatives.

14.6 Start the drafting with a *legal* and *factual* chronology. Include details of the dates of issue of relevant applications, the dates and content of all court orders and some basic factual information about the key people involved in the case (for example, dates of birth, marriage, death, entry to the UK). This information will assist in the analysis of the local authority's response (or lack of response) to significant life events for a child and/or family. It will also become apparent if a local authority has failed to comply properly with repeated directions to file particular pieces of evidence (for example, contact notes).

14.7

Key events to include in the lawyer's chronology

- Dates of birth

- Miscarriage or still-birth

- Marriage

- Separation

- Divorce

- Death

- Significant changes of address

- Moves to new schools or nurseries

- Changes of child's placement

- Entry to or departure from the UK

- Periods of imprisonment

- Periods of time in hospital or receiving medical treatment (whether as in-patient or out-patient)

- Relevant criminal convictions

- Relevant legal applications

- Relevant court orders or hearings

SECTION 2 – KEY MEETINGS

14.8 Then expand the chronology by including the dates and details of all key meetings at which social work decisions were made (or could have been made). An analysis of the chronology at this stage can reveal a useful picture of the local authority's work with the child and family so far. For example it may demonstrate:

- that the local authority failed to hold statutory reviews as regularly as required;

- that fundamental changes of plan (eg from rehabilitation to permanency) were never considered thoroughly at any formal local authority meeting;

- that the local authority failed to consider the extended family in seeking an alternative permanent placement for a child;

- that the local authority failed to consider the wishes and feelings of the child in an appropriate or adequate manner appropriate to their level of understanding and maturity;

- that the local authority failed to complete a core assessment;

- that the local authority failed to implement elements or recommendations of past plans; and

- that the local authority failed to work in partnership with families.

14.9

Key decision-making meetings

- Strategy meetings

- Meetings with families to formulate working agreements

- Family Group Conferences (or other family group meetings)

- Court hearings

- Advocates' meetings

- Child protection conferences (pre-birth, initial, review)

- Professionals' meetings

- Core group meetings

- Social worker's supervision sessions

- Assessment pre-planning meetings (with parents and/or with professionals)

- Assessment review meetings (with parents and/or with professionals)

- Meetings to consider changes in contact arrangements (with parents and/or with professionals)

- Post-assessment planning meetings

- Statutory reviews

- Child in need (CIN) meetings

- Permanency planning meetings

- Fostering panel

- Adoption panel

- Gatekeeping meetings dealing with the allocation of resources (eg for the approval of residential assessments)

- Rapid response meeting[1]

---

[1] Meeting held by a group of key professionals who come together for the purpose of enquiring into and evaluating each unexpected death of a child – Chapter 7 of *Working Together to Safeguard Children – A Guide to Inter-agency Working to Safeguard and Promote the Welfare of Children* (TSO, 4th edn, 2010).

SECTION 3 – KEY PERSONNEL

14.10   Then identify the dates of involvement of key professionals in the case, such as social workers, psychologists, family finding social workers, health visitors. Add the dates of the commencement and end of involvement of such professionals into the chronology.

14.11   For example, it may become apparent that there was a period of several months without any social worker being allocated to the case – this could assist a case strategy aimed at demonstrating that the family coped very well without any formal social work involvement.

14.12   It is also important to include dates of instruction of experts and dates of assessment interviews or appointments offered and attended – for example, it may become apparent that families were kept waiting for several months for an assessment to begin and that this had a detrimental effect on the family's functioning.

14.13   It is helpful to list any direct meetings with the child. How often was the child seen, who else was present and is there a clarity about the child being given sufficient time and opportunity to express their wishes and feelings? This is particularly important when representing older children, and when consideration is to be given for the child's lawyer to be separate from the child's guardian.

14.14   Explore whether the children's guardian has been involved in any decision-making meetings of the local authority, but check whether the guardian maintained their independence and did not contribute to the decision-making processes.

14.15

> **Key personnel**
>
> - Allocated social worker
>
> - Family finding social worker
>
> - Health visitor
>
> - Community psychiatric nurse (CPN)
>
> - Family support worker
>
> - Drugs or alcohol support worker
>
> - Voluntary organisation (such as Home Start or Domestic Violence Forum) support worker
>
> - Psychiatrist
>
> - Psychologist
>
> - Independent reviewing officers (IRO)
>
> - CAFCASS officer/Child's guardian

SECTION 4 – ANALYSIS OF THE SOCIAL WORKERS

What is the social worker's level of qualification and experience?

14.16 Most local authorities aim to ensure that complex child protection cases are only allocated to qualified and experienced social workers; namely, social workers who possess the old qualification of CQSW (Certificate of Qualification in Social Work) or the newer qualification of DipSW (Diploma of Qualification in Social Work). Such social workers should also routinely be encouraged to obtain post-qualifying qualifications (namely, PQ1 or 2 in Childcare). Similarly, social workers working in adoption and fostering teams or within specialist assessment units will often have a greater level of experience than social workers within children's teams. Statutory guidance requires adoption work to be carried out or be supervised by a qualified social workers with 3 years post-qualification experience in childcare social work, including direct experience of adoption. A student or unqualified social worker can do this work, but they must be supervised by a social worker with the above experience (who must sign written reports).

14.17 Information about the nature of a social worker's qualifications can assist lawyers in planning the case strategy whatever the level of the social worker's skill or experience: the most experienced workers can make errors or cut corners, conversely the most inexperienced workers are often more likely to seek out supervision or consultation with experienced staff to compensate for their own lack of knowledge or experience. This information can be obtained by:

- Confirming the nature of the social worker's qualifications (particularly if not stated in the social worker's statement or report) – it is not unusual for staff at residential units to be unqualified or to have non-social work qualifications (such as NNEB certificates (nursery nursing) or counselling diplomas). While, of course, such staff have very useful contributions to make during assessments, the statutory guidance makes it quite clear that the assessments of children in need should be led by suitably qualified and experienced staff.

- Checking the level of skills and experience of the assessing social workers when analysing the conduct and content of kinship assessments or assessments of prospective foster carers or adoptive carers.

What was the allocated social worker's involvement?

14.18 It is not unusual for local authority attention to a case to reach its highest point in the period leading up to an application for care proceedings and pending children being made subject of interim care orders. For the busy and overworked social worker the immediate pressure is often reduced once children are placed safely in foster care or residential units, and his or her attention is then inevitably redirected towards other more pressing cases.

14.19 It is therefore often useful to analyse the social worker's specific involvement in a case from the outset until the present. This can be done by:

- identifying the date of allocation to a social worker, and in a case where there has been more than one social worker, analysing the length of period of involvement of each worker;

- identifying any gaps between the involvement of different social workers, particularly if the local authority is seeking to argue that a high level of monitoring or statutory involvement is necessary in order to safeguard and promote the children's welfare; and

- exploring whether the nature of the relationship between the social worker and the parents and/or child has had an impact on the decision-making processes and if so in what way.

What was the extent of the social worker's direct involvement with the family?

14.20 It is not unusual for social workers to delegate visits to a child or family to other professionals (such as social work assistants or health visitors), particularly while assessments are under way. While this may not necessarily constitute poor practice, lawyers may wish to explore how the social worker was able to arrive at particular recommendations, observations or conclusions within a statement or care plan given a limited level of direct personal involvement. This can be done by:

- identifying the extent of an allocated social worker's direct contact with a child or family – this can often provide an accurate indication of the social worker's overall approach to working in partnership in respect of the specific case;

- identifying the number of statutory visits made by the social worker to looked-after children – this group also includes children subject to interim care orders or care orders who are placed at home with parents.[2] For such children, the dates of such visits (including an indication about whether the children were seen alone) should be noted within the statutory review minutes (if not specified within social work statements);

- identifying the dates, times and location of the social worker's visits or telephone calls to the family; and

- cross-referencing the social worker's account of such contact against the contemporaneous records in the case file (handwritten as well as typed).

What was the extent of the social worker's communication with other professionals?

14.21 Similarly, it is always important to explore the extent to which the allocated social worker communicated with other professionals involved with the family, particularly during any period of assessment. The extent of such contact with other professionals can often provide an indication of the social worker's overall approach to working in partnership in respect of the specific case. This can be done by:

- confirming the dates and content of the social worker's contact or meetings with other professionals;

- cross-referencing the social worker's account of such contact with reports, statements or records of other professionals; and

- cross-referencing the social worker's account of such contact against the contemporaneous records in the case file.

---

[2]   Subject to the Care Planning, Placement and Case Review (England) Regulations 2010, SI 2010/959.

14.22

Questions to consider in analysis of the decision-making process of the social worker

- Were there any periods of time when there was no permanent social worker allocated to the case?

- Has the allocated social worker visited the family at home or interviewed the parents and/or child regularly?

- Is there evidence that the social workers failed to make regular contact with the family?

- Is the allocated social worker sufficiently qualified and experienced?

- Has the allocated social worker discussed the case regularly with senior colleagues and/or his or her manager?

- Has the allocated social worker's direct manager signed the care plan?

SECTION 5 – ANALYSIS OF THE SOCIAL WORK ASSESSMENTS

14.23 One of the most common errors made by social workers completing assessments is to focus only on a *description* of the information completed, and to stop short of carrying out an *analysis* of the information and process of the assessment. A comprehensive guide to good practice in social work assessments is contained within Chapter 5.

14.24 A thorough analysis of social work assessments is often a fundamental and critical issue for lawyers seeking to challenge or protect the local authority's case. The conclusions of core assessments or kinship assessments may appear incontrovertible in written form, and a detailed deconstruction of such evidence is needed in order to challenge or protect the local authority's case.

14.25 Detailed analysis of social work assessments requires careful consideration of the following key issues.

Who conducted the assessment?

14.26 As stated in Chapter 5, the statutory guidance relating to the *Framework for Assessment*[3] clearly recommends that initial and core

---

[3]   The Department of Health *Framework for the Assessment of Children in Need and Their Families* (TSO, 2000).

assessments of children in need are led by suitably qualified and experienced social work staff. Information about the identity of assessors can be obtained by:

- confirming the nature of the assessor's qualifications (particularly if not stated in the assessment report);

- checking the length and scope of experience of the assessors in carrying out similar work in other cases;

- confirming that assessors have received suitable training in their particular area of expertise;

- confirming (where relevant) that assessors have:

  - suitable skills or experience in working with people from an appropriate range of cultural, linguistic, social and/or religious groups;
  - an appropriate knowledge of working with people with learning difficulties;
  - an appropriate knowledge of working with people with physical or sensory disabilities; and
  - suitable skills or experience in administering recommended exercises, tests or scales during the assessment (see Chapter 5);

- confirming that assessors sought and received regular supervision and consultation from senior colleagues.

What was the purpose of the assessment?

14.27 Ensuring that assessors have a clear understanding of the reasons for and purpose of an assessment is absolutely fundamental to good practice in social work assessment of any sort: if the purpose is unclear, ill-founded or misguided, then the recommendations and outcomes that flow from the assessment are inevitably likely to be deficient.

14.28 Clues to the likely adequacy of a social work assessment can often be gleaned from a careful reading of the details of the instructions to the assessor (whether internal or external to the local authority) and in the preamble at the start of the assessment report. For example, it is not uncommon to hear or read a social worker's reference to a core assessment of 'the mother' or 'the father', rather than to an assessment of the child. The use of such terminology should immediately alert lawyers to the likelihood that the social worker has failed to understand the holistic and tridimensional nature of good assessments (as described in Chapter 5); namely, that the purpose of a core assessment is to identify planning for *the child* taking account of the three domains of:

- the child's individual and developmental needs;

- the parenting capacity of the child's carers; and

- the family and environmental factors affecting the child.

14.29   Information about the purpose of an assessment can be obtained by:

- checking that the assessor has used appropriate terminology throughout the assessment report;

- identifying that the stated purpose of the assessment matches the stated purpose within any letter of instruction (or other local authority document) or court order;

- confirming that the reasons for the assessment were properly and adequately explained to the family (or people being assessed);

- cross-referencing written and/or oral explanations about the stated purpose of the assessment against:

    - contemporaneous case records (in the social work files or files belonging to the assessor's agency as appropriate);
    - planning meeting minutes;
    - statutory review minutes;
    - child protection conference minutes;
    - minutes of core group meetings;
    - minutes of fostering panel;
    - minutes of adoption panel;
    - social workers' reports to such meetings; and
    - the guardian's report.

What was the timing and context of the assessment?

14.30   It is important for lawyers to consider the context of any assessment undertaken with a child and/or family – it may be that the assessment would have been more likely to succeed if it had occurred at a different time, or it may be that parents were unable to sustain their motivation to succeed if there was a delay of several months before the assessment commenced. Information can be obtained by:

- identifying and evaluating whether the assessment started at an appropriate time (for example, not immediately after a significant life event such as birth or death); and

- evaluating the effect of any delay in commencing an assessment upon the family or the people being assessed.

What was the extent of the planning for the assessment?

14.31 It is not uncommon for social workers to pay insufficient attention to the planning of an assessment with parents before the assessment begins. Analysis of the extent of the professional preparation for an assessment can often act as a useful indicator of the assessor's general approach to working in partnership (or of the local authority's overall approach to the case). Information can be obtained by identifying:

- what specific discussions took place before the assessment commenced between family members (or people being assessed) and the assessor – if the assessment was not completed by the allocated social worker, then the social worker's role in such discussions should also be identified;

- what specific discussions about the timing, purpose and process of the assessment took place between the professionals before the assessment commenced;

- the form in which details about the timing, purpose and process of the assessment were given to the family (or people being assessed);

- the details about the likely consequences of non-compliance with the assessment that were given to the family (or people being assessed) before the assessment commenced;

- whether the family (or people being assessed) were given sufficient time to consider the implications of the assessment timing, process and consequences of non-compliance before actually commencing the assessment;

- whether the family (or people being assessed) were offered sufficient help and support by the local authority (or assessor) with practical arrangements to ensure that they could participate in the assessment (eg childcare, transport, fitting appointments around other commitments);

- what the family (or people being assessed) were told before the assessment commenced about the way in which information would be recorded during the assessment; and

- what the family (or people being assessed) were told before the assessment commenced about the way in which the progress of the assessment would be reviewed during and after the assessment.

What was the format and process of the assessment?

14.32 It is essential that lawyers carry out a detailed analysis of the specific process and format of assessment because of the critical link between assessment and planning. The absence of obvious reference to assessment information within social work plans should immediately alert lawyers to possible deficits in the local authority's planning process. Similarly, if assertions are made by the local authority about the family's poor co-operation or participation during the assessment process, a detailed analysis about the local authority's specific expectations may assist in challenging or supporting such arguments. Information about the format and process of the assessment can be obtained by:

- identifying that the location of the assessment was suitable and appropriate (eg confirming that the family (or people being assessed) were offered refreshments or suitable childcare);

- identifying that the family (or people being assessed) were offered the services of an interpreter at all appointments if necessary;

- identifying the dates and times of all appointments offered to the family (or people being assessed) before, during and after the assessment;

- identifying the length of each assessment appointment;

- identifying what contemporaneous records were made by the assessor(s) during the assessment;

- identifying what reviews were carried out by the assessor(s) during and after the assessment;

- identifying whether any reviews took place during the assessment to which the family (or people being assessed) were not invited to attend;

- identifying how long the family (or people being assessed) were given between assessment sessions to consider the issues being discussed and to develop and change;

- identifying how the assessor(s) evaluated the strengths and weaknesses of the family (or the people being assessed) during the assessment process;

- identifying (and examining if necessary) the specific tools, questionnaires and scales used by the assessor(s) during the assessment;

- confirming that any written materials used during the assessment were appropriate in light of the specific needs of the family (or people being assessed) (eg suitable for people with learning difficulties, physical or sensory impairment, or suitable for people whose first or chosen language is not English);

- confirming whether the family (or people being assessed) were given the opportunity to comment on and contribute to the contemporaneous records made by the assessor(s) during the assessment;

- identifying whether the assessment report does more than simply *describe* the family (or people being assessed) and goes on to *analyse* the information provided – see Chapter 5 for detailed discussion about analysis in assessments; and

- identifying that the assessment report has included discussion about the strengths as well as weaknesses of the family (or people being assessed).

What was the outcome of the assessment?

14.33 Analysis of the ending of an assessment can be just as revealing as analysis about the preparation and process of an assessment, particularly in cases where assessments have ended prematurely or been terminated. Analysis of the *chronology* of such endings is particularly useful. Information about the outcome of an assessment can be obtained by:

- clarifying the chronology of decision-making in cases where assessments ended prematurely or were terminated, and clarifying the nature of any discussions or reviews about progress before the assessment ended;

- checking whether there were any gaps between identifying the provision of services in any assessments past and present and actual provision;

- checking whether the family (or people being assessed) were given a copy of the assessment report to consider at the end of the assessment, and that they were given an opportunity to make their own comments on and contributions to such report;

- checking whether the assessor consulted senior colleagues or managers to discuss the likely outcome and recommendations of the assessment before discussions with the family (or people being assessed);

- checking that assessment reports have been signed by the family (or people being assessed);

- cross-referencing the dates of assessment appointments, reviews, discussions with other professionals and signatures of the family (or people being assessed) against contemporaneous case records, other written evidence or records of other professionals or agencies;

- identifying that the outcome and recommendations of the assessment report are SMART; namely that they are:

  – Specific;

- **M**easurable;
- **A**chievable;
- **R**ealistic;
- (have) **T**imescales.

14.34

Questions to consider in analysis of the decision-making process for social work assessments

- Was the assessment started at an appropriate time?

- Was there any delay between the decision to assess and the implementation of the assessment?

- Did the assessment allow sufficient time for family members to consider issues being discussed and to develop and change?

- Did the assessment allow sufficient time for the assessors to consider and evaluate any development or changes within the family?

- Was the assessment completed by suitably qualified and experienced professionals?

- Was there adequate and sufficient pre-assessment planning between professionals and with the family?

- Was the reason for the assessment properly explained to the family (including the child)?

- Were the consequences of non-compliance with the assessment properly explained to the family?

- Was the assessment conducted in a suitable and appropriate environment?

- Was the family offered suitable assistance with childcare, transport and employment issues during the assessment?

- Was the family (including the child) kept sufficiently and adequately involved and informed before, during and after the assessment?

- Did the assessment take account of any learning disabilities of family members, e g were suitable methods and materials used, did the assessors take account of any psychological assessments of individuals' cognitive functioning?

- Did the assessment take sufficient account of any cultural or language needs of family members, e g were interpreters used throughout all assessment sessions?   ➡

- Is there evidence that the social worker has done more than simply describe the family's situation? Is there evidence that the social worker has *analysed* the information gathered during the assessment?

- Did the assessor keep an open mind during the assessment and used new information to re-evaluate their hypotheses or beliefs about the family?

- Was the family given a copy of the assessment report to consider at the end of the assessment? Was the family given an opportunity to discuss the outcome of the assessment with social workers?

- Is the social work assessment signed by parents? Are their comments included within the assessment?

SECTION 6 – ANALYSIS OF THE CASE PLANNING

What was the context of the social worker's decision-making?

14.35 It is also helpful to consider the specific context of the social worker's decision-making. Analysis of this issue can often reveal that the social worker made such decisions in isolation or without sufficient consultation with more experienced or skilled managers. This analysis can be done by:

- exploring how, when and where the social worker actually made decisions about planning in the case. Social workers should receive at least monthly supervision and should expect to discuss fundamental issues about case planning within those supervision sessions – see Chapter 2;

- cross-referencing the social worker's account of such decision-making against the contemporaneous records in the case file. A discrete supervision note relating to a particular case should be placed within the child or family's case file. It is often the absence or presence of such records or supervision notes that can assist lawyers in challenging or protecting the local authority's case;

- confirming the chronology and nature of discussions within the local authority about important decisions (for example, removal of a child, change of plan from rehabilitation to permanency, or a move of foster placement);

- confirming the chronology, nature and extent of a social worker's informal discussions with colleagues or managers about case planning; and

- cross-referencing the social worker's account of such discussions against the contemporaneous records in the case file or other notes. It is often the absence or presence of such records that can assist lawyers in challenging or protecting the local authority's case.

Who signed the care plan?

14.36 The statutory guidance relating to care plans[4] makes it clear that one or more relevant senior officers within the local authority should endorse the care plan for the final hearing as an authority-wide statement of its commitment to the plan. The choice of one or more senior officers designated to endorse care plans on behalf of the local authority is for each local authority to determine, but should usually include the social worker's immediate line manager and/or next senior manager. Analysis of the extent of consultation regarding the care plan can be done by:

- identifying whether the relevant designated officer has signed the care plan. While the absence of a designated officer's signature from a care plan could represent nothing more than a simple oversight on the part of the local authority, it might also indicate a lack of consultation between the allocated social worker and his or her manager;

- considering whether a designated officer or other senior manager should be required to attend court and give evidence on behalf of the local authority in respect of the care plan. This might relate to the overall aim of the care plan, or the selection of a particular placement or resource.

When was the care plan signed?

14.37 The context of discussion or consultation between the social worker and the designated officer(s) may also provide useful information about the extent (if any) of such discussion. Analysis about the context of such discussion can be done by:

- checking the dates of signatures of the allocated social worker and endorsing designated officer(s) at the end of a care plan – are the dates reasonably close in time?

- cross-referencing the social worker's account of decision-making against the contemporaneous records in the case file. It is often the absence or presence of such records that can assist lawyers in challenging or protecting the local authority's case.

What is the content of the care plan?

14.38 Consideration of the fine detail within a care plan can often reveal inconsistencies or deficiencies in the local authority's decision-making or planning in a case. Analysis of the content of the care plan can be done by:

- identifying whether the care plan was informed by findings from relevant assessments;

---

4   Local Authority Circular (1999) 29 *Care Plans and Care Proceedings under the* Children Act 1989, paras 21–22.

- confirming that the social worker allowed sufficient time to consider the outcome of completed assessments before finalising the care plan;

- cross-referencing the social worker's *chronology* and *account* of decision-making against the contemporaneous records in the case file. It is often the absence or presence of such records that can assist lawyers in challenging or protecting the local authority's case;

- identifying whether the content of a care plan (particularly where it constitutes a change of direction in the local authority's planning) was discussed or endorsed by a multi-agency group of professionals involved with the family (such as a child protection conference, core group, or statutory review);

- identifying whether the social worker ensured that adequate discussion about the content of the care plan took place with the family;

- identifying whether specific elements of the care plan are sufficiently detailed so that:

    – there are detailed *reasons* for why a particular placement or course of action has been chosen;
    – the *timescales* for a particular course of action are achievable and realistic;
    – *specific outcomes* for overall implementation of the plan include the key steps required;
    – clear information is provided about the *contingency* plan (this section of the care plan often lacks detail); and
    – clear and specific information is provided about the *contact arrangements* for the child.

14.39

Questions to consider in analysis of the decision-making process of the case planning

- Was there sufficient time for the local authority to consider and evaluate the assessment before completing the plan?

- Is there clear evidence that the local authority's plan was informed by a thorough assessment? Were strengths as well as weaknesses taken into account?

- Did the social worker consult appropriate managers in formulating the plan?

- Did the local authority consult other professionals from a range of disciplines before completing the plan?

- Was the plan discussed properly and in detail with the family (including the child)?

- Was the plan considered in a formal meeting at which the parents were invited to attend and participate?

- Does the plan include specific proposals for intervention or treatment?

INDEX

References are to paragraph numbers.